Kraul

New Digital Services Act

New Digital Services Act

A Practitioner's Guide

edited by

Torsten Kraul

2024

BECK • HART • NOMOS

Published by
Nomos Verlagsgesellschaft mbH & Co. KG, Waldseestraße 3-5, 76530 Baden-Baden, Germany,
email: vertrieb@nomos.de

Co-published by
Verlag C.H.Beck oHG, Wilhelmstraße 9, 80801 München, Germany,
email: bestellung@beck.de

and

Hart Publishing, Kemp House, Chawley Park, Cumnor Hill, Oxford, OX2 9PH, United Kingdom,
online at: www.hartpub.co.uk

Published in North America by Hart Publishing,
An Imprint of Bloomsbury Publishing 1385 Broadway, New York, NY 10018, USA
email: mail@hartpub.co.uk

ISBN 978 3 7560 0318 1 (NOMOS Print)
ISBN 978 3 7489 3707 4 (NOMOS ePDF)
ISBN 978 3 406 80471 7 (C.H.BECK)
ISBN 978 1 5099 6998 2 (HART)

First Edition 2024

Preface

The Digital Agenda for Europe for the decade 2020–2030 is the European Commission's approach to promoting secure digital spaces and services, a level playing field in digital markets with large platforms, and Europe's digital sovereignty. To this end, European legislators are currently pursuing new regulatory initiatives at a rapid pace.

Among the key regulatory instruments are the Digital Markets Act (DMA), which is intended, as a special element of antitrust law, to counter unfair practices by large online platforms designated 'gatekeepers', and the Digital Services Act (DSA). The DSA came into force on 16.11.2022, with most of its obligations applying from 17.2.2024. It is relevant for all digital services that act as intermediaries and, in particular, give consumers access to goods, services and content, including search engines and online marketplaces. While the DSA, which evolved from the E-Commerce Directive, maintains the tried-and-tested rules on the liability privilege applying to intermediaries, it also imposes obligations on the intermediaries in a graduated regulatory regime depending on their type and size. The aim of these obligations is to ensure better protection for users and fundamental rights on the internet, provide a solid framework for the transparency and accountability of online platforms, and offer a single standardised framework throughout the EU.

This Practitioner's Guide sets out to provide a practical introduction to the far-reaching regulations of the DSA. Following the DSA's structure and against the backdrop of its new regulations, this book describes the scope of application and the provisions on the liability privilege of intermediaries, which have progressed compared to the E-Commerce Directive. A core part of this Practitioner's Guide focusses on the extensive obligations imposed on platforms as well as the system of official and private enforcement of those obligations and the sanctions for non-compliance with the DSA. This is followed by the provisions stating precisely when these obligations apply.

It is worth noting, though, that we are still in the early stages of dealing with the DSA. Many factual questions will only arise once its rules are applied in practice, and legal issues will be addressed over time by legal commentaries and the courts. This book is therefore also intended to aid future discussion among practitioners and academics. Feedback, questions and suggestions are most welcome.

As the editor, I would like to take this opportunity to thank all the co-authors for their contributions and the in-depth and productive discussions.

Berlin, May 2024 *Torsten Kraul*

Contents

CHAPTER 3
LIABILITY OF PROVIDERS OF INTERMEDIARY SERVICES

Patrick Neidinger/Julia Wildgans

CHAPTER 4
DUE DILIGENCE OBLIGATIONS OF PROVIDERS OF INTERMEDIARY SERVICES

Niklas Maamar

Authors

Dr. Marvin Bartels

Marvin Bartels is a tech lawyer, specialising on legal issues of innovative technologies (such as platforms, SaaS, artificial intelligence, internet of things, crypto) and the implementation of related business models. This includes commercial, regulatory and transactional aspects.

Dr. Torsten Kraul, LL.M. (London)

Torsten Kraul provides legal and strategic advice on digital business, IT, internet and e-commerce as well as privacy. One of his specialist areas is the implementation of innovative digital business models and the application of new technologies (internet of things, artificial intelligence, platforms, apps, blockchain, big data).

Dr. Niklas Maamar

Niklas Maamar specialises in legal issues relating to digital products and business models and advises companies on all aspects of European digital regulation. A focus of his work is the use of artificial intelligence as well as legal and strategic questions of online platforms.

Konstantina Nathanail

Konstantina Nathanail specialises in tech law and AI regulation. She completed her studies in Berlin and Geneva and is actively involved in shaping AI and digital policy within the United Nations' IGF network.

Patrick Neidinger, LL.M. (University of Southern California)

Patrick Neidinger has specialised experience in advising on large multi-jurisdictional projects including outsourcing transactions in the areas of financial services, facility management, logistics, information technology and telecommunications. His expertise encompasses all stages of the outsourcing process, including the transition and migration phase as well as the post-outsourcing phase. Additionally, Patrick Neidinger regularly advises on global technology transactions across all industries including legal support of software licensing, systems integration, innovation and cooperation projects and all matters related to internet, e-commerce, cloud computing and big data.

Dr. Julia Wildgans

Julia Wildgans is a lawyer specialising in German and European IP and IT law and associate at Grünecker Patent Attorneys and Attorneys-at-Law in Munich, Germany. She advises on all aspects of trademark and copyright law as well as IT law (including domain disputes) with a special focus on innovation and new technologies (IoT, AI, online platforms and the metaverse). She holds a Ph.D. in law from the University of Mannheim and regularly runs workshops for start-ups, multinational companies and users on various aspects of IP/IT law.

Abbreviations

AcP	Archiv für die civilistische Praxis (journal)
AEUV	Vertrag über die Arbeitsweise der Europäischen Union (Treaty on the Functioning of the European Union)
AG	Amtsgericht (German District Court)
AI	Artificial Intelligence
API	Application Programming Interface
Art.	Article(s)
BB	Betriebs-Berater (journal)
BGB	Bürgerliches Gesetzbuch (German Civil Code)
BGBl.	Bundesgesetzblatt (German Law Gazette)
BGH	Bundesgerichtshof (German Federal Court)
BT	Bundestag (German Federal Parliament)
BT-Drs.	Bundestags-Drucksache (German Federal Parliament Document)
BVerfG	Bundesverfassungsgericht (German Federal Constitutional Court)
cf.	see, compare
CFR	Charter of Fundamental Rights of the European Union
Ch.	Chapter
CJEU	Court of Justice of the European Union
CMLR	Common Market Law Review
CR	Computer und Recht (journal)
DG CNECT	Directorate-General for Communications Networks, Content and Technology (European Commission)
DG COMP	Directorate-General for Competition (European Commission)
DSC	Digital Services Coordinator
e.g.	for example
EBDS	European Board for Digital Services
EC	European Community
ECB	European Central Bank
ECJ	European Court of Justice
ECLI	European Case Law Identifier
ed(s)	editor(s)
edn	edition

EEC	European Economic Community
EP	European Parliament
et al.	and others
et seq./et seqq.	following
etc.	and so forth
EU	European Union
EuCML	Journal of European Consumer and Market Law
EUCO	European Council
EUR	Euro(s)
EuR	Europarecht (journal)
EUV	Vertrag über die Europäische Union (Treaty on European Union)
EuZW	Europäische Zeitschrift für Wirtschaftsrecht (journal)
GC	General Court
GG	Grundgesetz (German Constitution)
GRUR	Gewerblicher Rechtsschutz und Urheberrecht (journal)
GRUR-Int	Gewerblicher Rechtsschutz und Urheberrecht – International (journal)
GRUR-Prax	Gewerblicher Rechtsschutz und Urheberrecht – Praxis im Immaterialgüter- und Wettbewerbsrecht (journal)
GSZ	Zeitschrift für das gesamte Sicherheitsrecht (journal)
GWB	Gesetz gegen Wettbewerbsbeschränkungen (German Competition Act)
GWR	Gesellschafts- und Wirtschaftsrecht (journal)
HdB	Handbuch (handbook)
i.e.	that is
IIC	International Review of Intellectual Property and Competition Law
IMCO	Committee on Internal Market and Consumer Protection (European Parliament)
infra	below
IST	Implementing Technical Standards
IWRZ	Zeitschrift für Internationales Wirtschaftsrecht (journal)
JIPITEC	Journal of Intellectual Property, Information Technology and Electronic Commerce Law
LG	Landgericht (German Regional Court)

LIBE	Committee on Civil Liberties, Justice and Home Affairs (European Parliament)
MIS	Management Information System
MMR	Multimedia und Recht (journal)
mn.	margin number(s)
NetzDG	Netzwerkdurchsetzungsgesetz (German Network Enforcement Act)
NJW	Neue Juristische Wochenschrift (journal)
no.	number(s)
NVwZ	Neue Zeitschrift für Verwaltungsrecht (journal)
NZA	Neue Zeitschrift für Arbeits- und Sozialrecht (journal)
OECD	Organisation for Economic Co-operation and Development
OJ	Official Journal of the European Union
OLG	Oberlandesgericht (German Higher Regional Court)
OWiG	Gesetz über Ordnungswidrigkeiten (German Act on Regulatory Offences)
p.	page(s)
para.	paragraph(s)
RDi	Recht Digital (journal)
rec.	recital(s)
sent.	sentence(s)
subpara.	subparagraph(s)
T&Cs	Terms and Conditions
TEU	Treaty on European Union
TFEU	Treaty on the Functioning of the European Union
TMG	Telemediengesetz (German Telemedia Act)
UK	United Kingdom
UrhDaG	Urheberrechts-Diensteanbieter-Gesetz (German Copyright Service Provider Act)
UrhG	Urheberrechtsgesetz (German Act on Copyright and Related Rights)
US	United States (of America)
UWG	Gesetz gegen den unlauteren Wettbewerb (German Act against Unfair Competition)
v	versus
VLOP	Very Large Online Platform

VLOSE	Very Large Online Search Engine
VO	Verordnung (Regulation)
VwVfG	Verwaltungsverfahrensgesetz (German Administrative Procedure Act)
ZEuP	Zeitschrift für Europäisches Privatrecht (journal)
ZfDR	Zeitschrift für Digitalisierung und Recht (journal)
ZUM	Zeitschrift für Urheber- und Medienrecht (journal)

General bibliography

BeckOGK	Gsell et al. (eds), beck-online.Grosskommentar, Munich 2024
BeckOK BGB	Hau/Poseck (eds), Beck'scher Online-Kommentar BGB, 70th edn, Munich 2024
BeckOK InfoMedienR	Gersdorf/Paal (eds), Beck'scher Online-Kommentar Informations- und Medienrecht, 44th edn, Munich 2024
BeckOK VwGO	Posser/Wolff/Decker (eds), Beck'scher Online-Kommentar VwGO, 69th edn, Munich 2024
BeckOK VwVfG	Bader/Ronellenfitsch (eds), Beck'scher Online-Kommentar VwVfG, 63rd edn, Munich 2024
Calliess/Ruffert	Calliess/Ruffert (eds), EUV/AEUV – Das Verfassungsrecht der Europäischen Union mit Europäischer Grundrechtecharta, 6th edn, Munich 2022
Dauses/Ludwigs EU-WirtschaftsR-HdB	Dauses/Ludwigs (eds), Handbuch des EU-Wirtschaftsrechts, 60th edn, Munich 2024
Dürig/Herzog/Scholz	Dürig/Herzog/Scholz (eds), Grundgesetz-Kommentar, 103rd edn, Munich 2023
Geimer/Schütze Int. Rechtsverkehr	Geimer/Schütze (eds), Internationaler Rechtsverkehr in Zivil- und Handelssachen, 66th edn, Munich 2023
Grabitz/Hilf/Nettesheim	Grabitz/Hilf/Nettesheim (eds), Das Recht der Europäischen Union, 81st edn, Munich 2024
HK-UnionsR	Vedder/Heintschel von Heinegg (eds), Europäisches Unionsrecht, 2nd edn, Baden-Baden 2018
Hoeren/Sieber/Holznagel MMR-HdB	Hoeren/Sieber/Holznagel (eds), Handbuch Multimedia-Recht, 61st edn, Munich 2024
Immenga/Mestmäcker	Körber/Schweitzer/Zimmer (eds), Wettbewerbsrecht, 6th/7th edn, Munich 2019–2024
MüKoBGB	Säcker/Rixecker/Oetker/Limperg (eds), Münchener Kommentar zum Bürgerlichen Gesetzbuch, 9th edn, Munich 2021–2024
MüKoZPO	Krüger/Rauscher (eds), Münchener Kommentar zur ZPO, 6th edn, Munich 2020
Nomos-BR/Müller-Broich TMG	Müller-Broich (ed), Telemediengesetz, Baden-Baden 2012
Oppermann/Classen/Nettesheim EuropaR	Oppermann/Classen/Nettesheim, Europarecht, 9th edn, Munich 2021

Rengeling/Middeke/Gellermann Rechtsschutz-HdB	Rengeling/Middeke/Gellermann (eds), Handbuch des Rechtsschutzes in der Europäischen Union, 3rd edn, Munich 2014
Spindler/Schmitz	Spindler/Schmitz (eds), TMG, 2nd edn, Munich 2018
Spindler/Schuster	Spindler/Schuster (eds), Recht der elektronischen Medien, 4th edn, Munich 2019
Streinz	Streinz (ed), Vertrag über die Europäische Union (EUV), Vertrag über die Arbeitsweise der Europäischen Union (AEUV), Charta der Grundrechte der Europäischen Union, 3rd edn, Munich 2018

Legal acts

ADR Directive	Directive 2013/11/EU of the European Parliament and of the Council of 21 May 2013 on alternative dispute resolution for consumer disputes and amending Regulation (EC) No 2006/2004 and Directive 2009/22/EC (Directive on consumer ADR) (OJ 2013 L 165, 63)
AI Act (Draft)	Proposal for a Regulation of the European Parliament and of the Council laying down harmonised rules on Artificial Intelligence (Artificial Intelligence Act) and amending certain Union legislative acts, COM(2021) 206 final
AVMS Directive	Directive 2010/13/EU of the European Parliament and of the Council of 10 March 2010 on the coordination of certain provisions laid down by law, regulation or administrative action in Member States concerning the provision of audiovisual media services (Audiovisual Media Services Directive) (OJ 2010 L 95, 1)
Brussels I Regulation (recast)/ Brüssel Ia-VO	Regulation (EU) No 1215/2012 of the European Parliament and of the Council of 12 December 2012 on jurisdiction and the recognition and enforcement of judgments in civil and commercial matters (recast) (OJ 2012 L 351, 1)
Charter of Fundamental Rights/CFR	Charter of Fundamental Rights of the European Union (OJ 2016 C 202, 389)
Consumer Rights Directive	Directive 2011/83/EU of the European Parliament and of the Council of 25 October 2011 on consumer rights, amending Council Directive 93/13/EEC and Directive 1999/44/EC of the European Parliament and of the Council and repealing Council Directive 85/577/EEC and Directive 97/7/EC of the European Parliament and of the Council (OJ 2011 L 304, 64)
Data Act	Regulation (EU) 2023/2854 of the European Parliament and of the Council of 13 December 2023 on harmonised rules on fair access to and use of data and amending Regulation (EU) 2017/2394 and Directive (EU) 2020/1828 (Data Act) (OJ 2023 L 2854)
Data Act (Draft)	Proposal for a Regulation of the European Parliament and of the Council on harmonised rules on fair access to and use of data (Data Act), COM(2022) 68 final
Data Governance Act/DGA	Regulation (EU) 2022/868 of the European Parliament and of the Council of 30 May 2022 on European data governance and amending Regulation (EU) 2018/1724 (Data Governance Act) (OJ 2022 L 152, 1)

Decision No 1336/97/EC	Decision No 1336/97/EC of the European Parliament and of the Council of 17 June 1997 on a series of guidelines for trans-European telecommunications networks (OJ 1997 L 183, 12)
Digital Content Directive	Directive (EU) 2019/770 of the European Parliament and of the Council of 20 May 2019 on certain aspects concerning contracts for the supply of digital content and digital services (OJ 2019 L 136, 1)
Digital Markets Act/DMA	Regulation (EU) 2022/1925 of the European Parliament and of the Council of 14 September 2022 on contestable and fair markets in the digital sector and amending Directives (EU) 2019/1937 and (EU) 2020/1828 (Digital Markets Act) (OJ 2022 L 265, 1)
Digital Services Act/DSA	Regulation (EU) 2022/2065 of the European Parliament and of the Council of 19 October 2022 on a Single Market For Digital Services and amending Directive 2000/31/EC (Digital Services Act) (OJ 2022 L 277, 1)
Digital Services Act/DSA (Draft)	Proposal for a Regulation of the European Parliament and of the Council on a Single Market For Digital Services (Digital Services Act) and amending Directive 2000/31/EC, COM(2020) 825 final
Digital Single Market/DSM Directive	Directive (EU) 2019/790 of the European Parliament and of the Council of 17 April 2019 on copyright and related rights in the Digital Single Market and amending Directives 96/9/EC and 2001/29/EC (OJ 2019 L 130, 92)
Directive 90/387/EEC	Council Directive 90/387/EEC of 28 June 1990 on the establishment of the internal market for telecommunications services through the implementation of open network provision (OJ 1990 L 192, 1)
Directive 95/62/EC	Directive 95/62/EC of the European Parliament and of the Council of 13 December 1995 on the application of open network provision (ONP) to voice telephony (OJ 1995 L 321, 6)
Directive on Information Society services	Directive (EU) 2015/1535 of the European Parliament and of the Council of 9 September 2015 laying down a procedure for the provision of information in the field of technical regulations and of rules on Information Society services (codification) (OJ 2015 L 241, 1)
E-Commerce Directive	Directive 2000/31/EC of the European Parliament and of the Council of 8 June 2000 on certain legal aspects of information society services, in particular electronic commerce, in the Internal Market ('Directive on electronic commerce') (OJ 2000 L 178, 1)

Enforcement Directive	Directive 2004/48/EC of the European Parliament and of the Council of 29 April 2004 on the enforcement of intellectual property rights (OJ 2004 L 157, 45)
ePrivacy Directive	Directive 2002/58/EC of the European Parliament and of the Council of 12 July 2002 concerning the processing of personal data and the protection of privacy in the electronic communications sector (Directive on privacy and electronic communications) (OJ 2002 L 201, 37)
General Data Protection Regulation/GDPR	Regulation (EU) 2016/679 of the European Parliament and of the Council of 27 April 2016 on the protection of natural persons with regard to the processing of personal data and on the free movement of such data, and repealing Directive 95/46/EC (General Data Protection Regulation) (OJ 2016 L 119, 1)
Geoblocking Regulation	Regulation (EU) 2018/302 of the European Parliament and of the Council of 28 February 2018 on addressing unjustified geo-blocking and other forms of discrimination based on customers' nationality, place of residence or place of establishment within the internal market and amending Regulations (EC) No 2006/2004 and (EU) 2017/2394 and Directive 2009/22/EC (OJ 2018 L 60, 1)
InfoSoc Directive	Directive 2001/29/EC of the European Parliament and of the Council of 22 May 2001 on the harmonisation of certain aspects of copyright and related rights in the information society (OJ 2001 L 167, 10)
ODR Regulation	Regulation (EU) No 524/2013 of the European Parliament and of the Council of 21 May 2013 on online dispute resolution for consumer disputes and amending Regulation (EC) No 2006/2004 and Directive 2009/22/EC (Regulation on consumer ODR) (OJ 2013 L 165, 1)
P2B Regulation	Regulation (EU) 2019/1150 of the European Parliament and of the Council of 20 June 2019 on promoting fairness and transparency for business users of online intermediation services (OJ 2019 L 186, 57)
Portability Regulation	Regulation (EU) 2017/1128 of the European Parliament and of the Council of 14 June 2017 on cross-border portability of online content services in the internal market (OJ 2017 L 168, 1)
Product Safety Directive	Directive 2001/95/EC of the European Parliament and of the Council of 3 December 2001 on general product safety (OJ 2001 L 11, 4)

Recommendation 2003/361/EC	Commission Recommendation of 6 May 2003 concerning the definition of micro, small and medium-sized enterprises (OJ 2003 L 124, 36)
Recommendation (EU) 2018/334	Commission Recommendation (EU) 2018/334 of 1 March 2018 on measures to effectively tackle illegal content online (OJ 2018 L 63, 50)
Regulation on cooperation between national authorities responsible for the enforcement of consumer protection laws	Regulation (EU) 2017/2394 of the European Parliament and of the Council of 12 December 2017 on cooperation between national authorities responsible for the enforcement of consumer protection laws and repealing Regulation (EC) No 2006/2004 (OJ 2017 L 345, 1)
Regulation on market surveillance and compliance of products	Regulation (EU) 2019/1020 of the European Parliament and of the Council of 20 June 2019 on market surveillance and compliance of products and amending Directive 2004/42/EC and Regulations (EC) No 765/2008 and (EU) No 305/2011 (OJ 2019 L 169, 1)
Regulation on the free flow of non-personal data	Regulation (EU) 2018/1807 of the European Parliament and of the Council of 14 November 2018 on a framework for the free flow of non-personal data in the European Union (OJ 2018 L 303, 59)
Regulation on the marketing and use of explosives precursors	Regulation (EU) 2019/1148 of the European Parliament and of the Council of 20 June 2019 on the marketing and use of explosives precursors, amending Regulation (EC) No 1907/2006 and repealing Regulation (EU) No 98/2013 (OJ 2019 L 186, 1)
Representative Actions Directive	Directive (EU) 2020/1828 of the European Parliament and of the Council of 25 November 2020 on representative actions for the protection of the collective interests of consumers and repealing Directive 2009/22/EC (OJ 2020 L 409, 1)
Roaming Regulation	Regulation (EU) 2015/2120 of the European Parliament and of the Council of 25 November 2015 laying down measures concerning open internet access and amending Directive 2002/22/EC on universal service and users' rights relating to electronic communications networks and services and Regulation (EU) No 531/2012 on roaming on public mobile communications networks within the Union (OJ 2015 L 310, 1)
Rome I Regulation	Regulation (EC) No 593/2008 of the European Parliament and of the Council of 17 June 2008 on the law applicable to contractual obligations (Rome I) (OJ 2008 L 177, 6)

Rome II Regulation	Regulation (EC) No 864/2007 of the European Parliament and of the Council of 11 July 2007 on the law applicable to non-contractual obligations (Rome II) (OJ 2007 L 199, 40)
TCO Regulation	Regulation (EU) 2021/784 of the European Parliament and of the Council of 29 April 2021 on addressing the dissemination of terrorist content online (OJ 2021 L 172, 79)
UCP Directive	Directive 2005/29/EC of the European Parliament and of the Council of 11 May 2005 concerning unfair business-to-consumer commercial practices in the internal market and amending Council Directive 84/450/EEC, Directives 97/7/EC, 98/27/EC and 2002/65/EC of the European Parliament and of the Council and Regulation (EC) No 2006/2004 of the European Parliament and of the Council ('Unfair Commercial Practices Directive') (OJ 2005 L 149, 22)

CHAPTER 1
INTRODUCTION

Torsten Kraul

Bibliography: Bertuzzi, 'European Parliament rejects consolidated text of the Digital Services Act' (Euractiv, 10.6.2022) <https://www.euractiv.com/section/digital/news/european-parliament-rejects-consolidated-text-of-the-digital-services-act> (last accessed: 23.5.2024); Breyer, 'Digital Services Act: IMCO report is a missed opportunity in the fight against surveillance capitalism on the Internet' (Website of Patrick Breyer, 9.12.2021) <https://www.patrick-breyer.de/en/digital-services-act-imco-report-is-a-missed-opportunity-in-the-fight-against-surveillance-capitalism-on-the-internet/> (last accessed: 23.5.2024); Council of the European Union, 'Digital Services Act: Council and European Parliament provisional agreement for making the internet a safer space for European citizens' (23.4.2022) <https://www.consilium.europa.eu/en/press/press-releases/2022/04/23/digital-services-act-council-and-european-parliament-reach-deal-on-a-safer-online-space> (last accessed: 23.5.2024); Council of the European Union, 'DSA: Council gives final approval to the protection of users' rights online' (4.10.2022) <https://www.consilium.europa.eu/en/press/press-releases/2022/10/04/dsa-council-gives-final-approval-to-the-protection-of-users-rights-online/> (last accessed: 23.5.2024); De Gregorio/Pollicino, 'The European Constitutional Road to Address Platform Power' (Verfassungsblog, 31.8.2021) <https://verfassungsblog.de/power-dsa-dma-03> (last accessed: 23.5.2024); De Streel/Husovec, 'The e-commerce Directive as the cornerstone of the Internal Market' (Official Website of the European Parliament, May 2020), PE 648.797 <https://www.europarl.europa.eu/RegData/etudes/STUD/2020/648797/IPOL_STU(2020)648797_EN.pdf> (last accessed: 23.5.2024); Denga, 'Plattformregulierung durch europäische Werte: Zur Bindung von Meinungsplattformen an EU-Grundrechte', EuR 2021, 569; DG CNECT, 'Note for an orientation discussion at the DSM Steering Group' (June 2019) <https://cdn.netzpolitik.org/wp-upload/2019/07/Digital-Services-Act-note-DG-Connect-June-2019.pdf> (last accessed: 23.5.2024); European Commission, 'European Commission and IT Companies announce Code of Conduct on illegal online hate speech' (31.5.2016) <https://ec.europa.eu/commission/presscorner/detail/en/IP_16_1937> (last accessed: 23.5.2024); European Commission, 'Security Union: Commission steps up efforts to tackle illegal content online' (28.8.2017) <https://ec.europa.eu/commission/presscorner/detail/en/IP_17_3493> (last accessed: 23.5.2024); European Commission, 'A Europe fit for the digital age' <https://ec.europa.eu/info/strategy/priorities-2019-2024/europe-fit-digital-age_en> (last accessed: 23.5.2024); European Commission, 'Europe fit for the Digital Age: new online rules for platforms' <https://commission.europa.eu/strategy-and-policy/priorities-2019-2024/europe-fit-digital-age/digital-services-act-ensuring-safe-and-accountable-online-environment/europe-fit-digital-age-new-online-rules-platforms_en> (last accessed: 23.5.2024); European Commission, 'Statement by Executive Vice-President Vestager on the Commission proposal on new rules for digital platforms' (15.12.2020) <https://ec.europa.eu/commission/presscorner/detail/en/STATEMENT_20_2450> (last accessed: 23.5.2024); European Commission, 'The first 100 days' <https://ec.europa.eu/info/about-european-commission/what-european-commission-does/delivering-political-priorities/first-100-days_en> (last accessed: 23.5.2024); Hessel/Reusch, 'Kommentar: Der Digital Services Act – ein 'Grundgesetz für das Internet'?' (heise online, 27.4.2022) <https://www.heise.de/meinung/Kommentar-Der-Dgitial-Services-Act-ein-Grundgesetz-fuer-das-Internet-7066735.html> (last accessed: 23.5.2024); Holznagel, 'Zu starke Nutzerrechte in Art. 17 und 18 DSA', CR 2022, 594; Janal, 'Haftung und Verantwortung im Entwurf des Digital Services Acts', ZEuP 2021, 227; Klausa, 'Einigung zu Stay-Down-Pflichten im DSA' (Tagesspiegel Background, 15.6.2022) <https://background.tagesspiegel.de/digitalisierung/einigung-zu-stay-down-pflichten-im-dsa> (last accessed: 23.5.2024); Krause, 'Auf dem Weg zur unionsrechtlichen Regelung von Plattformtätigkeiten. Die Kommissionsinitiative zur Plattformarbeit', NZA 2022, 521; Kühl, 'Das neue Grundgesetz für Onlinedienste' (Zeit Online, 14.12.2020) <https://www.zeit.de/digital/internet/2020-12/digital-servcies-act-eu-kommission-facebook-google-amazon-gesetz> (last accessed: 23.5.2024); Nolte, 'Hate-Speech, Fake-News, das 'Netzwerkdurchsetzungsgesetz' und Vielfaltsicherung durch Suchmaschinen', ZUM 2017, 552; OECD, 'The Role of Internet Intermediaries in Advancing Public Policy Objectives' (September 2011) <https://www.oecd.org/sti/ieconomy/theroleofinternetintermediariesinadvancingpublicpolicyobjectives.htm> (last accessed: 23.5.2024); Oxford Economics, 'Digital Spillover' (Huawei, 5.9.2017) <https://www.huawei.com/minisite/gci/en/digital-spillover/files/gci_digital_spillover.pdf> (last accessed: 23.5.2024); Paal/Kumkar, 'Die digitale Zukunft Europas: Europäische Strategien für den digitalen Binnenmarkt', ZfDR 2021, 97; Podszun/Langenstein, 'Gatekeeper im Visier' (Legal Tribune Online, 16.12.2020) <https://www.lto.de/recht/hintergruende/h/eu-digital-wirtschaft-regulierung-plattformen-intermediaere-dsa-dma-kommission-datenschutz-kartellrecht> (last accessed: 23.5.2024); Raue, 'Plattformnutzungsverträge im Lichte der gesteigerten Grundrechtsbindung marktstarker sozialer Netze', NJW 2022, 209; Schmid/Grewe, 'Digital Services Act: Neues 'Grundgesetz für Onlinedienste'? Auswirkungen des Kommissionsentwurfs für die Digitalwirtschaft', MMR 2021, 279; Schultejans, 'Als Bayern das Internet 'zumachen' wollte' (t-online, 17.11.2019) <https://w

ww.t-online.de/digital/id_86819388/compuserve-prozess-in-muenchen-als-bayern-das-internet-zumache n-wollte.html> (last accessed: 23.5.2024); Siripurapu, 'Trump and Section 230: What to Know' (Council on Foreign Relations, 2.12.2020) <https://www.cfr.org/in-brief/trump-and-section-230-what-know> (last accessed: 23.5.2024); Smith/Van Alstyne, 'It's Time to Update Section 230' (Harvard Business Review, 12.8.2021) <https://hbr.org/2021/08/its-time-to-update-section-230> (last accessed: 23.5.2024); Staudenmayer, 'Die Anpassung des Privatrechts an die digitale Wirtschaft', IWRZ 2020, 147; Wilman, 'The EU's system of knowledge-based liability for hosting service providers in respect of illegal user content – between the e-Commerce Directive and the Digital Services Act', JIPITEC 2021, 317.

A. A 'Constitution' for Digital Services?

1 When the European Commission Executive Vice-President Margrethe Vestager presented the Digital Services Act (DSA) and the Digital Markets Act (DMA) in December 2020, she spoke of '**milestones** in our journey to make Europe fit for the **Digital Age**'.[1] The DSA, she said, could be compared to the first US traffic lights set up in Cleveland, Ohio at the beginning of the 20th century that brought order to the streets. Like those first traffic lights, the DSA, a little more than a hundred years later, is intended to create a regulatory system capable of application worldwide to make the online world a safe, reliable and secure place for all users. In pursuit of this aim, the DSA sets out three specific goals: first, to improve the safety of users; second, to increase the transparency of platforms; and third, to strengthen law enforcement *vis-à-vis* digital actors.

2 In brief, the DSA creates a **harmonised horizontal legal framework for digital services** offered in the EU, covering providers ranging from individual Wi-Fi networks to social media platforms with millions of users. The DSA addresses the intermediary services on the Internet, i.e. access, caching and hosting providers, and imposes **specific requirements and obligations** on them depending on their role, size and impact in the digital ecosystem. In pursuit of its goal to deliver a safe, predictable and trusted online environment (see Chapter 2 of this Practitioner's Guide), the DSA maintains a framework for the conditional exemption from liability of intermediary services providers established since the E-Commerce Directive (see Chapter 3). The DSA supplements existing rules regarding liability for third-party content with a system of far-reaching due diligence obligations tailored to certain specific categories of providers of intermediary services (on this, Chapter 4) and rules on the implementation and enforcement of the Regulation (on this, Chapter 5).

[1] European Commission, 'Statement by Executive Vice-President Vestager on the Commission proposal on new rules for digital platforms'.

The DSA has frequently been referred to as a **'constitution' for the Internet**.[2] It attempts to horizontally translate European constitutional values into private relationships between service providers and users to limit the power of digital platforms.[3] In this respect, the DSA reflects the position that, because of their central role as forum for public discourse, large platforms should increasingly be bound to respect the fundamental rights of users.[4] The rules set out by the DSA are thus a **balancing act** between the need for increased protection of users against illegal and harmful content and the preservation of freedom of expression in the digital space. Politically, the negotiations around the DSA were shaped by the controversial discussions taking place on the issues of hate speech, fake news and coordinated campaigns to manipulate and influence election processes. At the same time, the technical landscape of intermediary services is constantly changing. Recommender systems based on artificial intelligence present users with personalised suggestions for content to consume and goods to buy. Apps like TikTok are no longer designed to help users find the content they want to watch. Instead, the content itself finds the appropriate user – with the help of algorithms that control what the user sees. This further increases the importance of digital platforms as transmitters and disseminators of information. Meanwhile, entirely new risks are emerging, such as the phenomenon of echo chambers or filter bubbles. Against this background, the DSA should be seen as an attempt to **renegotiate the social compromise** between the opportunities and risks presented by intermediaries in the digital space. 3

Whether the DSA thereby acquires the character of a digital constitution is probably rightly doubted.[5] Nonetheless, with its **comprehensive and ambitious regulatory approach**, the DSA does provide a central regulatory framework for 'A Europe fit for the digital age',[6] though its effectiveness in combating illegal content and resolving social conflicts through intermediary services remains to be proven in the future. 4

B. The DSA as part of the EU Digital Strategy

The DSA represents a continuation in the development of the EU Digital Strategy. 5
European digital policy has a long history: initially focused on communication infrastructure,[7] with the development of the Internet the policy shifted its attention to e-commerce. In line with almost synchronous legal development worldwide, the European legislator enacted the **E-Commerce Directive in 2000** that featured a far-reaching liability exemption scheme for intermediaries and a basic regulatory framework for contracts concluded electronically. Since the exchange of information, goods and services beyond national borders is technologically inherent on the Internet, this was soon expanded with the **creation of a comprehensive Digital Single Market**. The cross-border nature of digital technologies, which are gradually detaching from static infrastructures and can be accessed globally, is thus both a driver of social and economic integration and a regulatory challenge from a European perspective.

[2] Kühl, 'Das neue Grundgesetz für Onlinedienste'; Schmid/Grewe MMR 2021, 279; Hessel/Reusch, 'Kommentar: Der Digital Services Act – ein 'Grundgesetz für das Internet'?'.

[3] De Gregorio/Pollicino, 'The European Constitutional Road to Address Platform Power'.

[4] Raue NJW 2022, 209; critical Denga EuR 2021, 569 (584 et seqq.).

[5] Podszun/Langenstein, 'Gatekeeper im Visier'.

[6] European Commission, 'A Europe fit for the digital age'.

[7] Cf. Directive 90/387/EEC, Directive 95/62/EC and Decision No 1336/97/EC.

I. The importance of the digital economy

6 The digital economy is of **paramount importance both for the competitiveness** of the EU and for the sustainable promotion of its economic growth.[8] It includes critical technologies such as content technologies and information management services, cloud computing, the Internet of Things and modern data infrastructures,[9] which form the basis for applications such as digital platforms, Big Data, artificial intelligence, the blockchain, and augmented and virtual reality. Today, the digital economy already accounts for 15.5 % of global gross domestic product and has grown two and a half times faster than the global economy over the past 15 years.[10]

7 However, digitalisation represents much more than just a sector of the overall economy; it is also the driver of an all-encompassing **process of transformation** that has very real effects on the **economic and social order**.[11] The widespread introduction of digital technologies and their integration into everyday life impact social inclusion, cultural participation, public sector services and labour.[12] From a regulatory perspective, digitalisation cuts across boundaries, its effects being seen in numerous domains, leading to a number of legal and factual challenges.

II. The creation of a Digital Single Market

8 In order to respond to the digital transformation and the significance of information and communication technology for EU citizens, the Commission adopted a **Digital Agenda** in 2010 as part of the ten-year 'Europe 2020 Strategy' to deliver sustainable economic and social benefits from a Digital Single Market based on fast and ultra-fast Internet and interoperable applications.[13] The political goal was a **Digital Single Market** whose harmonisation would positively impact both citizens and businesses throughout Europe. It should no longer matter whether one ordered goods online in Germany, Spain or Italy or used one's devices in France, Portugal or Greece. To this end, lighthouse projects such as the ban on roaming charges through the Roaming Regulation, the modernisation of the consumer's right of withdrawal from contracts through the Consumer Rights Directive, the modernisation of data protection through the Data Protection Regulation, the cross-border portability of online content through the Portability Regulation and the ending of digital access barriers through the Geoblocking Regulation were introduced. At the same time, the Digital Single Market acts as an enormous **driver of growth** for businesses, which enables businesses to access the entire EU market without having to comply with the individual legal systems of the 27 Member States, but rather with a single harmonised legal system. This reduces compliance costs and allows businesses to upscale their services across the Union. Based on Art. 114 TFEU, which lays down the EU's competence to harmonise Member States' laws that have as their object

[8] Paal/Kumkar ZfDR 2021, 97 (99).

[9] European Commission, 'Digital Economy and Social Index 2021, Research and Innovation: ICT projects in Horizon 2020', p. 6.

[10] Oxford Economics, 'Digital Spillover', p. 6.

[11] Staudenmayer IWRZ 2020, 147.

[12] Cf. International Telecommunications Union, 'Social and Economic Impact of Digital Transformation on the Economy, GSR-17 Discussion paper', p. 4, 20 et seqq.

[13] European Commission, 'Communication from the Commission to the European Parliament, the Council, the European Economic and Social Committee and the Committee of the Regions: A Digital Agenda for Europe' (19.5.2010), COM(2010) 245 final, p. 3 et seqq., 22 et seqq.

the establishment and functioning of the internal market, a large number of legislative acts implementing the Digital Strategy have emerged over the last decade.

1. ... through sector-specific regulation (2014–2019)

Starting in 2014, the Commission, under the leadership of Jean-Claude Juncker, presented the first legislative proposals for the European Digital Single Market. The Juncker Commission's approach was characterised by **sector-specific regulation**, which deliberately distributed the regulations for the Digital Single Market over numerous individual legislative acts, each with narrow areas of application limited to the respective sector. For example, there were separate Directives and Regulations for specific categories of services (audio-visual media services, telecommunications providers, online shops) and certain types of content (depictions of child abuse, terrorist content). Differentiation according to legal area was also applied (copyright, cybersecurity, data protection). This approach achieved success in a number of areas but, overall, turned out to be politically costly and failed to achieve the main goal of rendering the European digital economy competitive in the face of the technology leaders of Silicon Valley and Asia. **9**

2. ... through horizontal regulation (from 2019)

The Commission in office since 1.12.2019 under Commission President Ursula von der Leyen is building on the initiatives of its predecessor to create a Digital Single Market. Setting out its political priorities for the first 100 days of its mandate, it emphasised the importance of 'leading on the green and digital transformations in a changing world' as its primary objective[14] and set an agenda for shaping Europe's digital future to achieve that goal. In its guiding document, the Commission formulates three goals for future regulation: technology that works for people, a fair and competitive economy, and an open, democratic and sustainable society.[15] **10**

The Commission's proposals published after 2019, however, indicate an evident **change in the chosen regulatory approach**: instead of sector-specific legislative acts, the Commission is increasingly using **cross-sectoral ('horizontal') regulation**. This development represents a move away from a multitude of individual shorter legal texts towards the introduction of basic regulations that set a uniform legal framework for the Digital Single Market in terms of legislation. The Commission's major digital projects over the past two years exemplify this: the draft AI Act with its risk-based approach towards regulating artificial intelligence, the Data Act aimed at regulating access to and use of data, the Digital Markets Act to regulate the power of gatekeepers in digital markets and, most recently, the Cyber Resilience Act on the security of digital products, are all overarching legislative acts that transcend the boundaries of previous sector-specific regulation. **11**

---

[14] European Commission, 'The first 100 days'.

[15] European Commission, 'Communication from the Commission to the European Parliament, the Council, the European Economic and Social Committee and the Committee of the Regions: Shaping Europe's digital future' (19.2.2020), COM(2020) 67 final, p. 2 et seq.

C. Regulating intermediaries

I. The importance of intermediaries

12 Intermediary service providers are central players in the digital economy. These services enable communication and transactions between third parties and thus provide the basic infrastructure and platforms of the Internet.[16] Intermediaries are the **Internet communication network nodes** that transmit users' content, store it or make it available to the public.[17] The term intermediaries thus covers a **wide range of service providers**, from the technical service of transmitting information via the Internet (so-called 'mere conduit', Art. 3(g)(i) DSA) to complex algorithm-based services such as search engines, social networks and trading platforms.[18] Intermediaries thus represent an **essential interface** for data exchange, e-commerce, participatory networks and many other web services, significantly influencing how and which information, ideas and products are disseminated online.[19]

13 The role of intermediary services has always been to enable the dissemination of information, but without controlling each individual piece of information, thereby disrupting the existing rules regulating **responsibility for disseminating information** that applied to the analogue world. This was bound to create conflict and few cases illustrate this clash more vividly than the German case of CompuServe, one of the first Internet access providers. In May 1998, the managing director of CompuServe was convicted in the first instance as an accomplice to the dissemination of child pornography because such content was accessible online using CompuServe's lines.[20] The proceedings gave focus to the discussion about the responsibility of intermediaries for content uploaded or accessed by users. The judgement of the Munich District Court was sharply criticised and later overturned amid claims that 'Without the acquittal, the Internet in Germany would have been massively slowed down in its innovative power'.[21] The case illustrates the conflict raging in the background of the negotiations regarding the liability of intermediaries as their importance grew in parallel with the spread of the Internet in Germany, Europe and worldwide.

II. The E-Commerce Directive

14 The central legal instrument at the European level was the E-Commerce Directive of 2000. This lays down basic requirements for services on the Internet and establishes rules for commercial communications. In addition, Art. 12–15 of the E-Commerce Directive contain **exemptions from liability** for intermediaries, which are highly relevant in practice.

15 The E-Commerce Directive came into existence in the **early stages of the Internet development**. Amazon was just five years old at the time and had exclusively sold

[16] OECD, 'The Role of Internet Intermediaries in Advancing Public Policy Objectives', p. 11.
[17] Scientific Services of the German Parliament, 'Regulierung von Intermediären' (29.8.2018), WD 10-3000-062/18, p. 5.
[18] Scientific Services of the German Parliament, 'Regulierung von Intermediären' (29.8.2018), WD 10-3000-062/18, p. 5.
[19] Scientific Services of the German Parliament, 'Regulierung von Intermediären' (29.8.2018), WD 10-3000-062/18, p. 4.
[20] AG Munich 28.5.1998 – 8340 Ds 465 Js 173158/95, ZUM 1998, 685 – CompuServe.
[21] According to the business lawyer Malaika Nolde, quoted in Schultejans, 'Als Bayern das Internet 'zumachen' wollte'.

books,[22] Google had just celebrated its second birthday[23] and it would be several more years before Facebook arrived on the scene.[24] The regulations set out in the E-Commerce Directive, with their emphasis on removing obstacles to the development and dissemination of innovative Internet services, reflect the European legislator's **optimism regarding the potential of the Internet** for economic growth in the internal market. The aim of the Directive was to create a legal framework to ensure the free movement of information society services between Member States (rec. 8 and Art. 1(1) E-Commerce Directive). Above all, the E-Commerce Directive ensured that the liability issue would not stand in the way of intermediaries and thus the success of the Internet. Art. 12–14 of the E-Commerce Directive provide a solution that remains in force today: Intermediaries are not responsible for third-party content unless they have actual knowledge of the illegal content and can technically prevent its dissemination. With this compromise, the Directive has over time proved to be robust and fundamentally suitable for new digital business models, including the 'sharing economy'. The **exemption from liability** of intermediary services has acted as a **catalyst for the development and prosperity** of these business models and thus contributed significantly to the Internet as we know it today.[25]

III. Need for modernisation and supplementation

More than two decades later, the **social and economic conditions** that were the basis for enacting the E-Commerce Directive have **changed significantly**.[26] Today, digital intermediaries are among the most influential companies in the world. Providers such as Amazon, Google and Meta reach hundreds of millions of users worldwide and generate revenues in the triple-digit billions.[27] Large online platforms have attained central social significance as public discourse and commerce spaces. 16

At the same time, the compromise contained in the E-Commerce Directive on the question of liability does only partial justice to the technical reality: instead of the reporting of individual illegal content, which must then be removed or blocked by the intermediary, the focus is now on mass infringements, which are **automatically blocked** by the services **through algorithmic filters**.[28] On all major platforms, well over 90 % of blocked content is identified by automated filter technologies, which means that the principle of liability due to knowledge provided for in Art. 14 E-Commerce Directive has lost considerable significance.[29] Discussions on the spread of hate speech, disinformation[30] and the danger posed by algorithmic systems to users' physical and mental health 17

[22] Cf. History, 'Amazon opens for business' <https://www.history.com/this-day-in-history/amazon-opens-for-business> (last accessed: 23.5.2024).

[23] Cf. Google, 'From the garage to the Googleplex' <https://about.google/our-story> (last accessed: 23.5.2024).

[24] Cf. Britannica, 'Facebook' <https://www.britannica.com/topic/Facebook> (last accessed: 23.5.2024).

[25] See rec. 16 DSA; Gielen/Uphues EuZW 2021, 627 (632).

[26] For more details, see Krause NZA 2022, 521.

[27] Cf. Statista, 'Google, Amazon, Meta, Apple, and Microsoft (GAMAM) – Statistics & Facts' <https://www.statista.com/topics/4213/google-apple-facebook-amazon-and-microsoft-gafam/#topicHeader__wrapper> (last accessed: 23.5.2024).

[28] Holznagel CR 2022, 594 (603).

[29] Cf. Google, 'Transparency Report – YouTube Removed Videos and Comments Figures for the First Quarter of 2022' <https://transparencyreport.google.com/youtube-policy/removals?hl=en_GB> and Meta, 'Community Standards Enforcement Report for the Second Quarter of 2022' (22.11.2022) <https://transparency.fb.com/data/community-standards-enforcement> (each last accessed: 23.5.2024).

[30] Nolte ZUM 2017, 552 (553, 558).

throw into focus new risks around these services which were not addressed by the E-Commerce Directive.

18 Against this backdrop, there has been increased **criticism** of the E-Commerce Directive[31] and other similar regulations, such as Section 230 of Title 47 of the United States Code,[32] which highlights the shortcomings of the existing regulatory framework on the topic of how to effectively tackle illegal user content. In its study on the evaluation of the E-Commerce Directive, the Committee on the Internal Market and Consumer Protection of the European Parliament identified a need for reform, particularly concerning the following points:[33]

1. With its focus on liability, the E-Commerce Directive lacks safeguards to prevent violations of fundamental rights, in particular freedom of expression.
2. The E-Commerce Directive did not foresee that notifications may be sent by robots, rather than humans, and fails to incentivise the quality of sent and reviewed notifications.
3. The E-Commerce Directive fails to prevent fragmentation due to diverging applications of the passivity criterion by national courts.
4. The E-Commerce Directive fails to include hyperlinking and search engines; it also does not cover other new services.
5. The E-Commerce Directive serves only as a limiting force, rather than as a comprehensive tool for the removal of illegal content.

19 The Commission **initially used non-binding instruments** to encourage intermediaries to take more decisive action against illegal content. In 2016, for example, it published the Communication on 'Online Platforms and the Digital Single Market, Opportunities and Challenges for Europe'[34] and announced, together with IT companies, the Code of Conduct to combat illegal hate speech online.[35] In September 2017, it set out guidelines and principles for online platforms to increase the proactive prevention, detection and removal of illegal content inciting hatred, violence and terrorism online.[36] This was followed in March 2018 by the Commission's Recommendation on measures to effectively tackle illegal content online.[37] However, from the Commission's perspective, the non-binding instruments have not achieved sufficient success.[38]

D. The DSA

20 The central role of intermediary services as providers of a secure and trustworthy Digital Single Market led to the development of a new legislative act to **renegotiate and reassess questions on liability and risks in a digital era**. The European legislator was

[31] Wilman JIPITEC 2021, 317 (329 et seqq.).

[32] Smith/Van Alstyne, 'It's Time to Update Section 230'; Siripuranu, 'Trump and Section 230: What to Know'.

[33] De Streel/Husovec, 'The e-commerce Directive as the cornerstone of the Internal Market', p. 41.

[34] European Commission, 'Communication from the Commission to the European Parliament, the Council, the European Economic and Social Committee and the Committee of the Regions: Online Platforms and the Digital Single Market, Opportunities and Challenges for Europe' (25.5.2016), COM(2016) 288 final.

[35] European Commission, 'European Commission and IT Companies announce Code of Conduct on illegal online hate speech'.

[36] European Commission, 'Security Union: Commission steps up efforts to tackle illegal content online'.

[37] Commission Recommendation (EU) 2018/334 of 1 March 2018 on measures to effectively tackle illegal content online.

[38] European Commission, 'Impact Assessment', SWD(2020) 348 final, Part 1, p. 31 et seq.

forced to act in view of the fact that several Member States had already enacted national laws to deal with the risks of the new digital intermediaries, raising fears of a renewed **fragmentation of the Single Market.**[39] Through the DSA, the legislator seeks to counter illegal content distribution by imposing a binding obligation on intermediaries to act.

21 Despite their many common elements, the DSA represents a **paradigm shift away from the E-Commerce Directive.** Instead of viewing the Internet and the business models developing on its infrastructure exclusively as drivers of innovation and economic growth, the DSA introduces control mechanisms to minimise the social risks posed by intermediaries. Internet services, which have grown massively over the last two decades, are perceived by the legislator to be **'mature for regulation'** and to be capable of being more broadly held accountable.

I. Legislative process

22 The DSA was adopted with impressive speed, especially compared to other similarly complex European legislation. From the **presentation of the DSA draft by the Commission on 15.12.2020** to its publication in the Official Journal, less than two years elapsed.

23 Preparatory work within the Commission began in the summer of 2019 when the Directorate-General for Communications Networks, Content and Technologies developed the concept of comprehensive regulation for digital services as an update to the E-Commerce Directive.[40] In the summer of 2020, the Commission held a public consultation on the planned DSA.[41] A few months later, the DSA was presented simultaneously with the DMA. In the accompanying Impact Assessment, the Commission explained in detail why it had opted for the full harmonisation of measures to incentivise actions from service providers along with the introduction of asymmetric due diligence obligations for very large online platforms.[42]

24 The proposed regulation was then discussed in the European Parliament and the Council. In the European Parliament, the Committee on Internal Market and Consumer Protection (IMCO) was in charge, with Christel Schaldemose from the Social Democrats as the responsible rapporteur. In the **European Parliament's** discussions and subsequent negotiations with the Council, the challenge of finding a **balance** between the **protection of users** and the **promotion of innovative digital business models** became increasingly apparent.[43] On one side of the debate were those in favour of stronger user rights, such as the right to anonymity or a comprehensive ban on personalised advertising, as can be seen in particular in the amendments proposed by the Committee on Civil Liberties, Justice and Home Affairs (LIBE).[44] The other side of the debate argued that the economic interests of digital services should not be too greatly affected,

[39] Janal ZEuP 2021, 227 (230 et seq.) concerning national laws such as the German Network Enforcement Act (*Netzwerkdurchsetzungsgesetz* – NetzDG) and the French laws against false news and hate speech, as well as different measures on self-regulation.

[40] DG CNECT, 'Note for an orientation discussion at the DSM Steering Group'.

[41] European Commission, 'Open Public Consultation on the Digital Services Act Package, Summary Report' (15.12.2020), Ref. Ares(2020)7629347.

[42] European Commission, 'Impact Assessment', SWD(2020) 348 final, Part 1, p. 39 et seq., 67 et seqq.

[43] Council of the European Union, 'Digital Services Act: Council and European Parliament provisional agreement for making the internet a safer space for European citizens'.

[44] Cf. Breyer, 'Digital Services Act: IMCO report is a missed opportunity in the fight against surveillance capitalism on the Internet'.

claiming, for example, that personalised online advertising is an essential economic factor and a crucial source of funding for many services.

25 After intensive negotiations, the Council was the first to adopt its General Approach[45] on 25.11.2021, followed by the European Parliament's adoption of its proposed amendments[46] on 20.1.2022 in preparation for the **final discussions between the co-legislators.** Two essential demands of the Council were the extension of the DSA to online search engines and a more robust protection of minors. In addition, against a background of experience with the enforcement of the GDPR (→ Ch. 5 mn. 1 et seq.), the Council called for the Commission to supervise with its competence the very large services (those that reach more than 10 % of the EU's population) with pan-European significance. This proposal was primarily intended to counter concerns that inadequately equipped local authorities within individual Member States would use the de facto non-enforcement of the newly created rules to attract large online platforms. The European Parliament, meanwhile, demanded stricter regulations for content moderation in order to counter the risk of over-blocking, as well as for online advertising and recommender systems. The European Parliament and the Council also agreed to address the issue of manipulative design elements (so-called dark patterns, → Ch. 4 mn. 159 et seqq.) in the DSA.

26 Inter-institutional negotiations on the text of the regulation (**trilogue negotiations**) were initiated in January 2022 with the contribution of the French Council Presidency. Following closed-door negotiations, a preliminary political agreement was reached on 23.4.2022. The agreement almost broke down due to a subsequent dispute over the wording of the 'staydown' obligation of providers (→ Ch. 3 mn. 107 et seqq.).[47] Yet in June the dispute was settled[48] and the Draft was adopted by the European Parliament on 5.7.2022[49] and by the Council on 4.10.2022.[50] The main **changes compared to the Commission draft** include increased requirements for the justification of restrictions imposed on content (Art. 17 DSA), a ban on dark patterns (Art. 25 DSA), transparency requirements for recommender systems (Art. 27 DSA), provisions for the online protection of minors (Art. 28 DSA), equal treatment of very large online search engines with very large online platforms (Chapter III Section 5 DSA) and the responsibility of the Commission for the supervision of these very large services (Art. 56 DSA). In addition, against the backdrop of Russia's attack on Ukraine and concerns about coordinated disinformation campaigns, the trilogue negotiations led to an additional article (Art. 36 DSA) which provides for a crisis response mechanism. This had not previously been discussed in the European Parliament or the Council. The DSA was published in the Official Journal of the EU on 27.10.2022 as Regulation (EU) 2022/2065 and entered into force on 16.11.2022. Many of the obligations became applicable starting on 17.2.2024 (for temporal applicability → Ch. 2 mn. 40).

---

[45] Council of the European Union, 'General Approach of the Council' (18.11.2021), 13203/21.

[46] European Parliament, 'Amendments adopted by the European Parliament on 20 January 2022 on the proposal for a regulation of the European Parliament and of the Council on a Single Market For Digital Services (Digital Services Act) and amending Directive 2000/31/EC' (20.1.2022), P9_TA(2022)0014.

[47] Bertuzzi, 'European Parliament rejects consolidated text of the Digital Services Act'.

[48] Klausa, 'Einigung zu Stay-Down-Pflichten im DSA'.

[49] European Parliament, 'European Parliament legislative resolution of 5 July 2022 on the proposal for a regulation of the European Parliament and of the Council on a Single Market For Digital Services (Digital Services Act) and amending Directive 2000/31/EC' (5.7.2022), P9_TA(2022)0269.

[50] Council of the European Union, 'DSA: Council gives final approval to the protection of users' rights online'.

II. Principles of the DSA

The European legislator was confronted with two main challenges when designing the Digital Services Act. First, the current **need for changes and additions concerning large platforms** should be addressed without impairing the **advantages and growth potential** that the liability exemptions of the E-Commerce Directive had created for the digital economy. To this end, the DSA maintains the existing liability exemptions for intermediary services to provide 'the conditions for innovative digital services to emerge and scale up in the internal market' (rec. 4 DSA). Second, providers should address the systematic risks and increased potential risk of very large services (rec. 79 et seqq. DSA). The DSA's introduction of tiered due diligence obligations (Chapter III DSA) thereby holds the services accountable. The applicability of the regulation regardless of the provider's place of establishment (Art. 2(1) DSA) serves to further hold the services accountable despite their cross-border nature. 27

The Commission identifies the following elements of the DSA in particular as essential:[51] 28

- **Measures to counter illegal goods, services or content online**, such as a mechanism for users to flag such content and platforms to cooperate with 'trusted flaggers'.
- **New obligations on traceability of business users** in online marketplaces, to help identify sellers of illegal goods.
- **Effective safeguards for users**, including the possibility to challenge platforms' content moderation decisions.
- Wide-ranging **transparency** measures for online platforms, including for algorithms used for recommendation.
- **Obligations for very large platforms** that reach more than 10 % of the EU's population to prevent abuse of their systems by taking risk-based action and through independent audits of their risk management systems.
- **Researchers to be allowed access to data** of key platforms, in order to scrutinise how platforms work.
- **Codes of conduct and technical standards** to assist platforms and other players in their compliance with the new rules. Other codes will enhance measures taken to ensure accessibility of platforms to people with disabilities or to support further measures on advertising.
- **All online intermediaries offering their services in the single market**, whether they are established in the EU or outside, must comply with the new rules.
- **Oversight structure to match the complexity of the online space**: Member States will have the primary role, supported by a new European Board for Digital Services; for very large platforms, supervision and enforcement by the Commission.

III. Structure of the DSA

The DSA is divided into five chapters. Chapter I regulates the scope of application (see Chapter 2 of this book) and the underlying definitions. Chapter II incorporates the liability exemption from the E-Commerce Directive into the Regulation and supplements specific regulations on official orders to act against illegal content (see Chapter 3 of this book). Chapter III contains the due diligence obligations for intermediary services (see Chapter 4 of this book). Chapter IV regulates the system of official enforce- 29

[51] European Commission, 'Europe fit for the Digital Age: new online rules for platforms'.

ment of these obligations and the sanctions for non-compliance with the DSA (see Chapter 4 of this book). Chapter V contains the final provisions and rules on temporal application (→ Ch. 2 mn. 40).

CHAPTER 2
OBJECTIVES, SCOPE OF APPLICATION AND RELATIONSHIP TO OTHER LEGAL INSTRUMENTS

Konstantina Nathanail

Bibliography: Albrecht, 'Digital Markets Act kommt – Regulierung von Plattformen und Auswirkungen auf Unternehmen', GWR 2022, 181; Bomhard/Merkle, 'Der Entwurf eines EU Data Acts, Neue Spielregeln für die Data Economy', RDi 2022, 168; Busch/Mak, 'Putting the Digital Services Act in Context: Bridging the Gap Between EU Consumer Law and Platform Regulation', EuCML 2021, 109; De Streel/Husovec, 'The e-commerce Directive as the cornerstone of the Internal Market' (Official Website of the European Parliament, May 2020), PE 648.797 <https://www.europarl.europa.eu/RegData/etudes/STUD/2020/648797/IPOL_STU(2020)648797_EN.pdf> (last accessed: 23.5.2024); European Commission, 'Questions and Answers: Digital Markets Act: Ensuring fair and open digital markets' (23.4.2022) <https://ec.europa.eu/commission/presscorner/detail/en/QANDA_20_2349> (last accessed: 23.5.2024); European Commission, 'Commission welcomes the adoption of the Digital Services Package by the European Parliament' (5.7.2022) <https://digital-strategy.ec.europa.eu/en/news/commission-welcomes-european-parliaments-adoption-digital-services-package> (last accessed: 23.5.2024); European Commission, 'Digital Services Act: Commission designates first set of Very Large Online Platforms and Search Engines' (25.4.2023) <https://ec.europa.eu/commission/presscorner/detail/en/ip_23_2413> (last accessed: 23.5.2024); European Commission, 'Commission calls on Cyprus, Czechia, Estonia, Poland, Portugal and Slovakia to designate and fully empower their Digital Services Coordinators under the Digital Services Act' (24.4.2024) <https://digital-strategy.ec.europa.eu/en/news/commission-calls-cyprus-czechia-estonia-poland-portugal-and-slovakia-designate-and-fully-empower> (last accessed: 23.5.2024); Gielen/Uphues, 'Digital Markets Act und Digital Services Act. Regulierung von Markt- und Meinungsmacht durch die Europäische Union', EuZW 2021, 627; Heldt, 'EU Digital Services Act: The White Hope of Intermediary Regulation' in Flew/Martin (eds), Digital Platform Regulation, London 2022, p. 69; Hennemann/von Ditfurth, 'Datenintermediäre und Data Governance Act', NJW 2022, 1905; Hennemann/Steinrötter, 'Data Act – Fundament des neuen EU-Datenwirtschaftsrechts?', NJW 2022, 1481; Herbers, 'Der Digital Markets Act (DMA) kommt – neue Dos and Don'ts für Gatekeeper in der Digitalwirtschaft', RDi 2022, 252; ICANN, 'ICANN org Submission on the Proposal for a Regulation of the European Parliament and of the Council on a Single Market for Digital Services (Digital Services Act) and Amending Directive 2000/31/EC (COM/2020/825 final; 2020/0361 (COD)) Issued by the EU Commission. Executive Summary' <https://www.icann.org/en/system/files/files/icann-org-comments-proposed-dsa-regulation-01apr21-en.pdf> (last accessed: 23.5.2024); Janal, 'Haftung und Verantwortung im Entwurf des Digital Services Acts', ZEuP 2021, 227; Jaursch, 'The Digital Services Act is in effect – now what?' (Stiftung Neue Verantwortung, 8.2.2024) <https://www.stiftung-nv.de/en/publication/digital-services-act-now-what> (last accessed: 23.5.2024); Kogon, 'How the EU is Forcing Twitter to Censor (and Musk Can't Stop It)' (Brownstone Institute, 7.10.2022) <https://brownstone.org/articles/how-the-eu-is-forcing-twitter-to-censor-and-musk-cant-stop-it/> (last accessed: 23.5.2024); Llansó, 'An Opportunity to Build Human Rights Safeguards into Notice and Action' (Medium, 17.8.2020) <https://medium.com/global-network-initiative-collection/the-dsa-an-opportunity-to-build-human-rights-safeguards-into-notice-and-action-by-emma-llans%C3%B3-e0487397646f> (last accessed: 23.5.2024); Loos, 'The (Proposed) Transposition Of The Digital Content Directive In The Netherlands', JIPITEC 2021, 229; Nextiva, 'VoIP Examples: Who Uses VoIP?' (Nextiva, 15.5.2019) <https://www.nextiva.com/blog/voip-examples.html> (last accessed: 23.5.2024); Paal/Kieß, 'Digitale Plattformen im DSA-E, DMA-E und § 19a GWB', ZfDR 2022, 1; Picht/Richter, 'EU Digital Regulation 2022: Data Desiderata', GRUR-Int 2022, 395; Polčák, 'The Legal Classification of ISPs', JIPITEC 2010, 172; Rosati, 'The DSA's Trusted Flaggers' (Verfassungsblog, 22.2.2024) <https://verfassungsblog.de/the-dsas-trusted-flaggers/> (last accessed: 23.5.2024); Schmid/Grewe, 'Digital Services Act: Neues 'Grundgesetz für Onlinedienste'? Auswirkungen des Kommissionsentwurfs für die Digitalwirtschaft', MMR 2021, 279; Scott, 'The EU's online content rulebook isn't ready for primetime' (POLITICO, 14.2.2024) <https://www.politico.eu/article/european-union-digital-services-act-dsa-thierry-breton/> (last accessed: 23.5.2024); Seip/Berberich, 'Der Entwurf des Digital Markets Act', GRUR-Prax 2021, 44; Spindler, 'Der Vorschlag für ein neues Haftungsregime für Internetprovider – der EU-Digital Services Act (Teil 1)', GRUR 2021, 545; Spindler/Sein, 'Die endgültige Richtlinie über Verträge über digitale Inhalte und Dienstleistungen. Anwendungsbereich und grundsätzliche Ansätze', MMR 2019, 415; Staudenmayer, 'Die Richtlinien zu den digitalen Verträgen', ZEuP 2019, 663; Tolks, 'Die finale Fassung des Data Governance Act. Erste Schritte in Richtung einer europäischen Datenwirtschaft', MMR 2022, 444.

A. Objectives of the DSA

1 In recent decades, the rapid **development of digital services** has significantly impacted the European economy and the lives of EU citizens. This effect, as well as the population's increasing dependency on online services, have been analysed by the European Commission in an Impact Assessment. According to the Assessment, the transition of various activities into an exclusively digital and transnational environment leads to **three core issues** related to the governance of digital services in the European single market,[1] which the DSA is expected to address:

2 First, there are 'serious societal and economic **risks and harms of online intermediaries**', from which the European legislator should protect consumers and other users. These risks include in particular illegal online activities of users that take place on the intermediaries' platforms. Such activities multiply at varying degrees and their analysis

[1] European Commission, 'Impact Assessment', SWD(2020) 348 final, Part 1, p. 10.

has proven difficult due to the scarcity of data. Also at risk is a sufficient standard of protection of fundamental rights and freedoms in the digital sphere.[2] Second, perceived limitations in day to day cooperation between Member States weaken effective supervision and good **cooperation between administrative authorities**, thereby impairing the functioning of the European single market.[3] Third, **regulatory fragmentation** creates 'new barriers in the internal market and leads to high direct and opportunity costs, notably for SMEs, including innovative start-ups and scale-ups'.[4] This results in higher costs for consumers and businesses alike.

Subsequently, the DSA legislator aims to contribute to the proper functioning of the internal market for intermediary services by setting out harmonised rules for a safe, predictable and trusted online environment that facilitates innovation and in which fundamental rights enshrined in the Charter, including the principle of consumer protection, are effectively protected (Art. 1(1) DSA). This balancing act between harnessing the vast benefits of digital platforms and mitigating the associated risks poses the great challenge, yet it is also the central aim of the DSA. 3

I. The proper functioning of the internal market for intermediary services

The realisation of the European single market, as laid down in Art. 3(2) and (3) sent. 1 TEU and Art. 26 TFEU, is one of the **fundamental objectives of the European Union** and a core element of **European integration.**[5] Accordingly, under Art. 114 TFEU, measures for the harmonisation of the provisions laid down in Member State laws, regulation or administrative actions aiming at the establishment and functioning of the internal market fall within the competence of the European Parliament and the Council. 4

The traditional understanding of the internal market, which can already be found in the EEC Treaty of 1957, has evolved over time and has been adapted to the changing economic and social needs in the course of the digital transformation. As a result, the EU has taken various measures to create a **common Digital Single Market**, which in particular allows for the free movement of services (for more details → Ch. 1 mn. 8 et seqq.). 5

The realisation of the internal market is predominantly carried by the **fundamental freedoms**, which the CJEU understands as prohibitions of restrictions.[6] Given the cross-border nature of the internet as the basic infrastructure for intermediary services, the fundamental freedom of free movement of goods and services and the freedom of establishment increasingly take up a pivotal role in strengthening cross-border digital services (rec. 2 sent. 2 and rec. 32 sent. 3 DSA). In practice, these freedoms mean that goods and services purchased on the internet should reach buyers without significant obstacles, and that access to an intermediary service without hinderances must be ensured. At the same time, the freedom to take up and pursue activities as self-employed persons and to set up and manage undertakings (Art. 49(2) TFEU) must be guaranteed. 6

---

[2] European Commission, 'Impact Assessment', SWD(2020) 348 final, Part 1, p. 10, 12.
[3] European Commission, 'Impact Assessment', SWD(2020) 348 final, Part 1, p. 10, 21.
[4] European Commission, 'Impact Assessment', SWD(2020) 348 final, Part 1, p. 10, 23.
[5] Cf. Ruffert in Calliess/Ruffert EUV Art. 3 mn. 22.
[6] Terhechte in Grabitz/Hilf/Nettesheim EUV Art. 3 mn. 40.

II. Creating a safe, predictable and trustworthy online environment

7 The DSA aims to create a safe, predictable and trustworthy online environment that encourages innovation by harmonising the legal framework for digital services. To achieve this goal, the DSA establishes a 'clear, effective, predictable and balanced set of harmonised **due diligence obligations**', taking into account the nature and size of the intermediary service (rec. 40 sent. 1 and rec. 41 sent. 1 DSA).

1. Harmonisation of the legal framework

8 In its Impact Assessment for the preparation of the DSA, the Commission noted that, given the international dimension of illegal content, a **patchwork of national measures** could not provide effective protection for Union citizens.[7] At the same time, there is a need for harmonised safeguards to protect users' fundamental rights and prevent the excessive removal of legal content.[8] The legal harmonisation of rules within the internal market is expected to increase the volume of cross-border digital trade by 1 %–1.8 %.[9]

9 These considerations are also reflected in the recitals of the DSA. Since diverging national laws impair the European internal market (rec. 2 sent. 2 DSA), their harmonisation will offer businesses access to new markets and internal market advantages and provide users with a wider choice of products and services (rec. 2 sent. 3 DSA). Furthermore, harmonising the internal market should reduce uncertainty for developers and increase system **interoperability** (rec. 4 sent. 3 DSA).

10 The legislator selected the legal instrument of a **Regulation** to harmonise the existing regulatory regime, due to the instrument's direct and indirect effect (→ Ch. 3 mn. 7 et seqq.). A Regulation – unlike a Directive, such as the E-Commerce Directive – does not carry the risk of diverging implementation by national legislators. The harmonisation of the rules within the scope of a Regulation also prohibits Member States from enacting additional national requirements in the corresponding regulatory areas of the European law. Of course, national legislation remains permissible under Art. 3 E-Commerce Directive insofar as it serves a legitimate public interest beyond the objectives of the DSA (rec. 9 sent. 3 DSA).

2. Harmonisation of the exemptions from liability and the due diligence obligations for providers

11 The objective of the DSA is the **harmonisation of rules on the provision of intermediary services** in the internal market (Art. 1(2) sent. 1 DSA), including the already tested provisions of the E-Commerce Directive on conditional exemption from liability for providers of intermediary services (Art. 1(2) sent. 2(a) DSA). With regard to these liability exemptions, the European legislator could have been content with setting out the continued application of the provisions of the E-Commerce Directive – which have long been transposed into national law. However, given the divergences in the transposition and application of these provisions at the national level, and in order to achieve clarity and coherence, the legislator saw the need to incorporate them into the DSA with a few adjustments that take into account recent developments in case law (cf. rec. 16 sent. 3 DSA). The respective provisions of the E-Commerce Directive have been deleted

---

[7] European Commission, 'Impact Assessment', SWD(2020) 348 final, Part 1, p. 38.
[8] European Commission, 'Impact Assessment', SWD(2020) 348 final, Part 1, p. 38.
[9] European Commission, 'Impact Assessment', SWD(2020) 348 final, Part 1, p. 51.

(Art. 89(1) DSA), thereby narrowing the scope of application of the corresponding national transposition provisions significantly.

At the same time, **harmonised due diligence obligations** are introduced, which are tailored to certain categories of providers of intermediary services (Art. 1(2) sent. 2(b) DSA), namely in a tiered regulatory regime which differentiates between (all) intermediary services, hosting services, online platforms, online marketplaces[10] and very large online platforms and search engines. In this way, the DSA takes into consideration the results of the public consultation procedure on the DSA, in which citizens, companies, business associations, NGOs and public bodies supported far-reaching harmonisation of the obligations of online services.[11] 12

3. Implementation and enforcement

The DSA is intended to harmonise not only the requirements for the provision of intermediary services but also the implementation and enforcement of the obligations imposed (Art. 1(2) sent. 2(c) DSA). This includes **cooperation and coordination** between the competent authorities on a European and national level. In particular, the cross-border and cross-sectoral nature of intermediary services requires that national authorities cooperate consistently and effectively with each other and provide each other with the necessary information on issues, investigations and actions taken (rec. 127 sent. 3 DSA). This collaborative scheme, however, may prove to be challenging, as Digital Services Coordinators are implementing the Regulation at varying speeds, with some already initiating procedures against providers[12] as other Member States yet have to designate their competent authorities.[13] Furthermore, in order to ensure the effective enforcement of the DSA, national coordinators for digital services should carry out their cooperation with the help of a reliable and secure **information sharing system** (Art. 85 DSA, → Ch. 5 mn. 27 et seq.; cf. rec. 148 DSA), which should also enable mutual administrative assistance (Art. 57 DSA, → Ch. 5 mn. 20 et seq.). The new **European Board for Digital Services**, which enables the cooperation of Digital Services Coordinators, was established with effect from 17.2.2024 and will also contribute to this information exchange (Art. 61 et seqq. DSA, → Ch. 5 mn. 14 et seqq.). 13

III. Promotion of fundamental rights, in particular the principle of consumer protection

Protecting the fundamental rights guaranteed in the **Charter of Fundamental Rights** of the European Union is one of the central principles of the DSA (rec. 3 DSA). As such, fundamental rights and their protection are both the reason for the regulation of intermediary services and simultaneously the substantive limit on that regulation (rec. 9 sent. 1, rec. 22 sent. 2, rec. 40 sent. 2 and rec. 41 sent. 4 DSA). In addition, providers 14

---

[10] Referred to in the DSA as 'online platforms allowing consumers to conclude distance contracts with traders'.

[11] European Commission, 'Summary Report on the open public consultation on the Digital Services Act Package' (15.12.2020), Ref. Ares(2020)7629347. In particular, this concerned the harmonisation of notice and action procedures, which should be 'simple, standardised and transparent', cf. p. 5.

[12] Kroet, 'E-commerce platform Temu quizzed by Irish regulator' (13.3.2024) <https://www.euronews.com/next/2024/03/13/e-commerce-platform-temu-quizzed-by-irish-regulator> (last accessed: 23.5.2024).

[13] The European Commission sent a letter of formal notice to six Member States that had not yet designated their Digital Services Coordinator on 24.4.2024: European Commission, 'Commission calls on Cyprus, Czechia, Estonia, Poland, Portugal and Slovakia to designate and fully empower their Digital Services Coordinators under the Digital Services Act'.

of intermediary services are required to take fundamental rights into account when providing their services,[14] thereby establishing a kind of indirect third-party effect of (EU) fundamental rights.[15]

15 The European legislator emphasises, in particular, the **right to freedom of expression** and **information** and the **freedom and pluralism of the media** (Art. 11 CFR).[16] It also echoes the sentiment from the previously mentioned consultation process that combating illegal content should not unduly limit freedom of expression and media rights,[17] supporting the voices calling for effective mechanisms to prevent the removal of legitimate content. This view takes into consideration the gradual establishment of 'state-like dominant positions' of private companies, who are increasingly able to determine the framework and conditions of public discourse.[18] In particular, the issues of overblocking and collateral censorship that had been discussed with regard to Art. 14 E-Commerce Directive remain relevant after its transfer to Art. 6 DSA.[19]

IV. Conclusion

16 The success of the DSA in enhancing platform users' daily experiences and protecting them from dangers inherent to the internet will depend on its novel oversight structure designed to enforce the rules it establishes. So far, the views on the Regulation's impact have varied widely, with some describing it as legislation with 'momentous and disastrous implications for freedom of speech worldwide'[20] and others hinting at EU internal conflicts that effectively hinder its implementation.[21] Whether it will bring significant benefits or merely become a bureaucratic exercise with little improvement remains to be seen.[22]

B. Scope of application of the DSA

17 The scope of application of the DSA includes all intermediary services offered to users that have their place of establishment or are located in the Union, irrespective of where the providers of those intermediary services have their place of establishment (Art. 2(1) DSA, **marketplace principle**).[23]

---

[14] Rec. 47 sent. 1 and rec. 51 sent. 1, Art. 14(4), Art. 34(1) subpara. 2(b) and Art. 35(1) sent. 1 DSA.

[15] On the importance of incorporating specific fundamental rights in the DSA in contrast to the E-Commerce Directive cf. Llansó, 'The Digital Services Act: An Opportunity to Build Human Rights Safeguards into Notice and Action'.

[16] Rec. 3, rec. 22 sent. 2, rec. 47 sent. 2, rec. 81 sent. 1 and rec. 86 sent. 4, Art. 14(4) and Art. 34(1) subpara. 2 sent. 2(b) DSA.

[17] Cf. rec. 90 sent. 4 and rec. 153 sent. 2 and rec. 3 DSA; European Commission, 'Summary Report on the open public consultation on the Digital Services Act Package' (15.12.2020), Ref. Ares(2020)7629347, p. 5.

[18] BVerfG 6.11.2019 – 1 BvR 16/13, NJW 2020, 300 mn. 88 – Right to be forgotten I.

[19] In support of the balance struck by the European legislator Heldt, p. 79 et seq.

[20] Kogon, 'How the EU is Forcing Twitter to Censor (and Musk Can't Stop It)'.

[21] Scott, 'The EU's online content rulebook isn't ready for primetime'.

[22] Jaursch, 'The Digital Services Act is in effect – now what?'.

[23] Spindler GRUR 2021, 545 (547).

I. Material scope of application

According to the definition in Art. 3(g) DSA, the term intermediary service includes three specific kinds of information society services, namely **mere conduit** (Art. 3(g)(i) DSA), **caching services** (Art. 3(g)(ii) DSA) and **hosting services** (Art. 3(g)(iii) DSA). 18

The term **'information society service'** corresponds to that of the E-Commerce Directive and is defined according to the Directive on Information Society services as 'any service normally provided for remuneration, at a distance, by electronic means and at the individual request of a recipient of services' (Art. 3(a) DSA). 19

The term information society service is interpreted broadly[24] and, according to the case law of the CJEU, includes services that enable the initiation of contracts between consumers and service providers on an electronic platform,[25] the provision of free internet access via Wi-Fi[26] as well as certain online marketplaces.[27] Regarding the requirement of remuneration for services, the ECJ states in its *Papasavvas* decision that the term also includes online information services for which the service provider is remunerated, not by the recipient, but by income generated by advertisements posted on the website.[28] 20

However, the scopes of application of the DSA and the E-Commerce Directive differ. While the E-Commerce Directive regulates the provision of 'information society services', the DSA focuses on **'providers of intermediary services'**. It follows from Art. 3(g) DSA that the information society services covered by the DSA are a sub-category of information society services under the E-Commerce Directive, which is why the concept of intermediary services governed by the DSA is narrower.[29] Thus, the E-Commerce Directive remains applicable in particular to online services such as news sites or regular online shops where only the provider's content is made accessible. In contrast, the DSA only concerns **intermediaries**. 21

1. Intermediary services

The definitions of the individual categories of intermediary services from Art. 12–14 E-Commerce Directive were adopted verbatim. Which specific services fall within the respective terms has been specified primarily based on the case law of the CJEU. In addition, in rec. 29 DSA, the legislator gives **examples of services that fall within each cate-** 22

---

[24] Oster/Wagner in Dauses/Ludwigs EU WirtschaftsR-HdB E. V. mn. 88.

[25] ECJ 19.12.2019 – case C-390/18, ECLI:EU:C:2019:1112 para. 69 – Airbnb.

[26] ECJ 15.9.2016 – case C-484/14, ECLI:EU:C:2016:689 para. 43 and 54 – McFadden.

[27] Cf. ECJ 12.7.2011 – case C-324/09, ECLI:EU:C:2011:474 para. 123 et seq. – L'Oréal et al. For further examples, cf. De Streel/Husovec, 'The e-commerce Directive as the cornerstone of the Internal Market', p. 20.

[28] ECJ 11.9.2014 – case C-291/13, ECLI:EU:C:2014:2209 para. 30 – Papasavvas; on the question of renumeration, cf. in detail Oster/Wagner in Dauses/Ludwigs EU WirtschaftsR-HdB E. V. mn. 88.

[29] The relationship between the terms 'information society service', as defined in the E-Commerce Directive and 'intermediary service', as defined in the DSA and the general term of intermediary service is currently unclear. For example, ECJ 20.12.2017 – case C-434/15, ECLI:EU:C:2017:981 para. 35 and 42 – Asociación Profesional Elite Taxi, and ECJ 10.4.2018 – case C-320/16, ECLI:EU:C:2018:221 para. 19 and 22 – Uber France SAS, state that not all 'intermediary services' are to be understood as information society services within the meaning of the E-Commerce Directive. This shows that the ECJ considers the term 'intermediary service' to be broader. However, the ruling dates back to a time before the enactment of the DSA, so that the relationship between the terms requires further clarification in case law.

gory. The named examples represent a broad spectrum of services, some of whose categorisations contradict the assessments of national courts.[30]

a) Mere conduit

23 'Mere conduit' refers to an intermediary service which consists of **transmitting information provided by users in a communications network** or **providing access to a communications network** (Art. 3(g)(i) DSA).[31] According to rec. 28 sent. 2 and rec. 29 sent. 2 DSA, the term includes local wireless networks with internet access (Wi-Fi),[32] internet exchange points (such as DE-CIX), virtual private networks, DNS services and DNS resolvers, services of top-level domain name registries (such as DENIC, EURid), registrars,[33] certification authorities issuing digital certificates, internet voice telephony (VoIP such as WhatsApp or Skype)[34] and other communication services.[35] It remains noteworthy that according to rec. 28 sent. 2 DSA providers can benefit from the exemptions from liability set out in the Regulation 'to the extent' that their services qualify as 'mere conduit', 'caching' or 'hosting' services. DNS providers, which were concerned about a potentially 'extremely broad spectrum of actors' falling under the DSA, consider this formulation to be unclear, thereby leading to uncertainty for affected providers.[36]

24 In contrast to hosting providers, providers of mere conduit and caching services can only benefit from the exemptions from liability when they do not have any link to the transmitted information and, in particular, may not modify the information during transmission (rec. 21 sent. 1 and 2 DSA). Interventions of a technical nature during transmission or access do not constitute a modification, as long as they do not alter the integrity of the information (rec. 21 sent. 3 DSA).

b) Caching

25 Caching services, according to Art. 3(g)(ii) DSA include services of **transmission of information provided by users in a communications network**. In contrast to the concept of mere conduit, this term also includes cases in which intermediate storage of the transmitted information takes place (cf. Art. 3(g)(ii) DSA). However, this storage must be automatic, intermediate, limited in time, and only take place because the transmission of information to other users at their request can be done more efficiently (Art. 3(g)(ii) DSA). These services are characterized by their importance for the smooth and efficient transmission of information provided on the internet. Examples include the operation of networks for the provision of content (content delivery networks), reverse proxies and proxies for the adaptation of content (rec. 29 sent. 2 DSA). Since information is

---

[30] For example, the German Federal Court (*Bundesgerichtshof* – BGH) does not consider domain registrars to be service providers within the meaning of the TMG (transposition act of the E-Commerce Directive in Germany), BGH 15.10.2020 – I ZR 13/19, GRUR 2021, 63 mn. 16.

[31] In the literature, these providers are also called 'access providers', cf. Spindler in Spindler/Schmitz TMG § 8 mn. 5, 16, 18 and 21.

[32] ECJ 15.9.2016 – case C-484/14, ECLI:EU:C:2016:689 para. 43 – McFadden.

[33] ECJ 7.8.2018 – case C-521/17, ECLI:EU:C:2018:639 para. 52 – Coöperatieve Vereniging SNB-REACT.

[34] Cf. Nextiva, 'VoIP Examples: Who Uses VoIP?'.

[35] Cf. ECJ 6.10.2020 – cases C-511/18, C-512/18, C-520/18, ECLI:EU:C:2020:791 para. 212 – La Quadrature du Net et al.

[36] ICANN, 'ICANN org Submission on the Proposal for a Regulation of the European Parliament and of the Council on a Single Market for Digital Services (Digital Services Act) and Amending Directive 2000/31/EC (COM/2020/825 final; 2020/0361 (COD)) Issued by the EU Commission. Executive Summary', p. 2.

stored longer in caching services than in mere conduit, Art. 5(1) DSA requires additional technical conditions for the liability exemption to apply.

c) Hosting

In the case of hosting services, the **information provided by users is stored at their request** (Art. 3(g)(iii) DSA) with the service provider offering an infrastructure where user data is stored.[37] Examples of hosting services are cloud computing services, web hosting services, paid referencing services and services enabling sharing information and content online, including file storage and sharing (rec. 29 sent. 4 DSA). These refer to online marketplaces such as eBay and social networks such as Facebook and TikTok.[38] In addition, the provision of a video sharing or share hosting platform can also be understood as 'hosting' if the provider does not take an active role that includes knowledge of or control over the content uploaded to their platform.[39] 26

d) Hybrid services

The starting point for the application of the DSA and the corresponding due diligence obligations is the provision of an intermediary service. Therefore, each service must be assessed separately, even if the same provider offers several services. In the case of so-called hybrid services where the provider offers multiple services of which only some fall within the scope of application of the entire DSA or specific provisions, the respective provisions **apply only to those services falling within the scope of application** of the provisions (rec. 15 DSA). However, in the case of a uniform business model in which the services offered cannot be distinguished from one another, an assessment must be made as to whether the business model's focus is the provision of an intermediary service.[40] 27

2. No intermediary services

A service falls outside the DSA's definition of an intermediary service when no information provided by users is involved. This is the case, for instance, when **providers only upload and share their own content**, without allowing users to store their content. Accordingly, the exemptions from liability regulated in Art. 4–8 DSA (→ Ch. 3 mn. 43 et seqq.) do not apply to the providers of these services. This is compensated, of course, by the fact that these providers are not subject to the due diligence obligations under Chapter III DSA either. 28

However, the fact that a service does not meet the requirements of Art. 4–8 DSA does not automatically mean that there is no intermediary service within the definition of the DSA to which the information and due diligence obligations would apply. A provider can fall under the scope of application of the Regulation and be bound by the obligation it foresees, while not fulfilling the criteria of Art. 4–8 DSA that would grant a liability exemption. For example, in a case of mere conduit under Art. 3(g)(i) DSA, a provider that selects the information transmitted is not exempt from liability under Art. 4(1)(c) DSA. Nonetheless, the obligations under Chapter III DSA remain applicable to such a provider. 29

---

[37] Polčák JIPITEC 2010, 172 (175).

[38] Cf. ECJ 12.7.2011 – case C-324/09, ECLI:EU:C:2011:474 para. 124 – L'Oréal et al. and ECJ 3.10.2019 – case C-18/18, ECLI:EU:C:2019:821 para. 22 – Glawischnig-Piesczek.

[39] ECJ 22.6.2021 – cases C-682/18 and C-683/18, ECLI:EU:C:2021:503 para. 117 – YouTube and Cyando.

[40] Janal ZEuP 2021, 227 (235).

3. Exceptions

30 According to Art. 2(2) DSA, the Regulation does not apply to the provision of a service or the distribution of a product solely because an intermediary service is used for the provision of that service. In practice, this is the case, for example, with regard to remote information technology services, transport, accommodation and delivery services (rec. 6 sent. 1 DSA). Additionally, the DSA is intended to apply only to intermediary services and is without prejudice to the requirements laid down in Union or national law for products and services enabled through intermediary services. Finally, services provided through an intermediary service are not covered by the DSA even if the intermediary service is an integral part of another service which is not an intermediary service as recognised in the case law of the CJEU (cf. rec. 6 sent. 2 DSA).

4. Lack of distinction criteria

31 Interestingly, the legislator refrains from making two distinctions that are relevant in practice. First, the definition of intermediary services (Art. 3(g) DSA) does not distinguish between **content and transaction platforms**, although these were often separately regulated in earlier EU legislation. Specific obligations for online trading platforms are only included in Art. 30–32 DSA and focus on the traceability of traders operating on the platforms.[41] Furthermore, the DSA only distinguishes between **commercial users and consumers** in isolated cases (e.g. in Art. 6(3) and Art. 29–32 DSA) and otherwise refers to 'users' or 'recipients of the service' without further differentiation.

5. Case law

32 Despite the short amount of time since the entry into force of the DSA, the Commission already has a complaint in its hands: Following the adoption of the first designation decisions by the Commission on 25.4.2023, Zalando SE filed a complaint with the Court of Justice of the European Union.[42] Zalando, which alongside 16 other entities was designated as a VLOP,[43] challenges inter alia the application of the DSA on its services, claiming that it does not constitute an intermediary service provider within the scope of the Regulation. Zalando argues that it 'lacks the necessary provision of third-party content' and instead 'provides its own content through the sale of its articles'. With regard to third-party content published on its website, Zalando claims that it only adopts it following a 'strict onboarding process'.[44]

33 Thus, one can infer that Zalando understands third-party products sold on its platform not being 'information provided by a recipient of the service' or that the transaction does not include 'the provision of access to a communication network' within the meaning of Art. 3(g)(i) DSA. This argument, however, would narrow significantly the scope of application of Chapter III Section 4 DSA, which refers specifically to marketplaces (in detail → Ch. 4 mn. 188). The 'strict onboarding process' that Zalando points to simply seems to prove the platform's ability to fulfil the requirements with regard to traceability of traders (Art. 30 DSA) – it does not however exclude its services from the scope of application of the Section and the DSA in general. After all, Zalando itself clarifies in its terms and conditions that third parties ('Zalando partners') can become the

[41] Detailed information on the obligations for online marketplaces → Ch. 4 mn. 188 et seqq.
[42] Case T-348/23 – Zalando v Commission.
[43] European Commission, 'Digital Services Act: Commission designates first set of Very Large Online Platforms and Search Engines'.
[44] Case T-348/23 – Zalando v Commission.

contractual partner of the buyer.[45] Thereby, Zalando is offering distance contracts within the meaning of Art. 2(7) of Directive 2011/83/EU and within the scope of Art. 29–32 DSA, such that its activity is encompassed by the DSA.

II. Territorial scope of application

1. Offering a service in the Union

34 For the application of the E-Commerce Directive, the service provider had to be established in the territory of a Member State (Art. 3(1) E-Commerce Directive). This pushed the legislative instrument to its limits in cases where services were provided from outside the EU.[46] In order to ensure the effectiveness of the rules laid down in this Regulation and a level playing field within the internal market (rec. 7 DSA), it is now sufficient for the application of the DSA that the intermediary services are offered to **users that have their place of establishment or are located in the Union**, irrespective of the place of establishment of the provider of these intermediary services (Art. 2(1) DSA, **marketplace principle** or ***lex loci solutionis***).

35 However, to avoid a limitless application of the DSA, its scope is narrowed by the requirement that the providers must **'offer services in the Union'**, in Art. 3(d) DSA. For this to be the case, a **'substantial connection to the Union'** is required, which can be based on the provider's place of establishment or specific factual criteria such as a **significant number of users** in one or more Member States in comparison to its or their total population or the targeting of activity towards one or more Member States (Art. 3(e) DSA; see in detail → Ch. 4 mn. 31).

36 Rec. 8 sent. 2 DSA does, however, provide guidance as to when a provider's activity is **targeted at a Member State**. This is determined based on all relevant circumstances, including factors such as the use of a language or currency commonly used in the Member State concerned, the possibility of ordering products or services with delivery in the Member State and the use of a top-level domain of the Member State. Furthermore, the targeting of activities to a Member State can also be inferred from the availability of an application in the respective national app store, the placement of local advertising or advertisements in a local language or the management of customer relations, for example by providing customer service in a language commonly used in the Member State in question.

37 A substantial connection should also be assumed if a service provider **directs its activity within the meaning of Art. 17(1)(c) Brussels Ia Regulation to one or more Member States** (rec. 8 sent. 4 DSA). This is the case if the provider directs his activities to that State or to several States including that Member State, and the contract falls within the scope of such activities. Art. 17(1)(c) Brussels Ia Regulation is primarily intended to take into account the special features of internet commerce but is not limited to this area.[47] The contracting party pursuing the activity must seek customers in the Member State concerned, which is already the case when an offer or advertisement has reached the specific user.[48]

---

[45] Zalando, 'Summary of our general terms and conditions' <https://en.zalando.de/zalando-terms/> (last accessed: 23.5.2024).

[46] De Streel/Husovec, 'The e-commerce Directive as the cornerstone of the Internal Market', p. 39.

[47] De Streel/Husovec, 'The e-commerce Directive as the cornerstone of the Internal Market', p. 39.

[48] Gottwald in MüKoZPO Brüssel Ia-VO Art. 17 mn. 9.

2. Comparable regulations

38 A possible point of reference for the interpretation of Art. 2(1) DSA is provided by the TCO Regulation. According to Art. 1(2) TCO Regulation, it applies to hosting service providers 'offering services in the Union, irrespective of their place of main establishment'. According to Art. 2(4) TCO Regulation, in order to assume such an activity, a 'substantial connection' to one or more Member States is required. Art. 2(5) and rec. 16 TCO Regulation define the conditions under which such a substantial connection is to be assumed almost word-for-word identically with the corresponding passages of the DSA. However, the CJEU has not yet concretised these terms.

39 The marketplace principle of Art. 2(1) DSA was already introduced by the **General Data Protection Regulation (GDPR)**. In principle, Art. 3(1) GDPR requires the establishment of a controller or processor in the Union.[49] However, according to Art. 3(2) GDPR, the Regulation also applies to controllers or processors not established in the EU if the data subject is located in the EU and the data processing is carried out in connection with the offering of goods or services in the EU, or if they conduct monitoring of a behaviour and the behaviour takes place in the EU. The GDPR is materially and territorially applicable depending on the individual processing operation (Art. 2(1) GDPR), and therefore the applicability of the GDPR depends on the fulfilment of the requirements set out in Art. 3(1) and (2) GDPR (data processing in connection with offering goods or services or observing a person's behaviour) in the individual case. In contrast, Art. 3(e) DSA requires that the provider's activities generally exceed certain thresholds, which are user-related but require a plurality of users. Similarly, the Digital Markets Act (DMA) applies to 'core platform services provided or offered by gatekeepers to business users established in the Union or end users established or located in the Union' (Art. 1(2) DMA).

III. Temporal scope of application

40 The DSA came into force on 16.11.2022. As of **17.2.2024** the Regulation applies to all providers of intermediary services (Art. 93(2) subpara. 1 DSA). However, certain provisions of the DSA started applying to providers of VLOPs and VLOSEs earlier: Following the adoption of the first designation decisions under the DSA on 25.4.2023,[50] the 19 providers affected had to comply with the obligations under the DSA no later than **four months** after the Commission notified them of their designation as a provider of a VLOP or VLOSE (Art. 33(6), Art. 92 DSA).

C. Relationship between the DSA and other legal instruments

41 The DSA affects the scope of application of several sector-specific and horizontal legal acts that regulate digital content and intermediary services.

[49] Cf. also ECJ 15.6.2021 – case C-645/19, ECLI:EU:C:2021:483 para. 86 – Facebook Ireland et al.

[50] European Commission, 'Digital Services Act: Commission designates first set of Very Large Online Platforms and Search Engines'.

I. E-Commerce Directive

The DSA is intended to **supplement the E-Commerce Directive**. In principle, the DSA does not affect the Directive's application (Art. 2(3) DSA), except for the rules on exemptions from liability of Art. 12–15 E-Commerce Directive, which are removed from the Directive (Art. 89(1) DSA) and incorporated with few modifications into Art. 4–8 DSA. However, even after the removal of the provisions on exemption from liability in Art. 12–15 E-Commerce Directive, there remains a considerable scope of application for the provisions of the Directive. This applies particularly to the provisions on establishment and information requirements (Art. 4–8 E-Commerce Directive) and the rules on contracts concluded by electronic means (Art. 9–11 E-Commerce Directive). 42

II. Sector-specific legislation

1. General principle

As a horizontal regulation for all intermediary services, **the DSA is intended to supplement sector-specific regulations** but **not to replace** them (Art. 2(4) DSA).[51] Some voices in the literature criticise this, claiming that, as a new conceptualisation of regulation of social media, search engines and other platforms, the DSA should be tasked with unifying Union law and eliminating inconsistencies.[52] The enactment of the DSA as a further regulatory instrument, they argue, fails to exploit this potential and leads to further ambiguities regarding the rules applicable in individual cases.[53] 43

2. Audiovisual Media Services Directive

Regulations applicable alongside the DSA include the Audiovisual Media Services Directive (**AVMS Directive**), which is intended to promote the free distribution of audiovisual media services in the Digital Single Market.[54] The extension of the scope of the AVMS Directive to video-sharing platform services[55] means that many media service platforms regulated by the AVMS Directive fall within the scope of the DSA. This parallel regulation of platforms is particularly relevant for user-generated content websites, which are classified both as online platforms under Art. 3(i) DSA and as audiovisual media services under Art. 1(1)(a) AVMS Directive. 44

3. Copyright

The DSA also applies without prejudice to Union provisions in the field of copyright and related rights (Art. 2(4)(b) DSA). These include the **InfoSoc Directive**, the **Enforcement Directive** and the **DSM Directive** (rec. 11 DSA). 45

However, the relationship between the DSA and the DSM Directive in particular, especially with regard to Art. 17 DSM Directive on the liability of platforms for works protected by copyright, raises **questions of distinction and applicability**. According to **Art. 17(1) and (3) DSM Directive**, online content-sharing service providers under certain circumstances bear the responsibility for copyright infringements in content uploaded by their users and therefore cannot invoke the exemption from liability under 46

---

[51] Schmid/Grewe MMR 2021, 279 (282).
[52] Busch/Mak EuCML 2021, 109 (110).
[53] Busch/Mak EuCML 2021, 109 (110).
[54] Ukrow/Ress in Grabitz/Hilf/Nettesheim AEUV Art. 167 mn. 214.
[55] Through Directive (EU) 2018/1808.

Art. 14(1) E-Commerce Directive. This continues to apply under the DSA because, according to Art. 89(2) DSA, any reference to Art. 14(1) E-Commerce Directive shall be construed as a reference to Art. 6(1) DSA. Thus, copyright liability under the DSM Directive simultaneously excludes the exemption from liability under the DSA. This, of course, will not be the case, where providers comply with the cumulative requirements under Article 17(4)(b)–(c) DSM Directive.[56]

47 With regard to other provisions, the DSA supplements the DSM Directive, especially concerning procedural obligations (such as the creation of points of contact for users, Art. 12 DSA, and transparency reporting obligations, Art. 15 DSA).

4. Regulation for Combating Terrorist Content Online

48 The **TCO Regulation** imposes due diligence obligations on hosting service providers[57] to combat the public dissemination of terrorist content online, including short removal deadlines (Art. 4(4) TCO Regulation) as well as transparency and reporting requirements (Art. 7 and 8 TCO Regulation). These obligations apply in **addition** to the requirements of the DSA. This is evident because the term 'illegal content' includes terrorist content (rec. 12 sent. 2 and 3 DSA), which would be contradictory if the TCO Regulation as a *lex specialis* were to have a blocking effect *vis-à-vis* the DSA.

5. Regulation on platform-to-business relations

49 The **P2B Regulation**, which aims to ensure greater transparency and effective remedies for commercial users of online intermediation services within the EU in digital commercial transactions, also remains **applicable**. Since online intermediation services and online search engines mentioned in Art. 1(2) P2B Regulation will generally be qualified as providers of intermediary services within the meaning of the DSA, the two instruments share points of overlap.[58] Their common scope of application is further increased due to the broad understanding of the term 'recipients of a service' under the DSA, which refers to consumers as well as business and other users (rec. 2 sent. 4 DSA). The same applies to the requirements for internal complaint-handling systems (Art. 20 DSA and Art. 11 P2B Regulation) and the out of-court dispute settlement options (Art. 21 DSA and Art. 12 P2B Regulation). The question, therefore, arises as to whether the provisions apply cumulatively or whether the P2B Regulation takes precedence as a special regulation (→ Ch. 4 mn. 118 et seq.).[59] The latter would be rather impractical and, in the absence of clarity about the relationship between the systems, not user-friendly.

6. Consumer protection and product safety

50 Union legislation in the areas of consumer protection and product safety is not intended to be affected by the DSA. Such legislation includes, in particular, the Regulation on Cooperation between national authorities responsible for the enforcement of consumer protection laws, the Regulation on market surveillance and compliance of products, the Product Safety Directive and the ADR Directive (Art. 2(4)(f) DSA). Art. 2(4)

---

[56] Rosati, 'The DSA's Trusted Flaggers'.

[57] The definition of the term 'hosting service provider' according to Art. 2(1) TCO Regulation differs slightly from the definition according to Art. 3(g)(iii) DSA and has common elements with the term 'online platform' according to Art. 3(i) DSA.

[58] Cf. definition of 'online intermediary service' and 'online search engine' according to Art. 2(2) and (5) P2B Regulation accordingly.

[59] Busch/Mak EuCML 2021, 109 (114).

(d) DSA explicitly highlights the Regulation on the marketing and use of explosives precursors.

51 The **Digital Content Directive** also constitutes part of consumer protection law. This is a fully harmonising Directive (cf. Art. 4 Digital Content Directive), which prescribes obligations and warranty rights for digital content and digital services in order to 'contribute to the proper functioning of the internal market while providing for a high level of consumer protection' according to Art. 1 Digital Content Directive. The legislator has refrained from restricting the types of contracts covered by the Directive, just as he has also refrained from regulating the conclusion and termination of a contract.[60] Given the need for its adaptation to different legal systems as well as the need for flexibility in rules governing the digital domain,[61] such a 'contract type-neutral' regulation seems appropriate.[62] It applies alongside the DSA.[63]

7. Data protection

52 Union legislation on the protection of personal data **continues to apply** within the scope of the DSA.[64] This applies, in particular, to the GDPR and the ePrivacy Directive.

53 The **GDPR**, as the central instrument of data protection law in the EU, pursues two objectives according to its Art. 1: On the one hand, it aims to contribute to the protection of natural persons concerning the processing of personal data (Art. 1(1) and (2) GDPR) and, on the other hand, it is intended to protect the free movement of such data (Art. 1(1) and (3) GDPR). References to the GDPR can also be found in the substantive part of the DSA with regard to the definition of profiling (Art. 26(3), Art. 28(2) and Art. 38 DSA) and the examination of the permissibility of data disclosure processes (Art. 40(8) subpara. 1(g) and (13) sent. 2 DSA).

54 According to Art. 2(4)(g) DSA, the DSA shall be **without prejudice** to the applicability of the **GDPR**. This means that in the context of issuing orders to act against illegal content or to provide information, the provisions of the GDPR must be observed, in particular those concerning the prohibition of general obligations to monitor information or to actively seek facts, or circumstances indicating illegal activity (rec. 34 sent. 7 DSA). Furthermore, the requirement under the DSA to provide information concerning advertising is not intended to override the relevant GDPR provisions, particularly with regard to the right to object to automated decision-making in individual cases. This concerns profiling operations and the requirement to obtain consent of the data subject prior to the processing of personal data for targeted advertising (rec. 68 sent. 7 DSA).

8. Further provisions

55 Finally, according to Art. 2(4)(h)–(j) DSA, Union law in the areas of judicial cooperation in civil and criminal matters, legal acts establishing the rules governing contractual and non-contractual obligations and rules governing the appointment of legal representatives for the purpose of gathering evidence in criminal proceedings shall remain **unaffected**.

---

60 Spindler/Sein MMR 2019, 415.

61 Cf. Loos JIPITEC 2021, 229 (233 et seq.), also rec. 10 sent. 2 Digital Content Directive, according to which the substantive provisions must be 'future-proof'.

62 Staudenmayer ZEuP 2019, 663 (668).

63 Cf. Loos JIPITEC 2021, 229 (234) on the parallel implementation of the legal instruments.

64 Regarding the protection of data-related intellectual property rights cf. Picht/Richter GRUR-Int 2022, 395 (401).

III. Other instruments of the EU Digital Strategy

56 The DSA was prepared and implemented within the framework of the EU Digital Strategy (→ Ch. 1 mn. 5 et seqq.) and in connection with other relevant instruments. The DSA does not explicitly mention other legislative acts pertaining to the EU Digital Strategy, as they were proposed either simultaneously with the DSA proposal or at a later point. However, their relationship to the DSA remains of importance.

1. Data Governance Act

57 The Data Governance Act (DGA), adopted on 30.5.2022, is the first measure of the Commission's 2020 Data Strategy.[65] The DGA provides for the creation of data spaces within the EU to share and pool data. It aims to promote the cross-border Digital Single Market, to establish a level playing field in the data economy and to ensure that competition between companies is based on the quality of services offered and not on the accumulation of data (rec. 2(2) sent. 5 DGA). These data spaces must be 'findable, accessible, interoperable and reusable' (so-called 'FAIR data principles') and, at the same time, ensure a high level of cyber security (rec. 2(2) sent. 4 DGA). The DSA's scope of application includes both personal and non-personal data.[66] In order to strengthen the trust of data intermediation service providers in the market and thus increase the availability of data,[67] Art. 10–15 DGA introduce **various requirements for data intermediation services.**

58 Although the term 'data' demonstrates a central role within the DSA, the DSA itself does not regulate data availability in a narrow sense. Art. 40(1) DSA provides only that **VLOPs and VLOSEs** must grant the competent Digital Services Coordinator or the European Commission access to the data necessary for monitoring and assessing compliance with the rules of the Regulation. According to Art. 40(2) DSA, this data can only be used for this purpose and must take due account of the rights and interests of the providers. Additionally, according to Art. 40(8) and (12) DSA, such service providers are obliged to grant access to their data to certain groups of researchers for research purposes.

2. Digital Markets Act

59 The Digital Markets Act (DMA), which together with the DSA forms the 'digital services package', constitutes the first comprehensive set of rules for online platforms in the EU,[68] with the aim to create 'fair and open digital markets'.[69] The legislative project is partly interpreted as a pushback against the big US platforms.[70] More reserved voices focus on the goal of combating the anti-competitive market fragmentation effect of certain business practices and barriers to market entry.[71] While the principal aim of the DSA is to ensure a safe, predictable and trusted online environment (Art. 1(1) DSA) and it is primarily concerned with issues such as limiting the dissemination of illegal content, en-

---

[65] Tolks MMR 2022, 444.

[66] Hennemann/v. Ditfurth NJW 2022, 1905.

[67] Hennemann/v. Ditfurth NJW 2022, 1905 (1907).

[68] European Commission, 'Commission welcomes the adoption of the Digital Services Package by the European Parliament'.

[69] European Commission, 'Questions and Answers: Digital Markets Act: Ensuring fair and open digital markets'.

[70] Of the same opinion Gielen/Uphues EuZW 2021, 627 regarding the comparison drawn by EU Internal Market Commissioner Thierry Breton to the USA fight against terrorism.

[71] Seip/Berberich GRUR-Prax 2021, 44; Herbers RDi 2022, 252 (253).

suring consumer protection and fundamental rights, combating disinformation and protecting democratic elections,[72] the DMA aims to ensure the functioning of the internal market and **prevent the fragmentation of digital markets** (rec. 7 sent. 2 DMA).[73] Efforts by national legislators to address the particularly weak contestability of core platform services and their negative effects have, in the Commission's view, led to an inconsistent regulatory framework which may result in further fragmentation of the internal market and higher compliance costs (rec. 6 sent. 2 and 4 DMA). Nonetheless, according to Art. 1(5) sent. 2 DMA, national provisions that fall outside the purview of the DMA and therefore do not concern the guarantee of contestable and fair markets but pursue other legitimate public interests (e.g. in the field of consumer protection) remain permissible.

The DMA focuses on **gatekeepers**. According to Art. 3(1) DMA, these are undertak- **60**
ings that (i) have a significant impact on the internal market, (ii) operate a core platform service that serves as an important gateway for business users to reach end users and (iii) enjoy an entrenched and durable position in their operations or will foreseeably enjoy such a position in the near future. These platforms play an important part in digital markets and are, at the same time, involved in a substantial part of the interactions between end users and business users.[74] If a certain annual turnover or the enterprise fair market value threshold is reached in accordance with Art. 3(2) DMA, the fulfilment of these criteria is presumed (in contrast to the definition of very large services (VLOPs and VLOSEs) in the DSA. According to Art. 3(3) subpara. 1 DMA, it is incumbent upon the platform service provider to inform the Commission when these thresholds are reached.

Neither the DSA nor the DMA regulates its relationship to the other in its material **61**
part. This might be because the two sets of Regulations were proposed at the same time and passed through the legislative process almost simultaneously.[75] However, rec. 12 DMA states that the Regulation is intended to **supplement** the rules of other European legal acts, particularly the DSA. This suggests that while both instruments create obligations that depend on the size of the platforms, the DMA focuses on market imbalances that make digital markets less contestable, while the DSA is intended to address horizontal societal risks of illegal content. The two instruments consequently stand side by side and complement each other.

3. Data Act

One of the most recent projects of the European legislator is the Data Act (DA). **62**
In order to make full use of the **potential of data-driven technologies**, a regulatory framework has been created that is 'conducive to innovation and facilitates better **data portability**, **fair access to data** and ensures **interoperability**'.[76] The aim of the DA is, on the one hand, to create better data access and, on the other hand, to promote data production in order to increase data availability in the market and to break down data

[72] Paal/Kieß ZfDR 2022, 1 (10).
[73] Cf. also Seip/Berberich GRUR-Prax 2021, 44.
[74] Albrecht GWR 2022, 181.
[75] An exception can be found only in point 1.5.4 of the financial statement of the draft DMA on the compatibility of the regulation with other instruments and on possible synergy effects, where the regulatory content of the two Regulations is compared, cf. COM(2020) 842 final, Legislative financial statement.
[76] European Council, 'European Council meeting (21 and 22 October 2021)' (22.10.2021), EUCO 17/21, p. 2.

silos (rec. 2 sent. 2 DA).[77] As a cross-cutting area between data protection law and data trade, the Data Act considers both the principles of data minimisation and data protection (rec. 8 sent. 1 DA) as well as the advantages of assigning access and usage rights (rec. 6 sent. 3 DA).

63 According to Art. 1(3) DA, the Data Act applies to manufacturers of products and suppliers of related services placed on the market in the Union and the users of such products or services, data holders that make data available to data recipients, data recipients, public sector bodies and Union institutions, agencies or bodies that request data holders to make data available and providers of data processing services. For data holders, i.e. legal or natural persons who, depending on the type of data, are entitled, obliged or capable of providing data (cf. Art. 2(13) DA), the Data Act provides in Art. 3–5 for obligations to make user-generated data accessible. The Data Act is based on an 'access-by-default' approach, meaning that products are to be designed and services are to be provided so that data generated by their use are, by default, easily, securely and, where relevant and appropriate, directly accessible to the user (Art. 3(1) DA). In addition, generated non-personal data may only be used based on a contractual agreement with the user according to Art. 4(13) sent. 1 DA. Under Art. 8(1) DA, the provision of data must be 'under fair, reasonable and non-discriminatory terms and in a transparent manner', whereby any compensation given by the data recipient must be reasonable (Art. 9(1) DA). Exclusivity rules set up in data licensing agreements are only allowed at the request of the user (Art. 8(4) DA).

64 According to rec. 10 sent. 1 and 2 and Art. 1(6) subpara. 2 DA, the regulation should be without prejudice to the application of other instruments, including the DSA. The addressees of the DSA, i.e. the providers of intermediary services, may well be addressees of the Data Act as suppliers of services, data holders, data recipients and providers of data processing services within the meaning of Art. 2(1) DA, as long as the service is incorporated in or interconnected with a product in such a way that its absence would prevent the product from performing one of its functions (cf. Art. 2(6) DA). These addressees would then be subject to both the DSA and the DA.

4. AI Act

65 The final version of the **AI Act**[78] includes multiple references to the relationship between the DSA and the AI Act. Rec. 11 AI Act clarifies that the latter applies **without prejudice** to the provisions of the DSA. In particular, the AI Act will not affect the application of the provisions on the liability of providers of intermediary services in Chapter II DSA (Art. 2(5) AI Act). The requirement to label content generated by AI systems under the AI Act is without prejudice to the obligation in Art. 16(6) DSA for providers of hosting services to process notices on illegal content received pursuant to Art. 16(1) DSA and should not influence the assessment and the decision on the illegality of the specific content (rec. 119 AI Act).

66 According to rec. 118 AI Act, the AI Act complements obligations for providers of intermediary services that embed AI systems or models into their services that are already regulated by the DSA, whereas to the extent that such systems or models are embedded into designated VLOPs or VLOSEs, they are subject to the **risk-management** framework provided for in the DSA. Therefore, the corresponding obligations of the AI Act should be presumed to be fulfilled, unless significant systemic risks not covered by the DSA emerge and are identified in such AI models. AI systems subject to the AI Act

[77] Bomhard/Merkle RDi 2022, 168; Hennemann/Steinrötter NJW 2022, 1481 (1482).
[78] Corrigendum to the Artificial Intelligence Act (19.4.2024), P9_TA(2024)0138.

may be provided as intermediary services or parts thereof within the meaning of the DSA, which should be interpreted in a technology-neutral manner (rec. 119 sent. 2 AI Act).

CHAPTER 3
LIABILITY OF PROVIDERS OF INTERMEDIARY SERVICES

Patrick Neidinger/Julia Wildgans

Bibliography: Berberich/Seip, 'Der Entwurf des Digital Services Act', GRUR-Prax 2021, 4; Leistner, 'Grundlagen und Perspektiven der Haftung für Urheberrechtsverletzungen im Internet', ZUM 2012, 722; J. B. Nordemann, 'Die Haftung allgemeiner Zugangsprovider auf Website-Sperren. Der aktuelle Stand nach BGH 'Dead Island'', GRUR 2018, 1016; Rössel/Kruse, 'Schadensersatzhaftung bei Verletzung von Filterpflichten', CR 2008, 35; Schmid/Grewe, 'Digital Services Act: Neues 'Grundgesetz für Onlinedienste'? Auswirkungen des Kommissionsentwurfs für die Digitalwirtschaft', MMR 2021, 279; Spindler, 'Der Vorschlag für ein neues Haftungsregime für Internetprovider – der EU-Digital Services Act (Teil 1)', GRUR 2021, 545.

A. General

Digital intermediary services are an **essential part** of the economy of the EU and have become an indispensable **part of the everyday lives of its citizens**. It is, therefore, not surprising that the liability regulations and exemptions regulated in the DSA[1] play a significant role in this area. The recitals of the DSA explicitly emphasise the legal certainty provided by the legal framework laid down in the existing E-Commerce Directive and state that this framework should therefore be preserved (cf. rec. 16 sent. 1 and 2 DSA). 1

The DSA consequently largely maintains the **tried and tested liability regime for intermediaries** of the E-Commerce Directive, replacing the liability exemptions laid down in Art. 12–15 E-Commerce Directive with Art. 4, 5, 6 and 8 DSA (cf. Art. 89(1) DSA).[2] Intermediaries are therefore to date **not liable** for third-party content.[3] Only under certain circumstances (e.g. actual knowledge of illegal activity within the meaning of Art. 6(1)(a) DSA) may the providers of intermediary services be held accountable in individual cases (see in detail → mn. 43 et seqq.). Similarly, **providers of intermediary services are still not subject to a general duty to monitor** the information they transmit or store, **nor** are they subject to an obligation to **actively seek facts** or circumstances that indicate illegal activity (cf. Art. 8 DSA).[4] Since this does not entail a fundamental change of the previous liability exemptions in practice, case law is expected to continue to be guided by the principles previously developed for the E-Commerce Directive. 2

One innovation – albeit a rather minor one, since it follows previous case law – arises concerning the **liability of online platforms that allow consumers to conclude distance contracts with traders**. Art. 6(3) DSA now explicitly clarifies that the liability exemptions for these hosting services providers do not apply under certain circumstances, for instance where third parties post offers that violate **consumer protection law**. In such cases, the online platform itself may be held liable if, from the perspective of an average consumer, the third-party offer appears to have been provided by the online platform itself.[5] 3

To clarify, Art. 7 DSA now stipulates that **voluntary measures** carried out on their own initiative by intermediary services providers to identify illegal content do not lead to the inapplicability of the liability exemptions of Art. 4, 5 and 6 DSA. However, for these exemptions to apply, it is necessary that these measures be carried out in a diligent manner and in good faith.[6] 4

The central innovation introduced by the DSA is that the responsibility for implementing the liability exemptions no longer lies with each individual Member State. By transferring the tried and tested liability regime into a Regulation (→ mn. 6), the limitation of intermediary liability in the Member States constitutes **directly applicable EU law** according to Art. 288(1), (2) TFEU. 5

---

[1] The DSA is not intended to provide a positive basis for establishing when providers of intermediary services can be held liable, cf. rec. 17 sent. 1 DSA.

[2] Spindler GRUR 2021, 545 (548); Schmid/Grewe MMR 2021, 279 (280).

[3] Berberich/Seip GRUR-Prax 2021, 4.

[4] Berberich/Seip GRUR-Prax 2021, 4.

[5] Berberich/Seip GRUR-Prax 2021, 4; Schmid/Grewe MMR 2021, 279 (280).

[6] Rec. 26 DSA explains what the term 'good faith' means in this context.

I. Legal nature of the liability exemptions

6 By anchoring the liability exemptions **in a Regulation,** the European legislation, according to rec. 5 sent. 2 DSA, strives to react to the exponential growth of the use of digital services within the EU, which is accompanied by the increasing dissemination of unlawful or otherwise harmful information. Furthermore, the legal framework created by the E-Commerce Directive 'has allowed many novel services to emerge and scale up across the internal market' (rec. 16 sent. 1 DSA). For reasons of clarity and coherence, the relevant rules are now to be set down **by means of a Regulation** (Art. 288(2) TFEU).[7] In this way, the European legislation seeks to harmonise national rules for providers of intermediary services at the Union level and avoid fragmentation of the internal market (cf. rec. 4 sent. 3 DSA). This should result in a higher level of legal certainty, consumer protection and interoperability, and provide a further boost to cross-border economic activities (cf. rec. 3 and 4 DSA).

1. Nature of the Regulation

7 As already indicated in Chapter 2 of this Guide, the DSA, as a Regulation of the EU, has a **general application** in every Member State according to Art. 288(2) TFEU. The provisions of the DSA are, therefore, legal principles of secondary EU law that do **not require an act of transposition** by the Member States.[8] Irrespective of any existing liability regulations in national law, the liability exemptions of Art. 4–6 DSA are **directly applicable** in all EU Member States. They are thus part of the national legal system and can, in principle - like federal laws - confer rights and impose obligations on individuals.[9]

8 Unlike a Directive, the DSA as a Regulation also has a **horizontal effect on EU citizens**, in that the liability exemptions of Art. 4–6 DSA are directly applicable before national courts, e.g. in civil proceedings.[10]

9 In contrast to the previous framework of the E-Commerce Directive, which according to Art. 288(3) TFEU was only binding as to the result to be achieved, the DSA is **binding in all parts,**[11] in order to enable legal harmonisation within the EU.[12]

2. Primacy of application and adaption of national provisions

10 In the relationship between national standards and Union law, the so-called **primacy of application of EU law** applies.[13] This means that national law that conflicts with the requirements of the Regulation becomes inapplicable in the individual case examined. It does, however, remain valid in general.[14]

---

[7] Rec. 16 sent. 3 DSA; Schmid/Grewe MMR 2021, 279.

[8] Ruffert in Calliess/Ruffert AEUV Art. 288 mn. 17, 21; W. Schroeder in Streinz AEUV Art. 288 mn. 39, 43; Schmid/Grewe MMR 2021, 279.

[9] Ruffert in Calliess/Ruffert AEUV Art. 288 mn. 21; W. Schroeder in Streinz AEUV Art. 288 mn. 41, 43; Nettesheim in Grabitz/Hilf/Nettesheim AEUV Art. 288 mn. 89, 100.

[10] In general, on the topic of horizontal effect, cf. ECJ 17.9.2002 – case C-253/00, ECLI:EU:C:2002:497 para. 27 et seqq. – Muñoz and Superior Fruiticola; Opinion of Advocate General Geelhoed at the ECJ 13.12.2001 – case C-253/00, ECLI:EU:C:2001:697 para. 33 et seqq. – Muñoz and Superior Fruiticola; W. Schroeder in Streinz AEUV Art. 288 mn. 41.

[11] Ruffert in Calliess/Ruffert AEUV Art. 288 mn. 20; W. Schroeder in Streinz AEUV Art. 288 mn. 41.

[12] W. Schroeder in Streinz AEUV Art. 288 mn. 38

[13] Ruffert in Calliess/Ruffert AEUV Art. 288 mn. 21 with further references.

[14] Ruffert in Calliess/Ruffert AEUV Art. 1 mn. 18.

Concerning the provisions of the DSA, for example in Germany, this was of particular relevance for the liability exemptions in **§§ 8–10 of the German Telemedia Act (*Telemediengesetz* – TMG)**. Following the E-Commerce Directive, they had regulated liability exemptions for conduit, caching and hosting in Germany. Since the introduction of the DSA, the provisions had largely become legally superfluous but were still valid. In view of this and for the sake of coherence and legal clarity, the German legislator **repealed** most of them by the Act of 6.5.2024 (BGBl. 2024 I Nr. 149) as from 14.5.2024.[15] 11

To avoid ambiguities about authorship and the validity of liability exemptions, all EU Member States may examine on a case-by-case basis whether a **repeal of the national provisions** is necessary, in particular considering that, even if not contradicting the DSA, the existing parallel provisions are likely to cause 'an ambiguous state of affairs by keeping the persons concerned in a state of uncertainty as to the possibility of relying on Community law'.[16] The continuing existence of national liability exemptions could thereby hinder the unrestricted applicability of the DSA. 12

II. Personal and material scope of application

1. Providers of intermediary services

The new rules primarily affect **providers of intermediary services** within the meaning of Art. 3(g) DSA, i.e. access providers as providers of mere conduit (Art. 4 DSA), providers of caching services (Art. 5 DSA) and hosting providers (Art. 6 DSA).[17] For a more precise definition of mere conduit, caching and hosting → Ch. 2 mn. 23 et seqq. 13

Rec. 29 sent. 2 and 4 DSA clarify that providers of public Wi-Fi networks as well as virtual private networks (VPN), DNS services, VoIP and messaging services, top-level domain name registries, certificate authorities for digital certificates and providers for cloud computing services can also be considered **providers of intermediary services**, provided that their services are classified as mere conduit, caching or hosting.[18] 14

2. Special category: online search engines

In contrast to the Commission's draft, the final version of the DSA now also explicitly comments on the liability of **online search engine operators**.[19] 15

a) Status quo under the E-Commerce Directive

The E-Commerce Directive lacks an explicit response to the classification of **online search engine operators**.[20] Contrary to what is sometimes assumed in the **literature**,[21] Art. 21(2) of the E-Commerce Directive does not lead to the general conclusion that the EU legislator did not consider search engines to be affected by the liability exemptions of the E-Commerce Directive. The provision of Art. 21(2) E-Commerce Directive, by merely ordering an analysis of the 'need for proposals concerning the liability of providers [...] of location tool services [...]', makes no statement as to whether the scope of Art. 12–14 E-Commerce Directive covers online search engines. Regardless of 16

[15] BT-Drs. 20/10031, 69.
[16] ECJ 26.4.1988 – case 74/86, ECLI:EU:C:1988:198 para. 10 – Commission v Germany.
[17] Cf. rec. 5 sent. 2 DSA.
[18] Spindler GRUR 2021, 545 (548).
[19] Rec. 28 sent. 3 DSA.
[20] Spindler GRUR 2021, 545 (548).
[21] Spindler GRUR 2021, 545 (548); Spindler in Spindler/Schmitz TMG Vor §§ 7–10 mn. 84.

whether online search engines were already included in the term 'privileged parties' under Art. 12–14 E-Commerce Directive, corresponding proposals for the adaptation of the Directive in terms of online search engines might still be necessary. For one thing, the Directive contains further regulations that may affect online search engines beyond the liability exemptions in question and, for another, the term 'proposals' also refers to the creation and revision of rules.

17 The wording of rec. 18(4) of the E-Commerce Directive seems to suggest that online search engines, as services that provide tools for accessing and retrieving data, are covered by the concept of an 'information society service' within the meaning of Art. 2(a) of the E-Commerce Directive, but do not operate as mere conduit, caching or hosting services. Any other interpretation leads to difficulties explaining their explicit mention in rec. 18 of the E-Commerce Directive.

18 In the past, **case law** has expressed different views on this topic. An obiter dictum issued by the **German Federal Court of Justice (*Bundesgerichtshof* – BGH)**, for example, considered Art. 14(1) of the E-Commerce Directive to apply to the services provided by search engines 'if the relevant activity of the search engine operator is of a purely technical, automatic and passive nature and it has neither knowledge nor control over the information stored or forwarded by it [...]'.[22] In passing this judgement, it referred to rec. 42 of the E-Commerce Directive, which had previously been used in the **ECJ's Google France case law**:[23] The ECJ stated that Google's referencing service 'AdWords' constituted an information society service within the meaning of Art. 2(a) of the E-Commerce Directive in conjunction with Art. 1(2) of Directive 98/34/EC, which in principle could also benefit from the liability exemption of Art. 14 of the E-Commerce Directive if 'the conduct of that service provider [is] limited to that of an "intermediary services provider" within the meaning intended by the legislature in the context of Section 4 of [the E-Commerce Directive]'.[24] Following the wording of rec. 42 sent. 2 of the E-Commerce Directive, this presupposes that the activity of the information society service provider is 'of a mere technical, automatic and passive nature' and that the provider 'has neither knowledge of nor control over the information which is transmitted or stored'.[25]

19 The classification of online search engine operators concerning applicable liability law therefore depends on the **specific use of the search engine** in each individual case. In the case of a simple search query by a user, there may be a purely automatic transmission resulting in an overview of search results.[26] However, if this overview is influenced due to contractual relationships between the operators of the online search engine and

[22] BGH 29.4.2010 – I ZR 69/08, GRUR 2010, 628 mn. 39, translation by the authors. By contrast, former § 8 TMG (which corresponded in content to Art. 4 DSA or Art. 12 E-Commerce Directive) was negated and otherwise expressly left unanswered in LG Frankfurt a. M. 9.2.2017 – 2-03 S 16/16, GRUR-RR 2017, 458 mn. 50 et seqq.

[23] ECJ 23.3.2010 – cases C-236/08 and C-238/08, ECLI:EU:C:2010:159 para. 106 et seqq. – Google France and Google.

[24] ECJ 23.3.2010 – cases C-236/08 and C-238/08, ECLI:EU:C:2010:159 para. 112 – Google France and Google.

[25] ECJ 23.3.2010 – cases C-236/08 and C-238/08, ECLI:EU:C:2010:159 para. 113 – Google France and Google.

[26] On the corresponding liability exemptions resulting from the E-Commerce Directive: Hennemann in BeckOK InfoMedienR TMG § 8 mn. 25; Martini in BeckOK InfoMedienR TMG § 2 mn. 8; regarding search engines as comparable to access providers in the automatic generation of search results, but excluding search engines from the scope of the liability exemptions: Spindler in Spindler/Schmitz TMG Vor §§ 7–10 mn. 84; Hoffmann/Volkmann in Spindler/Schuster TMG § 8 mn. 25.

other websites, the activity may no longer be deemed merely passive, preventing the liability exemptions from applying.[27]

b) Status quo under the DSA

20 These principles can be **transferred to the liability exemptions of the DSA**.[28] At the suggestion of the Council during the legislative process,[29] online search engines are now explicitly mentioned as privileged services in rec. 28 sent. 2. This means that if a search engine provider plays an active role in generating search results, the liability exemptions of Art. 4–6 DSA cannot apply to them. However, if the search engine's activity is limited to the mere transmission or hosting of content of which the provider has no actual knowledge, there are good reasons to apply the liability exemptions of Art. 4–6 DSA to search engine providers.

21 In an attempt at clarification, the European Parliament also proposed a new rec. 27a in the legislative process, which, following the previous case law of the ECJ, would have stated as a principle: 'For example, a search engine could act solely as a "caching" service as to information included in the results of an inquiry. Elements displayed alongside those results, such as online advertisements, would however still qualify as a hosting service.'[30] This recital, however, was not included in the final version of the DSA.

3. Illegal content

22 The liability exemptions in Art. 4–6 DSA generally apply to all information, regardless of its legality. This establishes that providers of intermediary services should not be liable for information as a whole, provided that certain conditions are met. Consequently, an obligation for providers to examine whether content is illegal cannot exist. However, if the conditions of the liability exemptions of the DSA (→ mn. 43 et seqq.) are not met, the provider can still be held liable for so-called **illegal content**. This is explicitly defined in Art. 3(h) DSA as

> any information that, in itself or in relation to an activity, including the sale of products or the provision of services, is not in compliance with Union law or the law of any Member State which is in compliance with Union law, irrespective of the precise subject matter or nature of that law.

23 This covers all illegal information, regardless of whether it is national or EU law that is violated.[31] Rec. 12 DSA, which contains numerous examples, confirms this **broad understanding of the term**. In the case of 'illegal hate speech', discriminatory content or terrorist content, the information itself may violate applicable law. The sharing of images depicting child sexual abuse is also included in the concept of illegal content (cf. rec. 12 sent. 4 DSA), which additionally covers information ruled illegal due to its association with illegal activities, such as the sale of counterfeit products, the infringement of consumer protection law, illegal offers of accommodation services and the illegal sale of live animals.

---

[27] On the corresponding liability exemptions resulting from the E-Commerce Directive: Hennemann in BeckOK InfoMedienR TMG § 8 mn. 25; Hoffmann/Volkmann in Spindler/Schuster TMG § 8 mn. 24 (however, excluding search engines from the scope of the liability exemptions).

[28] Cf. now explicitly rec. 28 DSA.

[29] 'General Approach of the Council' (18.11.2021), ST 13203/21, Annex, mn. 27.

[30] 'Amendments adopted by the European Parliament on 20 January 2022 on the proposal for a DSA' (20.1.2022), P9_TA(2022)0014, Amendment 24; no longer included in the final version.

[31] Spindler GRUR 2021, 545 (548).

24 During the legislative process, the European Parliament intended to establish the following principle: '[W]hat is illegal offline should also be illegal online'.[32] This idea is now contained in rec. 12 sent. 1 DSA, according to which the concept of illegal content should 'broadly reflect the existing rules in the offline environment'.

25 Rec. 12 sent. 4 DSA also refers to the 'non-authorised use of copyright protected material'. At first glance, this is surprising since the legislator previously emphasised in rec. 11 and Art. 2(4)(b) DSA that the DSA was without prejudice to the provisions of Union law on **copyright and related rights**.[33] This referred in particular to the provisions of the InfoSoc Directive, the Enforcement Directive and the DSM Directive, as has now been clarified in rec. 11 DSA at the suggestion of the Council.[34] The specific provisions and procedures regarding the liability of intermediary services providers contained in these directives therefore remain unaffected, particularly Art. 17 DSM Directive, which refers to the use of copyright-protected content by online content-sharing service providers.

III. The regulatory concept of liability in the DSA

26 The regulatory concept of the DSA is based on the **concept of liability exemptions** pursued in the E-Commerce Directive.[35]

1. In principle: no liability of intermediaries

27 Art. 4–6 DSA contain no specific criteria for establishing liability and therefore provide **no positive basis for establishing liability** or the responsibility of providers of intermediary services.[36] As a result, like the corresponding provisions of the E-Commerce Directive, they cannot establish any civil or criminal liability that does not already exist in general liability law.[37] Therefore, no liability may exist due to a guarantor's status or the violation of a duty of care.[38] Instead – as can be seen from rec. 17 sent. 2 DSA – the positive basis for liability is to be determined by the applicable rules of Union or national law.

28 While there is no positive basis for liability in the DSA, the Regulation makes explicit statements on **cases in which the liability** of the provider of intermediary services **must be excluded** (→ mn. 43 et seqq.).[39] The DSA thus adopts the system already laid out in the liability exemptions of the E-Commerce Directive.[40] The DSA distinguishes between **three different liability exemptions**: 'mere conduit' in Art. 4 DSA (→ mn. 43 et seqq.),

[32] 'Amendments adopted by the European Parliament on 20 January 2022 on the proposal for a DSA' (20.1.2022), P9_TA(2022)0014, Amendment 12.

[33] Spindler GRUR 2021, 545 (548).

[34] Cf. rec. 11 in the 'General Approach of the Council' (18.11.2021), ST 13203/21, Annex, mn. 15.

[35] Schmid/Grewe MMR 2021, 279 (280).

[36] Schmid/Grewe MMR 2021, 279 (280); on the corresponding liability exemptions as a result of the E-Commerce Directive: ECJ 23.3.2010 – cases C-236/08 and C-238/08, ECLI:EU:C:2010:159 para. 107 – Google France and Google.

[37] Cf. also on the corresponding liability exemptions due to the E-Commerce Directive: German Parliament, 'Draft of a law on the legal framework for electronic commerce', BT-Drs. 14/6098, 23; Sieber/Höfinger in Hoeren/Sieber/Holznagel MMR-HdB Teil 18.1 mn. 14.

[38] Spindler GRUR 2021, 545 (548); cf. also on the corresponding liability exemptions as a result of the E-Commerce Directive: Hoffmann/Volkmann in Spindler/Schuster TMG Vor § 7 mn. 25; Spindler in Spindler/Schmitz TMG Vor § 7 mn. 33 with further evidence; Rössel/Kruse CR 2008, 35 (39).

[39] Cf. rec. 17 (1) DSA and Spindler GRUR 2021, 545 (548).

[40] Berberich/Seip GRUR-Prax 2021, 4 (6) see this as a 'rather cautious further development of the applicable rules'.

'caching' in Art. 5 DSA (→ mn. 57 et seqq.) and 'hosting' in Art. 6 DSA (→ mn. 68 et seqq.). Depending on the activity in question, the DSA links the liability exemption to different conditions, which are intended to take into account the different abilities of the providers to control and be aware of illegal content (cf. rec. 19 DSA). The primary purpose of Art. 4–6 DSA is to **limit liability**, as was the case with the corresponding provisions in the E-Commerce Directive (the so-called **filter function**).[41]

2. Concept of liability

29 In principle, liability exemption concerns **all areas of law**. It generally applies to (no-fault and fault-based) **civil law claims** for removal and injunction, for information and civil law claims for damages, irrespective of the precise subject matter, as well as to **criminal law sanctions** and administrative offences and claims.[42] The legislator thus uses a very broad concept of liability. According to rec. 17 DSA, the liability exemptions should apply in respect of any type of liability.[43] This is confirmed by the wording of Art. 6(1)(a) DSA, which distinguishes between (civil) claims for damages and other liability.[44] Additionally, a broad concept of liability seems appropriate to avoid contradictions within the legal system.[45]

30 Concerning criminal liability, the liability exemptions of Art. 4–6 DSA already **exclude the existence of an offence**; the same applies to liability in tort.[46] It should be noted, however, that the **competence of the EU** in the area of criminal law is significantly limited.[47] For this reason, rec. 8 of the E-Commerce Directive explicitly emphasised that the Directive's aim was not to harmonise the field of criminal law but merely to create a legal framework to ensure the free movement of information society services between Member States.[48] The DSA contains no such explicit clarification. However, Art. 9(6) DSA emphasises that the conditions and requirements laid down in the DSA shall be without prejudice to national, civil and criminal procedural law. In the absence of legislative competence of the EU for criminal law, an intention to harmonise criminal law through the DSA cannot be assumed.[49]

31 The DSA contains no statements on **product liability** (in particular of hosting providers as 'importers' within the meaning of Art. 3(2) of Directive 85/374/EEC).[50]

3. Liability for own content or due to an active role

32 According to rec. 18 sent. 1 DSA, the exemptions from liability apply only to providers who provide services **neutrally and by a merely technical and automatic processing** of the information provided by the recipient of the services. However, there is no liability exemption if a service provider provides its own content or plays an active

---

[41] Cf. also on the corresponding liability exemptions due to the E-Commerce Directive: German Parliament, 'Draft of a law on the legal framework for electronic commerce', BT-Drs. 14/6098, 23; Sieber/Höfinger in Hoeren/Sieber/Holznagel MMR-HdB Teil 18.1 mn. 14, 25.

[42] Sieber/Höfinger in Hoeren/Sieber/Holznagel MMR-HdB Teil 18.1 mn. 15.

[43] Spindler GRUR 2021, 545 (548).

[44] Spindler GRUR 2021, 545 (548).

[45] Cf. also on the corresponding liability exemptions contained in the E-Commerce Directive: Sieber/Höfinger in Hoeren/Sieber/Holznagel MMR-HdB Teil 18.1 mn. 23.

[46] Cf. also on the corresponding liability exemptions contained in the E-Commerce Directive: ECJ 23.3.2010 – cases C-236/08 and C-238/08, ECLI:EU:C:2010:159 para. 107 – Google France and Google; Sieber/Höfinger in Hoeren/Sieber/Holznagel MMR-HdB Teil 18.1 mn. 21 et seqq.

[47] ECJ 2.2.1989 – case 186/87, ECLI:EU:C:1989:47 para. 19 – Cowan v Trésor public.

[48] Spindler in Spindler/Schmitz TMG § 3 mn. 70.

[49] Spindler in Spindler/Schmitz TMG § 3 mn. 70.

[50] Spindler GRUR 2021, 545 (549).

role of such a kind as to give it knowledge of or control over the information or, in particular, develop editorial responsibility for the content (cf. rec. 18 sent. 2 DSA). The service provider's 'own content' therefore includes not only content which it has created, but also content from third parties which it has edited.[51]

33 Members of the German legal community will remember the Federal Court of Justice's case law on ***'Zu-eigen-Machen'***.[52] The BGH initially developed this in the highly regarded 'marions-kochbuch.de' decision, in which the plaintiff, the operator of an online recipe collection called marions-kochbuch.de, filed a claim against the operator of the internet portal chefkoch.de for injunctive relief, based on a violation of copyright law through making recipe photographs uploaded by its users publicly available:

> Own content is not only self-created content but also content the provider has made its own. Decisive for this is an objective view based on an overall consideration of all relevant circumstances [...]. [In the court's view], the defendant did not merely operate an auction platform [...] or an electronic marketplace on which third-party content is posted. Rather, it actually developed – publicly visibly – responsibility for the content of the recipes and illustrations published on its website.[53]

34 The **overall design** of the website was decisive for the assumption of ownership. The integration of content into the portal, as well as publication incorporating the website operator's emblem, were strong indicators of ownership by the provider. In addition, and even more crucially, the defendant expressly made the recipes publicly available as its own content only after an **editorial review of their completeness and correctness**.[54] In so doing, it created the 'attributable appearance of identifying with the third-party content and adopting it as its own'.[55] The defendant furthermore granted itself comprehensive **rights of use** to the recipes in the general terms and conditions and offered third parties rights of **commercial use** of the contributions.[56] By contrast, a mere reference to or identification of third-party content was not considered sufficient dissociation of the website operator from the content.[57]

35 The Federal Court of Justice has subsequently further substantiated this case law:

> Ownership is regularly deemed to exist if the third party's statement is inserted into one's own train of thought in such a way that the entire statement appears to be one's own. Statements by third parties that are merely reproduced in a distanced manner can also be attributed to the distributor if he has made them his own. However, whether this is the case must be examined with the restraint required in the interest of freedom of expression and the protection of the press. The external form of the publication alone may indicate that only a statement by another party is communicated without any evaluation or opinion of its own. This is the case, for example, when a press review is printed.[58]
>
> The operator of an internet website [furthermore] adopts content as its own if it has outwardly recognisably assumed responsibility for the content published on its website or has created the attributable appearance that it identifies with the third-party content [...]. Whether there is an attribution of ownership is [again] to be assessed from the perspective of a reasonable average user based on an overall consideration of all relevant circumstances. [...] The fact that the service provider has adopted the third-party information as its own is indicated by the fact that the provider checks

[51] Cf. reverse inference from rec. 21 sent. 2 and 3 DSA, according to which a provider is not connected with the information unless he modifies it (in terms of content).

[52] Thus expressly: Schmid/Grewe MMR 2021, 279 (280); Spindler GRUR 2021, 545 (550).

[53] BGH 12.11.2009 – I ZR 166/07, GRUR 2010, 616 mn. 23 et seqq. – marions-kochbuch.de; confirmed in BGH 27.3.2012 – VI ZR 144/11, GRUR 2012, 751 mn. 11 – RSS-Feeds; translation by the authors.

[54] BGH 12.11.2009 – I ZR 166/07, GRUR 2010, 616 mn. 25 – marions-kochbuch.de.

[55] BGH 12.11.2009 – I ZR 166/07, GRUR 2010, 616 mn. 27 – marions-kochbuch.de, translation by the authors.

[56] BGH 12.11.2009 – I ZR 166/07, GRUR 2010, 616 mn. 26 et seq. – marions-kochbuch.de.

[57] BGH 12.11.2009 – I ZR 166/07, GRUR 2010, 616 mn. 27 – marions-kochbuch.de.

[58] BGH 27.3.2012 – VI ZR 144/11, GRUR 2012, 751 mn. 11 – RSS-Feeds; translation by the authors.

> or selects the content uploaded by third parties for completeness and accuracy or integrates the third-party information into its own editorial offer. [...] However, the identification assumption with third-party content must be treated with caution.[59]

36 The European legislator refers to the corresponding **ECJ case law on active providers** in rec. 18 sent. 1 DSA. This states that the liability exemption of Art. 14 E-Commerce Directive does not apply if the provider of intermediary services has played an active role of such a kind as to give it knowledge of or control over the stored data.[60] If that provider has not played such a role, it 'cannot be held liable for the data which it has stored at the request of an advertiser, unless, having obtained knowledge of the unlawful nature of those data or of that advertiser's activities, it failed to act expeditiously to remove or to disable access to the data concerned'.[61] A liability exemption can thus only be considered if the service provider limits itself to 'providing [a] service neutrally by a merely technical and automatic processing of the data provided by its customers [...]'.[62]

37 The fact that the service is subject to payment or provides its users with general information can have no effect on any assessment of the neutrality of the service.[63] However, a provider plays an active role when it drafts commercial messages or establishes or selects key words to optimise third parties' sales offers.[64] In these cases, the provider has knowledge of the published information or exercises control over it, rendering a privileged liability within the meaning of Art. 12–14 E-Commerce Directive no longer justified.[65]

38 Furthermore, in the view of the European legislator, providers of intermediary services do not assume a neutral role if – as rec. 20 sent. 1 DSA makes clear – they **deliberately collaborate with third parties** to undertake illegal activities.[66] This includes the targeted offering of services whose main purpose is to facilitate illegal activities. Instances of this may include advertising statements by the service provider or indications that the services offered are suited to illegal activities. However, the fact alone that a service offers encrypted transmissions or other systems that make the identification of the user impossible should not in itself qualify as facilitating illegal activities (cf. rec. 20 sent. 3 DSA).

39 There are a number of **discrepancies** between the criteria developed by the ECJ and those of the German Federal Court of Justice. For liability exemptions, the ECJ's case law on active providers must be applied with priority over the case law of the German Federal Court of Justice or that of other Member States.[67] The Member States' case law can be used only insofar as it does not contradict the case law of the ECJ but merely complements it.

---

59 BGH 19.3.2015 – I ZR 94/13, GRUR 2015, 1129 mn. 25 – Hotel rating portal; principles reaffirmed in BGH 1.3.2016 – VI ZR 34/15, GRUR 2016, 855 mn.17 – www.jameda.de; translation by the authors.

60 Referring to this case law: Berberich/Seip GRUR-Prax 2021, 4.

61 ECJ 23.3.2010 – cases C-236/08 and C-238/08, ECLI:EU:C:2010:159 para. 120 – Google France and Google.

62 ECJ 12.7.2011 – case C-324/09, ECLI:EU:C:2011:474 para. 113 – L'Oréal and others.

63 ECJ 23.3.2010 – cases C-236/08 and C-238/08, ECLI:EU:C:2010:159 para. 116 – Google France and Google.

64 ECJ 23.3.2010 – cases C-236/08 and C-238/08, ECLI:EU:C:2010:159 para. 118 – Google France and Google; confirmed in ECJ 11.9.2014 – case C-291/13, ECLI:EU:C:2014:2209 para. 43 et seq. – Papasavvas.

65 ECJ 11.9.2014 – case C-291/13, ECLI:EU:C:2014:2209 para. 44 et seqq. – Papasavvas; confirmed in ECJ 7.8.2018 – case C-521/17, ECLI:EU:C:2018:639 para. 50 – SNB-REACT.

66 Spindler GRUR 2021, 545 (549).

67 ECJ 22.2.2022 – case C-430/21, ECLI:EU:C:2022:99 para. 52 – RS.

4. Exception for requests from judicial and administrative authorities

40 The liability exemptions of Art. 4–6 DSA do not affect the possibility for a **judicial or administrative authority** in accordance with a Member State's legal system to require the service provider to terminate or prevent an infringement. This is explicitly provided for in Art. 4(3), Art. 5(2) and Art. 6(4) DSA.[68] These Articles draw a clear line between the liability and the injunction regime with the injunction regime being subject to Member State law rather than the DSA.

41 By way of an example, it is worth mentioning that, in the context of civil claims for injunctive relief by hosting providers under German law, the principles of *Störerhaftung* (Breach of Duty of Care) are applied, which have been developed by case law in the context of extensive casuistry and are in accordance with the standards of the ECJ's **L'Oréal/ eBay decision**.[69] Initially, the German Federal Court of Justice derived a right to defence exclusively on a tortious basis in analogy to § 1004 of the German Civil Code (BGB).[70] Later, however, in a decision on media harmful to minors on eBay, it developed concrete duties of review for host providers according to § 3 of the German Act against Unfair Competition (*Gesetz gegen den unlauteren Wettbewerb* – UWG) based on the providers' role as indirect initiators in their own perpetration.[71] These inspection obligations presuppose a concrete indication of a certain offer and trigger extensive blocking and precautionary obligations on the provider's part.[72] However, according to ECJ case law, this does not include establishing a comprehensive, preventive filtering system.[73]

42 Despite the existing liability exemptions in Art. 4–6 DSA (→ mn. 43 et seqq.), service providers may therefore be required by general law to remove information or block access to information due to measures taken by the judiciary and the administration (in particular blocking and cease-and-desist orders). In this context, **Art. 9 DSA** places special requirements on orders to act against illegal content (→ mn. 95 et seqq.).

B. Liability for 'mere conduit' (Art. 4 DSA)

I. Principle of the liability exemption

43 Art. 4 DSA contains a **liability exemption for service providers in the case of a mere conduit of information**. Under certain circumstances, liability shall be excluded when information provided by users is transmitted in a communication network or where access to a communication network is provided.

44 This **corresponds** to the liability exemption for network providers, router operators, access providers and search engine providers previously provided in **Art. 12 E-Commerce Directive** (cf. on its restrictive application → mn. 15 et seqq.).[74] The legislator assumes that these service providers conduct an activity of a purely technical, automatic

---

[68] Only concerning access providers' liability: Spindler GRUR 2021, 545 (549).

[69] ECJ 12.7.2011 – case C-324/09, ECLI:EU:C:2011:474 para. 113 - L'Oréal and others.

[70] BGH 7.11.2002 – I ZR 64/00, GRUR 2002, 618 (619) – Meißner Dekor; BGH 30.1.2003 – I ZR 142/00, GRUR 2003, 624 (646) – Kleidersack.

[71] BGH 12.7.2007 – I ZR 18/04, GRUR 2007, 890 – Jugendgefährdende Medien bei eBay.

[72] BGH 16.5.2013 – I ZR 216/11, GRUR 2013, 1229 (1232) – Kinderhochstühle im Internet II; BGH 11.3.2004 – I ZR 304/01, GRUR 2004, 860 – Internet-Versteigerung I.

[73] ECJ 24.11.2011 – case C-70/10, ECLI:EU:C:2011:771 para. 44 et seqq. – Scarlet Extended; ECJ 16.2.2012 – case C-360/10, ECLI:EU:C:2012:85 para. 33 et seqq. – SABAM.

[74] Spindler GRUR 2021, 545 (549); Berberich/Seip GRUR-Prax 2021, 4; for the national standard of former § 8 TMG based on Art. 12 E-Commerce Directive and the activities privileged by it cf. Sieber/Höfinger in Hoeren/Sieber/Holznagel MMR-HdB Teil 18.1 mn. 62.

and passive nature, justifying a liability exemption in the absence of factual knowledge of the transmitted content.[75]

In the case of Germany and within the context of former § 8 TMG, the term **'transmission'** was understood to refer solely to the technical transmission process ('rooting').[76] Therefore, for the exemption to apply, the service provider had to be acting merely as a provider of transmission services.[77] For the purposes of former § 8 TMG, the term **'provision of access to a communications network'** meant that the service provider gives access to an electronic communications network, in particular the internet, to a third party via the third party's terminal equipment.[78] This access also includes reciprocal information flows between the terminal device and the communication network.[79] Such 'access providers' include universities and restaurants offering Wi-Fi access points to third parties. Even bearing in mind that EU law uses terminology which is peculiar to itself and engages legal concepts that do not necessarily have the same meaning as the corresponding concepts that may exist in the laws of Member States, there are no apparent reasons why the interpretation of Art. 4 DSA should not also be based on such an assessment.[80] 45

II. Limitations of the liability exemption

Art. 4(1)(a)–(c) DSA **incorporates the limitations of the liability exemptions** already contained in Art. 12(1)(a)–(c) E-Commerce Directive verbatim. It states that, in order to benefit from the liability exemption,[81] the provider 46

- must not initiate the transmission (Art. 4(1)(a) DSA);
- most not select the receiver of the transmission (Art. 4 (1)(b) DSA); and
- must not select or modify the information contained in the transmission (Art. 4(1)(c) DSA).

A transmission, in this sense, is **not initiated** by the service provider if it is initiated by the user (e.g. requesting specific information from other users by entering an address in a web browser).[82] In such cases, it is not the service provider who deliberately directs specific information to users. 47

Art. 4(1)(b) DSA further requires that the **service provider does not select the receiver**. The user himself must therefore select the receiver.[83] This does not preclude the service provider from assisting in the selection (e.g. through the purely passive facilitation of online communication via URLs, email address books etc.). 48

The first variant of Art. 4(1)(c) DSA requires that **no selection of information** takes place. This exception can be explained by looking at the operation mode of the 49

---

[75] Cf. rec. 42 sent. 2 E-Commerce Directive.

[76] Hoffmann/Volkmann in Spindler/Schuster TMG § 8 mn. 16. On the term 'rooting': Hoffmann/Volkmann in Spindler/Schuster TMG § 8 mn. 4.

[77] Hoffmann/Volkmann in Spindler/Schuster TMG § 8 mn. 16.

[78] Hoffmann/Volkmann in Spindler/Schuster TMG § 8 mn. 17.

[79] Hoffmann/Volkmann in Spindler/Schuster TMG § 8 mn. 17.

[80] Spindler in Spindler/Schmitz TMG § 8 mn. 40; concerning the autonomy of EU law most recently: ECJ 6.10.2021 – case C-561/19, ECLI:EU:C:2021:799 para. 45 – Consorzio Italian Management e Catania Multiservizi.

[81] In this respect, incorrectly referring to the entire provision of Art. 12 E-Commerce Directive or Art. 3 DSA: Spindler GRUR 2021, 545 (549).

[82] On former § 8(1) sent. 1 no. 1 TMG, which transposed Art. 12(1)(a) E-Commerce Directive: Hennemann in BeckOK InfoMedienR TMG § 8 mn. 21.

[83] Hennemann in BeckOK InfoMedienR TMG § 8 mn. 22.

widespread push services:[84] With the help of these services, providers control the flow of information from the senders by transmitting certain information to their users at a predetermined frequency. If this information is selected and editorially transmitted by a service provider, it can be assumed that the provider has knowledge of the content. A liability exemption does not appear justified in this case. If, on the other hand, the selection of information and topics is the sole responsibility of the user, the activity of the supporting service provider may be deemed to be of a purely technical or passive nature, meaning that a liability exemption can be considered.

50 Finally, according to rec. 21 sent. 3 DSA, a modification of information within the meaning of the second variant of Art. 4(1)(c) DSA is not deemed to exist if, in the course of transmitting information or providing access, the service provider carries out **manipulations of a technical nature** that do not alter the integrity of the information transmitted or to which access is provided. This is because such changes are purely technical and do not enable the control of the information, which would justify waiving the liability exemption.[85]

51 The liability exemption according to Art. 4(1) DSA ultimately means that the service provider is generally not liable for the transmitted information **even in the case of accidental knowledge of illegal content**, provided they have not initiated the transmission, have not selected the receivers of the transmitted information, and have not selected or modified the transmitted information.[86]

III. Clarification regarding automatic intermediate and transient storage (Art. 4(2) DSA)

52 Art. 4(2) DSA contains a clarification already provided in Art. 12(2) E-Commerce Directive. This states that acts of transmission and the provision of access within the meaning of Art. 4(1) DSA also include the **automatic intermediate and transient storage of the transmitted information**, insofar as (i) this only takes place in order to carry out the transmission in the communication network and (ii) the information is not stored for a period longer than is reasonably necessary for the transmission. This enables storage processes that are technically necessary to carry out the transmission, which is not directly covered by the wording of Art. 4(1) DSA.[87]

53 For an act to be considered a transmission within the meaning of Art. 4(1) DSA, it must firstly not be a **permanent** storage (as in Art. 6(1) DSA, → Ch. 2 mn. 26). Thus, the term of intermediate storage in Art. 4(2) DSA corresponds to the term in Art. 5(1) DSA (→ Ch. 2 mn. 25).[88] In contrast to Art. 5(1) DSA, however, Art. 4(2) DSA adds the requirement of **'transient'**. This suggests that storage covered by Art. 4(1) or (2) DSA is shorter in time than merely temporary storage in Art. 5(1) DSA. However, it is impossible to determine a maximum time limit, the concrete duration always being determined by the purpose of the transmission and the needs surrounding the storage.[89] If intermediate storage is carried out beyond the purpose of error-free data transmission (for example, for accelerated retrieval[90]), the liability exemption does not apply. In this case, Art. 5 DSA (→ mn. 57 et seqq.) comes into consideration.

[84] In detail: Hennemann in BeckOK InfoMedienR TMG § 8 mn. 24.
[85] Spindler GRUR 2021, 545 (549).
[86] Spindler GRUR 2021, 545 (549).
[87] Still on former § 8 TMG: Hennemann in BeckOK InfoMedienR TMG § 8 mn. 38.
[88] Still on former § 8 TMG: Hennemann in BeckOK InfoMedienR TMG § 8 mn. 40.
[89] Still on former § 8 TMG: Hennemann in BeckOK InfoMedienR TMG § 8 mn. 42.
[90] Still on former § 8 TMG: Hennemann in BeckOK InfoMedienR TMG § 8 mn. 43.

In addition, storage must **not** be **controlled by an act of will**, i.e. it must be 'automatic'. Otherwise, a lack of knowledge of the stored content cannot *a priori* be assumed, nor can a liability exemption be considered. 54

IV. Practical advice

Since Art. 4 DSA covers an **exceptional circumstance**, the **burden of proof** of the individual requirements of the liability exemption lies with the providers of intermediary services.[91] In most cases, they will be in a position to provide a substantiated demonstration of this proof since the circumstances are likely to be largely within their respective spheres of influence.[92] 55

Similar requirements **also apply to the negative elements** of Art. 4(1)(a)–(c) DSA. Although negative evidence can be more difficult to prove in practice than positive evidence, this does not preclude the burden of proof of a negative fact from being placed on the party which is generally obliged to prove it.[93] The requirements for a substantiated presentation are, however, reduced: the intermediary services provider is initially required only to present that it, for example, did not initiate the transmission; the opposing party may then – if it is reasonable to do so – be required to submit the opposing case within the scope of a substantiated denial (secondary burden of proof).[94] 56

C. Liability for 'caching' (Art. 5 DSA)

I. Principle of the liability exemption

Art. 5 DSA contains a **further liability exemption for service providers**. This applies when a service provider transmits the information provided by users in a communication network and stores it automatically and for a limited time to make the transmission of the information to other users, on their request, more efficient (so-called **'caching'**). 57

Caching must be distinguished from final storage. The purpose of caching information is not to open it up and use it but rather to speed up the data processing operation by eliminating the need to retrieve the information from the storage location each time it is requested.[95] It is, therefore, a **temporary copy of the actual information**.[96] 58

The intermediate storage must be **limited in time**, whereby the wording correctly does not contain any default concerning the duration of such time limitation (e.g. short-term). The permissible period of time depends entirely on the purpose of the intermediate storage, which is, after all, precisely to increase efficiency and security in future data processing operations.[97] It is the responsibility of the service provider to ensure that data are not being stored for an unlimited period of time.[98] 59

---

[91] Still on former § 8 TMG: Hennemann in BeckOK InfoMedienR TMG § 8 mn. 45.

[92] Still on former § 8 TMG: Hennemann in BeckOK InfoMedienR TMG § 8 mn. 45.

[93] Already BGH 13.5.1987 – VIII ZR 137/86, NJW 1987, 2235 (2236) – Beweislast des Käufers für Zugang der empfangsbedürftigen Mängelanzeige.

[94] Similarly, BGH 24.3.2010 – XII ZR 175/08, NJW 2010, 1813 mn. 19 et seqq. – Darlegungs- und Beweislast bei der Herabsetzung und Befristung des nachehelichen Unterhalts; still on former § 8 TMG: Hoffmann/Volkmann in Spindler/Schuster TMG § 8 mn. 46.

[95] Cf. still on former TMG: Hoffmann/Volkmann in Spindler/Schuster TMG § 9 mn. 8.

[96] Cf. still on forner TMG: Hoffmann/Volkmann in Spindler/Schuster TMG § 9 mn. 9.

[97] Cf. still on former TMG: Hoffmann/Volkmann in Spindler/Schuster TMG § 9 mn. 12.

[98] Cf. still on former TMG: Hoffmann/Volkmann in Spindler/Schuster TMG § 9 mn. 12.

II. Limitations of the liability exemption

60 In regard to caching, a liability exemption is only justified if the service provider

- does not modify the information (Art. 5(1)(a) DSA);
- complies with conditions on access to the information (Art. 5(1)(b) DSA);
- complies with rules regarding the updating of the information, specified in a manner widely recognised and used by industry (Art. 5(1)(c) DSA);
- does not interfere with the lawful use of technology, widely recognised and used by industry, to obtain data on the use of the information (Art. 5(1)(d) DSA); and
- acts expeditiously to remove or disable access to the information they have stored upon obtaining actual knowledge of the fact that the information at the initial source of the transmission has been removed from the network, or access to it has been disabled, or that a judicial or an administrative authority has ordered such removal or disablement (Art. 5(1)(e) DSA).

61 Art. 5 DSA therefore **largely corresponds to** the regulation of **Art. 13(1) E-Commerce Directive.**[99] The minimal changes in some language versions of the DSA are likely to be due to translation inaccuracies and do not contain any changes in meaning (e.g. 'widely recognised and used by industry' in Art. 5(1)(c) and (d) DSA instead of 'industry standards' in the German version of Art. 13(1)(c) and (d) E-Commerce Directive). However, the retention of the previous regulation also leads to problems of interpretation. The **legal classification of content delivery networks**, i.e. networks of regionally distributed servers connected via the internet and with which content is delivered, remains unclear.[100]

62 Since the wording of Art. 5 DSA has a large linguistic overlap with former § 9 TMG in Germany, it should be considered to refer to the corresponding evaluations – even if, once again, it should be borne in mind that EU law uses terminology which is peculiar to itself and engages legal concepts that do not necessarily have the same meaning as the corresponding concepts that may exist in the law of Member States. The **modification of information** (cf. Art. 5(1)(a) DSA) under former § 9 TMG required a deliberate alteration;[101] a change due to a technical error was not sufficient.[102] Information was also not altered if only a smaller version of an image was stored in addition to the actual information ('thumbnail').[103]

63 In addition, the conditions for access to information may **not be circumvented** by caching (Art. 5(1)(b) DSA); in particular, laws for the protection of minors and copyright law need to be observed.[104] It is also the case that merely making an already freely accessible but hidden piece of information more accessible does not constitute a case of circumventing the access conditions.[105] Circumvention does occur, however, if the intermediate storage takes place against the will of the information owner.[106]

---

[99] Again incorrectly referring to identical wording: Spindler GRUR 2021, 545 (549).

[100] Spindler GRUR 2021, 545 (549).

[101] Cf. still on former TMG: Hoffmann/Volkmann in Spindler/Schuster TMG § 9 mn. 17.

[102] Cf. still on former TMG: Hoffmann/Volkmann in Spindler/Schuster TMG § 9 mn. 17; concerning the autonomy of EU law most recently: ECJ 6.10.2021 – case C-561/19, ECLI:EU:C:2021:799 para. 45 – Consorzio Italian Management e Catania Multiservizi.

[103] Cf. still on former TMG: Hoffmann/Volkmann in Spindler/Schuster TMG § 9 mn. 18; Spindler in Spindler/Schmitz TMG § 9 mn. 17.

[104] Cf. still on former TMG: Hoffmann/Volkmann in Spindler/Schuster TMG § 9 mn. 19; Spindler in Spindler/Schmitz TMG § 9 mn. 18.

[105] Cf. still on former TMG: Hoffmann/Volkmann in Spindler/Schuster TMG § 9 mn. 20.

[106] Spindler in Spindler/Schmitz TMG § 9 mn. 19.

Regarding the **updating of information** in a manner widely recognised and used by industry (cf. Art. 5(1)(c) DSA), it should be noted that such industry standards often do not currently exist.[107] Therefore, when applying this rule, no excessively strict requirements should be placed on the legal assessment of the period between updating processes.[108] 64

In addition, according to Art. 5(1)(d) DSA, the service provider may **not interfere with lawful data collection** by information providers,[109] since these data are regularly used to finance the information providers.[110] Once again, there is a reference to industry standards but, if relevant standards existed, it would not be the service providers that would have to observe them, but the owners of the information.[111] 65

Finally, the service provider must **act expeditiously to remove or to disable access** to information it has stored in the situations mentioned above (Art. 5(1)(e) DSA). As regards former German TMG, Spindler considers a period of three to five days after obtaining relevant information to be appropriate.[112] It remains to be seen whether case law will adopt a similarly short deletion timeframe. 66

III. Practical advice

Concerning the **burden of proof** in liability claims for caching, the same rules apply as for liability claims for mere conduit (→ mn. 55 et seqq.). 67

D. Liability for hosting (Art. 6 DSA)

I. Principle of the liability exemption

Art. 6 DSA contains a **liability exemption for hosting activities**. According to this provision, service providers are not liable for the information stored at the request of users if they have no actual knowledge of illegal activity or illegal content and – as regards claims for damages – are also not aware of any facts or circumstances from which an illegal activity or illegal content becomes apparent (Art. 6(1)(a) DSA), or if, upon obtaining such knowledge or awareness, they act expeditiously to remove or to disable access to the illegal content (Art. 6(1)(b) DSA). This liability exemption **corresponds to the provision of Art. 14(1) E-Commerce Directive.**[113] 68

Rec. 22 sent. 3 DSA additionally clarifies when such knowledge or awareness is to be assumed.[114] Service providers can obtain **knowledge of (allegedly) illegal content** through investigations on their own initiative or through precise notices submitted by third parties. These must be sufficiently substantiated as to enable the service providers 69

---

[107] Cf. still on former TMG: Hoffmann/Volkmann in Spindler/Schuster TMG § 9 mn. 26; Spindler in Spindler/Schmitz TMG § 9 mn. 24.

[108] Cf. still on former TMG: Hoffmann/Volkmann in Spindler/Schuster TMG § 9 mn. 27; Spindler in Spindler/Schmitz TMG § 9 mn. 24.

[109] Cf. still on former TMG: Hoffmann/Volkmann in Spindler/Schuster TMG § 9 mn. 29; Spindler in Spindler/Schmitz TMG § 9 mn. 27.

[110] Cf. still on former TMG: Hoffmann/Volkmann in Spindler/Schuster TMG § 9 mn. 29; Spindler in Spindler/Schmitz TMG § 9 mn. 27.

[111] Cf. still on former TMG: Hoffmann/Volkmann in Spindler/Schuster TMG § 9 mn. 32.

[112] Spindler in Spindler/Schmitz TMG § 9 mn. 31.

[113] Reference can be made to the corresponding commentary on former TMG: Hoffmann/Volkmann in Spindler/Schuster TMG § 10 mn. 13 et seqq.; Spindler in Spindler/Schmitz TMG § 10 mn. 11 et seqq.

[114] The provision is not to be understood conclusively, cf. Spindler GRUR 2021, 545 (549).

to identify and evaluate the allegedly illegal content and, where appropriate, to take action against it (rec. 22 sent. 3 DSA). Art. 16 DSA obliges hosting providers to offer a procedure for reporting illegal content (→ Ch. 4 mn. 61 et seqq.). According to Art. 16(3) DSA, if a notice 'allows a diligent provider of hosting services to identify the illegality of the relevant activity or information without a detailed legal examination', the hosting provider is presumed to have knowledge within the meaning of Art. 6 DSA. The liability exemption therefore does not apply in these cases.

70 This largely corresponds to the principles developed in **German case law** on pre-procedural notices of infringements. According to these principles, a notice must 'enable the provider of an internet trading platform, who is in principle not obliged to carry out preventive checks, to find those offers for sale that infringe the rights of third parties in the multitude of offers for sale posted without his knowledge by the registered members of the platform with the help of the platform software made available. This requires that the notice is formulated in **such concrete terms that** the addressee of the notice can **easily** – i.e. without a detailed legal or factual examination – **determine the infringement**. The extent of the examination effort to be demanded from the operator of an internet trading platform in this respect depends on the circumstances of the individual case, in particular on the severity of the reported infringements on the one hand and the possibilities of the operator to detect them on the other hand.'[115]

71 However, rec. 22 sent. 4 DSA does not consider **an operator's general awareness** that their services are also used to store illegal content to be sufficient to establish liability. Similarly, automatic indexing of uploaded content, a search function or a recommendation function is not a sufficient reason to suppose 'specific' knowledge (rec. 22 sent. 5 DSA).

72 Rec. 22 sent. 2 DSA further clarifies that removal or disabling of access should always be undertaken in compliance with the fundamental rights of the recipients of the hosting services. In this context, the DSA explicitly refers to the **right to freedom of expression** regulated in Art. 11(1) CFR, which includes the freedom to hold opinions and the freedom to receive and impart information and ideas without interference by public authority and regardless of frontiers.

II. Exclusion of the liability exemption

1. Influence of the service providers (Art. 6(2) DSA)

73 Like the corresponding provision in Art. 14(2) E-Commerce Directive, Art. 6(2) DSA provides that the liability exemption of Art. 6(1) DSA (or Art. 14(1) E-Commerce Directive) does not apply to third-party content if users are under the control of the service providers or are acting under their authority. A requirement for this is the service providers' ability to influence the users.[116]

74 Such a **subordination** may exist, for example, within an employer-employee context, whereas in these situations special attention must be paid to the actual foreignness of the information. Where employees act within the scope of their assigned field of activity, the information usually belongs to the employer providing the service.[117] The liability ex-

---

[115] BGH 17.8.2011 – I ZR 57/09, GRUR 2011, 1038 mn. 28 – Stiftparfüm, translation by the authors.

[116] Cf. also on the German transposition norm of Art. 14(1) E-Commerce Directive in former § 10 TMG: Hennemann in BeckOK InfoMedienR TMG § 10 mn. 49.

[117] Cf. also on the German transposition norm of Art. 14(2) E-Commerce Directive in former § 10 TMG: Müller-Broich in Nomos-BR TMG § 10 mn. 7; Hennemann in BeckOK InfoMedienR TMG § 10 mn. 52.

emption of Art. 6(1) DSA, which applies only to third-party content, is therefore excluded from the outset in such cases.[118]

In Germany, for example, a **supervisory relationship** was confirmed in case law for the fact check on Facebook. A research centre was commissioned to conduct fact checks, the results of which were integrated into the Facebook platform through a fact check notice. The content was to be marked as objectionable according to the defendant's business principles. The court considered the question of whether and to what extent Facebook actually supervised the content of these third parties to be irrelevant. It was sufficient for the existence of a supervisory relationship that Facebook could have reserved such supervisory powers for itself, 'especially since it must be assumed that [Facebook] already makes the fundamental decision as to which companies it grants the position of being able to provide [it] with fact-checking results in such a way that they appear automatically and without further verification by [Facebook] on [the] platform'.[119] 75

By contrast, the mere operation of an internet forum in which users can post their own contributions, even where there is moderation of the platform by the provider, is not sufficient for a supervisory relationship between users and service providers. The mere possibility of subsequent control does not constitute supervision of the formal creation of contributions.[120] In addition, supervision within the meaning of Art. 6(2) DSA may come into question in particular in cases of controlled subsidiaries' dependency within a group of companies but is generally determined on a case by case basis according to applicable criteria set out by company law.[121] 76

2. (Appearance of) control by online trading platforms (Art. 6(3) DSA)

Art. 6(3) DSA contains one of the few innovations in the DSA compared to the E-Commerce Directive:[122] If products or services are presented on **online trading platforms** in such a way that an average consumer believes that the object of the transaction is provided by the online platform itself or by a user who is acting under its authority or control, a liability exemption with respect to the liability under consumer protection law shall not apply.[123] Examples include marketplaces and app stores that do not clearly distance themselves from the information provided by third parties.[124] Online platforms that enable consumers to conclude distance contracts where the provider determines the price of goods and services offered by these third parties on that platform are covered by Art. 6(3) DSA as set out in rec. 23 DSA following a proposal by the Council. 77

For members of the German legal community, the exception in Art. 6(3) DSA may be reminiscent of the **'*Zu-eigen-Machen*'** case law (→ mn. 33 et seqq.); the European legislator meanwhile was guided by ECJ case law on active providers (→ mn. 36 et seqq.).[125] 78

[118] Cf. also on the German transposition norm of Art. 14(2) E-Commerce Directive in former § 10 TMG: Hennemann in BeckOK InfoMedienR TMG § 10 mn. 52.

[119] OLG Karlsruhe 14.7.2021 – 6 W 8/21, GRUR-RS 2021, 22158 mn. 42 – Faktencheck-Hinweis, translation by the authors.

[120] Cf. also on the German transposition norm of Art. 14(2) E-Commerce Directive in former § 10 TMG: Hennemann in BeckOK InfoMedienR TMG § 10 mn. 55.

[121] In detail: Hoffmann/Volkmann in Spindler/Schuster TMG § 10 mn. 50; Hennemann in BeckOK InfoMedienR TMG § 10 mn. 54.

[122] Schmid/Grewe MMR 2021, 279 (280).

[123] Berberich/Seip GRUR-Prax 2021, 4.

[124] Spindler GRUR 2021, 545 (549).

[125] Thus expressly: Schmid/Grewe MMR 2021, 279 (280); Spindler GRUR 2021, 545 (550).

III. Practical advice

79 Concerning the **burden of proof**, general principles apply. The provision favours the **service providers**, which will therefore be considered to carry the burden of proof. In the case of Germany, parallels to former § 10 TMG, where a partial burden of proof on the other party was advocated for, can probably not be drawn.[126] The relevant ruling of the Federal Court of Justice[127] was still based on an earlier version of § 5(2) TDG. However, with its clear wording to the disadvantage of the other party ('only responsible if ...'), this provision already suggested a corresponding reversal of the burden of proof.

E. 'Good Samaritan' privilege: consequences of own-initiative investigations (Art. 7 DSA)

80 Art. 7 DSA contains one of the main innovations of the DSA. Providers of intermediary services may, in principle, also claim the above-mentioned liability exemptions where they **conduct investigations on their own initiative** that identify illegal content and result in its removal or the disabling of access to it.

81 This special rule may be explained by the following:[128] In the past, there was **little incentive** for hosting providers **to carry out monitoring measures**. This was because such measures could result in the hosting providers becoming aware of illegal content and thus losing the right to claim the liability exemptions which generally presuppose a lack of awareness of the illegal content. Increased efforts to discover illegal content therefore led to a potential liability trap. Compared to hosting providers who did not carry out such monitoring measures, those who did were consequently disadvantaged. This did not seem appropriate and set the wrong incentives.[129]

82 Art. 7 DSA attempts to resolve this **dilemma** by emphasising the applicability of the liability exemptions for hosting providers, even if they undertake voluntary monitoring measures. This is intended to give smaller service providers greater legal certainty.[130]

83 Whether such increased legal certainty can actually be achieved based on the provision in Art. 7 DSA, however, remains to be seen in the future application of the law. At present, the DSA contains **no statement on the consequences of inaction** on the provider's part subsequent to the gaining of knowledge through own-initiative investigative measures. There is agreement in the literature that a **literal interpretation** of the provision in Art. 7 DSA would **not be appropriate** as this would render a provider of intermediary services who, despite positive knowledge of the illegality of the content, fails to remove that content expeditiously, to be exempt from liability.[131] This would counter the intended protection of fundamental rights on the internet.[132]

84 However, a liability exemption appears to be appropriate only if providers of intermediary services act immediately – i.e. **without undue delay** – to remove the content in question or disable access to it. Due to the 'good Samaritan' privilege, in individual cases

---

[126] Cf. Spindler in Spindler/Schmitz TMG § 10 mn. 74 et seq.

[127] BGH 23.9.2003 – VI ZR 335/02, NJW 2003, 3764.

[128] On the following already Spindler GRUR 2021, 545 (549).

[129] European Commission, 'Explanatory Memorandum of the DSA' (15.12.2020), COM(2020) 825 final, 3; Leistner ZUM 2012, 722 (726); Spindler GRUR 2021, 545 (549).

[130] European Commission, 'Explanatory Memorandum of the DSA' (15.12.2020), COM(2020) 825 final, 3.

[131] Similarly Spindler GRUR 2021, 545 (550).

[132] European Commission, 'Explanatory Memorandum of the DSA' (15.12.2020), COM(2020) 825 final, 3.

there may be a **considerable time gap** between the gaining of knowledge of illegal content and the actual removal or disabling of access to it,[133] but Art. 7 DSA should not be interpreted so broadly that the mere taking of monitoring measures justifies a far-reaching exemption from liability.

The Council's addition to Art. 7 DSA in the legislative procedure also confirms this. 85
It states that voluntary investigations and measures to remove content and disable access to it are to be carried out **'in good faith'**.[134] Investigations by providers of intermediary services are carried out in good faith so long as these providers have either no knowledge or grossly negligent ignorance of the illegal content. If providers remain inactive for an excessive period of time after gaining possession of objective knowledge of illegal content, they are no longer acting in good faith and cannot claim the 'good Samaritan' privilege.

F. Monitoring and information obligations

Although there is **no general duty to monitor or actively investigate** according to 86
the principle of Art. 8 DSA, specific monitoring duties may be required in individual cases, and judicial or administrative authorities may issue orders to stop or prevent infringements (Art. 9 DSA) or to provide information (Art. 10 DSA).

I. Exclusion of the general obligation to monitor or to actively investigate (Art. 8 DSA)

Like the corresponding provisions of the E-Commerce Directive, the liability-related 87
provisions of the DSA do not establish a duty of general monitoring.[135] This is explicitly stated in Art. 8 DSA, as it was in Art. 15(1) E-Commerce Directive. Rec. 30 sent. 1 DSA confirms this position. Even if a reaction may be required where circumstances indicate an illegal activity, there is no duty to actively search for and investigate specific facts (cf. Art. 8 DSA or Art. 15(1) E-Commerce Directive). Consequently, a general active 'fact-finding' obligation cannot be established by the DSA (cf. rec. 30 sent. 1 and 3 DSA).

The ECJ has already specified these non-obligations in several decisions in the past. 88
It ruled that the prohibition of general monitoring extends in particular to national measures that would oblige a provider of intermediary services to **actively monitor** 'all the data of each of its customers **in order to prevent any future infringement of intellectual property rights** via that provider's website'.[136] In this context, it considered any filtering systems for providers of social networks and peer-to-peer programmes to be impermissible.[137]

---

[133] European Commission, 'Explanatory Memorandum of the DSA' (15.12.2020), COM(2020) 825 final, 3.

[134] Cf. Art. 6 DSA (Draft) in the 'General Approach of the Council' (18.11.2021), ST 13203/21, Annex, mn. 118.

[135] Schmid/Grewe MMR 2021, 279 (280).

[136] ECJ 12.7.2011 – case C-324/09, ECLI:EU:C:2011:474 para. 139 – L'Oréal and others; following this: ECJ 24.11.2011 – case C-70/10, ECLI:EU:C:2011:771 para. 36 et seqq. – Scarlet Extended.

[137] ECJ 24.11.2011 – case C-70/10, ECLI:EU:C:2011:771 para. 54 – Scarlet Extended; ECJ 16.2.2012 – case C-360/10, ECLI:EU:C:2012:85 para. 52 – SABAM.

89 This ban on general monitoring was justified based on the **fundamental rights** applicable in the EU, between which an appropriate balance must be struck.[138] The right to intellectual property, which is protected in Art. 17(2) CFR, must be weighed against the freedom of the providers of intermediary services to conduct a business (Art. 16 CFR) as well as against the right to protection of personal data (Art. 8(1) and (2) CFR) and the right to freedom of expression (Art. 11(1) CFR).[139]

II. Specific monitoring obligations

90 This absence of a duty of general monitoring does not, however, preclude the **need for specific monitoring** in individual cases. Rec. 30 sent. 2 DSA clarifies in this context that monitoring obligations can be established in specific cases, in particular as a result of orders issued by national authorities.[140]

91 In this, the European legislator is guided by previous ECJ case law. '**Such a specific case** may, in particular, [according to the ECJ] be found [...] in a **particular piece of information** stored by the host provider concerned at the request of a certain user of its social network, the content of which was examined and assessed by a court having jurisdiction in the Member State, which, following its assessment, **declared** it **to be illegal**'.[141]

92 As a result, hosting providers can be **ordered** by a court to disable access to or remove stored illegal (and similar) information, in particular to prevent the rapid dissemination of illegal information through 'sharing'.[142] It is clear, however, that such an order does not create a general duty to monitor - which is inadmissible under Art. 8 DSA.[143] Furthermore, specific (as opposed to general) monitoring duties are inherent in any **warning** or **cease-and-desist action.**[144] Consequently, to avoid a claim for injunctive relief, the provider is required to prevent similar infringements and ultimately to carry out corresponding (specific) checks for this purpose.

93 A duty of general monitoring is similarly not established when a court directs a specific order to providers of an IP address rental and registration service allowing the anonymous use of internet domain names to **bring an end to or prevent the risk of infringement** of an intellectual property right.[145]

94 However, an order directed at access providers to check all communications passing through an internet connection would be a **violation** of the prohibition of a general duty of monitoring.[146]

---

138 ECJ 24.11.2011 – case C-70/10, ECLI:EU:C:2011:771 para. 43 et seqq. – Scarlet Extended; ECJ 16.2.2012 – case C-360/10, ECLI:EU:C:2012:85 para. 41 et seqq. – SABAM; following this: European Commission, 'Explanatory Memorandum of the DSA' (15.12.2020), COM(2020) 825 final, 13.

139 ECJ 24.11.2011 – case C-70/10, ECLI:EU:C:2011:771 para. 43, 46, 50 – Scarlet Extended; following this concerning the right to freedom of expression, freedom of information as well as the freedom to conduct a business: European Commission, 'Explanatory Memorandum of the DSA' (15.12.2020), COM(2020) 825 final, 13.

140 Spindler GRUR 2021, 545 (550).

141 ECJ 3.10.2019 – case C-18/18, ECLI:EU:C:2019:821 para. 35 – Glawischnig-Piesczek.

142 This is particularly the case where a hosting provider has recourse to automated techniques and means of investigation, see ECJ 3.10.2019 – case C-18/18, ECLI:EU:C:2019:821 para. 37 – Glawischnig-Piesczek.

143 Still on Art. 15(1) E-Commerce Directive, ECJ 3.10.2019 – case C-18/18, ECLI:EU:C:2019:821 – Glawischnig-Piesczek; ECJ 16.2.2012 – case C-360/10, ECLI:EU:C:2012:85 – SABAM.

144 LG Frankfurt a. M. 8.4.2022 – 2-03 O 188/21, MMR 2022, 494 (495); similar: LG Hamburg 24.1.2014 – 324 O 264/11, ZUM-RD 2014, 511 (526) on the deletion by the 'notice and takedown' method.

145 ECJ 7.8.2018 – case C-521/17, ECLI:EU:C:2018:639 para. 51 et seq. – SNB-REACT.

146 ECJ 15.9.2016 – case C-484/14, ECLI:EU:C:2016:689 para. 85 et seqq. – McFadden.

III. Orders to take action against illegal content (Art. 9 DSA)

Rec. 25 sent. 1 DSA emphasises that the liability exemptions contained in Art. 4–6 DSA are without prejudice to the possibilities of 'injunctions of different kinds against providers of intermediary services [...]'. This means it will also be possible in the future to issue orders on the part of national judicial or administrative authorities requiring the cessation or prevention of an infringement. 95

However, these orders do not find their legal basis in the DSA itself (in particular, not in Art. 9 DSA) but are to be based on legal grounds found in Union or Member State law. This is implicit in Art. 9(2)(a)(i) DSA, which requires 'a reference to the legal basis under Union or national law for the order'. Such a reference obligation only seems logical if Art. 9 DSA does not itself already constitute the legal basis and, in fact, rec. 31 sent. 5 DSA states that the DSA neither provides the legal basis for issuing orders nor regulates their territorial scope or cross-border enforcement. 96

Within the context of such orders, however, it is important to take into consideration the **principle of subsidiarity of liability** constituted in rec. 27 sent. 1 and 3 DSA. According to this principle, the users (referred to as 'recipients' in the DSA) of the intermediary services should primarily be liable for the illegal content they provide and disseminate and, if possible, conflicts should be settled without the involvement of the intermediary services providers. 97

In cases where this is not possible and the involvement of the intermediary services provider in the conflict is required, the necessary orders should, in principle, be **addressed to the party with the technical and operational capabilities** to take action against specific illegal content, thereby eliminating, or at least minimising, the risk of any negative effects on the availability and accessibility of non-illegal information. 98

Members of the German legal community are probably already familiar with these principles from the existing BGH case law on **subsidiarity of liability by analogy to former § 7(4) sent. 1 TMG**. According to this principle, the subsidiarity requirement has the effect that a claim for redress against access providers exists only if the same claim against the website operators is ruled out in the specific case. In this respect, the latter (and their hosting providers) are 'significantly closer to the infringement [...] than the party generally providing access to the Internet'.[147] 99

1. Minimum formal requirements for orders

For the first time, Art. 9 DSA contains numerous **formal minimum requirements** for admissible orders. According to Art. 9(2)(a) DSA, the orders must include the following: 100

- a reference to the **legal basis** under Union or national law for the order;
- a **statement of reasons** explaining why the information is **illegal content** (→ mn. 22 et seqq.), by reference to one or more specific provisions of Union law or national law in compliance with Union law;
- information identifying the issuing **authority**;
- clear information enabling the provider of intermediary services to identify and locate the illegal content concerned, such as one or more **exact URL** and, where necessary, additional information;

[147] BGH 26.11.2015 – I ZR 174/14, GRUR 2016, 268 para. 83, translation by the authors; confirmed by BGH 15.10.2020 – I ZR 13/19, GRUR 2021, 63 para. 31; critical: Nordemann GRUR 2018, 1016 (1018).

- information about **redress mechanisms** available to the provider of intermediary services and to the recipient of the service who provided the content;
- where applicable, information about which authority is to receive the information about the effect given to the orders.

101 Whether the statement of reasons for the order is required to contain **information on the weighing of the legal interests affected** and on the appropriate balance between protected fundamental rights is not clarified in Art. 9 DSA, though such a statement was required by the ECJ in the kino.to decision[148] and was concretised in the McFadden decision[149]. By contrast, the wording of the provision suggests a rather narrow interpretation.[150]

102 Art. 9(2)(c) DSA is further intended to ensure that there are no **linguistic barriers to understanding** the order. Orders are therefore to be issued in one of the languages specified in Art. 9(2)(c), Art. 11(3) DSA (→ Ch. 4 mn. 21 et seqq.).

103 Following a suggestion by the Council in the legislative process, Art. 9(5) DSA contains the **obligation of the service provider to inform the affected user** about the order and its formal requirements. When an order is issued to take action against illegal content, the service provider, without the involvement of courts or authorities, must inform the individually affected users that the order has been received and why, as well as how it has been complied with and what avenues for redress are available to the user. This notification must occur at the latest when the order comes into force or at a time stipulated in the order by the issuing authority. The service provider thereby becomes an 'extended arm' of the executive or judiciary.

2. Territorial scope of validity of orders

104 Art. 9(2)(b) DSA further provides for a **limit in territorial terms**, in that the scope of an order may not exceed what is strictly necessary to achieve its objective. According to rec. 36 sent. 2 DSA, the issuing authority should balance the objective that the order seeks to achieve with the rights and legitimate interests of all third parties potentially affected by the order, in particular their fundamental rights under the CFR.

105 According to the conviction of the European legislator, the order will generally be limited to the **territory of the issuing Member State** (cf. rec. 36 sent. 3 DSA). However, rec. 36 sent. 3 DSA provides for two **exceptions**: The first is when a cross-border order is needed to remove illegal content that may arise directly from Union law; the second is when the balancing of the various rights affected may require a larger territorial scope (e.g. in the case of illegal content on websites accessible in several Member States).

106 Regarding legal policy, this possibility for **cross-border deletion orders** is viewed in two ways: On the one hand, there is the desire for Europe-wide, effective tools against infringements of rights; on the other hand, there is concern about possible censorship and extensive use of the deletion order to enforce political goals. It remains to be seen how the use of the cross-border deletion order will turn out in practice.

3. 'Stay down' or just 'takedown'?

107 Concerning the scope of the authorities' orders (Art. 9 DSA), a legislative discussion has taken place as to whether providers should be required not only to 'takedown' illegal content but also to ensure that it 'stays down'. The latter includes the obligation to not

[148] ECJ 27.3.2014 – case C-314/12, ECLI:EU:C:2014:192 para. 62 et seqq. – UPC Telekabel Wien.
[149] ECJ 15.9.2016 – case C-484/14, ECLI:EU:C:2016:689 para. 83 et seq. – McFadden.
[150] So also Spindler GRUR 2021, 545 (549).

only selectively delete illegal content but to delete the same or similar content or deny platform access.

The recital discussed in this regard, which did not become part of the final version, read: 108

> However, such orders may require a provider of hosting services to remove information which it stores, the content of which is identical or equivalent to the content of information which was previously declared to be unlawful, or to block access to that information, irrespective of who requested the storage of that information, provided that the monitoring of and search for the information concerned is limited to information properly identified in the order, such as the name of the person concerned by the infringement determined previously, the circumstances in which that infringement was determined and equivalent content to that which was declared to be illegal, and does not require the provider of hosting services to carry out an independent assessment of that content, as interpreted by the Court of Justice of the EU.

However, the final version of the DSA seems to assume that a **'stay down'** obligation 109 does **not prevail**. According to rec. 34 sent. 7 DSA, orders should be issued in compliance with the GDPR and the prohibition of general obligations to monitor information or actively seek facts or circumstances indicating illegal activities. Similarly, the DSA is intended to be without prejudice to the possibility for a Member State to require an intermediary services provider to prevent an infringement under Union law, including this Regulation, particularly with regard to the prohibition of general obligations to monitor. This clearly expresses the principle that there should be no general duty of monitoring. However, such a duty could be introduced 'through the back door' if official orders also contained a duty to ensure 'stay down'. The intermediaries would then have to review the uploaded information for an indefinite period of time.

IV. Orders to provide information (Art. 10 DSA)

Finally, Art. 10 DSA contains certain requirements for information orders. These are 110 to be applied when national judicial or administrative authorities issue orders against providers of intermediary services under Union or national law and require them to provide information about their users. In this respect, Art. 10 DSA is not an individual legal basis for authorities but instead regulates **harmonised procedural requirements** for existing official information orders.

In formal terms, such a requirement under Art. 10(2)(a) DSA must contain at least 111 the following:

- a reference to the **legal basis** under Union or national law for the order;
- information identifying the issuing **authority**;
- clear information enabling intermediary services providers to identify the specific recipient(s) on whom information is sought, such as one or more **account names or unique identifiers**;
- a **statement of reasons** explaining the objective for which the information is required and why the requirement to provide the information is necessary and proportionate to determine compliance by the recipients of the intermediary services with applicable Union law or national law in compliance with Union law, unless such a statement cannot be provided for reasons related to the prevention, investigation, detection and prosecution of criminal offences;

- information about **redress mechanisms** available to the service provider and the recipients of the service concerned;
- where applicable, information about which authority is to receive the information about the effect given to the orders.

G. Conclusion

112 It is obvious that the DSA contains **little that is new concerning liability exemptions**. For one thing, nothing changes for providers. In the case of Germany, the liability regulations largely adopted by the DSA were already implemented in former §§ 7 et seqq. TMG following the E-Commerce Directive. Intermediaries are still **not responsible for third-party content**[151] and only under certain circumstances can the liability of providers of intermediary services arise. Also, a **general duty of monitoring content** and an active duty of clarification concerning illegal activities still need to be individually established. By way of clarification, Art. 7 DSA now explicitly states that **own-initiative activities** of the intermediary services to identify illegal content independently do not lead to the inapplicability of the liability exemptions in Art. 4, 5 and 6 DSA. What is new, however, is that the directly applicable provisions of the Regulation are now the primary legal basis.

[151] Berberich/Seip GRUR-Prax 2021, 4.

CHAPTER 4
DUE DILIGENCE OBLIGATIONS OF PROVIDERS OF INTERMEDIARY SERVICES

Niklas Maamar

Bibliography: Akerlof, 'The Market for 'Lemons': Quality Uncertainty and the Market Mechanism', 84 The Quarterly Journal of Economics 1970, 488; Allen/Stockhem, 'Due Diligence in Content Moderation' (Center for Democracy & Technology, 10.8.2022) <https://cdt.org/insights/a-series-on-the-eu-digital-services-act-due-diligence-in-content-moderation> (last accessed: 23.5.2024); Berberich/Seip, 'Der Entwurf des Digital Services Act', GRUR-Prax 2021, 4; Busch/Mak, 'Putting the Digital Services Act in Context: Bridging the Gap Between EU Consumer Law and Platform Regulation', EuCML 2021, 109; Castellaro/Penfrat, 'The DSA fails to reign in the most harmful digital platform businesses – but it is still useful' (Verfassungsblog, 8.11.2022) <https://verfassungsblog.de/dsa-fails> (last accessed: 23.5.2024); Cauffman/Goanta, 'A New Order: The Digital Services Act and Consumer Protection', European Journal of Risk Regulation 2021, 758; Council of the European Union, 'DSA: Council gives final approval to the protection of users' rights online' (4.10.2022) <https://www.consilium.europa.eu/en/press/press-releases/2022/10/04/dsa-council-gives-final-approval-to-the-protection-of-users-rights-online> (last accessed: 23.5.2024); Edelson et al., 'Understanding engagement with U.S. (mis)information news sources on Facebook', Proceedings of the 21st ACM Internet Measurement Conference 2021, 444; Eifert et al., 'Taming the Giants: The DMA/DSA Package', CMLR 2021, 987; Electronic Frontier Foundation, 'Preserve What Works, Fix What is Broken: EFF's Policy Principles for the Digital Services Act' (2020) <https://www.eff.org/files/consolidatedeupolicyprinciples.pdf> (last accessed: 23.5.2024); European Commission, 'Europe fit for the Digital Age: New online rules for businesses' <https://commission.europa.eu/strategy-and-policy/priorities-2019-2024/europe-fit-digital-age/digital-services-act-ensuring-safe-and-accountable-online-environment/europe-fit-digital-age-new-online-rules-businesses_en> (last accessed: 23.5.2024); European Commission, 'Disinformation: Commission welcomes the new stronger and more comprehensive Code of Practice on disinformation' (16.6.2022) <https://ec.europa.eu/commission/presscorner/detail/en/IP_22_3664> (last accessed: 23.5.2024); European Commission, 'Sneak Peek: How the Commission will enforce the DSA & DMA – Blog of Commissioner Thierry Breton', Statement 22/4327 (5.7.2022) <https://ec.europa.eu/commission/presscorner/detail/en/STATEMENT_22_4327> (last accessed: 23.5.2024); European Commission, 'Questions and Answers: Digital Services Act' (25.4.2023) <https://ec.europa.eu/commission/presscorner/detail/en/QANDA_20_2348> (last accessed: 23.5.2024); European Commission, 'Digital Services Act: Application of the Risk Management Framework to Russian disinformation campaigns' (30.8.2023) <https://data.europa.eu/doi/10.2759/764631> (last accessed: 23.5.2024); European Commission, 'Guidelines for providers of Very Large Online Platforms and Very Large Search Engines on the mitigation of systemic risk for electoral processes pursuant to the Digital Services Act' (26.4.2024) <https://digital-strategy.ec.europa.eu/en/library/guidelines-providers-vlops-and-vloses-mitigation-systemic-risks-electoral-processes>; Fiala/Husovec, 'Using experimental evidence to improve delegated enforcement', 71 International Review of Law & Economics 2022, 106079; Genç-Gelgeç, 'Regulating Digital Platforms: Will the DSA Correct Its Predecessor's Deficiencies?', 18 Croatian Yearbook of European Law and Policy 2022, 25; Gerpott, 'Das Gesetz über digitale Dienste nach den Trilog-Verhandlungen', CR 2022, 516; Gielen/Uphues, 'Digital Markets Act und Digital Services Act. Regulierung von Markt- und Meinungsmacht durch die Europäische Union', EuZW 2021, 627; Gömann, Das öffentlich-rechtliche Binnenkollisionsrecht der GDPR, Tübingen 2021; Gomez-Uribe/Hunt, 'The Netflix Recommender System: Algorithms, Business Value, and Innovation', 6 ACM Transactions on Management Information Systems 2015, 13; Griffin, 'Tackling Discrimination in Targeted Advertising' (Verfassungsblog, 23.6.2022) <https://verfassungsblog.de/targeted-ad> (last accessed: 23.5.2024); Helberger et al., 'Regulation of news recommenders in the Digital Services Act: empowering David against the Very Large Online Goliath' (Internet Policy Review, 26.2.2021) <https://policyreview.info/articles/news/regulation-news-recommenders-digital-services-act-empowering-david-against-very-large> (last accessed: 23.5.2024); Ho-Dac/Lehmann, 'Digital Services Act – Part Two: Inside the Belly of the Beast' (European Association of Private International Law, 24.2.2023) <https://eapil.org/2023/02/24/digital-services-act-part-2-inside-the-belly-of-the-beast> (last accessed: 23.5.2024); Holznagel, 'Chapter II des Vorschlags der EU-Kommission für einen Digital Services Act', CR 2021, 123; Holznagel, 'Zu starke Nutzerrechte in Art. 17 and 18 DSA', CR 2022, 594; Holznagel, 'A Self-Regulatory Race to the Bottom through Out-of-Court Dispute Settlement in the Digital Services Act' (Verfassungsblog, 22.3.2022) <https://verfassungsblog.de/a-self-regulatory-race-to-the-bottom-through-art-18-digital-services-act> (last accessed: 23.5.2024); Husovec, 'Will the DSA work? – On money and effort' (Verfassungsblog, 9.11.2022) <https://verfassungsblog.de/dsa-money-effort> (last accessed: 23.5.2024); Husovec/Laguna, 'Digital Services Act: A Short Primer', forthcoming in Husovec/Laguna (eds), Principles of the Digital Services Act, Oxford 2023 <https://ssrn.com/abstract=4153796> (last accessed: 23.5.2024); Janal, 'Haftung und Verantwortung im Entwurf des Digital Services Acts', ZEuP 2021, 227; Kuclar Stiković, 'The EU's Digital Services Act and Its Impact on Online Platforms', European Union Law Working Papers 2024, No. 85; Kuczerawy/Dutkiewicz, 'Accessing Information about Abortion' (Verfassungsblog, 28.7.2022) <https://verfassungsblog.de/accessing-information-about-abortion> (last accessed: 23.5.2024); Kühling/Sauerborn, ''Dark patterns' unter der DSGVO und dem DSA – Neue Herausforderung für die digitale Rechtsordnung', CR 2022, 226; Kuhlmannn/Trute, 'Die Regulierung von Desinformationen und rechtswidrigen Inhalten nach dem neuen Digital Services Act', GSZ 2022, 115; Leerssen, 'An end to shadow banning? Transparency rights in the Digital Services Act between content moderation and curation', 48 Computer Law & Security Review 2023, 105790; Legner, 'Der Digital Services Act – Ein neuer Grundstein der Digitalregulierung, ZUM 2024, 99; Mantelero, 'Fundamental rights impact assessments in the DSA' (Verfassungsblog, 1.11.2022) <https://verfassungsblog.de/dsa-impact-assessment> (last accessed: 23.5.2024); Martini et al., 'Dark Patterns. Phänomenologie und Antworten der Rechtsordnung', ZfDR 2021, 47; Nosák, 'The DSA Introduces Important Transparency Obligations for Digital Services, but Key Questions Remain' (Center for Democracy & Technology, 18.6.2021) <https://cdt.org/insights/the-dsa-introduces-important-transparency-obligations-for-digital-services-but-key-questions-remain> (last accessed: 23.5.2024); Ortolani, 'If You Build It, They Will Come – The DSA's 'Procedure Before Substance' Approach' (Verfassungsblog, 7.11.2022) <https://verfassungsblog.de/dsa-build-it> (last accessed: 23.5.2024); Pernice, 'Einigungsmängel im EU-Mitentscheidungsverfahren. Zum Umgang mit Korrekturen durch die Rechts- und Sprachendienste der Institutionen', EuZW 2004, 743; Peukert, 'Five Reasons to be Skeptical About the DSA' (Verfassungsblog, 31.8.2021) <https://verfassungsblog.de/power-dsa-dma-04> (last accessed: 23.5.2024); Peukert et al., 'European Copyright Society – Comment on Copyright and the Digital Services Act Proposal', IIC 2022, 358; Plummer, 'This is how Netflix's top-secret recommendation system works' (Wired, 22.8.2017) <https://wired.co.uk/article/how-do-netflixs-algorithms-work-machine-learning-helps-to-predict-what-viewers-will-like> (last accessed: 23.5.2024); Quintais/Schwemer, 'The Interplay between the Digital Services Act and Sector Regulation: How Special Is Copyright?', European Journal of Risk Regulation 2022, 1; Schechner/Horwitz/Glazer, 'How Facebook Hobbled Mark Zuckerberg's Bid to Get America Vaccinated' (Wall Street Journal, 17.9.2021) <https://wsj.com/articles/facebook-mark-zuckerberg-vaccinated-11631880296> (last accessed: 23.5.2024); Schmidt/Grewe, 'Digital Services Act: Neues 'Grundgesetz für Onlinedienste'?', MMR 2021, 279; Spindler, 'Der Vorschlag für ein neues Haftungsregime für Internetprovider – der EU-Digital Services Act. Teil 1', GRUR 2021, 545; Spindler, 'Der Vorschlag für ein neues Haftungsregime für Internetprovider – der EU-Digital Services Act. Teil 2: Große und besonders große Plattformen', GRUR 2021, 653; Turillazzi et al., 'The Digital Services Act: an analysis of its ethical, legal, and social implications' (12.1.2022) <https://ssrn.com/abstract=4007389> (last accessed: 23.5.2024); Wells/Horwitz/Seetharaman, 'Facebook Knows Instagram Is Toxic for Teen Girls, Company Documents Show' (Wall Street Journal, 14.9.2021) <https://wsj.com/articles/facebook-knows-instagram-is-toxic-for-teen-girls-company-documents-show-11631620739> (last accessed: 23.5.2024); Wilman, 'The Digital Services Act (DSA) – An Overview' (16.12.2022) <https://ssrn.com/abstract=4304586> (last accessed: 23.5.2024); Wimmers, 'The Out-of-court dispute settlement mechanism in the Digital Services Act – A disservice to its own goals', 4 JIPITEC 2021, 421; Zech, 'General and specific monitoring obligations in the Digital Services Act' (Verfassungsblog, 2.9.2021) <https://verfassungsblog.de/power-dsa-dma-07> (last accessed: 23.5.2024).

A. Introduction

1 'The time of online platforms behaving like they are "too big to care" is coming to an end.' With these striking words, EU Internal Market Commissioner Thierry Breton announced that an agreement on the DSA had been reached.[1] The allusion to the 2008 financial crisis and the so-called 'too big to fail' banks underlines the significance and impact the Commission attaches to the **regulatory framework for the digital space**. The DSA is a **first-of-its-kind legislation**, creating binding obligations for online intermediary services, large and small, which apply directly and uniformly across the European Union.

2 The starting point for discussions on the harmonisation of due diligence obligations in the DSA was the realisation that the problem of illegal content and illegal activities online cannot be dealt with by focusing on liability provisions for intermediaries alone (rec. 27 DSA).[2] Instead, the DSA takes a dual approach by adopting the previous liability exemptions known from the E-Commerce Directive (→ Ch. 3 mn. 26) and supplementing them with specific due diligence obligations. The regulatory system aims to minimise the **negative externalities of intermediary services** – in particular, the spread of illegal goods, fake news and hate speech – through organisational and procedural requirements, and to internalise the social costs among the providers without relying on the heavy-handed instrument of imposing liability for third-party content.[3] The due diligence obligations are therefore designed as **genuine obligations to act** on the part of the **intermediary services** which are independent of the question of liability for third-party illegal content under Art. 4–10 DSA and are therefore regulated in a separate chapter of the DSA (rec. 41 DSA).

3 The following chapter provides an overview of the structure of the due diligence obligations and their scope of application before going on to discuss individual obligations. It will show that, in contrast to the issue of liability for third-party content, in this regard the DSA pursues many **novel regulatory concepts** and introduces **very comprehensive duties** for various digital services.

---

[1] European Commission, 'Sneak Peek: how the Commission will enforce the DSA & DMA – Blog of Commissioner Thierry Breton', Statement 22/4327', @ThierryBreton on X (23.4.2022 at 2:17 AM) <https://x.com/thierrybreton/status/1517658796927164417> (last accessed: 23.5.2024).

[2] European Commission, 'Impact Assessment', SWD(2020) 348 final, Part 1, p. 25. Mere liability provisions are insufficient, e.g. for tackling fake news and disinformation or the danger of overblocking.

[3] Eifert et al. CMLR 2021, 987 (995 et seq.).

B. Tiered due diligence obligations for intermediary services

Online business models are subject to constant change and have become significantly more diverse in the two decades since the introduction of the E-Commerce Directive. In 2000, the E-Commerce Directive distinguished between **three basic intermediary services**: the mere conduit of information by access providers, temporary storage for caching and the hosting of third-party information. 23 years later, a wide variety of intermediary services have been developed, in particular in the field of hosting services, which pose various and quite different risks that were hardly foreseeable at the time the E-Commerce Directive was adopted. The DSA takes account of this diversification by refining the category of hosting services into several subcategories and providing for a **tiered system of due diligence obligations** for different intermediary services, where these obligations increase with the size and risk profile of the service.[4] 4

The European legislator's aim was to create a **safe and transparent online environment** by establishing due diligence obligations. These obligations are intended to protect the fundamental rights of users, especially vulnerable groups such as minors, potential victims of hate speech and consumers on online marketplaces, and to strengthen trust in digital markets (rec. 40 DSA). In the public perception, this centers around **regulation of the Silicon Valley big tech companies** (Amazon, Facebook, YouTube, X & Co.). However, the scope of obligations in the DSA is much broader. According to a Commission study, there are **about 10,000 online platforms in the EU**, of which more than 90 % are small and medium-sized services.[5] A uniform European legal framework should allow these smaller providers to scale their services by eliminating the costs of fragmented national regulations.[6] At the same time, the legislator faced the challenge that far-reaching due diligence and information obligations tend to burden smaller providers disproportionately. While the already dominant platforms are able to cope with stronger regulation and the resulting higher regulatory costs due to their size, the same obligations may create a barrier to market entry for new services because of the significant initial investment required. This would contradict the economic policy goal to build a digital economy in the EU that can compete with Silicon Valley. 5

In pursuit of these political goals, the DSA seeks to strike a balance between **strict due diligence obligations for the very large platforms and search engines**, on the one hand, and a more lenient regulation with less obligations for smaller services, on the other, to allow such smaller services to grow at the beginning of the innovation cycle. This is intended to enable them to compete with large intermediary services. Whether this **balancing act** is successful will likely only become apparent in a few years or decades – just as the consequences of the liability privileges of the E-Commerce Directive for the digital economy only became apparent over time. 6

---

[4] Gerpott CR 2022, 516 (517).

[5] European Commission, 'A Europe fit for the Digital Age: New online rules for businesses'.

[6] European Commission, 'Impact Assessment', SWD(2020) 348 final, Part 1, p. 55 and Part 2, p. 49.

I. Categories of intermediary services

7 Firstly, the DSA incorporates the three categories of intermediary services as defined in the E-Commerce Directive:

- Section 1 covers general obligations that apply to providers of all three types of intermediary services.
- Sections 2–5 set out obligations for different types of hosting services, which supplement the general provisions.

8 Secondly, the DSA introduces **new subcategories of hosting providers**, differentiated by the type of service and number of users, to reflect the specific risks of certain services (rec. 13 and 41 DSA):

- Section 2 addresses all hosting services.
- Section 3 addresses **online platforms**. These hosting services make content uploaded by users publicly available to other users (e.g. social networks).
- Section 4 addresses **online marketplaces**. These hosting services allow consumers to conclude distance contracts with traders.
- Section 5 addresses **very large online platforms and very large online search engines**. These are online platforms and online search engines that have more than 45 million monthly active users in the European Union ('very large services', also known as VLOPs and VLOSEs).

II. Exemption for micro and small enterprises

9 To protect small service providers, certain due diligence obligations of the DSA do not apply to **micro and small enterprises** as defined in the Commission Recommendation 2003/361/EC concerning the definition of micro, small and medium-sized enterprises (→ mn. 103). According to Art. 2 of the Annex to the Recommendation 2003/361/EC, a provider is considered a microenterprise if it employs fewer than ten persons (full-time equivalents) and the annual turnover or balance sheet total does not exceed two million EUR. A provider is considered a small enterprise if it employs fewer than 50 persons (full-time equivalents) and the annual turnover or balance sheet total does not exceed ten million EUR.

10 The DSA provides a **counter-exception** for services that meet the criteria for a micro or small enterprise but at the same time reach more than 45 million monthly active users and are therefore classified by the Commission as a very large service. In this case, according to Art. 19(2) DSA, all obligations apply without exception.

11 The proposal to exempt **non-profit organisations** of any size from the application of due diligence obligations upon request was not implemented.[7] Therefore, the DSA applies to platforms like Wikipedia without restrictions.

III. Tabular overview of the due diligence obligations

12 The due diligence obligations can be roughly systematised into five broad groups that correspond to the objectives of the DSA: (1) the designation of contact points and (2) the transparency obligations serve to build trust among users and to support the effective enforcement of the DSA by public authorities; (3) the due diligence obligations

---

[7] Gerpott CR 2022, 516 (519).

for dealing with illegal content and implementing effective content moderation create the basis for the uniform liability framework; (4) the specifications for the design of services ensure that consumer protection rules are applied effectively; and (5) the specific rules for very large services address the particular social importance and specific risks associated with the largest digital players. The obligations presented in the following overview are explained in detail in later sections of this chapter.

		All services	Hosting services	Online platforms	Online marketplaces	Very large services
Point of contact	Point of contact for authorities	Art. 11	Art. 11	Art. 11	Art. 11	Art. 11
	Point of contact for users	Art. 12	Art. 12	Art. 12	Art. 12	Art. 12
	Legal representative (if the service has no establishment in the EU)	Art. 13	Art. 13	Art. 13	Art. 13	Art. 13
Transparency	Fair T&Cs	Art. 14	Art. 14	Art. 14	Art. 14	Art. 14
	Transparency reports	Art. 15*	Art. 15*	Art. 15* Art. 24*	Art. 15*	Art. 15 Art. 24 Art. 42
Dealing with infringing content	Notice and takedown mechanism		Art. 16	Art. 16	Art. 16	Art. 16
	Statement of reasons and documentation of moderation decisions		Art. 17	Art. 17	Art. 17	Art. 17
	Reporting of criminal offences		Art. 18	Art. 18	Art. 18	Art. 18
	Internal complaint-handling system			Art. 20*	Art. 20*	Art. 20
	Out-of-court dispute settlement			Art. 21*	Art. 21*	Art. 21
	Cooperation with trusted flaggers			Art. 22*	Art. 22*	Art. 22
	Safeguards against misuse of the service or notice and complaints procedures			Art. 23*	Art. 23*	Art. 23

		All services	Hosting services	Online plat-forms	Online market-places	Very large services
Consumer protection through service design	Prohibition of dark patterns			Art. 25*	Art. 25*	Art. 25
	Transparency of online advertising			Art. 26*	Art. 26*	Art. 26 Art. 39
	Recommender system transparency			Art. 27*	Art. 27*	Art. 27 Art. 38
	Protection of minors			Art. 28*	Art. 28*	Art. 28*
	Traceability of traders (know your business customer)				Art. 30*	Art. 30
	Compliance by design				Art. 31*	Art. 31
	Duty to check for illegal products and services				Art. 31*	Art. 31
	Duty to inform the customer in case of ille-gal products and services				Art. 32*	Art. 32
Systemic risks of large services	Risk assessment and mitigation					Art. 34 Art. 35
	Crisis response mechanism					Art. 36
	Independent audit					Art. 37
	Data access for authori-ties and researchers					Art. 40
	Compliance function					Art. 41
	Supervisory fee					Art. 43

* Exemption for micro and small enterprises

C. Due diligence obligations for all services (Art. 11–15 DSA)

13 Art. 11–15 DSA contain due diligence obligations that apply to **all providers of intermediary services** (for the definition of intermediary service → Ch. 2 mn. 22). Therefore, these generally applicable obligations apply to all three types of intermediary services, namely access, caching and hosting services.

14 The aim of the generally applicable obligations of Section 1 is to obtain relevant **information about the service and to identify contact persons necessary for the application and the enforcement of the DSA**. To this end, all providers of intermediary services are obliged to designate points of contact and to publish annual transparency reports. In addition, Art. 14 DSA sets out specific requirements for the content of general terms and conditions (T&Cs).

15 The **scope of application is very broad** and likely includes services that are not the intended addressees of the regulation. According to the case law of the CJEU, a public Wi-Fi network operated in connection with the offering of goods or services (e.g. in a

coffee shop) would also be considered an intermediary service.[8] Following the wording of the DSA, the said coffee shop would be a service provider obliged to designate points of contact both for authorities and users and to publish annual transparency reports.[9]

I. Point of contact for authorities (Art. 11 DSA)

According to Art. 11 DSA, providers of intermediary services must designate a **single point of contact for authorities**, to ensure smooth and efficient communication with the service provider regarding the obligations imposed by the DSA (rec. 42 DSA). 16

The purpose of the point of contact is to provide authorities with fast and direct means of contact with the service provider. It follows from paragraph 1 that the point of contact must be reachable **by electronic means**. It is therefore not sufficient to provide a postal address. In general, an email address will serve as an electronic means of contact. However, other means of communication that allow 'direct' electronic communication are also acceptable. In this context, 'direct' refers to any communication in which no third party is involved.[10] The authorities must be able to communicate directly with the service provider and not through a third party (for the legal representative → mn. 29). A chat tool or telephone number can be used for this purpose. In principle, a contact form on the website may also be appropriate, provided that the service provider responds promptly to messages sent via the contact form, for example by email. While rec. 42 DSA requires 'two-way communications' between authorities and the service provider, in accordance with the wording of Art. 11(1) DSA, it is sufficient if the communication tool provided enables the establishment of a two-way communication at a later stage. 17

The **point of contact serves purely operational purposes** and should be seen as additional to the indication of a summonable address or a legal representative in the legal notice (rec. 42 sent. 3 DSA). In particular, the point of contact is not the correct recipient for formal decisions of authorities. Therefore, the point of contact is not required to be physically located in the European Union (rec. 42 sent. 3 DSA). 18

The point of contact should be available to the authorities of the Member States, the Commission and the European Board for Digital Services (the 'Board' according to Art. 61 DSA).[11] In addition, trusted flaggers (→ mn. 138) and commercial users who have an existing contractual relationship with the provider, as in the case of traders on an online marketplace, may also use the point of contact (rec. 42 sent. 2 DSA). Other users may be referred to the point of contact according to Art. 12 DSA (→ mn. 24). 19

According to Art. 11(2) DSA, information on how to reach the point of contact shall be **published in an easily accessible manner** and kept **up to date**. This corresponds to the requirements regarding the mandatory information to be provided in the legal notice as set out in Art. 5 E-Commerce Directive. Therefore, it is advisable for providers to include the point of contact in their legal notice as the 'point of contact for authorities according to Art. 11 DSA'. The DSA explicitly allows for the designation of the same single point of contact for the purposes of other Union acts (rec. 42 sent. 4 DSA). 20

---

[8] ECJ 15.9.2014 – case C-484/14, ECLI:EU:C:2016:689 – McFadden.

[9] With regard to the transparency report, Art. 15(2) DSA provides an exception for micro and small-sized enterprises (→ mn. 57).

[10] ECJ 16.10.2008 – case C-298/07, ECLI:EU:C:2008:572 para. 29 – Verbraucherzentrale Bundesverband eV v deutsche internet versicherung AG.

[11] The title of Art. 11 DSA in the German language version refers to a point of contact for the '*Vorstand*' (executive board of the company). This is based on a translation error. 'Board', in the sense of Art. 61 DSA, was translated incorrectly.

21 Paragraph 3 addresses the question of in **which language(s)** the point of contact should be able to communicate. In principle, the provider must offer communication in two languages. Specifically:

1. In one of the official languages of the Member State in which the provider has its **main establishment** or, if the provider has no main establishment within the Union, of the country where the legal representative (→ mn. 29) resides or is established.
2. In a language broadly understood by the largest possible number of Union citizens. The DSA is not clear whether only the language understood by the greatest number of Union citizens, namely English, should be used or whether the provider is free to choose some other widely understood language. However, given that the purpose of Art. 11 DSA is to enable the European institutions (Commission and Board) to communicate with the provider without the need for translation services, there are good arguments that one of the three working languages of the Commission should be acceptable, namely **English, German and French**.

22 Art. 11(3) DSA does not specify whether the provider must offer communication in a second language if the official language at its main establishment is widely understood in the Union. Is a provider based in Ireland, for example, required to communicate in a second language in addition to English? On the one hand, the requirement of a widely understood language, which was included in the trilogue negotiations, is introduced with the words 'in addition'. This suggests that at least two languages must be offered. Similarly, rec. 42 DSA uses the plural 'languages to be used'. On the other hand, Art. 11(3) DSA speaks of 'official language or languages', which implies that it is acceptable to designate only one language.

23 Providers must also consider that the chosen language(s) should **not constitute an obstacle to effective communication** (rec. 42 sent. 5 DSA). This could be the case if a provider were to choose an official language not widely used or recognised only regionally. Rec. 42 sent. 6 DSA clarifies that the provider may also communicate in languages other than those chosen if a separate language agreement has been reached with the authorities or may seek alternative means to overcome a language barrier, such as (automated) translation. This kind of translation of a message does not render the communication not 'direct' within the meaning of Art. 11(1) DSA as it does not involve an intermediary. The provider must specify the languages which can be used by authorities to communicate with the point of contact when providing details on how to reach the point of contact. The obligation to designate a point of contact for authorities applies to all providers of intermediary services. There is no exception for small enterprises or start-ups.[12]

II. Point of contact for recipients (Art. 12 DSA)

24 Art. 12 DSA obliges providers to **designate a single point of contact for users**. This provision was added at the request of the European Parliament in the trilogue negotiations to allow users to communicate directly with the provider, similar to the point of contact for authorities under Art. 11 DSA.

[12] Art. 19 DSA, which is part of the third section, explicitly limits the exemption for micro and small-sized enterprises to 'this section'. Therefore, the obligations of the first and second section apply to micro and small-sized enterprises as well, subject to specific exceptions in relevant Articles of the DSA.

The point of contact for users must enable **direct and rapid communication** by electronic means.[13] This can take the form of a telephone number, an email address, a live chat, an electronic contact form or instant messaging (rec. 43 sent. 1 DSA). According to the case law of the CJEU, efficient and rapid communication requires that the user should generally receive an answer within a period of time compatible with their needs and legitimate expectations.[14] For general enquiries during normal business hours, the provider should **respond within 30–60 minutes.**[15] For more complex issues, especially those requiring in-depth legal or factual examination, a time period of several hours or days may still meet the user's reasonable expectations. The provider is obliged to allocate reasonable human and financial resources to ensure the legally required communication speed (rec. 43 sent. 4 DSA). 25

The use of automated means of communication, such as chatbots, is permissible. In such cases, the provider must explicitly indicate to the user that communication will take place via an automated chatbot (rec. 43 sent. 2 DSA). At the same time, according to Art. 12(1) DSA, the user must be provided with the possibility to choose a means of communication that is not exclusively based on automated tools. A chatbot may, therefore, only be used as an additional tool or for first-level support. The user has a right to request direct communication with a human. However, the provider may use automated tools for filtering, sorting and assigning requests to a human. 26

Art. 12 DSA also requires that all routes of communication with the point of contact be **user friendly**. In particular, this means ensuring that the user is not effectively discouraged from contacting the provider directly, for example by complicated click paths or unnecessarily long contact forms. Unlike Art. 11 DSA, Art. 12 DSA does not contain any requirements regarding the **languages to be offered by the provider**. However, the requirement for user-friendly communication will in effect lead to a similar legal standard by requiring the provider to use a language that does not constitute an obstacle to communication for the user. The provider must therefore, at the very least, offer communication with the point of contact in the language in which the service is provided or the language of the audience at which the service is targeted, or translate the user's enquiry and the provider's response. 27

According to paragraph 2, information on how to reach the point of contact must be **published in an easily accessible manner** and kept **up to date**. As with Art. 11(2) DSA, these requirements correspond to the provisions on mandatory information in the legal notice under Art. 5 E-Commerce Directive. The point of contact should be included in the legal notice as the 'point of contact for users according to Art. 12 DSA'. Paragraph 2 clarifies that the obligation to designate the point of contact for users applies in addition to the obligation regarding general information in the legal notice under Art. 5 E-Commerce Directive and does not replace it. 28

III. Legal representative (Art. 13 DSA)

According to Art. 13 DSA, providers of **intermediary services without an establishment in the Union** are obliged to designate a legal representative.[16] This provision is in- 29

[13] This obligation largely corresponds to the trader's duty to provide contact information in case of distance contracts under Art. 6(1)(c) Consumer Rights Directive.

[14] ECJ 16.10.2008 – case C-298/07, ECLI:EU:C:2008:572 para. 2 – Verbraucherzentrale Bundesverband eV v deutsche internet versicherung AG.

[15] ECJ 16.10.2008 – case C-298/07, ECLI:EU:C:2008:572 para. 35 – Verbraucherzentrale Bundesverband eV v deutsche internet versicherung AG.

[16] For a similar obligation see Art. 17 TCO Regulation.

tended to facilitate communication and has considerable practical significance, in particular regarding the **enforcement of DSA provisions in the case of non-EU providers.**[17]

30 The obligation applies to all providers who (1) do not have an establishment in the Union and are based exclusively in a non-EU country, and (2) offer services in the Union. The term **'establishment'** is not defined separately in the DSA and is therefore based on the general understanding of the term in Union law.[18]

31 According to Art. 3(d) DSA, an intermediary services provider **offers services in the Union** if it enables natural or legal persons in one or more Member States to use those services and the provider has a **substantial connection to the Union**. Since intermediary services can generally be used worldwide via the internet, the primary criterion will be whether the provider has a substantial connection to the Union.[19] According to Art. 3(e) DSA, for providers without an establishment in the Union this is deemed to be the case if a connection to the Union can be established based on specific factual criteria (→ Ch. 2 mn. 35). The DSA gives two examples:

- The provider has a **significant number of users** in one or more Member States relative to its or their populations. This means that in at least one Member State a significant percentage of the population uses the service. The DSA does not specify a percentage value which it considers to be 'significant'. Given that the largest social networks reach a share of 20–30 % of the population in countries such as Germany, a significant number of users within the meaning of the DSA might be defined – at least in the case of large Member States – to be around 5–10 % of the population.
- The provider targets its activity at one or more Member States (***lex loci solutionis*** or marketplace principle). This shall be determined based on all circumstances. For example, the language and currency used, the top-level domain of the service and the placement of local advertising all need to be considered. In addition, the availability of an application in the relevant national app store, as well as the provision of customer support in the language commonly used in the Member State, indicate that the activity is targeted at that Member State (rec. 8 sent. 2 and 3 DSA).

32 In addition, according to rec. 8 sent. 4 DSA, a substantial connection to the Union is deemed to exist if the provider has directed its activities towards a Member State within the meaning of Art. 17(1)(c) of the **Brussels I Regulation** (recast). This provision, which is largely identical to Art. 6(1) Rome I Regulation, covers all activities directed towards that Member State 'by any means'.[20] According to the case law of the CJEU, the direction of activities is determined by 'all clear expressions of the intention to solicit the custom of that State's consumers'.[21] The criteria developed for this in both case law and the literature largely correspond to the criteria referred to above with regard to the *lex loci solu-*

[17] Berberich/Seip GRUR-Prax 2021, 4 (4); Spindler GRUR 2021, 545 (551); cf. rec. 44 sent. 5 DSA.

[18] ECJ 5.6.2018 – case C-210/16, ECLI:EU:C:2018:388 para. 54 – Unabhängiges Landeszentrum für Datenschutz v Wirtschaftsakademie Schleswig-Holstein; ECJ 25.7.1991 – case C-221/89, ECLI:EU:C:1991:320 para. 20 – Factortame.

[19] According to rec. 8 sent. 5 DSA, the mere technical accessibility of a website in the Union is not sufficient to assume a substantial connection. Cf. ECJ 7.12.2010 – case C-585/08 and case C-144/09, ECLI:EU:C:2010:740 para. 74 et seqq. – Peter Pammer v Reederei Karl Schlüter/Hotel Alpenhof v Oliver Heller.

[20] According to the reference in rec. 8 sent. 4 DSA, only the substantial connection within the meaning of Art. 17(1)(c) Brussels I Regulation (recast) is relevant, not the other criteria of Art. 17 Brussels I Regulation (recast), such as a consumer contract.

[21] ECJ 7.12.2010 – case C-585/08 and case C-144/09, ECLI:EU:C:2010:740 para. 80 – Peter Pammer v Reederei Karl Schlüter/Hotel Alpenhof v Oliver Heller.

tionis. In this respect, the reference to the Brussels I Regulation does not entail a significant extension of the scope of application.

The legal representative may be a **natural or legal person**. This person must be provided with the necessary powers and sufficient resources to cooperate efficiently and in a timely manner with the competent authorities and to comply with their decisions. In particular, the legal representative shall serve as an agent for service of process on behalf of the provider. In addition, the provider must ensure that decisions made by the legal representative are implemented in a timely manner. In principle, it is possible to appoint a **subsidiary or parent company** of the same group as the provider to be the legal representative if such subsidiary or parent company is established in the Union (rec. 44 sent. 3 DSA). However, companies that are subject to restructuring or insolvency are excluded as they cannot guarantee efficient cooperation (rec. 44 sent. 4 DSA). An **independent external person** can also be appointed legal representative – similar to an external data protection officer. Given the personal liability of the legal representative (→ mn. 37), contractual safeguards will in this case be necessary with regard to how the legal representative can ensure the implementation of the decisions of the relevant authorities. A legal representative is allowed to act on behalf of several providers (rec. 44 sent. 6 DSA). In contrast to an authorised representative for the service of documents (e.g. under § 5 of the German Network Enforcement Act (*Netzwerkdurchsetzungsgesetz* – NetzDG)), who is a mere receiving agent, the legal representative must also be authorised to react to the service of documents and requests from the authorities. 33

The DSA does not explicitly regulate the **requirements regarding the qualifications and language** of the legal representative. However, efficient cooperation with public authorities requires that the legal representative is sufficiently informed about the provider's business processes and its user numbers and can obtain and pass on information on issues relevant to the enforcement of the DSA within a short period of time. 34

According to Art. 13(2) DSA, the legal representative is the **contact person for all competent authorities** of the Member States, the Commission and the Board. In line with the broad understanding of the term 'authorities' in Union law, courts are included as judicial authorities.[22] The authorities can choose to address the legal representative in addition to or instead of the provider. However, the legal representative's power may be limited to communication with authorities on 'decisions issued in relation to this Regulation'. This is a **very significant restriction, especially from the users' point of view**. Users can only address the point of contact according to Art. 12 DSA and may not serve documents on the legal representative. Therefore, courts will send documents to the legal representative only in proceedings under the DSA, such as orders under Art. 9 and 10 DSA, but not in actions by users, for example for or against the deletion of content. Users must continue to serve relevant documents on the provider in accordance with applicable procedural law. As a result, for contractual disputes or the enforcement of personality rights, the existing problems of enforceability against non-EU providers remain unsolved. 35

The legal representative may, **at the same time, act as a point of contact** for authorities and users within the meaning of Art. 11 and 12 DSA, provided the relevant requirements of the DSA are complied with (rec. 44 sent. 7 DSA). With regard to external legal representatives, the requirement of 'direct' communication with the provider will have particular significance. Direct communication, as interpreted by the CJEU, requires that no third party be involved between the parties.[23] This is in line with the purpose of the 36

[22] Spindler GRUR 2021, 545 (551).

[23] ECJ 16.10.2008 – case C-298/07, ECLI:EU:C:2008:572 para. 29 – Verbraucherzentrale Bundesverband eV v deutsche internet versicherung AG.

point of contact to maintain direct operational contact with the provider. Whether this requirement would still be met if an external legal representative acts as a point of contact is questionable. In this case, communication with the provider only takes place via the legal representative as a third party. However, the external legal representative may not be considered an intermediary third party in the communication if the representative has operational powers allowing him to implement relevant measures.

37 According to Art. 13(3) DSA, **the legal representative is personally liable** for non-compliance with obligations under the DSA and may, therefore, also be held liable by the authorities to pay fines or penalty payments. The liability of the legal representative applies in addition to the liability of the provider and the right of authorities to assert claims directly against the provider remains unaffected. The provision constitutes a case of **joint and several liability**, in which the liability in the relationship between the legal representative and the provider of intermediary services lies solely with the provider (unless the non-compliance is based on the conduct of the legal representative). According to the clear wording of Art. 13(3) DSA, the legal representative is only liable for non-compliance with obligations under the DSA and not generally liable for any violation of laws by the provider (insofar as the liability privileges of the DSA do not already apply).[24]

38 The designation of a legal representative must be notified to the Digital Services Coordinator of the Member State in which the legal representative resides or is established in accordance with Art. 13(4) DSA. The name, postal address, email address and telephone number of the legal representative must be provided. In addition, this information on the legal representative must be **published in an easily accessible manner** and kept up to date. This corresponds to the requirements for the publication of points of contact according to Art. 11 and 12 DSA. In the case of service providers without an establishment in the Union, the legal representative must therefore be included in the legal notice. Art. 13(5) DSA clarifies that the designation of a legal representative does not constitute an establishment in the Union.

39 In principle, the Member State in which the appointed legal representative resides or is established is competent for the **supervision** of the intermediary service (→ Ch. 5 mn. 17). If a provider without an establishment in the Union does not appoint a legal representative in the Union, he is in **breach of Art. 13 DSA**, and according to Art. 56(7) DSA all Member States have the power to enforce the DSA and may therefore initiate proceedings against that provider.

IV. General terms and conditions (Art. 14 DSA)

40 Art. 14 DSA provides **transparency requirements for the general terms and conditions** (T&Cs) of intermediary services. The provision does not affect the provider's freedom of contract (rec. 45 DSA). Therefore, providers remain free to decide in their T&Cs which content they wish to 'provide', for example by community standards or content policies. However, Art. 14 DSA requires the provider to disclose this decision transparently and enforce the T&Cs without discrimination.[25] This approach is based on two **regulatory principles** that recur frequently within the DSA: (1) building the trust of

[24] Spindler GRUR 2021, 545 (551), however, argues that the DSA leaves the question open as to whether the legal representative is liable for violations other than obligations under the DSA.

[25] For a critique of this approach see Peukert, 'Five Reasons to be Skeptical About the DSA'.

users through transparency of the service and (2) enforced self-regulation[26] of providers through binding contracts with users.

1. Content of T&Cs

Art. 14(1) DSA contains the **minimum information to be provided in T&Cs**. The T&Cs should disclose all restrictions that apply in relation to the content provided. According to Art. 14(1) and rec. 45 DSA, the following information is required: 41

- information on any policies and procedures used for the purpose of content moderation, such as community standards or content policies;
- information on any measures and tools used for the purpose of content moderation, including any human review of reported content or the use of automated detection or decision-making technologies;
- information on the procedural rules of the internal complaint-handling system within the meaning of Art. 20 DSA (→ mn. 110);
- information on the provider's right to terminate the use of the service, such as the right to terminate the contract with the user extraordinarily.

Pursuant to Art. 14(1) sent. 3 DSA, the information must be provided in clear, plain, user-friendly and unambiguous language. Considering the highly detailed technical information required, on paper these are quite demanding transparency obligations. However, they will in practice likely correspond to the existing requirements for T&Cs under consumer protection law, for example in Germany according to the case law on §§ 305 et seqq. of the German Civil Code (*Bürgerliches Gesetzbuch* – BGB). 42

In addition to the existing requirements, the DSA also obliges providers to make the T&Cs publicly available in an **easily accessible and machine-readable format**. This means that, similar to the legal notice, T&Cs of intermediary services must be quickly retrievable for users of the service, for example via a link to the T&Cs in the footer of the website. The T&Cs are machine-readable if they are available as text that can be processed electronically, for example by text-to-speech programs. It is not necessary that individual contractual terms can be understood and interpreted by a computer. Such machine-processable contracts are not commonly used and there is currently no common standard.[27] Consequently, such a requirement would limit the providers' freedom of contract and therefore be in contradiction to rec. 45 DSA. Providers may, in addition to the text, use graphical elements such as icons or images to illustrate the main elements of the T&Cs (rec. 45 sent. 5 DSA). 43

Art. 14(3) DSA applies even stricter requirements to the T&Cs of **intermediary services that are primarily directed at minors** or are predominantly used by minors (→ mn. 184). This includes providers who specifically address minors based on the design or marketing of their service (rec. 46 DSA). Following the letter of the law, a service is used predominantly by minors if more than 50 % of the users of the intermediary service are minors. Such services must make special efforts to phrase their T&Cs in such a way that minors can understand them. This obligation acknowledges that minors sign up for intermediary services on their own initiative, without a legal guardian, even if they are usually unable to agree to the T&Cs in a legally effective manner under national civil law. 44

---

[26] Also referred to as 'meta regulation', cf. Kuclar Stiković EU Law Working Papers No. 85, 1 (86).

[27] Machine-readable contract terms are, for example, required in the USA with regard to certain health insurance policies for transparency reasons. On machine-processable contracts, see the concept of 'Ricardian contracts'.

45 Art. 14(2) DSA introduces a specific transparency obligation in the case of a **significant change** to the T&Cs. As far as ongoing contractual relationships between users and providers are concerned, a duty to inform the user about any changes to the T&Cs typically arises from (national) contract law. Where such contract law allows for changes without notice to the user, Art. 14(2) DSA limits the provider by requiring a notice for significant changes. Significant changes in this sense are in particular those that affect the user's contractual rights and obligations. Rec. 45 sent. 5 DSA mentions, by way of example, changes to the community guidelines prohibiting certain content on the service and other changes which could directly impact the user's ability to make use of the service.

2. Enforcement of T&Cs

46 As stated in Art. 14(4) DSA, intermediary services are bound by their self-imposed rules and must apply and enforce the restrictions in their T&Cs in a diligent, objective and proportionate manner, with due **regard to the relevant fundamental rights**. When enforcing the restrictions on permissible content in particular, the provider must act in a non-arbitrary and non-discriminatory manner (rec. 47 DSA).

47 In addition, Art. 14(4) DSA establishes an **indirect third-party effect of fundamental rights**, meaning that fundamental rights apply to the (private) providers of intermediary services. Providers must consider the rights and legitimate interests of all parties involved when applying and enforcing their T&Cs. In most cases, there is (at least) a triad of rights to be taken into account.[28] Firstly, the right to freedom of expression and media freedom (Art. 11 CFR) of users who wish to publish content online is affected. Secondly, users who wish to access the content can invoke the right to freedom of information (Art. 11 CFR). Thirdly, the provider's interest in moderating or deleting content is protected by the freedom to conduct a business (Art. 16 CFR).[29] The provider must weigh and balance these fundamental rights when applying its T&Cs. This is an example of an indirect third-party effect of EU fundamental rights (**horizontal effect**) established through legal text.[30] However, Art. 14(4) DSA does not solve the problem that employees of large service providers usually do not have time to comprehensively consider all fundamental rights at stake, given the large number of content moderation decisions to be taken each day.[31] Rec. 47 sent. 3 DSA only includes a reference to the relevant standards for the protection of human rights, which providers must take into account.[32]

48 According to rec. 47 of the DSA, fundamental rights considerations should also be taken into account in the 'design'[33] of restrictions, namely in the question of what content is permissible under the T&Cs. The recital may at first glance be understood in a way that providers are bound by fundamental rights when setting up their T&Cs and may not prohibit content on their services if this inhibits free speech.[34] However, such a restriction of the contractual freedom of providers is not supported by the legally bind-

---

[28] Eifert et al. CMLR 2021, 987 (1026).

[29] This contrasts with the US view, which considers the deletion of content as part of the provider's freedom of expression; Janal ZEuP 2021, 227 (232).

[30] Spindler GRUR 2021, 545 (551); Wilman, 'The Digital Services Act (DSA) – An Overview', p. 9 et seq.

[31] Gielen/Uphues EuZW 2021, 627 (635).

[32] Cf. UN Guiding Principles on Business and Human Rights, <https://www.ohchr.org/sites/default/files/documents/publications/guidingprinciplesbusinesshr_en.pdf> (last accessed: 23.5.2024).

[33] In the German ('*Gestaltung*') and French ('*conçoivent*') language versions, it is clear that what is at issue is the conception and formulation of the contractual conditions limiting the types of content which are permitted on the service.

[34] Legner ZUM 2024, 99 (105).

ing normative text of the DSA and would contradict the regulatory concept of Art. 14 DSA and the freedom of contract of the provider.[35]

3. Special duties for very large services

49 Art. 14(5) and (6) DSA contain **increased transparency obligations for very large online platforms and very large search engines (very large services)**, which are justified by the special role and reach of very large services (rec. 48 DSA). Systematically, these obligations belong in the fifth section, but are regulated in the context of Art. 14 DSA because of the close connection to T&Cs.

50 Art. 14(5) DSA requires very large services to provide a **concise summary of the T&Cs** in clear and unambiguous language. The provider must sum up the main elements of the T&Cs in an easily readable manner and make the summary accessible in the same way as the T&Cs (rec. 48 sent. 2 DSA). This can be implemented by a summary preceding the T&Cs which is visually separated. Contrary to the ideas initially discussed in the legislative process, graphic elements in the summary, such as icons, may only be used as an additional visualisation. Art. 14(5) DSA requires a 'readable' summary in 'language', not in pictures. Regarding the main elements of T&Cs to be included in the summary, the DSA mentions the minimum information required under Art. 14(1) DSA as well as the available remedies and dispute resolution mechanisms (rec. 48 sent. 3 DSA). According to rec. 48 sent. 3 DSA, very large services must also provide information on how users can easily opt out of optional clauses. This addition was made in the trilogue procedure at the request of the European Parliament. It goes back to a report of the Committee on the Internal Market and Consumer Protection (IMCO), according to which users should have the possibility to change or reject optional clauses in the T&Cs of providers.[36] Since users do not have such a right under the final version of the DSA and very large services will not accept individually negotiated contracts, the recital is likely to have no practical relevance.

51 According to Art. 14(6) DSA, the T&Cs of very large services are to be published in the official national **languages of all Member States** in which the service is offered. This is to ensure that users can understand the T&Cs. In which Member States a service is 'offered' depends on the number of users in the territory and whether the service is targeted at the respective Member State (→ mn. 31 and → Ch. 2 mn. 35). In contrast to Art. 11(3) DSA, 'all' official languages are explicitly mentioned and not just 'one of' the official languages. Accordingly, for Member States with several official languages, the T&Cs must be translated into each of these official languages.

4. Critical analysis: information obligations equal information costs

52 Art. 14 DSA is in line with a regulatory approach that is common in the consumer protection acquis: by imposing far-reaching information obligations on businesses, the European legislator intends to create transparency and, in turn, strengthen consumers' trust in businesses and the internal market.[37] Whether this approach has been successful in the past is rather questionable. Instead of creating the desired transparency, in prac-

---

[35] Cf. Eifert et al. CMLR 2021, 987 (1012 et seq.).

[36] Art. 12(2a) DSA (Draft) in European Parliament, 'Report of the Committee on the Internal Market and Consumer Protection (IMCO)' (20.12.2021), A9-0356/2021, Amendment 190.

[37] Cf. Art. 5 et seqq. Consumer Rights Directive or Art. 38 et seqq. Directive (EU) 2015/2366 of the European Parliament and of the Council on payment services in the internal market.

tice consumers are subjected to an **'information overload'**[38] as they are flooded with highly detailed and technical information which they are unable to process. In addition, the information obligations have the potential to cause considerable information costs. When a user wishes to conclude a new contract or change his service provider, he is required first to sift through and accept ever-lengthening T&Cs. Given the huge number of users of very large services, if even a modest proportion of them were to actually read the T&Cs, this would result in enormous economic costs – which, in reality, are not incurred because users generally accept the T&Cs without actually reading them. This suggests that T&Cs are not an effective tool for creating market transparency.

53 Recognising that consumers require targeted and highly simplified information about the contractual terms to which they are subject when using the service, the DSA attempts to remedy this problem by introducing an additional information obligation, requiring very large services to provide an easily readable summary of their T&Cs. Under the DSA, the **providers of very large services** will therefore be responsible (and liable) to **reduce complexity**. For providers, this significantly increases the difficulty of drafting T&Cs. In addition to the legal questions involved, drafting T&Cs will become a communicative challenge, in which complex technical systems have to be broken down into a language that is easy to understand for the general consumer.

54 Structurally, however, the question remains whether information obligations are the right legislative instrument to address the trust deficit of consumers in digital services. Statutory transparency requirements can remedy a market failure caused by one contracting party having incomplete information.[39] While there certainly is an **asymmetry of information** and users can often neither assess what (personal) data is being stored nor what information the providers can derive from this data, transparency may not be the main issue that needs to be dealt with. Users' mistrust seems to be based more often on a perceived powerlessness in the face of the influence of platforms on public discourse than on incomplete information regarding which types of content are permitted on a service. Therefore, the main factor to consider is the **power imbalance**: users depend on providers that have achieved positions of near monopoly due to the network effects typical for digital services.[40]

V. Transparency reporting obligation (Art. 15 DSA)

55 Art. 15 DSA obliges intermediary services to **publish annual transparency reports** on their content moderation. The reports are to be made publicly available in a machine-readable electronic format, for example on the provider's website. The reports provide the public and the authorities with a factual basis for political discussion about content moderation on digital services. The minimum details the report must contain result from Art. 15(1) DSA. The points covered are listed below.

point (a): The number of **orders issued** by Member States' authorities to take down or moderate content, including orders to take action against illegal content in accordance with Art. 9 DSA (→ Ch. 3 mn. 95) and information orders in accordance with Art. 10 DSA (→ Ch. 3 mn. 110), each broken down by

[38] Gielen/Uphues EuZW 2021, 627 (636). Cf. the literature on information obligations under the law on payment service providers.

[39] For the textbook example of the 'Market for Lemons', see Akerlof 84 The Quarterly Journal of Economics 1970, 488.

[40] Eifert et al. CMLR 2021, 987 (990 et seq.).

- the Member State issuing the order;
- the median time taken to confirm receipt of the order;
- the median time taken to give effect to the order;
- the type of illegal content concerned.

What the **'type of illegal content concerned'** refers to is not further explained in Art. 15 DSA. A mere categorisation according to the format of the content (e.g. text, image, video) would not achieve the goal of the transparency report. Therefore, an interpretation in the spirit of the law requires a categorisation according to abstract types of illegal content. In December 2023, the Commission published a draft of the transparency report template that includes 15 categories of illegal content to be used for standardised reporting (animal welfare, consumer information infringements, data protection and privacy violations, illegal or harmful speech, IP infringements, negative effects on civic discourse or elections, non-consensual behaviour, pornography or sexualized content, protection of minors, risk for public security, scams and fraud, self-harm, unsafe or prohibited products, violence, and content in violation of the platform's T&Cs).[41] This understanding of the provision was also the basis of the Commission's impact assessment prior to the introduction of the DSA.[42]

point (b): Only for hosting service providers, the **number of notices in the notice and action mechanism** in accordance with Art. 16 DSA (→ mn. 60), broken down by

- the type of alleged illegal content concerned;
- the measures taken as a result of the notification differentiating whether they were taken on the basis of statutory law or following the provider's T&Cs;
- the median time to take action;
- where applicable, the number of notices processed exclusively by automated means;
- where applicable, the number of notices submitted by trusted flaggers (Art. 22 DSA).

point (c): Information on content moderation engaged in on the provider's own initiative (→ Ch. 3 mn. 80), in particular

- the use of automated tools;
- the measures taken to train and assist employees or users responsible for content moderation;
- the number and type of measures taken on own initiative, broken down by the type of illegal content or violation of the T&Cs and the detection method, including measures that affect the visibility or accessibility of content (e.g. shadow banning[43]).

The fact that the violation of the T&Cs is listed in Art. 15(1)(c) DSA separately from 'illegal content' can be explained by the narrow understanding of the term 'illegal content'. According to Art. 3(h) DSA, only content that is not in compliance with the law is illegal (cf. rec. 12 DSA). The wording of Art. 15(1)(c) DSA, which is broader than (a) and (b), therefore ensures that

[41] European Commission, 'Annex I to Draft Commission Implementing Regulation laying down templates concerning the transparency reporting obligations of providers of intermediary services and of providers of online platforms' (8.12.2023), Ref. Ares(2023)8428591.

[42] European Commission, 'Impact Assessment', SWD(2020) 348 final, Part 2, p. 182.

[43] On shadow banning cf. Leerssen 48 Computer Law & Security Review 2023, 105790.

the moderation of content with regard to violations of the T&Cs is also included in the transparency report.

point (d): **Number of complaints** received via internal complaint-handling systems in accordance with Art. 20 DSA (→ mn. 111), broken down by
- the basis of the complaint;
- the decisions taken on these complaints;
- the median time taken to make a decision;
- the number of cases where the decision was later overturned (e.g. through dispute settlement or other legal remedies).

point (e): Description of the **use of automated means** for content moderation, in particular
- the purposes of the use;
- indicators of the accuracy (detection rate) and the possible rate of errors (false positives and false negatives);
- the safeguards applied against such errors.

56 According to Art. 15(3) DSA, the Commission may adopt a **template for the transparency report**. In December 2023, the Commission published a draft of an implementing act setting out a mandatory transparency report template and a harmonised reporting period from 1 January until 31 December of each year.[44] Following adoption of the Implementing Regulation, providers are obliged to use the detailed template and publish their transparency reports using the CSV (comma-separated values) format. The Draft Implementing Regulation includes obligations regarding detailed information that go well beyond the wording of Art. 15 DSA. For example, the Draft Implementing Regulation requires all information to be broken down, at a minimum, per calendar month. Transparency reports have to be provided no later than two months after the end of the harmonised reporting period, i.e. by end of February of the following year.

57 Art. 15(2) DSA exempts **micro and small enterprises** from the Regulation because they should not be burdened with the cost-intensive reporting obligation.[45]

D. Obligations for hosting services (Art. 16–18 DSA)

58 Section 2 of the third chapter of the DSA establishes due diligence obligations applicable to all hosting services. These obligations relate to how services manage and deal with illegal content. As per Art. 3(g)(iii) DSA, the term **'hosting service'** applies to any service that stores information provided by a user on the user's behalf (→ Ch. 2 mn. 26). Such hosting services play a pivotal role in the mitigation and containment of illegal content. This is mainly because of their inherent features that facilitate easy storage, transmission and the sharing of information (rec. 50 sent. 1 DSA). Art. 16–18 DSA, therefore, provide for certain procedural provisions that complement the liability exemption under Art. 6 DSA with specific obligations to act. Violations of these provisions can lead, in addition to the penalties for non-compliance with the DSA, under specific circumstances to the loss of the liability exemption for user content.

59 There is **no exemption for micro and small-sized enterprises**. The European legislator assumed that the volume of illegal content disseminated via a service correlates roughly with the service's size. Consequently, duties associated with illegal content

[44] European Commission, 'Annex I to Draft Commission Implementing Regulation laying down templates concerning the transparency reporting obligations of providers of intermediary services and of providers of online platforms' (8.12.2023), Ref. Ares(2023)8428591.

[45] Rec. 49 sent. 2 DSA; Spindler GRUR 2021, 545 (552).

should, in theory, not lead to an excessive burden for smaller services. In the few cases where a small service contributes disproportionately to the spread of illegal content, the societal damage is so severe that the due diligence obligations have to be upheld and the additional effort imposed on the small service is justified.[46]

I. Notice and action mechanisms (Art. 16 DSA)

Art. 16 DSA creates a harmonised **notice and takedown mechanism** for reporting illegal content. Loosely inspired by the US Digital Millennium Copyright Act (DMCA), this mechanism aims to provide a procedural framework around the liability exemption for hosting services under Art. 6 DSA. Following the DMCA approach, persons or institutions may use a standardised form to notify providers of illegal content, thereby providing them with actual knowledge of illegal content on their service. Providers, in turn, must then decide whether to remove the content or disable access to it (rec. 50 sent. 2, rec. 52 DSA). Otherwise, they risk losing the liability exemption. 60

1. Procedure for notices

Art. 16(1) DSA provides for a **fully digital procedure** for transmitting the information that the notifying party considers content to be illegal ('notice', rec. 50 sent. 2 DSA). The form for reporting content as illegal must be displayed near any user-provided content and be as easy to locate and use as the mechanism for reporting content that violates the provider's T&Cs (rec. 50 sent. 3 DSA). 61

The subject of the notice can be any kind of allegedly illegal content within the meaning of Art. 3(h) DSA, namely any content that may not be in compliance with national or EU law (on the problems → mn. 81). Conversely, the procedure according to **Art. 16 DSA does not apply to content that only violates the provider's T&C**. 62

The reporting procedure is limited to **'specific items of information'**. Therefore, notices must identify specific illegal content on the service and cannot merely report systematic violations with exemplary evidence. According to rec. 50 sent. 4 DSA, however, it must be possible to combine several individual allegedly illegal contents in one notice to allow for efficient reporting procedures. 63

Art. 16(2) DSA lists certain information that is necessary for a **sufficiently precise and substantiated notice**. The provider must design the reporting form in a way that the notifying party can provide such necessary information. This allows the provider to quickly check whether the allegedly illegal content is in fact illegal (rec. 53 sent. 1 DSA). The necessary information which a notifying party must be able to provide includes the location of the allegedly illegal content (e.g. URL), an explanation of why the content is considered unlawful, and a statement that the individual or entity believes in good faith that his notice is accurate. As the provider is only required to enable notifying parties to provide the relevant information, the reporting form should include these fields, but they should not be made mandatory for submission. Notices missing information considered necessary by the European legislator may still be submitted. The provider may also add additional fields that make it easier for the provider to process the notice, provided that the additional information is optional and does not unnecessarily complicate the notice procedure. 64

An **open question is whether the notifying party must identify themselves**. According to Art. 16(2)(c) DSA, the reporting form must allow the name and email address 65

[46] European Commission, 'Impact Assessment', SWD(2020) 348 final, Part 1, p. 55 et seq.

of the individual or entity submitting the notice to be stated, unless the notice reports depictions of child abuse[47]. In line with this, rec. 50 sent. 5 DSA states that the 'notification mechanism should allow, but not require, the identification of the individual or the entity submitting a notice', in essence implying a right to anonymous reporting of illegal content. Rec. 53 sent. 4 DSA, on the other hand, requires providers to 'ask the individual or the entity submitting a notice to disclose its identity in order to avoid misuse'. In order to find a practicable solution to these – at first sight, contradictory – requirements of the DSA, the reporting form should provide an optional field for name and contact address and the notifying party should be asked but not required to fill out the relevant fields. However, in certain cases, such as violations of personal rights or copyright, it will not be possible for a provider to determine whether the reported content is illegal without identifying the notifying party (rec. 50 sent. 6 DSA).

2. Legal consequence of notices

66 According to Art. 16(3) DSA, the legal effect of a notice is that the provider is considered to have actual knowledge or awareness of the illegal content if the illegality can be determined without a detailed legal examination. This is an **irrebuttable presumption of knowledge** that directly affects the liability exemption under Art. 6 DSA.

67 For the presumption to apply, it is necessary that the content can be identified as illegal by a **reasonably diligent provider** based on the notice without a detailed legal examination (rec. 53 sent. 3 DSA). This criterion codifies the recent case law of the CJEU regarding the reporting of illegal content.[48] Infringement of the law must be evident based on the information provided in the notice. The standard of care to be applied depends on the type and size of the service: generally, small services will not be required to have notices processed by trained staff, whereas large services must have sufficient capacity to evaluate complex or extensive notices with fundamental rights implications.

68 The **requirements for the legal examination** must not be overly taxing. It should be taken into account that the standard for judging the unlawfulness of content varies across Member States and that the weighing of fundamental rights can yield divergent results depending on the legal system. Rec. 52 DSA states that the rights of all affected parties should be guaranteed 'irrespective of the Member State in which those parties are established or reside and of the field of law at issue', and lists various fundamental rights under the EU Charter of Fundamental Rights,[49] such as the freedom of expression and information, the respect for private and family life, data protection, non-discrimination and the right to an effective remedy, the freedom to conduct a business, the right to human dignity and the rights of the child, as well as the protection of (intellectual) property. Whenever a complex balancing of such fundamental rights is required, this will necessitate an in-depth legal examination which exceeds the requirements to be placed on a diligent provider (rec. 22 sent. 3 DSA). In such cases, the DSA may extend the liability privileges of the hosting service in spite of a justified notice, since the liability exemption according to Art. 6 DSA continues to apply in complex legal cases until the legal questions are resolved.

---

[47] Within the meaning of Art. 3–7 Directive 2011/93/EU of the European Parliament and of the Council on combating the sexual abuse and sexual exploitation of children and child pornography.

[48] ECJ 22.6.2021 – case C-682/18, ECLI:EU:C:2021:503 para. 116 – Frank Peterson v Google LLC; ECJ 26.4.2022 – case C-401/19, ECLI:EU:C:2022:297 para 91 – Poland v Parliament and Council.

[49] Whether this standard is correct, however, seems questionable since the unlawfulness of the content can also result from national law, and in this respect, national fundamental rights (and not the EU Charter of Fundamental Rights) are to be applied.

69 If the requirements of Art. 16(3) DSA are met, it is assumed for the purpose of Art. 6(1)(a) DSA that the provider possesses **actual knowledge of the illegality of the content** (rec. 53 sent. 3 DSA). In this case, the hosting service can only preserve the exemption from liability by removing the illegal content or blocking access to it without delay. A clarification proposed by the European Parliament that the provider should not be liable for the period between the receipt of the notice and its (speedy) processing was not included in the DSA. However, this already follows from the wording of Art. 6(1)(b) DSA, according to which the liability exemption is upheld if the provider acts expeditiously in deleting the illegal content in response to the notice.

70 If a hosting provider does not delete the illegal content or does not act expeditiously in deleting the illegal content in spite of a justified notice, the **liability exemption ceases to apply**. The provider's liability for the illegal content is then determined by national law.[50] It is important to note that Art. 16(3) DSA is not an exhaustive provision for the provider gaining knowledge of illegal content.[51] The provider can also become aware of illegal content through formally incorrect notices, investigations carried out on their own initiative or information gained outside of the notice and action mechanism (rec. 22 sent. 3 DSA).

71 Unlike the DMCA, the DSA does not exempt the hosting provider from liability towards the user whose content is wrongfully removed in response to a notice.[52] Hosting services must protect themselves against such claims in their T&Cs.

3. Notice processing

72 Upon receipt of a notice, the hosting provider must send an **electronic confirmation of receipt** to the notifying party pursuant to Art. 16(4) DSA, provided that a contact address is specified in the notice. Unlike the DMCA, the notice and action mechanism in **Art. 16 DSA does not provide for the mandatory participation of the user** who provided the allegedly illegal content.[53] In particular, the hosting provider is not required to obtain a statement from the user before deleting the content in question or blocking access to it. Nevertheless, the provider may choose to do so where it is reasonable or necessary to process the notice in a timely and thorough manner.

73 The DSA does not mandate a human review of notices received, thus **allowing the use of automated means.**[54] If such automated means are used in the processing of notices or decision-making, this must be communicated to the parties involved as set out in Art. 16(6) sent. 2 DSA.

74 The obligation to **inform the persons concerned**, namely the notifying party and the user who provided the allegedly illegal content, of the decision taken by the provider follows from Art. 16(5) DSA. The provider must also inform them about the possible legal remedies against the decision. Possible remedies include the internal complaint-handling system and out-of-court dispute settlement, as well as judicial redress (rec. 39 DSA).

---

[50] Holznagel CR 2021, 123 (126).

[51] Holznagel CR 2021, 123 (126); Spindler GRUR 2021, 545 (549).

[52] Schmidt/Grewe MMR 2021, 279 (280).

[53] Genç-Gelgeç 18 Croatian Yearbook of European Law and Policy 2022, 25 (51); However, national media or contract law may require a hearing of the user. Under German law, according to BGH 29.7.2021 – III ZR 179/20, NJW 2021, 3179 para. 88, such a hearing of the user before the removal of individual content is not mandatory.

[54] Spindler GRUR 2021, 545 (552).

4. Timeline and scope of obligation to delete illegal content

75 If a notice is justified and the content is deemed illegal, the hosting provider is obliged to remove the illegal content or block access to it. In contrast to the former German Network Enforcement Act (*Netzwerkdurchsetzungsgesetz* – NetzDG), which generally required illegal content to be deleted within 24 hours of receipt of a notice, the **DSA does not specify a fixed deadline for deletion of illegal content**. This is based on the understanding that strict timelines may prevent providers from doing a diligent examination of complex cases, thereby triggering a false incentive for the excessive deletion of content ('overblocking').[55]

76 Instead of a strict deadline for deletion, the DSA uses a flexible approach and the timeframe granted for a provider to react to a notice depends on the type and size of the platform, the type of illegal content concerned, and the complexity of the legal and factual issues involved. In general, a distinction must be made between two points of reference:

- Art. 6(1)(b) DSA imposes on providers an **obligation to delete illegal content expeditiously**. Otherwise, the hosting provider's liability exemption ceases to apply. This aligns with the wording of the former Art. 14 E-Commerce Directive, leaving it unchanged. Discrepancies in other language versions between Art. 14 E-Commerce Directive and Art. 6 DSA are based on a modified translation of the English version and do not imply any change in substance (e.g. the German wording of Art. 6 DSA ('zügig') differs from Art. 14 E-Commerce Directive ('unverzüglich')).
- Art. 16(6) DSA obliges providers to **process notices 'in a timely manner'**. This requirement is part of the due diligence obligations which should be seen as separate from the liability exemption in Art. 6 DSA. In particular, the violation of the due diligence obligation to process notices in a timely manner can lead to fines by the competent authorities. The standard is somewhat more lenient than in Art. 6(1)(b) DSA since the processing of notices may require complex fact-finding enquiries or legal examinations.[56] Hosting services must take the urgency of the specific notice into account when processing it (rec. 52 sent. 3 DSA). Prompt reaction – as specified in Art. 6(1)(b) DSA – can be expected in cases where threats to the life or safety of persons are involved (rec. 52 sent. 4 DSA), such as incitements to violence or the publication of private addresses or other sensitive personal data. The person filing the notice must inform the hosting service of any possible threat posed by the allegedly illegal content if such threat is not already evident from the type of reported content.

77 The hosting service is obliged to remove the specific piece of content reported via the notice and action mechanism (**'takedown'**). A notification under Art. 16 DSA does not provide the provider with knowledge of similar infringements on the service or of future identical infringements ('staydown').

78 If it is technically or operationally **impossible to remove the specific content** or block access to it, the provider must inform the notifying person (rec. 51 sent. 3 DSA). This is likely to be an **exceptional case**, as when an encrypted folder uploaded by the user contains only one illegal file that cannot be removed individually. Additionally, if blockchain technology is used, there may be content that cannot be deleted for technical reasons.

[55] Gielen/Uphues EuZW 2021, 627 (635); Kuhlmannn/Trute GSZ 2022, 115 (117).

[56] Art. 6(1)(b) DSA, in contrast, assumes a situation in which the hosting provider already has knowledge or awareness of an infringement by the content.

5. Critical analysis: illegality of content determined by national law

The key issue under Art. 16 DSA is **what content should be classified as illegal.** 79 With regard to this crucial question, the DSA contains a **regulatory gap**. This gap could perpetuate the existing legal fragmentation instead of effecting a much-to-be-desired harmonisation.

Art. 3(h) DSA defines content as illegal if it 'is not in compliance with Union law or 80 the law of any Member State'. Illegality, therefore, means any infringement of Union law or national law. The definition goes back to the 'general idea that what is illegal offline should also be illegal online'.[57] Based on this approach, illegal content is defined very broadly (→ Ch. 3 mn. 22) and includes, for example, the sale of counterfeit products as well as the illegal sharing of private images or copyright-infringing content (rec. 12 sent. 3 DSA). In contrast to the former German Network Enforcement Act (*Netzwerkdurchsetzungsgesetz* – NetzDG)[58] and the French Avia Law (*Loi contre les contenus haineux sur internet*), the DSA targets not only criminal content, but also infringements of any other law, including consumer protection law and copyright law.

An assessment of illegality of content depends mainly on the law of Member States, as 81 directly applicable Union law rarely classifies content as illegal.[59] However, the **DSA does not specify which national law applies.**[60] For example, if a user based in Germany publishes content in Spanish on an online platform based in Ireland, it is not clear which Member State's law will govern whether the content is illegal. There is no conflict-of-law rule within the DSA system that determines which Member State's law is applicable.[61] In general, the DSA uses both the *lex loci solutionis* or marketplace principle (in Art. 2(1) DSA) and the country of origin principle (in Art. 56(1) DSA). With regard to the illegality of content, however, the DSA is silent on the question of applicable law. This problem arises because the DSA harmonises the procedural rules and liability exemptions for intermediary services, but leaves the establishment of liability to national law. There was no political consensus to agree on provisions in Union law to determine illegal content – or even the applicable law that defines which content is illegal. The rules of private international law, which remain unaffected by the DSA according to Art. 2(4)(h) DSA, will likely not help to fill the regulatory gap. This is because the notice and action mechanism lacks a clear reference point to determine the applicable law under private international law. From the notifying party's point of view, the takedown of content usually is a tortious claim (governed by Rome II Regulation), while the removal of the affected user's content is, from his point of view, part of his contractual relationship with the service provider (governed by Rome I Regulation). Under private international law, the applicable law would therefore vary depending on the point of view.

If the conflict of law is resolved **according to the letter of Art. 3(h) DSA, the content** 82 **is deemed illegal if it violates the national law of a (single) Member State.** In the absence of a conflict-of-law rule, the law of any Member State concerned by the publication of content online may assert applicability. It is therefore not by accident that the wording of Art. 3(h) DSA refers to 'the law of any Member State'. In fact, the English

[57] This was explicitly stated in rec. 12 DSA (Draft) in the Council's General Approach of 18.11.2021, ST 13203/21 (EN), Annex, p. 16. In the final rec. 12 DSA, the wording is somewhat softer.

[58] See the explanatory memorandum in the German parliament (Bundestag), BT-Drs. 20/2308, 5.

[59] Husovec/Laguna, 'Digital Services Act: A Short Primer', p. 11; Turillazzi et al., 'The Digital Services Act: an analysis of its ethical, legal, and social implications', p. 10.

[60] Wimmers 4 JIPITEC 2021, 421 (431 et seqq.).

[61] Ho-Dac/Lehmann, 'Digital Services Act – Part Two: Inside the Belly of the Beast'; Kuclar Stiković EU Law Working Papers No. 85, 1 (88 et seq.). Regarding 'conflict-of-law' provisions within Union law at the example of the GDPR, see Gömann.

language version of Art. 3(h) DSA was changed during the trilogue negotiations from 'the law of *a* Member State' to 'the law of *any* Member State'.[62] Following the letter of the law, this means that all national laws must be applied cumulatively. If one Member State, for example, prohibits certain information on abortion[63] or homosexuality, this content would be considered illegal in the entire European Union.[64] This would result in the most restrictive interpretation of freedom of expression prevailing across the European digital space. The DSA would thereby find itself in open conflict with the EU Charter of Fundamental Rights.

83 In order to avert this untenable outcome, the DSA should be **interpreted in conformity with primary Union law**. To protect the fundamental rights of users, either a conflict-of-law rule has to be applied to restrict the applicable law determining the illegality of content or the legal effect of the DSA has to be limited to the Member State(s) which defines such content as illegal.

84 The applicable Member State law could be determined by **applying the *lex loci solutionis* or marketplace principle as the conflict-of-law rule**. The illegality of any content would then be assessed based on the law of the Member State at whose citizens the content is targeted (analogous application of Art. 2(1) DSA). For example, content in Spanish on a Spanish online platform would be subject to Spanish law.

85 However, the wording and the history of Art. 3(h) DSA speak against such an analogy. As shown by the clarification introduced by the Council during the trilogue negotiations ('the law of *any* Member State'), the European legislator did not intend to create a conflict-of-law rule applicable to the illegality of content. This is probably not least due to the fact that the *lex loci solutionis* or marketplace principle is hard to implement as a criterion in practice. After all, the goal of the European Union's digital regulation is to create a **European digital single market** in which content is in principle targeted at all Union citizens. Much digital content already lacks a suitable connecting factor because neither the language nor the online platform used is targeted at just one Member State. Today's intermediaries provide cross-border services and content in English, German and French that can be addressed to users in more than one Member State. In addition, this approach cannot resolve a hard conflict between two national legal systems: if the distribution of a product or information is illegal under the law of one Member State but expressly permitted or even required in another Member State, the content would – depending on the applicable national law – either have to be taken down or kept online in the entire Union.[65] By determining which national law applies, and thereby deciding whether the content has to be deleted throughout the Union regardless of other conflicting national laws, the DSA would in effect prevail over Member State law on the illegality of content. According to Art. 2(2) DSA, such harmonisation is expressly not intended.

86 Alternatively, the **legal effect of the illegality of content could be restricted geographically** to the specific Member State. Content would then have to be deleted only in the Member State in which it is considered illegal, rather than in the entire Union. This is in line with the approach taken regarding takedown orders by authorities in accordance with Art. 9 DSA which are also limited to the ordering Member State's territory (rec. 36 sent. 3 DSA, → Ch. 3 mn. 104). This type of restriction of the legal effect is also

---

[62] Cf. the proposed amendment to Art. 2(g) DSA (Draft) in the General Approach of the Council, 18.11.2021, ST 13203/21 (EN), Annex, p. 111.

[63] Kuczerawy/Dutkiewicz, 'Accessing Information about Abortion'.

[64] According to Art. 3(h) DSA this is of course subject to the condition that such national law is compatible with Union law ('law of any Member State which is in compliance with Union law'). This clarification is missing in the German language version of Art. 3(h) DSA due to a translation error.

[65] Husovec/Laguna, 'Digital Services Act: A Short Primer'.

reflected in a Commission statement on questions on the DSA: 'Where a content is illegal only in a given Member State, as a general rule it should only be removed in the territory where it is illegal'.[66] The downside of this solution is that it places a heavy burden on hosting services to review content upon notice under all 27 Member State jurisdictions and, if necessary, take down content restricted to specific territories. Localised takedowns likely include the obligation to take effective measures to ensure that users in the Member State affected by such a takedown cannot access the content that is illegal for them, for example by ensuring that the content is not visible even if accessing the service via a different top-level domain.[67] This would require hosting services to install geo-filters to block content for users from certain Member States,[68] which would be a setback for the European digital single market.

II. Statement of reasons (Art. 17 DSA)

Art. 17 DSA requires that providers of hosting services give a **clear and specific explanation when they remove or restrict content** provided on the service, for example by deleting or blocking content or banning users. 87

1. Scope of application

The obligation to inform and justify any content restrictions refers to restrictions imposed due to both **violations of the law (illegal content)** and **violations of the provider's T&Cs**. The term 'restrictions' is to be understood broadly and, according to Art. 17(1) DSA, includes: 88

point (a): The **removal, disabling of access to content or demoting of content** and other measures to reduce the visibility of the content (rec. 54 sent. 1 DSA). This includes demotion of content in rankings and recommender systems (rec. 55 sent. 1 DSA). Where the line is drawn between demotion that requires a statement of reasons and the general ranking of content by a hosting service, as in the sorting of search results or the order of posts in social network timelines, is not specified. Rec. 55 DSA also mentions the process of 'shadow banning', in which a hosting service neither formally blocks nor deletes an account but ceases to display a user's content to other users, thereby clandestinely depriving the user of his reach.[69] This practice is now covered by Art. 17 DSA, which requires that the user be informed and offered an explanation, thus rendering the process more or less pointless since it cannot be implemented without the user being aware.

point (b): **Demonetisation** by suspending or discontinuing monetary payments. This also includes the restriction of future income if the user is blocked from earning money through advertising for future content uploaded to the hosting service (rec. 55 sent. 2 DSA).

point (c): The permanent or temporary **blocking of access to the service** or parts of the service.

point (d): The permanent or temporary **blocking of the user's account**.

---

[66] European Commission, 'Questions and Answers: Digital Services Act'.

[67] See ECJ 24.9.2019 – case C-507/17, ECLI:EU:C:2019:772 para. 70 – Google v CNIL; ECJ 27.3.2014 – case C-314/12, ECLI:EU:C:2014:192 para. 62 – UPC Telekabel Wien v Constantin Film Verleih.

[68] Users would have to be informed of the reasons for this access restriction by the provider, see Art. 3(3) Geo-blocking Regulation.

[69] On shadow banning cf. Leerssen 48 Computer Law & Security Review 2023, 105790.

89 The provider of a hosting service must inform the user who provided the content concerned of these restrictions. According to Art. 17(2) subpara. 1 sent. 1 DSA, this applies only if the provider is aware of the **user's electronic contact details**. Art. 17 DSA does not contain any further specifications on the means of communication. In this respect, it remains open whether a notification in the account or in an app is sufficient to fulfil the duty to inform and to give reasons. In principle, the **addressee of the statement of reasons is the affected user** whose content or account is restricted. In the case of collaborative content, however, there may also be groups of persons affected, such as several authors of a Wikipedia article.

90 Excluded from the scope of application is 'deceptive high-volume commercial content', as set out in Art. 17(2) subpara. 2. This refers to the use of fake accounts or **bots and comparable spam content** (rec. 55 sent. 3 DSA). It is unclear why the word 'commercial' was included in Art. 17(2) subpara. 2 DSA. In the past, bots have been particularly active in spreading political propaganda and fake news without commercial interests. It is unlikely that the legislator wanted to exclude such politically motivated bots.

91 The conclusive list of decisions to be justified under Art. 17(1) DSA does not cover accompanying information that the hosting provider associates with the content, such as **'fact checks'** or the labelling of content as misleading.[70] In addition, according to Art. 17(5) DSA, a statement of reasons is not required in the case of judicial or official orders to take action against illegal content (Art. 9 DSA, → Ch. 3 mn. 95). In such cases, the obligation to state reasons already arises from Art. 9(5) DSA and the reasoning has to be provided by the relevant authority.

2. Content of the statement of reasons

92 Art. 17(3) DSA contains **minimum requirements for the statement of reasons**. The provider must name the restrictive measure taken and its temporal and territorial scope, provide the legal basis and inform the user about the possibilities to contest the decision. In addition, the user must be informed about how the hosting service became aware of the content. If automated means were used in the process, this must be stated. If the restriction is based on a report within the notice and action mechanism according to Art. 16 DSA, the reporter's identity should only be disclosed if this is necessary to identify whether the content is illegal, as in cases of infringements of intellectual property rights (rec. 54 sent. 3 DSA).

93 Pursuant to Art. 17(4) DSA, the statement of reasons must be sufficiently precise to effectively exercise any possible legal remedies. In particular, it must be made possible for the user to realistically assess the prospects of success in judicial or extrajudicial action against the decision taken by the provider.

94 The DSA does not provide for a general claim by the user to restore wrongfully removed or blocked content (on the claim to restore access to content during internal complaint-handling → mn. 115).[71] However, the right to put-back content can arise from national law, in particular from the user's contractual relationship with the hosting provider.[72]

---

[70] Holznagel CR 2022, 594 (596).

[71] So-called put-back claims are an essential legal instrument against hosting services from the user's point of view, see Zech, 'General and specific monitoring obligations in the Digital Services Act'.

[72] Janal ZEuP 2021, 227 (253); Spindler GRUR 2021, 545 (553). Cf. rec. 55 sent. 4 DSA.

III. Notification of suspicions of criminal offences (Art. 18 DSA)

95 According to Art. 18 DSA, hosting services are obliged to immediately report to state authorities if they become **aware of a past, present or imminent criminal offence** that endangers the life or safety of a person.

96 Art. 18 DSA does not specify which criminal offences trigger a reporting obligation on the part of the provider. The abstract criterion is that the **crime threatens the life or safety** of one or more persons. As examples, rec. 56 DSA cites human trafficking, child abuse and incitement to terrorism.

97 It is the provider's responsibility to check whether the user's activity or the content provided constitutes a criminal offence within the meaning of the DSA.[73] According to the wording of Art. 18 DSA, the provider is obliged to report a **suspicion**. The required level of suspicion is not specified. In order to minimise erroneous accusations by users, there should be sufficient factual evidence of an offence to justify a reasonable initial suspicion. However, hosting services will have to be granted a certain amount of leeway when examining criminal provisions that vary from one Member State to another.

98 **The addressees of the notification** are the law enforcement or judicial authorities in the Member State concerned. According to Art. 18(2) subpara. 2 DSA, the Member State concerned is the state in which the offence has taken place, takes place or is suspected to take place, as well as the state of residence or domicile of the victim and the suspect. If several Member States are involved according to these criteria, in particular in cross-border cases, the hosting service must, in principle, inform all Member States concerned. If a Member State cannot be identified with sufficient certainty, the provider may, according to Art. 18(2) subpara. 1 DSA, choose to inform the competent authorities at the place of the provider (or, in the case of non-EU providers, the place of the legal representative) or Europol or both.

99 The notification should provide the authorities with **all relevant information** available to the provider. This includes the content in question, the time of publication including time zone, an explanation of the suspicion as well as the information necessary to locate and identify the relevant user (rec. 56 sent. 4 DSA). The hosting service must therefore disclose the user's personal data. Art. 18 DSA does not provide a legal basis for the transfer of this data to the authorities.[74] However, the provider is covered by Art. 6(1)(c) GDPR since he is fulfilling a (Union) legal obligation by sending the notification to authorities. Rec. 56 sent. 5 DSA clarifies that the DSA provisions do not provide a legal basis for the profiling of users to identify possible criminal offences.

E. Obligations for online platforms (Art. 19–28 DSA)

100 Section 3 contains due diligence obligations for **online platforms**, a **sub-category of hosting service providers**, including social networks and online marketplaces (rec. 13(1) sent. 2 DSA).

101 The **term online platform** is defined in Art. 3(i) DSA as a hosting service that stores and makes information available to the public on behalf of a user. Unlike other hosting services, an online platform must not only store content but also publicly disseminate it. According to Art. 3(k) DSA, public dissemination means **making content available to a potentially unlimited number of third parties** at the request of the user who provided the content. Mere online storage services are therefore considered hosting services but

---

[73] Kuhlmann/Trute GSZ 2022, 115 (118).

[74] Cf. rec. 56 sent. 6 DSA.

do not fall under the definition of an online platform since the content is available only to the user and not to an unlimited number of third parties. The aspect of dissemination to an unlimited number of third parties is generally also missing in email or messenger services used for communication between a finite number of persons (rec. 14 sent. 3 DSA). This is different in the case of public chat groups or channels where the sender of the communication does not determine the possible recipients (rec. 14 sent. 4 DSA). In this respect, the messenger service Telegram, for example, can be classified in part as an online platform. Public dissemination can also be present in closed user groups if new users are automatically added to the group upon their request, without a human decision or selection process determining to whom access is granted (rec. 14 sent. 2 DSA).

102 Excluded from the definition of online platforms are services where the storage and dissemination of user content is **merely an ancillary feature** to another (main) service and cannot be used without the main service for objective or technical reasons. Rec. 13 of the DSA cites the comments section of an online newspaper as an example. The comments section allows the dissemination of user content as an ancillary feature to the main service, namely the publication of news. Services are also not covered by the provisions on online platforms if the dissemination of content is a minor functionality of the main service, such as the sharing function in an image editing app. In contrast, in the case of a social network, it must be assumed that the comment function is not a mere ancillary feature (rec. 14 sent. 5 DSA). The communicative aspect is the main function of social networks which are therefore considered online platforms. For cloud storage such as Dropbox, it depends on whether the possibility to share stored content (e.g. via a link) is an ancillary feature or an **essential feature of the service** (rec. 14 sent. 6 DSA). In practice, this will largely depend on the design of the individual service. However, the definition in Art. 3(i) DSA makes it clear that providers cannot rely on the exception if they want to circumvent the applicability of Art. 19–28 DSA by labelling or designing the dissemination of content as an ancillary feature.

I. Exemption for micro and small enterprises (Art. 19 DSA)

103 To avoid disproportionate burdens, micro and small-sized enterprises are largely excluded from the due diligence obligations for online platforms in Section 3 (rec. 57 DSA). This is intended to create a **protected space for services in the growth phase**, shielding them from the considerable compliance and implementation costs of the DSA. For these micro and small enterprises, of the obligations contained in Section 3, only Art. 24(3) DSA applies. Art. 24(3) DSA requires (micro and small) services to provide information on the number of average monthly active users to the competent Digital Services Coordinator or the Commission upon request.

104 According to Art. 2 of the Annex to Recommendation 2003/361/EC, a provider is considered a micro enterprise if it employs fewer than ten persons (full time equivalent) and its annual turnover does not exceed two million EUR and a small enterprise if it **employs fewer than 50 persons and its annual turnover does not exceed ten million EUR**. The calculation of the number of employees and turnover is based on the methodology set out in Art. 4, 5 of the Annex to Recommendation 2003/361/EC. For affiliated enterprises, consolidated values are calculated according to Art. 6 of the Annex to Recommendation 2003/361/EC (rec. 57 sent. 5 DSA). The data are calculated annually with the applicable accounting or financial year as the reference period. If a provider loses its status as a micro or small enterprise, the privileged status under the DSA continues to apply for a **transitional period of 12 months** according to Art. 19(1) subpara. 2 DSA.

Due to their reach in terms of users, very large services within the meaning of Art. 33 DSA (→ mn. 212) cannot invoke the status of micro or small enterprises. They are subject to the full scope of due diligence obligations, even if they have only a small number of employees or a low turnover. 105

II. Internal complaint-handling system (Art. 20 DSA)

Art. 20–23 DSA establish a complex **private-order legal review mechanism** against decisions of online platforms outside the public judicial system. In this way, the DSA creates a level of legal protection upstream of the state courts that is intended to be particularly effective and fast.[75] The additional and often very user-friendly review regimes take account of the negative economic and social impact of wrongful content moderation decisions on users and society as a whole. 106

The starting point for the legal protection of users is the **internal complaint system, which is obligatory** under Art. 20 DSA. The complaint system gives users the right to defend themselves against decisions made by providers without incurring any costs and, at the same time, allows providers to review their moderation decisions – which may have been made automatically.[76] The procedure is comparable to Art. 11 P2B Regulation.[77] 107

1. Scope

The subject of a complaint by a user can be any **restrictive measure imposed by the provider** mentioned in Art. 17 DSA (→ mn. 87), as well as a decision taken in response to a **notice in the notice and action mechanism** according to Art. 16 DSA. According to Art. 20(1) DSA, the complaints procedure applies both to allegedly illegal content and to content that may violate the provider's T&Cs. 108

In the Commission's draft of the DSA, the right of complaint was limited to the user. A party submitting a notice in the notice and action mechanism (e.g. victims of hate speech, rightsholders) could not file a complaint if the provider failed to delete the reported content. After this asymmetrical design of the complaints procedure was strongly criticised with regard to the constitutionally protected positions of both groups,[78] Art. 20 DSA now provides for a **symmetrical complaints procedure**. Users and all persons or institutions that have sent a notice within the meaning of Art. 16 DSA are entitled to lodge a complaint using the internal complaint-handling system (rec. 58 sent. 4 DSA). In addition, Art. 86(2) DSA extends the group of persons entitled to complain to consumer protection organisations and similar institutions acting in the user's interests. The provider must handle complaints of consumer protection organisations as a matter of priority. 109

2. Procedure

According to Art. 20(3) DSA, the complaint system must be **easy to access and user-friendly**. In general, this requires that the user should be able to access the form to lodge 110

---

[75] Ortolani, 'If You Build It, They Will Come'.

[76] Under German law, the obligation to review the decision after the user has submitted a statement also follows from national contract law. T&Cs deviating from this procedure have been held to be ineffective by the German Federal Court, cf. BGH 29.7.2021 – III ZR 179/20, NJW 2021, 3179 para. 83 et seqq.; BGH 27.1.2022 – III ZR 12/21, NJW-RR 2022, 625 para. 52.

[77] Busch/Mak EuCML 2021, 109 (111).

[78] Eifert et al. CMLR 2021, 987 (1010 et seq.); Spindler GRUR 2021, 653 (654).

a complaint directly from the notification of any decision which negatively affects him, for example via a link. Providing access to the complaints procedure via a FAQ page or the imprint is not sufficient.[79]

111 The **complaints form** must not impose complex requirements on the user. In particular, service providers may not set out formal requirements such as a detailed statement of reasons or the indication of legal provisions (rec. 58 sent. 3 DSA). However, the provider must enable the user to submit a sufficiently precise and substantiated complaint. This will usually require a free text field with sufficient space to present even complex facts or considerations. In addition, it should be possible to upload files to explain the complaint or provide evidence, for example regarding the grant of rights by the rightsholder in the case of an alleged violation of intellectual property rights.

112 According to Art. 20(2) DSA, the complaint is admissible for a period of at least **six months from the date on which the user was informed of the decision** he wishes to contest. In the case of complaints filed after this deadline, the provider may still decide on the complaint, as the time limit protects only the interests of the provider. A decision on a late complaint is only questionable in the case of complaints against a refusal of the provider to delete content in the notice and action mechanism. In such cases, the complaint affects a triangular relationship between provider, user and the party notifying the provider of allegedly illegal content. The user is interested in his content not being removed in response to the complaint and may have, on first sight, a legitimate interest in the complaint of a notifying party becoming time-barred. In this event, however, the notifying party could simply use the notice and action mechanism to send a new notice or could seek legal protection in the state courts. The user can therefore have no legitimate expectation that the content will not be deleted once the time limit for making an internal complaint has expired.

113 The DSA does not contain a provision regarding the start of the time limit in cases where a user or notifying party could not be informed of a decision because the provider was not aware of an electronic contact address. Based on the wording of Art. 20(1) DSA, it is highly likely that the time limit, in this case, runs for six months from the provider's decision, **regardless of the knowledge of the user or notifying party**.

114 Online platforms must decide on complaints in a timely manner. The **standard of review** is whether the complaint contains sufficient grounds to conclude that the content is neither illegal nor in breach of the provider's T&Cs or – if the content was not removed in response to a notice – the decision not to remove the content was erroneous (Art. 20(4) sent. 2 DSA). In the case of the blocking of a user account, the complaint can also be based on the fact that the conduct of the user does not justify the measure taken. The provider must decide on the **lawfulness and expediency of the measure**.

115 If the complaint is justified, the provider must reverse the measure without undue delay. The obligation to reverse the initial decision according to Art. 20(4) sent. 2 DSA in effect establishes a **'put-back' claim of the user** limited to the complaints procedure.[80] The provider must therefore ensure that the content is not irretrievably deleted until the complaints procedure is concluded.[81] Content that has been blocked or removed wrongfully must be made available again and must not be subject to any restrictions on visibility. However, the DSA does not preclude the provider from adding a note that the content was temporarily blocked as long as this does not affect the visibility or ranking of the

[79] Holznagel CR 2022, 594 (598).

[80] Holznagel CR 2022, 594 (598); to the contrary Spindler GRUR 2021, 653 (654).

[81] Under German contract law, this is already required because the provider must be able to reverse a decision after receiving a statement from the user, cf. BGH 27.1.2022 – III ZR 12/21, NJW-RR 2022, 625 para. 52.

content. The wording of Art. 20(4) sent. 2 DSA lacks a clear obligation in the case of complaints against a refusal of the provider to delete content in the notice and action mechanism. This is based on the fact that the notifying party's right to lodge a complaint was only subsequently included as part of the symmetrical complaints procedure. In the case of a successful complaint by a notifying party, the obligation to reverse the initial decision means that the reported content should be blocked or removed, after all.

Art. 20(6) DSA requires that decisions on complaints are **not to be taken solely by** 116 **automated means** but are to be made under the supervision of appropriately qualified staff. In this respect, the provider's procedural freedom is restricted. Automated procedures can assist the procedure, but each decision must be manually reviewed by a human being (rec. 58 sent. 2 DSA). The criterion of 'supervision' means that not every single decision needs to be reviewed by qualified personnel, but the provider should establish a general quality control procedure and ensure that complex complaints are passed on internally to specially trained personnel for processing.

The decision taken shall be **communicated to the complainant** according to 117 Art. 20(5) DSA without undue delay, stating the reasons. At the same time, the provider must also inform the user about the possibility of out-of-court dispute settlement according to Art. 21 DSA and other available legal remedies, such as legal protection in state courts.

3. Relationship to complaint systems in other Union acts

The DSA does not address the relationship between the complaint-handling system 118 pursuant to Art. 20 DSA and internal complaint mechanisms imposed by other (Union) legal acts. In particular, there is a **large overlap of the DSA mechanism with Art. 11 P2B Regulation, Art. 17(9) DSM Directive and Art. 28b(3)(i) AVMS Directive**. It is unclear whether these apply in parallel to Art. 20 DSA or whether online platforms can refer users to one or other of the procedures.

There is much to suggest that at least **the P2B Regulation and the DSM Directive** 119 **will remain applicable in parallel**. A complaint under the P2B Regulation has a different scope of application than Art. 20 DSA, as it also covers technical problems in the service provision, but is limited to commercial users. In this respect, commercial users can choose between the two types of complaints.[82] The provisions enacted to implement the DSM Directive concern the special area of copyright, which is to remain unaffected according to Art. 2(4)(b) DSA.[83] In addition, the takedown procedure under copyright law has certain specific functions and procedural safeguards which are not reflected in the DSA and should therefore remain applicable in parallel.[84] By contrast, the **complaints procedure under the AVMS Directive is likely overridden by the DSA**.[85] The AVMS Directive, like Art. 20 of the DSA, regulates the handling of content moderation decisions for a subgroup of online platforms, namely video-sharing platforms, and contains less detailed provisions on the complaints procedure compared to the DSA.

---

[82] Holznagel CR 2022, 594 (596) and Busch/Mak EuCML 2021, 109 (114) argue that the P2B Regulation takes precedence over the DSA for commercial users and commercial users may only use the complaint mechanism of the P2B Regulation.

[83] On the interplay between the DSA and the DSM Directive cf. Quintais/Schwemer European Journal of Risk Regulation 2022, 1 (with regard to complaint mechanisms in particular p. 24 et seqq.).

[84] See, e.g. the German implementation in the Copyright Service Provider Act (*Urheberrechts-Diensteanbieter-Gesetz* – UrhDaG) which contains specific procedural rules, such as a decision period of one week and the possibility to immediately block content during the complaint procedure.

[85] Holznagel CR 2022, 594 (596).

III. Out-of-court dispute settlement (Art. 21 DSA)

120 Art. 21 DSA **obliges online platforms to participate in out-of-court dispute settlement** proceedings with certified dispute settlement bodies. The settlement reached in front of a dispute settlement body provides a level of external control in addition to the internal complaint-handling system. However, this is not a 'second instance' or an appeals process against the internal complaint system. The user can choose whether to proceed with an internal complaint or directly seek out-of-court dispute settlement or start judicial proceedings in public courts (rec. 59 sent. 6 DSA). Dispute settlement bodies may be established throughout the Union, with **users free to choose which dispute settlement body to use**. The provider is then obliged to participate in the proceedings before this body chosen by the user.

1. Scope

121 The subject of out-of-court dispute settlement can be **complaints** that the provider has not remedied, **as well as all moderation decisions listed in Art. 17 DSA** (→ mn. 87) and the decision taken in response to a notice in the notice and action mechanism according to Art. 16 DSA.

2. Procedure

122 According to Art. 21(1) subpara. 2 DSA, online platforms must state the possibility of out-of-court dispute settlement in a clear and user-friendly manner. A **reference to out-of-court dispute settlement in a general form** on the provider's website is sufficient. Since the user is free to choose a dispute settlement body, a link to a specific body is not required.

123 The provider and the user shall engage in **good faith** with the dispute settlement body to resolve the dispute according to Art. 21(2) DSA. The DSA does not set a legal standard for the settlement of disputes. This is not surprising as the DSA does not even specify which Member State's law is applicable to determine whether the content is illegal (→ mn. 81).[86] The dispute settlement bodies will therefore enjoy considerable legal and procedural autonomy. This will mostly benefit the user since the user has the right to choose the dispute settlement body.

124 The providers of **online platforms are obliged to participate in the proceedings before the body chosen by the user**. According to Art. 21(2) subpara. 2 DSA, an exception applies only if the dispute has already been settled or is still pending in front of a state court or another out-of-court dispute settlement body (rec. 59 sent. 5 DSA). This is comparable to the principles of *lis alibi pendens* and *res judicata* in court judgments.

125 Decisions of the dispute settlement body are – except for the decision on costs – **non-binding** (Art. 21(2) subpara. 3 DSA). They have the legal effect of information provided to the parties. However, the parties are free to declare the decision binding. In this case, it depends on national civil procedure law whether the decision of the dispute settlement body itself is an enforceable order once declared binding by the parties or whether the relevant party needs a court judgment to enforce claims under a binding settlement decision.

---

[86] Holznagel CR 2022, 594 (598); Wimmers 4 JIPITEC 2021, 421 (432 et seqq.).

3. Establishment of dispute settlement bodies

Out-of-court dispute settlement bodies are external bodies certified by the national Digital Services Coordinator in the procedure according to Art. 21(3), (7) and (8) DSA. The **certification of the dispute settlement body** is valid for all Member States (rec. 59 sent. 4 DSA). Dispute settlement bodies are subject to an annual reporting obligation according to Art. 21(4) DSA. 126

The main requirement for certified dispute settlement bodies is their **impartiality and independence** in terms of personnel and finances. Dispute settlement bodies need to ensure independence both from the providers of online platforms and from users and those reporting illegal content. Personal impartiality must be ensured through rules on conflicts of interest (rec. 59 sent. 2 DSA). With regard to monetary impartiality, the remuneration of dispute settlement body's employees must not depend on the outcome of the proceedings. 127

The DSA **restricts the procedural autonomy of the dispute settlement body** regarding two aspects: 128

- According to Art. 21(4) subpara. 3 DSA, a **decision has to be reached within 90 days** after the receipt of a complaint (the time limit may be extended to a maximum of 180 days in highly complex cases).
- In addition, Art. 21(5) DSA contains requirements for the **fees charged by the dispute settlement body**, which are intended to protect the user (for a critical analysis of this → mn. 133). Fees must be reasonable, inexpensive and attractive to the user, particularly in comparison to the costs of legal action in the public courts system. Fees shall generally not exceed the cost of the dispute settlement body and must be assessed on a case-by-case basis (rec. 59 sent. 3 DSA). However, a degree of generalisation (e.g. lump sums for certain types of cases) will be permissible and necessary to develop the scale of fees required by Art. 21(5) subpara. 3 DSA. The privileged position of the user becomes apparent in the decision on costs mandated by the DSA:
  - If the dispute settlement body decides in favour of the user, the online platform shall bear all fees and reimburse any reasonable costs incurred by the user in relation to the dispute settlement.
  - If the dispute settlement body decides in favour of the online platform, the dispute settlement body may charge the user a nominal fee. Apart from this nominal fee and his own costs, the user shall not bear any other costs. Therefore, the online platform needs to cover the remainder of the fee for the dispute settlement body[87] and does not receive any reimbursement for its own costs. The user shall be obliged to bear these costs only in the exceptional case that he has clearly used the dispute settlement procedure in bad faith.

Dispute settlement bodies should possess **specific expertise concerning certain types of illegal content or certain types of online platforms**. Member States may establish such bodies but are not obliged to do so (rec. 59 sent. 9 DSA). In general, Member States should already have out-of-court redress mechanisms in place for video-sharing platform services as this is required by Art. 28b(7) AVMS Directive. One such example is the arbitration board for video-sharing platform services at the German Federal Office of Justice (*Schlichtungsstelle Videosharingplattform-Dienste*). In addition, private out-of- 129

[87] The dispute settlement body receives a fee to cover its costs independent of the outcome of the proceedings. If it can only demand a nominal fee from the user, the online platform must be responsible for the remainder of the fee.

court dispute settlement bodies may be established. Such private settlement bodies are well established in consumer arbitration, particularly in the banking and transport sectors.

4. Relationship to judicial action

130 According to Art. 21(1) subpara. 3 DSA, the **user may at any time take legal action before a (public) court** against decisions of the online platform. Even an ongoing dispute settlement procedure does not prevent the user from initiating judicial proceedings against the provider.[88] The user can therefore unilaterally remove the dispute settlement body's jurisdiction over the case in the same way as he is free to choose the competent body. The dispute settlement body will then only have to decide on the costs of the initiated procedure based on the scale of fees communicated in advance.

5. Relationship to dispute settlement systems in other Union acts

131 As with the internal complaint-handling system, the relationship between Art. 21 DSA and out-of-court dispute settlement systems under other (Union) legal acts has yet to be clarified. According to Art. 21(9) DSA, dispute settlement under the **Consumer ADR Directive**[89] **remains unaffected**. The corresponding ODR Regulation[90] is not mentioned explicitly. However, since it is based on the instruments of the Consumer ADR Directive, any dispute settlement on contractual disputes between consumers and traders regarding the purchase of goods or services applies in parallel to Art. 21 DSA (rec. 60 DSA).

132 With regard to other Union acts, the same considerations as for the internal complaint-handling system apply (→ mn. 118). Accordingly, the dispute settlement procedures established in the implementation of **Art. 17(9) subpara. 2 DSM Directive remain applicable,**[91] **as does Art. 12 P2B Regulation**, which provides for a special mediation procedure. On the other hand, dispute settlement according to **Art. 28b(7) AVMS Directive is likely superseded by the DSA.**[92]

6. Critical analysis: moral hazard overrides the internalisation of external costs

133 A key aspect of out-of-court dispute settlement is the intention to **internalise the external costs of excessive content removal (overblocking)**. By providing the user with an effective remedy and making the online platform bear the costs in case its moderation decision later turns out to be wrong, a price tag is put on overblocking. This structure highlights the intermediary position of online platforms. If the online platform does not remove illegal content, the provider faces liability to the infringed party. If, on the other hand, the provider of the platform removes legal content, he is liable to the user and now runs the risk of having to bear settlement costs. This price tag for overblocking

---

[88] Berberich/Seip GRUR-Prax 2021, 4 (5); cf. rec. 59 sent. 6, 7 DSA.

[89] Directive 2013/11/EU of the European Parliament and of the Council on alternative dispute resolution for consumer disputes (Directive on consumer ADR).

[90] Regulation (EU) No 524/2013 of the European Parliament and of the Council on online dispute resolution for consumer disputes (Regulation on consumer ODR).

[91] On the interplay between the DSA and the DSM Directive cf. Quintais/Schwemer European Journal of Risk Regulation 2022, 1 (with regard to dispute settlement in particular p. 24 et seqq.).

[92] The German implementation of Art. 28b(7) AVMS Directive in §§ 3e, 3f of the German Network Enforcement Act (*Netzwerkdurchsetzungsgesetz* – NetzDG) has, therefore, been repealed.

aims to shift the balance from the existing structural tendency towards overblocking and provide an incentive for diligent content moderation by online platforms.[93]

134 However, this incentive structure is undermined by the structure of fees set out in Art. 21(5) DSA, which was introduced for the purpose of consumer protection. According to this provision, the vast **majority of dispute settlement costs are to be borne by the online platforms, regardless of the outcome**. If the platform loses, the provider must reimburse the user for all fees and costs and, if the platform wins, the provider must also bear most of the fees in addition to his own costs. The intended economic incentive for diligent moderation is therefore reduced to the reimbursement of the user's out-of-court legal costs – which are likely to be minimal in digital dispute settlement proceedings initiated typically without professional legal support. Instead of providing an incentive for diligent moderation decisions, Art. 21(5) DSA therefore leads to an additional cost factor for online platforms which affects both correct and incorrect moderation decisions equally. In this respect, the economic incentive described above does not work against overblocking but is an **incentive to carry out as little content moderation as possible,** since any content moderation decision may be subject to a complaint and a costly dispute settlement. This incentive is likely to contradict the political goals of the DSA.

135 The attempt to internalise external costs is also superseded by an economic effect that allows users to **attack controversial moderation decisions at the expense of third parties without risk**:

- According to Art. 21(5) subara. 2 sent. 2 DSA, the dispute settlement procedure shall be available to users free of charge or at a nominal fee. Since the user is free to choose the dispute settlement body and these bodies compete for cases throughout the Union, free dispute settlement will be the rule.[94] At the same time, the user will not risk incurring any costs even if he loses, as long as the dispute settlement body does not find that he manifestly acted in bad faith. A clear determination of bad faith will hardly be possible, and it is not in the interests of the dispute settlement body to go down this route. After all, no user will turn to a dispute settlement body that regularly holds that users act in bad faith and obliges them to pay the full fees.
- Dispute settlement bodies have a structural incentive to decide in favour of users. Since the user can choose the dispute settlement body and the settlement bodies are paid per case, there is an economic motivation for the bodies to attract users through a user-friendly decision-making practice.
- The mechanisms against misuse do not apply to out-of-court dispute settlement (→ mn. 144).

136 All of this means that **dispute settlement almost always has a positive expected value for an affected user**. A rational user who regularly publishes controversial content will make use of the dispute settlement instrument in as many cases as possible because he runs little to no risk and enjoys the potential upside of the content being restored to the platform. The data at this point confirms that users are taking up offers for free dispute settlement in large numbers when it comes to often emotionally charged moderation decisions on online platforms. In the first quarter of 2022 alone, about half a million cases were filed with the Meta Oversight Board, an external complaints body for moder-

[93] Fiala/Husovec 71 International Review of Law & Economics 2022, 106079; criticised by Holznagel, 'A Self-Regulatory Race to the Bottom through Out-of-Court Dispute'.

[94] Holznagel, 'A Self-Regulatory Race to the Bottom through Out-of-Court Dispute Settlement in the Digital Services Act'.

ation decisions taken by Facebook and Instagram.[95] Art. 21 DSA creates a classic **moral hazard** problem, because the individual (cost) risk of the user is collectivised by shifting it to the online platform. The provider will ultimately pass on the additional costs of the dispute settlement to the other users of the service, for example through higher prices or more advertisements.

137 There is also the fundamental question of **whether out-of-court dispute settlement is a suitable instrument for dealing with content moderation**. The removal or blocking of content is usually a binary decision that is not suitable for mediation because there is no middle ground.[96] Dispute settlement bodies therefore have to take a decision balancing the fundamental rights of the user, the platform and the affected third parties. There is, however, no uniform legal standard in the DSA for such a decision (→ mn. 79). In addition, it is questionable whether decisions of dispute settlement bodies are suited to solve fundamental rights conflicts. The decisions do not have to be published and are therefore neither subject to public scrutiny nor do they provide a decision-making standard for the future.[97]

IV. Trusted flaggers (Art. 22 DSA)

138 Art. 22 DSA expands the notice and action mechanism to include the concept of trusted flaggers, whose reports must be given priority by the providers of online platforms.[98] Trusted flaggers are **entities with particular expertise in a specific field**. These can be public bodies, such as the national police units for internet content or Europol, but also non-governmental organisations and private bodies, such as the members of the INHOPE network for reporting child sexual abuse material and organisations for reporting hate speech (rec. 61 sent. 4 DSA).[99] Trusted flaggers must be independent of any provider of online platforms. However, Art. 22 DSA does not require a trusted flagger to be neutral within their area of expertise. Therefore, trade associations or associations of right holders can also be trusted flaggers (rec. 61 sent. 6 DSA).

139 The status of a trusted flagger is granted by the national Digital Services Coordinator in the procedure according to Art. 22(2), (6) and (7) DSA. The **award of the status of 'trusted flagger' by the competent Digital Services Coordinator** has effect for all Member States (rec. 61 sent. 2 DSA). Trusted flaggers are subject to an annual reporting obligation pursuant to Art. 22(3) DSA. In this report, they must indicate how much content was reported per provider and what measures the provider has taken. Trusted flaggers are thus obligated to implement an internal quality management, since they have to track the success of their notices. In addition, according to Art. 22(4) and (5) DSA, the contact details of trusted flaggers will be published in a database maintained by the Commission.

140 The reports of trusted flaggers in the notice and action mechanism according to Art. 16 DSA are to be treated by the provider **with priority and without delay**. This requirement is based on the consideration that reports from these bodies can be processed more quickly and with less effort due to their special expertise and competence (rec. 62(1) sent. 3 DSA). However, the DSA refrains from imposing a strict deadline for

[95] Oversight Board, 'Q1 2022 Transparency Report' (3.8.2022) <https://oversightboard.com/attachment/731010438013851> (last accessed: 23.5.2024), p. 5.

[96] Holznagel CR 2022, 594 (595); Janal ZEuP 2021, 227 (265).

[97] Eifert et al. CMLR 2021, 987 (1012).

[98] Cf. Husovec, 'Will the DSA work?'.

[99] E.g. the German anti-hate speech organisation 'Hate Aid' and the youth protection organisation *'jugendschutz.net'*.

the removal of content due to the considerable differences depending on the type of illegal content (rec. 62(1) sent. 3 and 4 DSA). To comply with the obligation, online platforms should offer a fast-track procedure for trusted flaggers to ensure priority treatment of their reports. This requires an option to indicate the status as trusted flagger in the notice and action mechanism, for example by providing a specific form only for trusted flaggers or by adding a checkbox to the general notice form. Provided that the report of a trusted flagger does not require any further factual or legal clarification, the period for immediate removal or blocking of content should be in the range of a few hours to a maximum of one day. However, the privileged status of trusted flaggers is limited to reports within their recognised area of expertise. In addition, violation of the obligation to process reports 'without delay' according to Art. 22 DSA does not affect the liability exemption according to Art. 6 DSA. In this respect, providers remain exempt from liability if they delete content 'expeditiously' – though it is not apparent from the DSA what the difference in substance between 'without delay' and 'expeditiously' is (→ mn. 76).

If a trusted flagger submits a significant number of **inaccurate or false reports**, the online platform should draw this to the attention of the competent Digital Services Coordinator. The latter may initiate proceedings to revoke the status as a trusted flagger according to Art. 22(6) DSA. For the duration of the procedure, the privileged status is suspended. 141

Rec. 62(2) sent. 3 DSA clarifies that online platforms may also cooperate with trusted flaggers on content that violates the provider's T&Cs. The proposal to include the status of 'trusted user', whereby a user takes specific liability for the content he provides and the disputed content remains online during a complaints procedure on the user's responsibility, has not been implemented in the DSA.[100] 142

The concept of trusted flaggers is known in German law from § 14(4) of the Copyright Service Provider Act (*Urheberrechts-Diensteanbieter-Gesetz* – UrhDaG). § 14(4) German Copyright Service Provider Act is the national implementation of Art. 17 DSM Directive and includes specific provisions on a notice and takedown mechanism for online platforms from which the DSA has taken inspiration. 143

V. Safeguards against misuse of the service or the reporting and complaints procedures (Art. 23 DSA)

Art. 23 DSA obliges online platforms to sanction **two cases of misuse** of their service: 144

- Art. 23(1) DSA concerns the misuse of the online platform by users of the service who frequently provide manifestly illegal content.
- Art. 23(2) DSA concerns the misuse of reporting and complaints procedures by users and notifying parties who frequently submit manifestly unfounded notices or complaints.

According to rec. 63 sent. 3 DSA, **'manifestly'** means that it is evident to a layperson, without any substantive analysis, that the content is illegal or that the notice or complaint is unfounded. The legal standard for content to be considered manifestly illegal is likely to be quite high. The action of the user must show a deliberate disregard for the readily apparent illegality or intent. The reference point is the average user of the platform, without taking any special knowledge of the specific user into account. In determining whether the use is a misuse, the provider must consider both the absolute num- 145

[100] Peukert et al. IIC 2022, 358 (372 et seq.).

ber and the relative proportion of illegal content, as well as the gravity and type of illegal content and the user's intentions, according to Art. 23(3) DSA.

146 In cases of misuse, Art. 23 DSA provides for a **two-step approach**. As a first step, the online platform must send a **prior warning to the user**, which has to include the reasons for the imminent suspension of the service and the possible remedies against such a decision by the provider (rec. 64 sent. 4 DSA).

147 If the user continues to provide manifestly illegal content despite the warning or submits further manifestly unfounded notices or complaints, the online platform must **temporarily suspend the user's access**. The suspension of access consists in the online platform not processing further notices and complaints or discontinuing its service for the user in question. Since, according to rec. 64 DSA, only the 'relevant services' are to be stopped, it will generally be permissible to block only the upload function of the service and to continue to grant the user read access to the online platform. The user must remain blocked for a reasonable time. Art. 23(4) DSA obliges online platforms to provide **detailed examples in their T&Cs** of the circumstances constituting a misuse and the respective duration for which the user will be suspended in such cases. Art. 23 DSA does not affect the provider's right to take measures for other or further cases of misuse of the online platform based on the T&Cs (rec. 64 sent. 2, 3 and 6 DSA). In particular, online platforms may also suspend users without prior warning or indefinitely if so provided for by the T&Cs in accordance with Union and national law.

VI. Transparency obligations for online platforms (Art. 24 DSA)

148 Art. 24 DSA contains **three separate transparency obligations** for online platforms.

1. Extended transparency reporting obligation (para. 1 and 6)

149 For online platforms, the **obligation to provide transparency reports according to Art. 15 DSA is extended** to include information on the number and outcomes of proceedings before out-of-court dispute settlement bodies as well as the number of suspensions due to misuse pursuant to Art. 23 DSA. Regarding the draft template for the transparency report published by the Commission → mn. 57.

2. Monitoring of user numbers (para. 2–4)

150 In order to be able to identify very large services (→ mn. 213), all online platforms and online search engines are obliged to regularly **publish on their website the average monthly number of active users in the European Union** (rec. 65 sent. 2 DSA). The information must be provided in an area of the website which is accessible to the public without registration. Calculation of the number of users is based on the methodology set out in Art. 33 DSA (→ mn. 216).

151 According to Art. 24(2) DSA, the average number of monthly active recipients had to be published for the first time on 17.2.2023 and, subsequently, at least every six months. The wording of the DSA is not entirely clear on whether online platforms have to publish the exact number of users or whether it is sufficient to indicate that the number of users is well below the 45 million user threshold to be considered a very large service. While Art. 24(2) DSA refers to 'information on the average monthly active recipients' which may point to a more abstract information than the actual number of users, Art. 24(4) DSA generally places the responsibility to determine whether the threshold of a very large service was passed with the competent Digital Services Coordinator. However, given the challenge to calculate an accurate number of monthly active recipients,

the current market standard for smaller services seems to be to only disclose that the number of users is **below the threshold**.

The competent Digital Services Coordinator and the Commission may also request the online platform or online search engine to provide the current number of users at any point in time, for example in the case of services that have grown particularly rapidly. Indicators of a rapidly growing user base may be the annual turnover and market capitalisation (rec. 78 DSA). In addition, the authorities may request additional explanations and justifications to verify the calculation of the number of users, provided that this information does not contain personal data. 152

The **inclusion of search engines in Art. 24(2)–(4) DSA** does not fit within the structure of the DSA since Section 3 sets out due diligence obligations for online platforms, which by definition do not include search engines. However, it is necessary to monitor the number of users of online search engines in order to identify the very large search engines subject to increased due diligence obligations under Section 5 (→ mn. 222). As there is no specific Section on search engines, the obligation to publish user numbers was placed in Art. 24 DSA. This, however, means that the obligation also applies to very small search engines, because the exception for micro and small enterprises in Art. 19 DSA only refers to online platforms. 153

3. DSA Transparency Database (para. 5)

Art. 24(5) DSA is the legal basis for establishing a **Union-wide database for all moderation decisions taken by online platforms (DSA Transparency Database)**.[101] Providers must transmit all decisions taken in content moderation on their platform to the Commission, which operates the database. The database was inspired by the 'Lumen Database', an independent project for archiving notice and takedown requests used, for example, by Google and X.[102] The database is intended to create transparency concerning the moderation of content and to enable an informed political discussion and public control over the decisions taken by online platforms (rec. 66 DSA). 154

The DSA Transparency Database includes **all decisions of an online platform covered by Art. 17(1) DSA**,[103] which is to say every removal, blocking, restriction on visibility or demonetisation of content and every suspension or blocking of users. The subject matter covered by Art. 24(5) DSA thus goes far beyond the original Lumen Database remit. In particular, the DSA covers both illegal content and content removed or blocked due to alleged violations of the provider's T&Cs and is not limited to decisions taken based on a notice, but also includes any decision taken by the provider on its own account. 155

The provider has to **communicate every moderation decision to the Commission, along with the statement of reasons** provided for in Art. 17(3) DSA. The statement of reasons shall contain the minimum information required by the DSA, which includes information on the legal basis on which the content was deleted and whether the content was detected by automated means. The provider of the system must ensure that no personal data is transmitted to the database. Accordingly, the username concerned and the identity of the person making the notification may not be disclosed and must not be recognisable from the statement of reasons submitted to the database. The DSA does 156

---

[101] See <https://transparency.dsa.ec.europa.eu> (last accessed: 23.5.2024).

[102] See <https://www.lumendatabase.org> (last accessed: 23.5.2024).

[103] It is not clear whether official orders to act against illegal content according to Art. 9 DSA must also be recorded in the database, because such official orders are excluded from the scope of Art. 17 DSA, see Art. 17(5) DSA. The purpose of the database to control content moderation by providers clearly speaks against including official orders.

not contain an obligation to archive the content in dispute in the database. In this respect, the database is not intended to review whether content moderation decisions of platforms were correct in individual cases. Rather, it allows for statistical analyses designed to monitor structural changes in the decisions taken by online platforms.

157 The data must be transmitted to the Commission without delay, which generally means in **real time** (rec. 66 sent. 2 DSA). The Commission provides the option to submit data via an API or a webform to the database.[104] The question of timeframe of the obligation is subject to technical feasibility and proportionality for the providers, whereby in particular the size of the online platform should be taken into account.

158 Given the large scope of provider actions subject to reporting to the DSA Transparency Database, it is still not clear whether the **gigantic size of the data collection** is justified and practically manageable. In the two decades since the original Lumen Database was launched, it has archived about 20 million reports, but these figures were dwarfed in no time by those of the DSA Transparency Database. With only 16 very large services onboarded, in the few months the DSA Transparency Database has been implemented so far nearly 17 billion reports have been submitted to the database. In the future, platforms such as Wikipedia will also have to submit a report to the Commission whenever an article is deleted or a revision is rejected. Given that the German-language version of Wikipedia alone currently has ten million page edits per year, the volume of data submitted to the database in the future can reasonably be expected to be significant.

VII. Prohibition of dark patterns (Art. 25 DSA)

159 Art. 25 DSA contains a **prohibition on online platforms using manipulative design in their online interface** (so-called **'dark patterns'**). The ban is intended to protect users' ability to make autonomous and informed decisions (rec. 67 DSA). In this way, the DSA addresses the problem that, through the use of certain technical designs, interactive services can make it difficult or even impossible for users to exercise their rights.[105]

160 The DSA defines a dark pattern as any practice that, either on purpose or in effect, manipulates or otherwise impairs or hinders the user's ability to make a free and informed decision (cf. rec. 67(1) sent. 1 DSA). This **definition of a dark pattern** has three essential elements: a dark pattern is (1) an interactive element that (2) persuades the user to act (or refrain from acting) in a way that (3) does not correspond to the user's autonomous decision.

161 **Persuading an action** means more than simply influencing a purchase decision through traditional advertising.[106] The key characteristic of a dark pattern is that it exploits human weaknesses and gaps in rational decision making, such as the user's inattention, convenience or cognitive biases.[107] This is typically achieved by redirecting the attention (by differently designed buttons), manipulating the flow of information (by highlighting or omitting information) or artificially limiting the decision space (by creating urgency).[108]

---

[104] See the API at <https://github.com/digital-services-act/transparency-database> and the corresponding documentation at <https://transparency.dsa.ec.europa.eu/page/api-documentation> (last accessed: 23.5.2024).

[105] Gerpott CR 2022, 516 (524 et seq.).

[106] Rec. 67 sent. 6 and 7 DSA; cf. Gerpott CR 2022, 516 (526).

[107] Kühling/Sauerborn CR 2022, 226 (227); Martini et al. ZfDR 2021, 47 (49).

[108] Kühling/Sauerborn CR 2022, 226 (227).

Whether the design **impairs the user's decision making and autonomy** depends on an objective evaluation of the specific design. Usually, but not necessarily, a dark pattern has an unintended or negative consequence for the user because he fails to assert the rights to which he is entitled or is unaware of alternative choices.[109] However, in the context of Art. 25 DSA, the effectiveness or success of the dark pattern in an individual case is irrelevant.[110] What matters is whether the provider of the online platform unilaterally places its own interests above those of the user by impairing his ability to make a self-determined decision.[111] By looking at the alignment of a design with the user's (presumed) interest, positive nudging can be distinguished from malicious nudging in the form of dark patterns. A dark pattern is generally used in the sole interest of the online platform provider and ignores or overrides the preferences of the user.[112] 162

The Commission may issue guidelines for a more precise definition of dark patterns (on guidelines → mn. 277). By way of example, Art. 25(3) DSA defines three types of dark patterns that may fall under Art. 25 DSA: 163

- The provider highlights certain choices visually, acoustically or in some other way when the user is asked to make a decision (**'misdirection pattern'**). In this case, the platform presents the desired decision to the user in such a large and conspicuous way that he is barely aware of the alternative offered. This design pattern can be found in the checkout process of many online retailers. Often the option to add additional services like insurance is highlighted in colour and immediately recognisable as a continuation of the ordering process, while the option to continue the order without additional services (and thus costs) is presented in a smaller font with low contrast.
- The provider repeatedly asks the user to make a choice when the user has already made a decision (**'nagging pattern'**). This is the case when a cookie banner is displayed every time a user visits a website, in spite of the fact that the user has previously refused to accept cookies.
- The provider makes it more difficult to terminate a service than to subscribe to the service (**'roach motel pattern'**). This includes designs where it is very easy to register as a user, but the provider hides the mechanism for unsubscribing from the platform or deleting the customer account in deeply branched menus or help pages that are difficult to find. Similarly, a design that makes it disproportionately difficult to cancel a purchase or checkout process once it has begun is considered a deceptive design pattern (rec. 67(2) sent. 1 DSA).

A wide range of other misleading or manipulative designs are conceivable.[113] According to rec. 67(2) sent. 1 DSA, default settings that are very difficult to change, as well as practices that push users to conclude unwanted transactions, should also be prohibited. Many online platforms also use elements inspired from behavioural psychology that artificially keep users on the platform or increase the number of interactions (addictive design), such as infinite scrolling or gamification. The **line between prohibited dark patterns and permissible design elements will be difficult to draw**. 164

[109] Rec. 67 sent. 2 DSA; Gerpott CR 2022, 516 (524).

[110] Martini et al. ZfDR 2021, 47 (50).

[111] Kühling/Sauerborn CR 2022, 226 (227); Martini et al. ZfDR 2021, 47 (52 et seq.).

[112] Martini et al. ZfDR 2021, 47 (50). In this respect, it is irrelevant whether the choice in an individual case actually corresponds to the user's interests.

[113] An overview of different types of dark patterns is given by the Dark Pattern Detection Project <https://dapde.de/en/dark-patterns-en/types-and-examples-en/> and Harry Brignull <www.deceptive.design/types> (last accessed: 23.5.2024).

165 The wording of Art. 25 DSA refers to the use of dark patterns on the online interface of a platform. According to Art. 3(m) DSA, this means any kind of software, including **websites or apps**. As the term 'recipient' is defined broadly in the DSA, the prohibition of dark patterns applies both to consumers and commercial users of online platforms.

166 According to Art. 25(2) DSA, the prohibition of dark patterns does not apply to practices that are covered by the UCP Directive[114] or the GDPR. The legal effect of this provision is not entirely clear. It may be understood to completely **exclude online interfaces in B2C commerce and data protection from the scope** of Art. 25 DSA. However, given rec. 67(2) sent. 4 DSA, it may also be construed that the UCP Directive and the GDPR are to be examined first as *leges speciales* and that Art. 25 DSA applies as a fallback option.[115] In any case, the unfairness of commercial practice standard and the voluntariness of consent under data protection law are likely to lead to similar results as Art. 25 DSA.[116]

167 In addition to enforcement under competition and data protection law, individual users are also able to enforce the prohibition of dark patterns under Art. 25 DSA against online platforms if they are manipulated to make disadvantageous decisions (Private Enforcement, → Ch. 5 mn. 112). The use of dark patterns may justify a claim for damages by the user under contract or tort law, which can result in the cancellation of a contract or indemnification against claims by third parties.

168 Art. 25 DSA was not included in the Commission's draft of the DSA but was added later during the legislative process. The adopted version represents a compromise between the proposal of the European Parliament,[117] which envisaged a very detailed ban on dark patterns applicable to all types of intermediary services, and the much more industry-friendly solution of the Council,[118] which wanted to limit the ban to online marketplaces.

VIII. Advertising on online platforms (Art. 26 DSA)

169 In regulating online advertising, the legislator was faced with the challenge that, while **advertising plays an important role in the financing of many online platforms,**[119] some advertisements may be illegal or **contribute to the financing of illegal content and services** (rec. 68(1) sent. 1 and 2 DSA). Art. 26 DSA therefore contains specific obligations for online platforms if the provider or a user disseminates advertising on the platform.[120] The term advertising is defined in Art. 3(r) DSA as a message that is presented by an online platform against remuneration paid specifically for promoting this information.

---

[114] Directive 2005/29/EC of the European Parliament and of the Council concerning unfair business-to-consumer commercial practices in the internal market.

[115] '[...] should be interpreted as covering prohibited practices [...] to the extent that those practices are not already covered under Directive 2005/29/EC or Regulation (EU) 2016/679'.

[116] See the decisions of the French data protection authority CNIL against Google and Facebook (31.12.2021) No. SAN-2021-023 and No. SAN-2021-024; European Data Protection Board, 'Draft Guidelines 3/2022 on Dark patterns in social media platform interfaces' (14.3.2022).

[117] Art. 13a DSA (Draft) in the Negotiating Mandate of the European Parliament, 'Amendments on the proposal for a DSA' (20.1.2022), P9_TA(2022)0014, Amendment 202.

[118] Art. 24b(-1) [sic] DSA (Draft) in the General Approach of the Council (18.11.2021), ST 13203/21, Annex, p. 152.

[119] European Commission, 'Impact Assessment', SWD(2020) 348 final, Part 2, p. 196.

[120] For a critique of the rules on advertising on online platforms see Castellaro/Penfrat, 'The DSA fails to reign in the most harmful digital platform businesses – but it is still useful'.

1. Labelling obligation for advertising of the provider

170 Art. 26(1) DSA contains **transparency requirements for advertising placed on the online platform by the provider**. The user should know when he is exposed to advertising and have clarity about who is paying for it and why this particular piece of advertising is being displayed to him. To this end, the DSA provides four information requirements that must be fulfilled each time advertising is displayed and which should be highlighted by standardised visual or acoustic markings (rec. 68(2) sent. 4 DSA):

point (a): The content must be **labelled as advertising**. The label needs to be in a language generally understood by the users of the platform and consistent with the design of the service. For non-English platforms the indication 'Ad' will only be sufficient if it is broadly understood by the typical target audience of the platform.[121] Online platforms can adhere to the standards of the standardisation bodies within the meaning of Art. 44 DSA.

point (b): It must be stated **on whose behalf** the advertisement is presented, namely which natural or legal person is placing it.

point (c): It must be stated **who paid for the advertisement**, if this is not the person referred to in point (b). This requirement is akin to the obligation to disclose the funding of election campaign ads in the United States ('Paid for by ...').

point (d): Directly next to the advertisement, the user must be able to access information to determine **based on which parameters** the advertisement is being displayed to him. The online platform must disclose the method used to display the advertisement (such as contextual advertising, profiling) and the main parameters used to determine the target group (rec. 68(1) sent. 4 and 5 DSA). If profiling is used to display advertisements, the platform must provide meaningful information on the underlying logic and inform the user as to how he can change the relevant profiling parameters (rec. 68(1) sent. 5 DSA). It is not sufficient for this information to be provided in the platform's T&Cs; it must also be directly accessible from the advertisement in question, for example via an info icon next to the advertisement.

171 These obligations are intended to **make personalised advertising more easily recognisable**, in particular micro-targeting.[122] Although the scope of Art. 26 DSA is now much broader, the regulation of online advertising must be seen against the background of political disinformation campaigns, such as on Brexit and the Covid pandemic (rec. 69 sent. 2 DSA). The DSA is only one piece in a larger set of rules that is complemented by the Regulation on the transparency and targeting of political advertising.[123] According to rec. 51 of the Regulation (EU) 2024/900, the Regulation should go hand in hand with the DSA and lay down additional requirements for political advertising on online platforms.

172 It is not entirely clear from the wording of Art. 26(1) DSA, whether providers must label content as advertising if the provider charges all users a fee for the distribution of content on the platform, for example in the case of online marketplaces that charge a commission for each product offered on the marketplace. However, based on the purpose of Art. 26(1) DSA to make advertising more easily recognisable, the obligation should apply only if the provider has highlighted the content or otherwise increased its

[121] This is in line with the case law on labelling of advertising under German press and media law, cf. OLG Celle 8.6.2018 – 12 U 53/17, MMR 2017, 769.

[122] Berberich/Seip GRUR-Prax 2021, 4 (5).

[123] Regulation (EU) 2024/900 of the European Parliament and of the Council on the transparency and targeting of political advertising.

visibility in return for a payment by the user. The labelling obligation is intended to enable users to identify 'paid content'. If, for example, all product listings on an online marketplace had to be labelled as advertising, this would be contrary to the purpose of Art. 26 DSA, since users would not be able to identify which content is displayed to them because of a specific remuneration to the provider. In addition, in order to be considered an 'advertisement' within the definition of Art. 3(r) DSA, the remuneration paid to the provider must be specifically for the purpose of 'promoting that information'. A general fee to use the platform or a sales-based commission is not linked to a specific promotion of the content and should therefore not constitute paid advertising.

2. Option to label advertising posted by users

173 Art. 26(2) DSA contains the obligation for online platforms to **enable their users to label commercial communication** posted on the platform. Online platforms must provide a function which allows users to declare any content uploaded by them as advertising. This obligation applies in addition to the similar obligation for video-sharing platforms in Art. 28b(2) subpara. 2, Art. 9(1) AVMS Directive and is intended to make it easier for users to comply with Union and national obligations to disclose the commercial background of content (rec. 68(2) sent. 4 and 5 DSA). Such obligations arise for traders from the UCP Directive and, under German law, from § 5a(4) of the Act against Unfair Competition (*Gesetz gegen den unlauteren Wettbewerb* – UWG).

174 If the user has declared uploaded content to be advertising, the online platform must ensure that the label is **clear and unambiguous for other users**. This requires visual, acoustic, or other highlighting according to Art. 26(2) subpara. 2 DSA, for which online platforms can follow the standards of standardisation bodies within the meaning of Art. 44 DSA.

3. Prohibition of advertising based on sensitive data

175 Art. 26(3) DSA prohibits **targeting based on 'special categories of personal data'** as defined in Art. 9(1) GDPR. This aims to prevent manipulative targeting techniques that discriminate against or harm certain groups (rec. 69 DSA). Under the GDPR, information on the racial or ethnic origin, political opinions, religion, trade union membership, genetic or biometric data, health and sexual orientation of an individual are considered to be specially protected.

176 The prohibition covers both the direct use of data covered by Art. 9(1) GDPR as well as **indirect profiling** with categories based on special categories (rec. 69 sent. 4 DSA). This means that online platforms are prohibited from deriving specially protected data from existing data in order to target groups of users based on whether they are likely to fall into a specific group. However, the use of data that are not covered by Art. 9(1) GDPR but have a high correlation with the specially protected categories and therefore achieve a de facto identical targeting effect (proxy data) remains a possible loophole.[124]

177 Although it was demanded during the legislative process, in particular by the European Parliament,[125] the **DSA does not contain a complete ban on personalised advertising**. To minimise the risks of this data-intensive business model, the DSA follows the path of increased transparency requirements and targeted restrictions where the individual's rights are particularly affected or where vulnerable groups are at risk (on minors

[124] Griffin, 'Tackling Discrimination in Targeted Advertising'; Kuclar Stiković EU Law Working Papers No. 85, 1 (95 et seq.).

[125] Cf. Art. 2b DSA (Draft) according to European Parliament, 'Opinion of the Committee on Civil Liberties, Justice and Home Affairs (LIBE)' (28.7.2021), LIBE_AD(2021)692898, Amendment 58.

→ mn. 186). In general, however, the GDPR approach of self-determined consent by well-informed users remains the standard for targeting and data processing.[126]

IX. Recommender system transparency (Art. 27 DSA)

178 Recommender systems are one of the **transformative technologies of online platforms**. Platforms can curate and rank content or display personalised information to users according to their preferences to increase content consumption and time spent on the service. The streaming service Netflix generates about 80 % of its total streaming time by displaying personalised recommendations for movies and series.[127] Many social networks also use recommender systems to rank posts in the timelines of their users. This has a significant impact – both positive and negative – on the spread of certain messages. On the one hand, recommender systems help users to quickly access information that is of interest to them and lead to the viral effect that is typical and desired for the internet.[128] On the other hand, they also increase the spread of particularly controversial content, such as hate speech and fake news, that affects users emotionally and keeps them on the platform for extended periods of time.[129]

179 In light of this, Art. 27 DSA contains two due diligence obligations for the use of recommender systems on online platforms. **Art. 3(s) DSA defines a recommender system** as any

> fully or partially automated system used by an online platform to suggest […] specific information to recipients of the service or to prioritise that information, including as a result of a search initiated by the recipient of the service or otherwise determining the relative order or prominence of information displayed.

This includes ranking systems based on user behaviour or user data, a search function which sorts by relevance as well as automatically – including chronologically – compiled timelines. It, however, does not include purely manual curation of content.

180 Art. 27(1) and (2) DSA provide for an **information obligation** that online platforms must fulfil when using recommender systems. Providers must state in their T&Cs the main parameters according to which content is suggested to the user and the reasons for the weighting of these parameters. The provider should also explain how these parameters influence the presentation of content as well as if and how the user can change or influence the parameters (rec. 70 sent. 6 DSA).

181 There is a **strong overlap** with the transparency obligation for ranking systems according to Art. 5 P2B Regulation, which, however, only applies to online marketplaces (a subgroup of online platforms). In addition, with regard to online marketplaces, Art. 6a Consumer Rights Directive applies which requires similar information to be presented in a specific section of the interface of an online marketplace.

182 Separate from the information obligation, Art. 27(3) DSA requires an **easy option to choose the recommender system** if the provider offers different types of ranking. The user must be able to select the desired recommender system using a button located in immediate proximity to the content ranked by the platform, for example by switching

---

[126] Gerpott CR 2022, 516 (524).

[127] Gomez-Uribe/Hunt 6 ACM Transactions on Management Information Systems 2015, 13; Plummer, 'This is how Netflix's top-secret recommender system works'.

[128] Rec. 70 sent. 4 and 5 DSA; European Commission, 'Staff Working Document Online Platforms accompanying the document Communication on Online Platforms and the Digital Single Market', SWD(2016) 172 final, p. 6 et seq.

[129] See Edelson et al. Proceedings of the 21st ACM Internet Measurement Conference 2021, 444.

from sorting content by relevance to alphabetical sorting. However, the DSA does not oblige online platforms to offer more than one recommender system to their users (except in the case of very large online platforms, which are subject to additional obligations under Art. 38 DSA, → mn. 246). If an online platform uses only one system for sorting content, the obligation in Art. 27(3) DSA does not apply.

183 The demand by civil society organisations to mandate interoperability of recommender systems so that users are able to employ third-party ranking systems on online platforms was not met by the European legislator.[130] In addition, Art. 27 DSA contains no provisions on the ranking of search results by search engines, as these do not fall within the definition of an online platform.[131]

X. Online protection of minors (Art. 28 DSA)

184 In order to protect minors, a particularly vulnerable group, online platforms must ensure a high level of privacy and security when targeting minors. Art. 28 DSA applies to all **online platforms that are accessible to minors**. Rec. 71 of the DSA lists **four groups of cases** in which this requirement is considered to be fulfilled:

1. The platform permits the use by minors in its T&Cs, for example by setting a minimum age below the age of majority. This is the case for Facebook's terms of service, which exclude (only) users under 13 years of age from the platform.[132]
2. The platform is directed at minors. The target audience is to be determined in particular based on the platform's content and design.
3. The platform is predominantly used by minors. In this case, the applicability of Art. 28 DSA is based only on the actual proportion of minors among all users, without considering whether minors were intentionally targeted as users.
4. The platform provider knows that some of the users are minors because the online platform processes the age of users, for example when they register for the service.

185 According to Art. 28(1) DSA, these online platforms must take **appropriate measures, proportionate to the nature of the platform**, to ensure the privacy and security of minors. An appropriate measure may be the pre-selection of the strictest data protection settings for minors (rec. 71 sent. 3 DSA). The Commission has announced that it will develop a code of conduct for the age-appropriate design of digital services, which may assist online platforms in fulfilling their due diligence obligations according to Art. 28(4) DSA.[133]

186 Art. 28(2) DSA provides for a **complete ban on personalised advertising to minors**. Providers who fall within the scope of Art. 28(1) DSA and have reasonable certainty that the user in question is a minor may not use any personal data of the user for profiling for advertising purposes. This goes beyond the scope of the general provisions on online advertising in Art. 26(3) DSA (→ mn. 175), as it covers not only sensitive data but all personal data of minors. Regardless of whether the minor has given its consent to advertis-

---

[130] Cf. European Parliament, 'Draft Amendments 1592-1872 in the Internal Market and Consumer Protection Committee (IMCO)' (8.7.2021), IMCO_AM(2021)695161, Amendments 1700, 1703, 1707 and 1806; Electronic Frontier Foundation, 'Preserve What Works, Fix What is Broken: EFF's Policy Principles on the Digital Services Act', p. 9.

[131] Spindler GRUR 2021, 653 (660).

[132] Facebook Terms of Service (12.1.2024) <https://facebook.com/terms.php> (last accessed: 23.5.2024).

[133] European Commission, 'Communication from the Commission to the European Parliament, the Council, the European Economic and Social Committee and the Committee of the Regions: A Digital Decade for Children and Young People' (11.5.2022), COM(2022) 212 final, 12 et seq.

ing, providers are not allowed to show personalised advertising to the minor.[134] The DSA does not specify when a provider is considered to be reasonably certain that a user is a minor. In general, the provider is certain if the user has disclosed his age during sign-up. A platform may also obtain reasonable certainty about the age of a user through other factors, such as user behaviour or reports of third parties. It should be noted, however, that the platform must be 'aware' of the age and platforms are not obliged to actively investigate their users' age.

Art. 28(3) DSA clarifies that online platforms are **not obliged to verify the age of their users**. In accordance with the principle of data minimisation, they are not required to ask the user's age during sign-up or registration (rec. 71 sent. 6 and 7 DSA). 187

F. Obligations for online marketplaces (Art. 29–32 DSA)

Section 4 of the third chapter of the DSA contains additional due diligence obligations for online platforms that allow consumers to conclude distance contracts with traders (hereinafter **'online marketplace'**). This refers to marketplaces such as Amazon Marketplace and eBay. The rules are intended to protect consumers and deter traders from selling illegal products and services (rec. 72 DSA). 188

The scope of application largely coincides with the **definition of the online marketplace** under Art. 2(17) Consumer Rights Directive. It covers online platforms on which traders can conclude contracts with customers within an organised sales system exclusively using means of distance communication.[135] A slight difference compared to the Consumer Rights Directive is that the **DSA only covers business-to-consumer (B2C) platforms**. While the Consumer Rights Directive refers to 'other traders or consumers' as the seller and, therefore, also applies to consumer-to-consumer platforms (C2C), the DSA explicitly refers to platforms that enable consumers to conclude contracts with traders. This difference is the reason why there is no legal definition included in the DSA for the category of services covered by the obligations in Section 4. The Council had proposed to insert such a definition under the term 'online marketplace' in Art. 3 DSA.[136] However, in order to avoid confusion with the slightly different understanding of the online marketplace under the Consumer Rights Directive, the proposal was not implemented. The definition of 'online intermediation services' in Art. 2(2) P2B Regulation, which also has a comparable scope, could not be applied in the context of the DSA because the DSA already uses the term 'intermediary service' with a different meaning. Instead, the DSA now repeats the relevant criteria in each Article of Section 4. 189

The new obligations under the DSA come on top of the existing requirements imposed on online marketplaces under Union law. This creates a regulatory web that is rightly described as **'chaotic at first sight'**.[137] This web can be untangled by looking at the **objectives of the different legal acts**. The DSA – like Art. 6a of the Consumer Rights Directive – primarily protects consumers by creating market transparency. The P2B Regulation protects commercial traders registered as sellers on the platform (rec. 3 and 7 190

[134] In this respect, the capacity of minors to give consent under Art. 8 GDPR is superseded by the DSA.

[135] Regarding the term distance contract, Art. 3(l) DSA refers to the definition in Art. 2(7) Consumer Rights Directive.

[136] Cf. the proposed amendment to Art. 2(ia) DSA (Draft) in the General Approach of the Council (18.11.2021), ST 13203/21, Annex, p. 112.

[137] Eifert et al. CMLR 2021, 987 (1016); cf. Cauffman/Goanta European Journal of Risk Regulation 2021, 758 (760 et seqq.).

P2B Regulation). The Digital Markets Act (DMA) strengthens the position of companies that place advertisements on online marketplaces.[138]

I. Exemption for micro and small enterprises (Art. 29 DSA)

191 According to Art. 29 DSA, the due diligence obligations of Section 4 do not apply to micro and small enterprises. This provision corresponds to Art. 19 DSA (→ mn. 103).

II. Traceability of traders (Art. 30 DSA)

192 Art. 30 DSA contains specific **know-your-business-customer obligations for online marketplaces**. Providers must store the data of traders on their marketplace in order to make it easier for consumers and rightsholders to enforce their rights when traders offer illegal products or services.[139]

193 According to Art. 30(1) DSA, the provider is required to store the contact details (name, address, telephone number, email address) and a copy of the identification document of the trader as well as the trader's payment account details and self-certification to offer only legally compliant products and services. Since no specific form is required for this self-commitment, a checkbox to be ticked by the trader when registering on the platform should generally be sufficient. If the trader is registered in a trade register or similar public register, his identification number must also be stored. The minimum mandatory information is extended by different sector- or product-specific Union acts. For example, Art. 62(6) of the Battery Regulation requires online platforms to store the producer's registration number in the public registry of battery producers and to obtain a self-certification that the batteries offered are in compliance with the Battery Regulation.[140] The obligation to additionally indicate the person responsible for product safety (manufacturer or importer)[141], which was included in the Commission draft[142], has been moved to Art. 31(1) subpara. 2 DSA in the legislative procedure.

194 The relevant data must be **provided by the trader before he can use the marketplace** to offer or advertise products or services (Art. 30(2) DSA). Therefore, use of the marketplace may only be activated once all the necessary information is available and has been checked (→ mn. 195). Generally, the relevant information should be obtained during the sign-up process when a new trader joins the marketplace. For traders already registered on the marketplace when the DSA became applicable, a transition period of 12 months from 17.2.2024 applies according to Art. 30(2) subpara. 2 DSA, during which the information must be obtained by the provider.

195 In principle, the trader is liable for the correctness and completeness of the information provided. However, Art. 30(2) DSA requires the **marketplace provider to conduct a plausibility check**. In this respect, the DSA attempts to strike a balance between a strict obligation to actively investigate, which would protect consumers, and the interests

[138] Eifert et al. CMLR 2021, 987 (1017).

[139] Rec. 72 sent. 1 and 5 DSA; European Commission, 'Impact Assessment', SWD(2020) 348 final, Part 1, p. 42.

[140] Regulation (EU) 2023/1542 of the European Parliament and of the Council concerning batteries and waste batteries.

[141] Cf. Art. 3(13) in conjunction with Art. 4 Regulation (EU) 2019/1020 of the European Parliament and of the Council on market surveillance and compliance of products.

[142] Art. 22(1)(d) DSA (Draft) in the Proposal for a Regulation on a Single Market for Digital Services (Digital Services Act) of the Commission (15.12.2020), COM(2020) 825 final.

of the marketplace providers, who are in a neutral position and should not be burdened with disproportionate requirements.[143] The result is a vaguely-worded obligation for providers to use their best efforts to assess the reliability and completeness of the information, which, however, leaves considerable legal uncertainty for online marketplaces.[144] Art. 30(2) DSA imposes an obligation to check each trader registered on the platform and only allow traders to use the marketplace after their information has been checked – possibly by automated means. In particular, the provider must compare the information provided by the trader with information available in freely accessible official databases (rec. 73 DSA).[145] Alternatively, or if the database request is inconclusive, the provider may ask the trader to provide appropriate evidence from reliable sources, for example register certificates or other official documents (rec. 73 sent. 2 DSA). Bank account statements are also admissible as evidence since credit institutions are usually subject to strict customer identification obligations. The provider may also search freely available sources on the internet, as long as they are of comparable reliability (rec. 73 sent. 3 DSA). However, he does not have to carry out time-consuming and expensive on-site checks or inspections (rec. 73 sent. 4 DSA).

The provider must store and retain the information for the entire duration of the con- **196** tractual relationship with the trader concerned and a period of six months after that. The **subsequent obligation to store** the information ensures that the provider can fulfil his obligation to inform consumers according to Art. 32 DSA if the trader has sold illegal products or services via the online marketplace (→ mn. 204).

According to Art. 30(7) DSA, the online platform must display the trader's contact **197** details and identification number in the trade register as well as his self-certification **on the relevant product page**. Designing the marketplace in such a way is in the provider's own interest because it clearly shows that the offers are provided by third-party traders and not the marketplace provider. Otherwise, the average consumer could get the impression that he is entering into a contract with the marketplace provider. In cases where the information is presented in such a misleading way, the marketplace provider does not benefit from the liability exemption of the DSA for intermediary services and may be liable for illegal products and services, even if he has no actual knowledge or control over the information (Art. 6(3) and rec. 24 DSA). The remaining data not presented on the online interface (identification document and payment details of the trader) may only be disclosed by the marketplace provider pursuant to Art. 30(6) DSA if there is a legal obligation to do so or if an information order is issued against the provider according to Art. 10 DSA.

If a trader fails to provide relevant information or if the information is incorrect or **198** incomplete, the platform must **suspend the trader's access to the service** in accordance with Art. 30(3) subpara. 2 DSA. According to the clarification in Art. 30(4) DSA, the trader can take action against this decision using the internal complaint-handling system (→ mn. 106) as well as by way of out-of-court dispute settlement (→ mn. 120). In addition, the trader has the legal remedies available under the P2B Regulation.

The know-your-business-customer obligation under Art. 30 DSA applies without **199** prejudice to the existing identification requirements (rec. 72 DSA), such as the obligation under Art. 5 E-Commerce Directive, according to which intermediary services must provide certain information to the authorities, as well as the tax obligations under

---

[143] Spindler GRUR 2021, 653 (656 et seq.).

[144] Gerpott CR 2022, 516 (520).

[145] For example, by verifying the provided VAT ID number using the VIES VAT number validation or a similar system provided on Member State level, cf. <https://ec.europa.eu/taxation_customs/vies> and for Germany <https://evatr.bff-online.de/eVatR/xmlrpc> (last accessed: 23.5.2024).

Art. 8ac Council Directive 2011/16/EU on administrative cooperation in the field of taxation.

III. Compliance by design (Art. 31 DSA)

200 According to Art. 31 DSA, online marketplaces must **design their websites and apps in such a way that traders are able to fulfil their information obligations under applicable Union law towards consumers**. In addition, Art. 31(3) DSA includes an obligation to assess the completeness of the information as well as the legality of the products and services offered by traders through randomised checks.

201 Art. 31(1) and (2) DSA requires the online interface of a marketplace to **enable compliance with the obligations under Union law** concerning pre-contractual information, compliance, and product safety information. For this purpose, marketplace providers must ensure that it is possible to indicate the person responsible for product safety (manufacturer or importer).[146] In addition, rec. 74 sent. 1 DSA lists information obligations according to the relevant Union law on distance contracts,[147] competition law,[148] price indications on consumer products[149] and the E-Commerce Directive.[150] The online marketplace must allow all traders on the platform to provide this information in a way that is compliant with Union law. Art. 31(2) DSA includes additional minimum information to identify the trader and the products or services offered.

202 The wording of Art. 31 DSA only obliges marketplaces to provide technical means for traders to provide the relevant information to consumers. Following this wording, online marketplaces generally do not have to enforce that traders actually provide the legally required information. In particular, not all of the information mentioned can and must be provided for all types of products or services. However, Art. 31(3) DSA contains two **verification obligations for online marketplaces**:

- According to Art. 31(3) sent. 1 DSA, the provider must **assess whether the information provided by the trader is complete** before allowing the trader to offer the product or service (rec. 74 sent. 2 and 3 DSA). This is not intended to imply a general duty to monitor or a duty to actively review the accuracy of the information provided (rec. 74 sent. 4 DSA). The provider must only ensure that all the legally mandatory information is provided but not that it is factually accurate. Depending on the product type, online marketplaces should therefore require specific information from traders as a mandatory input before the offer becomes visible to consumers on the platform.
- According to Art. 31(3) sent. 2 DSA, after activating a specific offer, the provider must **conduct random checks to determine whether the products or services offered by traders on the marketplace are illegal**. For this purpose, the provider shall use freely accessible and machine-readable official online databases and check whether the products or services have been identified as illegal by the authorities.[151] In essence, this is a general monitoring obligation that applies regardless of suspi-

[146] Cf. Art. 3(13) in conjunction with Art. 4 Regulation (EU) 2019/1020 of the European Parliament and of the Council on market surveillance and compliance of products.

[147] Art. 6 and 8 Consumer Rights Directive.

[148] Art. 7 UCP Directive.

[149] Art. 3 Directive 98/6/EC of the European Parliament and of the Council on consumer protection in the indication of the prices of products offered to consumers.

[150] Art. 5 and 6 E-Commerce Directive.

[151] For example, via the European Commission's 'Information and Communication System for Market Surveillance' (ICSMS) or the Safety Gate rapid alert system (formerly RAPEX).

cions in a specific case. However, marketplace providers do not themselves need to assess whether products or services are illegal and may rely solely on assessments carried out by authorities. Therefore, the checks can be partly automated by filtering for terms or product numbers relating to products identified as illegal.

Unlike Art. 30(2) subpara. 2 DSA, **Art. 31 DSA does not contain a transition period** 203 for offers already active when the DSA came into effect. Regarding these offers, the obligation to carry out random checks applies since 17.2.2024.

IV. Obligation to inform consumers about illegal products or services (Art. 32 DSA)

According to Art. 32 DSA, the provider of an online marketplace must **inform consumers who have purchased illegal products or services** via the platform. The duty to inform users applies regardless of how the provider became aware of the illegality of the product or service. 204

A product or service is illegal according to the definition in Art. 3(h) DSA if it violates Union or national law (on the question of applicable law → mn. 79). The term is therefore **not limited to safety-related defects**. It also covers products that infringe trademarks and products that lack a mandatory certification. The wording may be understood to also cover any individual defect of a product, because the product in question would not be provided in conformity with applicable sales or contract law. In this respect, however, Art. 32 DSA must be **construed restrictively**. According to the meaning and purpose of the duty to inform, the obligation only covers defects that systematically occur in the product and therefore affect the group of consumers as a whole, as in the case of a defect which leads to a product recall by the manufacturer. 205

In the case of illegal products or services, all buyers of the product or service must be informed of the illegality and the identity of the trader. In addition, the supplier must point out the relevant means of redress, such as the possibility of asserting statutory defect-related rights before the competent courts or out-of-court dispute settlement bodies. 206

The information must be addressed to all consumers who have purchased the product or service in the six months prior to the marketplace provider becoming aware of the illegality. The DSA does not set out formal requirements regarding how the information is communicated. If the provider does not have the contact details of all consumers concerned – for example, because a consumer has deleted his account or if the provider did not collect the contact details when the order was placed – the provider is obliged to publish the relevant information on the marketplace's website according to Art. 32(2) DSA. The information must be published so that affected consumers can easily take note of it. For this purpose, it is likely to be necessary to set up a separate section for product warnings and to add a link to it at appropriate places typically visited by users of the marketplace. The DSA does not specify how long the information on products and services identified as illegal must be kept on the website. 207

Despite multiple demands for such provisions during the legislative process, **Art. 32 DSA does not provide for liability of online marketplaces for illegal products or services offered by third-party traders**, nor does it regulate specific legal protection mechanisms for affected consumers.[152] The right to information is only intended to make consumers aware that they were provided an illegal product or service and to give help- 208

[152] Busch/Mak EuCML 2021, 109 (110 et seq.).

ful information so as to enable them to exercise their rights *vis-à-vis* the relevant trader. In practice, some uncertainty remains around how providers are supposed to handle unclear cases where the illegality of a product or service cannot be determined by the marketplace provider.

G. Obligations for very large online platforms and online search engines (Art. 33–43 DSA)

209 Section 5 imposes the strictest level of due diligence obligations applicable to very large online platforms and very large online search engines (**'very large services'**). Due to their reach, very large services have a significant impact on the accessibility and dissemination of information, in facilitating public debate and enabling economic transactions in the internal market (rec. 75 sent. 1 and 2 DSA). The strong network effects and economies of scale in intermediary services have led to technology-based oligopolies, where a large proportion of users are concentrated on a few platforms, which thereby gain systemic importance. Today, such platforms are the arena for political debate and an important forum for social and societal discussion.[153] At the same time, the size of the platforms gives rise to new types of risks, such as the viral spread of (illegal) content or the phenomenon of echo chambers (rec. 76 DSA). The specific obligations in Art. 33–43 DSA are linked to this particular **social and economic importance** of very large services.[154] In essence, these are regulatory measures (rec. 75 sent. 3 DSA) based on fundamental rights considerations.[155]

210 On 25.4.2023, the Commission designated the social networks Facebook, Instagram, Twitter, LinkedIn, Snapchat, TikTok, Pinterest; online marketplaces Alibaba, Amazon, Zalando, Apple AppStore, Google Play, Booking.com; the video-sharing platform YouTube, as well as Wikipedia, Google Maps and Google Shopping as very large online platforms and Google Search and Bing as very large online search engines. Both Amazon and Zalando have challenged their designation as very large services before the General Court of the EU.[156] On 20.12.2023, the Commission designated the adult entertainment sites Pornhub, XVideos and Stripchat as very large online platforms. All three have challenged their designation before the General Court of the EU.[157] On 26.4.2024, the Commission designated the online marketplace Shein as a very large online platform. On 31.5.2024, the online marketplace Temu was designated as a very large online platform as well.

211 Art. 92 DSA provided for the early applicability of the entire due diligence obligations of the DSA, including Section 5, to very large services. Deviating from the 15-month transition period under Art. 93(2) DSA, the DSA's obligations applied to very large services four months after their designation by the Commission. For the first batch of services designated on 25.4.2023, the obligations of the DSA therefore needed to be implemented by 25.8.2023. With the general application of the DSA since 17.2.2024, this provision is now obsolete.

[153] European Commission, 'Impact Assessment', SWD(2020) 348 final, Part 2, p. 62 speaks of 'de facto public spaces'.

[154] Cf. Mantelero, 'Fundamental rights impact assessments in the DSA'.

[155] Spindler GRUR 2021, 653 (658).

[156] See GC cases T-348/23 (Zalando v Commission) and T-367/23 (Amazon Services Europe v Commission).

[157] See GC cases T-134/24 (Technius Ltd. v Commission), T-138/24 (Aylo Freesites Ltd. v Commission) and T-139/24 (WebGroup Czech Republic v Commission).

I. Very large online platforms and very large online search engines (Art. 33 DSA)

Art. 33 DSA contains the **definition of a very large service** and the related procedural rules and calculation methods. An online platform or online search engine is subject to Section 5 if it both exceeds the threshold for very large services of 45 million users and is designated as a very large service by a Commission's decision. 212

1. Threshold for very large services

According to Art. 33(1) DSA, a service is considered to be very large if it has an **average monthly number of at least 45 million active users in the Union**. This corresponds to approximately 10 % of the population of the EU Member States, which totals 447 million people (rec. 76 sent. 3 DSA). Should the number of inhabitants change significantly, the Commission must adjust the threshold to 10 % of the then-current population by a delegated act according to Art. 33(2) DSA.[158] 213

The threshold value was set in the legislative process in order to cover those services which, according to the experts and stakeholders, present the highest risks and have a pan-European relevance.[159] The figure of 10 % of the EU population that has be active on the platform each month to allow the designation as a very large service has been **criticised** as being too undifferentiated and too high. Social and political discussions are often still segregated along national and language borders so that the discourse-steering effect of online platforms can start well before this figure has been reached, especially in smaller Member States or sub-groups of the population.[160] 214

The definition of a very large service in the DSA **differs from the definition of a gatekeeper under the Digital Markets Act** (DMA). Designation as a gatekeeper under the DMA (cf. Art. 3 DMA) is based on a combination of economic relevance in terms of turnover or market capitalisation as well as number of end users. By contrast, under the DSA, only the number of users is relevant. Both the DSA and the DMA use the threshold of 45 million monthly active users. However, in the DSA, this includes both private and commercial users, while the DMA counts only private users and additionally requires a minimum of 10,000 commercial users.[161] The most significant difference between the two definitions is the **different legal effect of the threshold values**: under the DSA, the number of users is a necessary criterion and once the threshold is passed, the Commission must designate the service as a very large service, whereas, under the DMA, exceeding the threshold only gives rise to a presumption of the service's important role. Consequently, under the DMA, platforms with lower user numbers can still be designated as gatekeepers and platforms with higher user numbers may not be considered gatekeepers despite meeting all the thresholds.[162] 215

2. Calculating the number of users

The relevant number of users for the DSA is the **number of active recipients of the platform or search engine per month in the Union**, calculated as a running average over six months. A 'recipient' is defined in Art. 3(b) DSA as 'any natural or legal person who uses an intermediary service'. Art. 33 DSA does not contain any information on the 216

---

[158] This would also apply when a Member State enters or leaves the Union.
[159] European Commission, 'Impact Assessment', SWD(2020) 348 final, Part 1, p. 45.
[160] Eifert et al. CMLR 2021, 987 (997 et seq.); Gerpott CR 2022, 516 (519).
[161] Cf. the definition of 'end user' in Art. 2 no. 20 DMA.
[162] For a critical view on this approach, see Eifert et al. CMLR 2021, 987 (997 et seq.).

methodology to be used to determine the average monthly number of recipients. However, some indications can be found in rec. 76 and 77 DSA:

- All recipients who have used the service at least once during the month by **calling up information or providing information themselves** (rec. 77(1) sent. 2 DSA) are taken into account. Simply calling up the website is sufficient. It is not required that the user has interacted with the platform's content: the user does not have to click on, comment on or share content (rec. 77(2) sent. 1 DSA).
- The number of recipients is **independent of the number of registered users** of the service (rec. 77(2) sent. 2 DSA).
- The number of recipients refers to the **number of individual recipients (unique visitors)**, not the number of times the website is accessed (rec. 77(2) sent. 4 DSA). A person who visits the website several times is therefore only counted once. If a person accesses a service via two different interfaces, such as the website and an app, he is counted as only one recipient (rec. 77(2) sent. 5 DSA). However, providers are not required to implement online tracking to uniquely identify users across interfaces or multiple site visits (rec. 77(2) sent. 7 DSA) and will generally be prohibited to do so without the user's consent by data protection laws.[163]
- Automated or technically induced calls to the website, for example by bots, scrapers or crawlers, or in the context of framing, or embedded like buttons, should not be counted (rec. 77(2) sent. 6 and 8 DSA).

217 Rec. 77 DSA thus describes the number of **'monthly unique visitors'**, which, in order to avoid fluctuations, is to be calculated according to rec. 76 sent. 3 DSA as a **running average of the past six months**. Only those users who use the service from within the Union are relevant.

218 Art. 33(3) DSA gives the Commission the right to supplement the calculation methodology by delegated acts in order to **respond to technological changes and market developments**. This does not constitute a general power to establish a methodology for determining the number of users. The Commission may only react to a changed situation, such as a new way of interacting with services, by adapting the rules (rec. 77(2) sent. 9 DSA). On 1.2.2023, the Commission published guidance on the identification and counting of active recipients of a service, which mostly mirrors the wording of the DSA and provides generic explanations without binding effect.[164]

3. Designation as a very large service

219 If a service exceeds the threshold of 45 million recipients, it will be **designated as a very large service by a decision of the Commission** according to Art. 33(4) DSA. This is generally done on the basis of the number of recipients reported by the service according to Art. 24(2) and (3) DSA. Prior to the designation, the competent Digital Services Coordinator shall be consulted, but not the service provider concerned, unless the Commission bases its decision on data other than the user numbers reported by the provider. In making the designation, the Commission has **no discretion** and must base its decision solely on the number of recipients. If the number of service recipients falls below

[163] From the provider's point of view, this leads to an artificially increased number of users. Wikipedia has tried to minimise this effect by dividing the number of site visits by the conversion factor of 2.4 to reflect the average number of devices per person, cf. <https://foundation.wikimedia.org/wiki/Legal:EU_DSA_Userbase_Statistics> (last accessed: 23.5.2024).

[164] Cf. <https://digital-strategy.ec.europa.eu/en/library/dsa-guidance-requirement-publish-user-numbers> (last accessed: 23.5.2024).

the relevant threshold for an uninterrupted period of one year, the designation must be terminated according to Art. 33(5) DSA.

The designation decision has a **constitutive effect**. The legal consequences, in particular the due diligence obligations under Section 5 of the DSA, take effect four months after notification of the decision to the provider according to Art. 33(6) subpara. 2 sent. 2 DSA. The service may bring an action for annulment of the designation decision before the General Court of the EU (→ Ch. 5 mn. 95).[165] According to Art. 278 TFEU, the action for annulment does not suspend the designation. **220**

In addition to the obligations under the DSA, designation as a very large service has **legal consequences outside the DSA**. For example, the European Media Freedom Act and the Regulation (EU) 2024/900 on the transparency and targeting of political advertising provide for special obligations of very large services, such as faster processing of complaints.[166] **221**

4. Extension to online search engines

Art. 33 et seqq. DSA also **apply to very large online search engines**. The term 'online search engine' is defined in Art. 3(j) DSA and means a service that allows users to input queries in order to perform searches of websites and to have results displayed.[167] The service must, in principle, allow users to search all websites or all websites in a particular language. Therefore, the search function on a specific website is not considered a search engine within the meaning of the DSA. The term 'users' includes all visitors to the search engine but not crawlers or the owners of the indexed web pages (rec. 77(2) sent. 3 DSA). As of 25.4.2023, Google Search and Bing have been designated as very large search engines by the Commission. **222**

Following the designation as a very large service, providers of search engines are bound by the obligations of Section 5, which are explicitly addressed only to very large online platforms. Since online search engines are not covered by the definition of an online platform, Art. 19–32 DSA do not apply.[168] **223**

II. Risk assessment (Art. 34 DSA)

Art. 34 DSA is the **focal point of the due diligence obligations for very large services** and contains an obligation to **assess the systemic risks** arising from the design, functioning and use of the online platform or search engine. Providers of very large services are thus obliged to deal with the economic and social impact of their service and to bring these negative externalities into a fair balance with their growth and profit ambitions. **224**

---

[165] See GC cases T-348/23 (Zalando v Commission), T-367/23 (Amazon Services Europe v Commission), T-134/24 (Technius Ltd. v Commission), T-138/24 (Aylo Freesites Ltd. v Commission) and T-139/24 (WebGroup Czech Republic v Commission).

[166] Cf. Art. 18 of Regulation (EU) 2024/1083 of the European Parliament and of the Council establishing a common framework for media services in the internal market (European Media Freedom Act) and Art. 15 of Regulation (EU) 2024/900 of the European Parliament and of the Council on the transparency and targeting of political advertising.

[167] This definition corresponds to Art. 2(5) P2B Regulation.

[168] The applicability of Art. 16–18 DSA depends on whether a search engine is classified as a hosting provider. This decision has to be made on a case-by-case basis, looking at the specific function, cf. ECJ 23.3.2010 – case C-237/08, ECLI:EU:C:2008:389 para. 106 et seq. – Google France v Louis Vuitton and → Ch. 3 mn. 16 et seqq.

1. Nature and scope of risk assessment

225 Very large services must carry out a **risk assessment once a year** according to Art. 34(1) subpara. 2 DSA. They must conduct the first assessment within four months after notification of their designation as a very large service. In addition, the service must conduct a risk assessment if it introduces a new feature that has a critical impact on the systemic risks, such as the introduction of the 'like' button. The DSA identifies **four categories of systemic risks**:

point (a): The **dissemination of illegal content** through the service, such as child sexual abuse material and other criminal content, or the distribution of counterfeit goods. This category also includes the risk of systematic infringement of copyright or other intellectual property rights.[169] In this context, the provider may not rely on the argument that the dissemination of illegal content is prohibited by the T&Cs (rec. 80 sent. 4 DSA). Very large platforms need to consider that their service may be misused by users. The provider must also take into account that illegal content can spread particularly quickly on very large platforms due to the viral effect (rec. 80 sent. 3 DSA).

point (b): Negative **impacts on fundamental rights**, in particular human dignity, personal rights, freedom of expression and the media, the right to non-discrimination and consumer protection. This risk category reflects the increasing impact of online platforms on the exercise of fundamental rights in the digital age as platforms are increasingly considered to be public spaces.[170] As a result, freedom of expression may be restricted if a user is prevented from posting certain content on a very large online platform, since, without dissemination via the platform, the user cannot reach an audience and is effectively silenced (cf. rec. 81 sent. 2 DSA).

In addition, rec. 81 DSA emphasises the **rights of children**. Very large services should consider whether minors understand how the service works, for example that users 'pay' with their personal data. Specific risks may also arise where minors have access to content that may impair their physical, mental, or moral development (rec. 81 sent. 3 DSA). In addition, providers must assess whether their service is appropriate for use by minors. In doing so, consideration must be given to whether the design of the online interface intentionally or unintentionally exploits the weaknesses or inexperience of minors, for example through a design or technical feature that causes addictive behaviour (rec. 81 sent. 4 DSA). The significant expansion of the scope of risk assessment in point (b) compared to the original draft of the DSA can be attributed, at least in part, to the speech of Facebook whistleblower Frances Haugen before the European Parliament.[171] In contrast to the general duty to protect minors in Art. 28 DSA (→ mn. 184), the obligation to assess the systemic risk for minors applies to all very large services, regardless of whether the service is targeted at minors. Simply due to their reach, it can be assumed that the service is actually used by minors.

In essence, Art. 34(1)(b) DSA establishes a mandatory **'human rights impact assessment'** for very large services.[172] This is similar to the data protection

[169] Peukert et al. IIC 2022, 358 (369).

[170] Cf. for a view from German constitutional law BVerfG 22.5.2019 – 1 BvQ 42/19, NJW 2019, 1935; BGH 29.7.2021 – III ZR 179/20, NJW 2021, 3179 para. 55 et seq.

[171] Gerpott CR 2022, 516 (522).

[172] Mantelero, 'Fundamental rights impact assessments in the DSA'.

impact assessment according to Art. 35 GDPR but with a much broader scope.[173] Some services have already used human rights impact assessments as a tool in the past.[174] So far, however, there are no uniform standards or methodologies.[175] The special feature of the human rights impact assessment under the DSA is that very large services are bound by the **fundamental rights of the EU Charter of Fundamental Rights**, regardless of where they are located.

point (c): Negative **impact on democratic processes**, such as civic discourse, elections and voting, and public security. This includes, for example, the dissemination of fake news in the context of elections as possibly lawful but socially harmful content.[176] 'Public security' is to be interpreted in the sense of Union law and not in the sense of national (criminal or police) law (on the term → mn. 235).

point (d): Negative **effects on individual or public health**, in particular in the form of gender-based violence and serious negative consequences to a person's physical and mental well-being. Risks may arise from both the design of the service and the content disseminated. Services that stimulate addictive behaviour in users put their health at risk: the recommendation algorithms of social networks, for example, are known to affect the mental health of minors.[177] The coordinated spread of disinformation may also endanger public health, as in the case of fake news about vaccinations.[178]

In its risk assessment, the provider must take into account the **probability and the** 226 **severity of the potential negative impact of the service** (rec. 79 sent. 5 DSA). The severity of a risk is determined by the number of people affected, the intensity of impairment and the reversibility of the damage (rec. 79 sent. 6 DSA). Relevant risks may also occur limited to certain regions or linguistic areas (rec. 84 sent. 6 DSA). As an example, on 30.8.2023, the Commission published a study applying the risk management framework of the DSA on Russian disinformation campaigns.[179]

2. Subject of risk assessment

According to Art. 34(2) DSA, risk assessments must refer in particular to **algorithmic** 227 **systems and the collection and use of data**. Recommender systems and other algorithms used, content moderation systems, the service's T&Cs, advertising and profiling technologies, as well as the processing of personal data are therefore all within the scope

[173] Eifert et al. CMLR 2021, 987 (1022); Schmidt/Grewe MMR 2021, 279 (281).

[174] See Business for Social Responsibility, 'Human Rights Impact Assessment: Meta's Expansion of End-to-End Encryption' (2022) <https://www.bsr.org/reports/bsr-meta-human-rights-impact-assessment-e2ee-report.pdf> (last accessed: 23.5.2024).

[175] Allen/Stockhem, 'Due Diligence in Content Moderation'.

[176] The notion of 'legal but harmful content' is controversial from a fundamental rights perspective because content which is not illegal may, in principle, be freely expressed and disseminated; cf. Berberich/Seip GRUR-Prax 2021, 4 (6); Kuclar Stiković EU Law Working Papers No. 85, 1 (47 et seq.); Turillazzi et al., 'The Digital Services Act: an analysis of its ethical, legal, and social implications', p. 10. However, the line may be difficult to draw in some cases, as, for example, in the textbook case of 'shouting fire in a crowded theatre'.

[177] Wells/Horwitz/Seetharaman, 'Facebook Knows Instagram Is Toxic for Teen Girls, Company Documents Show'.

[178] Rec. 83 sent. 2 DSA; Schechner/Horwitz/Glazer, 'How Facebook Hobbled Mark Zuckerberg's Bid to Get America Vaccinated'.

[179] European Commission, 'Digital Services Act: Application of the Risk Management Framework to Russian disinformation campaigns'.

of the risk assessment required by the DSA. In addition, the provider must assess whether its technical and human resources are sufficient to enforce the T&Cs (rec. 84 sent. 2 DSA).

228 Art. 34(2) subpara. 2 DSA requires providers to take into account the **misuse of their service**, for example by bots and fake accounts, and for the dissemination of misleading or deceptive content (rec. 84 sent. 4 DSA). Very large services must also consider that the dissemination of disinformation is often based on intentional and coordinated actions in systematic violation of the service's T&Cs (rec. 84 sent. 7 DSA). Rec. 84 sent. 3 DSA speaks in this context of content 'which is not illegal, but contributes to the systemic risks identified in this Regulation'.

3. No publication of risk assessment

229 Art. 34 DSA includes **no obligation to publish the risk assessment**. However, providers must keep the relevant documents, including preparatory data and the data on which the assessment is based, for at least three years in order to enable monitoring of the obligations by the authorities (Art. 34(3) DSA and rec. 85 DSA). In addition, a report containing the main results of the risk assessment must be made available on the website of the service as part of the transparency obligations according to Art. 42(4) DSA (→ mn. 266). The Commission and the competent Digital Services Coordinator may request the complete risk assessment at any time.

III. Mitigation of risks (Art. 35 DSA)

230 Based on the risk assessment, very large services are obliged under Art. 35 DSA to take **measures to mitigate the identified risks**. This is intended to make providers take **preventive measures** to stop or limit the negative effects of their services on society.[180] The obligation must be proportionate for the provider in the individual case and should not cause unnecessary restrictions on the use of the service. In particular, it may not unduly restrict the users' freedom of expression (rec. 86 sent. 3 and 4 DSA). To determine the appropriate measures, very large services should base their decisions on the best available information and scientific evidence and, where possible and appropriate, on discussions with representatives of users, civil society organisations or affected parties (rec. 90 DSA). However, there is no formal right of participation for people impacted by the service.[181]

1. Risk mitigation measures

231 The DSA lists 11 measures that providers can take to minimise specific risks.

point (a): Adapting the **design and functioning of the service**, for example by implementing changes to the app or website.
point (b): Adapting the **T&Cs** or the procedures for enforcing the T&Cs.
point (c): Adapting the **internal content moderation** procedures, for example by using more or better qualified staff or automated tools. These measures may affect both the quality and the speed of the handling of notices (rec. 87 sent. 4 DSA). In particular, with regard to illegal hate speech, rec. 87 sent. 5 of the DSA refers to a benchmark for removing reported content within less than

[180] Kuhlmann/Trute GSZ 2022, 115 (120).
[181] Spindler GRUR 2021, 653 (658 et seq.).

24 hours.[182] Providers should ensure that they can meet these deadlines. However, depending on the type of content reported, longer or shorter timelines may be required (rec. 87 sent. 7 DSA). Rapid processing of reports may be needed, for example, with regard to the illegal dissemination of intimate recordings ('revenge porn'), depictions of violence or abuse, and technically manipulated images, sounds or videos ('deepfakes') (rec. 87 sent. 6 DSA).

point (d): Adapting **recommender systems** or other algorithmic systems that affect the user experience. This should take into account possible negative effects of personalised recommendations, such as the impairment of users' mental health or the reinforcement of echo chambers. If necessary, the criteria used for personalisation must be adapted or limited (rec. 88 sent. 2 DSA). In particular, providers should take measures to avoid or minimise algorithmically induced bias and discrimination (rec. 94 sent. 1 DSA). Providers can also add reliable sources of information next to controversial content. This can include fact-checking by journalists or information from official sources.[183]

point (e): Adapting the **display of advertisements**, for example by not allowing certain types of content to be monetised by users, in order to reduce the incentive for its dissemination (rec. 88 sent. 4 DSA). Alternatively, it may also be appropriate to allow only verified advertising or advertising that is neither contextual nor based on profiling alongside such content.

point (f): Reinforcing the **identification of systemic risks** and the monitoring of risk mitigation measures by conducting more frequent or targeted risk assessments, particularly when introducing new functions (rec. 88 sent. 5 DSA).

point (g): Increasing the implementation of decisions by out-of-court dispute settlement bodies under Art. 21 DSA (→ mn. 120) or **cooperation with trusted flaggers** under Art. 22 DSA (→ mn. 138).

point (h): Participating in drafting and implementing relevant codes of conduct and other **self-regulatory measures** (→ mn. 274).

point (i): Taking measures to **raise user awareness of systemic risks**, in particular as a means of countering disinformation campaigns (rec. 88 sent. 7 DSA). This may include advertising campaigns, whether online or offline, highlighting the risks of disinformation and enabling users to fact-check information and find reliable sources.

point (j): Taking specific **measures to protect minors**, for example by ensuring that minors can report illegal content using the notice and action mechanism (rec. 89 DSA). Depending on the nature of the service and the content distributed, means of age verification and parental control of the use of the service may also be appropriate measures to prevent minors from accessing content harmful to their development (rec. 89 sent. 3 DSA).

point (k): **Labelling deepfakes** which would falsely appear to users to be authentic or truthful. The European Parliament had originally called for a general obligation to label deepfakes.[184] However, labelling has only been included as

---

[182] Cf. European Commission, 'Code of Conduct on countering illegal hate speech online' (30.6.2016) <https://ec.europa.eu/newsroom/just/document.cfm?doc_id=42985> (last accessed: 23.5.2024). First, Facebook, Microsoft, Twitter and YouTube joined the Code of Conduct, followed by Instagram, Snapchat, Dailymotion, TikTok, LinkedIn, Rakuten Viber and Twitch.

[183] Cf. LG München I 10.2.2021 – 37 O 15720/20, MMR 2021, 431 – Google Knowledge Panels.

[184] Art. 30a DSA (Draft) in the Negotiating Mandate of the European Parliament, 'Amendments on the proposal for a DSA' (20.1.2022), P9_TA(2022)0014, Amendment 339.

one of the possible measures to mitigate risks such as fake news.[185] A separate labelling obligation for deepfakes is included in the AI Act, but this obligation is directed at users rather than online platforms.[186]

232 Providers may choose risk mitigation measures from this broad catalogue or develop other appropriate measures. In this respect, the reaction to systemic risks is largely **at the discretion of the individual provider**, who usually has no interest in fundamentally changing the functional logic and business model of his service.[187] In the DSA, the European legislator opted for this approach of **enforced self-regulation** instead of comprehensive obligations to disclose algorithms or liability claims by users for algorithmically caused damage.[188] This should also be seen in light of the Commission's separate proposal on liability for algorithms, published in September 2022.[189]

2. Best practices and guidelines (para. 2 and 3)

233 According to Art. 35(2) DSA, the European Board for Digital Services (EBDS) gathers data on the typical systemic risks identified by very large services or by the EBDS itself and publishes its findings in an annual report, indicating proven mitigation measures ('best practices'). In addition, the Commission may, after public consultation, issue guidelines on best practices in relation to specific risks (Art. 35(3) DSA). In April 2024, in light of the elections to the European Parliament held in June 2024, the Commission adopted guidelines regarding the mitigation of systemic risks for electoral processes.[190]

IV. Crisis response mechanism (Art. 36 DSA)

234 Against the background of the war in Ukraine and the danger of the manipulative use of fake news, which can spread rapidly and make an effective state response to the crisis more difficult, a **crisis response mechanism** was added to Art. 36 DSA in the trilogue.[191] In the original Commission proposal this was intended as a voluntary cooperation model.[192] Despite the extensive wording of Art. 36 DSA, the obligatory mechanism still has **rather limited legal effect**. Ultimately, the crisis response mechanism is a specific risk assessment and mitigation obligation of very large services.[193] In practice, public and political pressure in crisis situations are likely to have a much greater impact than Art. 36 DSA.

235 A **crisis, as defined in Art. 36(2) DSA**, is the occurrence of extraordinary circumstances leading to a serious threat to public security or public health in the Union or in significant parts of the Union. Public security within the meaning of Union law is threat-

185 Gerpott CR 2022, 516 (522 et seq.).

186 Cf. Art. 50(4) of Regulation of the European Parliament and of the Council laying down harmonised rules on artificial intelligence (Artificial Intelligence Act).

187 Kuhlmann/Trute GSZ 2022, 115 (120 et seq.).

188 Gerpott CR 2022, 516 (521).

189 European Commission, 'Proposal for a Directive of the European Parliament and of the Council on the liability for defective products' (28.9.2022), COM(2022) 495 final and 'Proposal for a Directive of the European Parliament and of the Council on adapting non-contractual civil liability rules to artificial intelligence' (28.9.2022), COM(2022) 496 final.

190 European Commission, 'Guidelines for providers of Very Large Online Platforms and Very Large Search Engines on the mitigation of systemic risk for electoral processes pursuant to the Digital Services Act'.

191 Council, 'DSA: Council gives final approval to protect users' rights online'.

192 European Commission, 'Impact Assessment', SWD(2020) 348 final, Part 1, p. 60.

193 Wilman, 'The Digital Services Act (DSA) – An Overview', p. 14.

ened if the internal or external security of a state is endangered, for example in the event of armed conflict, riots or terrorist acts.[194] A threat can also arise from natural disasters, such as earthquakes or hurricanes. Pandemics and other serious cross-border health threats[195] are to be covered by the term 'public health' (rec. 91 sent. 3 DSA). According to the wording of Art. 36(2) DSA, the Union must be affected as a whole or at least in significant parts. A threat limited to a single Member State or region is therefore not sufficient to trigger a crisis in the sense of Art. 36 DSA.

In the event of a crisis, the Commission may, upon a recommendation of the EBDS, adopt a **decision requiring one or more very large services to respond to the crisis**. Art. 36(1) DSA lists the following as possible responses to a crisis: 236

- assess whether and how the service contributes to the crisis;
- identify and apply appropriate and effective measures to prevent or limit the identified risks, in particular through measures from the catalogue of risk mitigation measures in Art. 35 DSA (→ mn. 231);
- report to the Commission which risks have been identified and which measures have been taken.

The Commission may request one or more of these responses from providers of very large services. However, according to Art. 36(5) DSA, the Commission has no right to impose specific risk mitigation measures. It is **up to the provider to decide whether and which measures the service implements**. If the Commission considers the measures chosen to be insufficient, it may request the provider to reconsider them as set out in Art. 36(7) subpara. 2 DSA. However, Art. 36 DSA does not include any means that force providers to implement specific measures.[196] In this respect, Art. 36 DSA is only a specific case of the general duty to assess and mitigate risks which follows a self-regulatory approach. 237

The Commission's decision is initially valid for a **maximum of three months** ('sunset clause') pursuant to Art. 36(3)(c) DSA. Art. 36(8)(b) DSA provides for the possibility of extending the decision for a further maximum of three months. Since the wording only refers to an extension of the initial period, it is unclear whether a repeated extension is permissible. A clear argument against the possibility of repeated extensions is the fact that Art. 36(9) DSA, which declares certain parts of Art. 36 DSA applicable to the extension, does not include a reference to the right of the Commission to extend the term according to Art. 36(8)(b) DSA. 238

V. Independent audit (Art. 37 DSA)

Art. 37 DSA obliges very large services to undergo an **annual audit by an independent body** to verify compliance with the due diligence obligations and self-regulatory 239

[194] Rec. 91 sent. 3 DSA; cf. ECJ 23.11.2010 – case C-145/09, ECLI:EU:C:2010:708 para. 43 et seq. – Baden-Württemberg v Tsakouridis; ECJ 2.5.2018 – case C-331/16, ECLI:EU:C:2018:296 para. 42 – K. v Staatssecretaris van Veilingheid en Justitie. Slightly different is the understanding in ECJ 5.4.2022 – case C-140/20, ECLI:EU:C:2022:258 para. 62 – Commissioner of An Garda Síochána; ECJ 20.9.2022 – case C-793/19, ECLI:EU:C:2022:702 para. 93 et seq. – Bundesrepublik Deutschland v SpaceNet, where the ECJ differentiates between the concepts of 'national' and 'public' security.

[195] Cf. Art. 168(1) TFEU and the definitions of the World Health Organization, 'International Health Regulations' (2005) <https://apps.who.int/iris/rest/bitstreams/1031116/retrieve> (last accessed: 23.5.2024).

[196] Wilman, 'The Digital Services Act (DSA) – An Overview', p. 14.

measures. This independent audit complements the risk assessment and mitigation carried out by the provider.

240 Auditors must have the necessary expertise and technical competence and meet **strict requirements on independence** according to Art. 37(3) DSA. The auditor may not have any connection with the service provider and, in particular, may not provide or have provided any services other than the audit for the very large service or any company connected to the service in the year preceding and following the audit. This could discourage major accounting and consulting firms from acting as auditors.[197] In addition, the DSA provides for a **rotation of auditors**. Art. 37(3)(a)(ii) DSA requires that the auditor has 'not provided auditing services pursuant to this Article [for the service in question] during a period longer than 10 consecutive years'. This provision was inserted in the trilogue without having had any predecessor in the negotiation mandates of the European Parliament or the Council. The wording of the provisions is not entirely consistent in the different language versions of the DSA. According to the wording of the German,[198] French,[199] Spanish[200] and Italian[201] versions, auditors would be allowed to act only once for a very large service and would have to observe a standstill period of ten years before performing the next audit of the same service. However, the English language version allows for a different understanding, namely that the auditor is allowed to perform the audit for ten consecutive years, at the end of which the service is required to employ a different auditor. This interpretation is supported by the fact that it is in line with the rotation principle for auditors set out in Art. 17(1) subpara. 2 of the Audit Regulation[202].

241 The provider must **grant the auditor full access**, including access to data and algorithms, and must answer his questions (rec. 92 sent. 2 DSA). Since the auditor must maintain confidentiality, the provider cannot invoke the protection of business secrets or intellectual property rights against the requests of the auditor (rec. 92 sent. 6 and 7 DSA). Where appropriate, auditors may also use other sources, such as scientific studies (rec. 92 sent. 3 DSA).

242 The auditor prepares a substantiated audit report, the minimum content of which is listed in Art. 37(4) DSA. The report contains an **audit opinion based on the categories 'positive', 'positive with comments', and 'negative'** with regard to what extent the provider has fulfilled its obligations, in particular whether it has carried out sufficient risk assessment and mitigation. A 'positive with comments' opinion may be issued in the case of findings that do not have a substantial impact on the audit result (rec. 93 sent. 7 DSA). When the audit result is not entirely positive, the auditor must state the operational measures the provider should implement to comply with its obligations. The provider is obliged under Art. 37(6) DSA to review the recommendations, take the necessary measures and report back within one month. If the provider decides against im-

---

[197] However, it is unclear whether the independence requirements are also violated if an affiliate of the auditor provides the non-audit services, cf. Spindler GRUR 2021, 653 (659).

[198] The German version reads: 'während eines Zeitraums von mehr als zehn aufeinanderfolgenden Jahren keine Prüfungsleistungen gemäß diesem Artikel erbracht haben'.

[199] The French version reads: 'elles n'ont pas fourni de services d'audit [...] pendant une période supérieure à dix années consécutives'.

[200] The Spanish version reads: 'no hayan prestado servicios de auditoría [...] durante un período superior a diez años consecutivos'.

[201] The Italian version reads: 'non devono aver fornito servizi di revisione [...] per un periodo superiore a dieci anni consecutivi'.

[202] Regulation (EU) No 537/2014 of the European Parliament and of the Council on specific requirements for the statutory audit of public interest entities.

plementing the recommended measures, the report must include the reasons for this decision and any alternative measures proposed to address the concerns of the auditor.

According to Art. 37(7) DSA, the Commission may adopt rules on the audit through delegated acts. On 20.10.2023, the Commission adopted a Delegated Regulation including **detailed procedural provisions** regarding the performance of audits and a template for the audit report to be used by auditors.[203] The Regulation sets out numerous obligations of the provider to cooperate in the audit and substantiates the criteria to be used when auditing the provider's risk analysis and mitigation measures. **243**

The audit report shall be transmitted to the Commission, the competent Digital Services Coordinator and the EBDS (rec. 93 sent. 3 DSA). Art. 42(4)(c) and (d) DSA includes an **obligation to publish audit reports**. However, according to Art. 42(5) DSA, the provider may remove any confidential information from the report prior to publication. This also applies to information that could endanger the security of the service or the public safety of users. In such cases, in addition to the full report, a justification as to why the provider has removed the information must be sent to the authorities. **244**

VI. Recommender systems (Art. 38 DSA)

Because of the enormous impact of recommender systems on the visibility and dissemination of content on very large online platforms, Art. 38 DSA contains an **obligation to offer a recommender system that is not based on profiling with personal data**. The obligation for very large online platforms consequently goes beyond the general due diligence obligation in Art. 27 DSA (→ mn. 178). To comply with the additional obligation, social networks must offer a view of the timeline that is not personalised according to the user's preferences. This option must be directly accessible from the online interface (rec. 94 sent. 3 DSA). As this obligation applies to 'each of their recommender systems', search and filter functions, for example, of very large online marketplaces, are also covered. **245**

However, contrary to what was requested in the negotiations, there is no right to a 'chronological timeline'.[204] The DSA does not specify the alternative recommender system which has to be provided and therefore allows platforms to prioritise content by relevance rather than by date. The provider is simply obliged to provide an alternative to personalised recommendations. This means that Art. 38 DSA can be complied with either by offering only one recommender system that is not based on profiling or by giving users the possibility to switch from personalised recommendations to any other non-personalised recommender system. The proposal to require non-personalised ranking as the default was rejected during the negotiations.[205] Providers are therefore allowed to use **personalised recommender systems as the default**. It remains to be seen whether users will actually select the option to switch to an alternative recommender system.[206] **246**

According to the wording of Art. 38 DSA, the obligation to offer an alternative recommender system **also applies to very large online search engines**. The extension to **247**

203 Commission Delegated Regulation (EU) 2024/436 supplementing Regulation (EU) 2022/2065 of the European Parliament and of the Council, by laying down rules on the performance of audits for very large online platforms and very large online search engines.

204 Cf. Art. 29(2a) DSA (Draft) according to European Parliament, 'Opinion of the Committee on Civil Liberties, Justice and Home Affairs (LIBE)' (28.7.2021), LIBE_AD(2021)692898, Amendment 201.

205 Cf. European Parliament, 'Draft Amendments 1302-1591 in the Internal Market and Consumer Protection Committee (IMCO)' (8.7.2021), IMCO_AM(2021)695162, Amendment 1518.

206 Gerpott CR 2022, 516 (521 et seq.); Helberger et al., 'Regulation of news recommenders in the Digital Services Act: empowering David against the Very Large Online Goliath'.

online search engines leaves some room for controversy. The version of Art. 38 DSA adopted by the European Parliament and the Council only referred to very large online platforms.[207] It was only during the final formal check before publication in the Official Journal that the legal and linguistic services of the European institutions inserted 'and very large online search engines' into the Regulation's wording. Whether this was a proper correction of an obvious editorial mistake is not clear. In the provisional political agreement of the European Parliament and the Council, there was a separate Article on very large search engines which provided that (almost) all provisions for very large online platforms shall also apply to very large online search engines. This general Article was deleted in a corrigendum provided by the European Parliament. Instead, most of the obligations in Section 5 were changed to apply to 'very large online platforms and very large search engines'. However, this change has not been made in Art. 38 DSA.

248 Whether this is an obvious editorial mistake which could only be corrected in one way seems questionable. Although the corresponding rec. 94 sent. 3 DSA also speaks of an obligation of online platforms and online search engines, this conflict between the Article and the recital could have been resolved in two ways. In line with the negotiation mandate of the European Parliament, it would also have been possible to limit the application of Art. 38 DSA to online platforms. This is supported by the wording of Art. 38 DSA which stipulates that the obligation contained therein shall apply in addition to the general transparency obligation according to Art. 27 DSA (→ mn. 178). Art. 27 DSA does not apply to online search engines, as online search engines are not covered by the definition of an online platform. Looking at the negotiation documents, it is therefore not clear whether the corrigendum was intended to correct a mistake made in the provisional political agreement or whether the corrigendum itself was the mistake. The decision of the legal and linguistic services thus overrode the wording voted on in the legislative procedure and has the effect of a de facto extension of the scope of application, even though there was no clear mandate by the legislator. Since the published Article deviates from the wording approved by the European Parliament and the Council, there are good arguments for a (partial) invalidity of Art. 38 DSA.[208]

VII. Repository for online advertising (Art. 39 DSA)

249 Art. 39 DSA obliges the very large services, in addition to the general transparency requirements of Art. 26 DSA (→ mn. 169), to **set up a database of the advertising displayed on the service ('repository')**. The repository is intended to facilitate oversight and enable research into new risks posed by online advertising, such as the use of manipulative techniques and disinformation, which may have a negative impact on social discourse and the political participation of users (rec. 95 sent. 2 DSA).

250 The repository must be accessible and searchable on the service's website according to Art. 39(1) DSA. It must contain all advertisements placed on the platform within the meaning of Art. 3(r) DSA for **at least one year** after the advertisement was last displayed on the service. Art. 39(2) DSA defines **the minimum content of the repository** as the following:

[207] This is consistent in all language versions and not a translation error.

[208] On limits to corrections of the language services after the legislative procedure see Pernice EuZW 2004, 743; cf. on the possibility of corrections in the legislative procedure ECJ 12.12.2006 – case C-380/03, ECLI:EU:C:2006:772 – Germany v Parliament and Council.

point (a): The **content of the advertisement**, for example as text, image or video, as well as the name of the advertised product, service or brand and the subject matter of the advertisement.
point (b) and (c): The **identity of the advertiser**, namely on whose behalf the advertisement was displayed and who paid for the advertisement.
point (d): The time **period** during which the advertisement was displayed.
point (e): If applicable, the criteria according to which advertising was or was not presented to certain user groups (**targeting**), namely the advertisement's target group(s).[209]
point (g): The total number of users in each of the target groups reached by the advertisement, broken down by Member State (**reach**). The provider must ensure that no personal data of users can be accessed in the repository.

The provision of Art. 39(2)(f) DSA contains a substantial extension of the scope of application. In addition to the advertising placed on the service by the provider, **commercial communication by users** of very large online platforms must also be included in the repository if it was marked as commercial content using the function provided for in Art. 26(2) DSA. This obligation was only added in the trilogue and covers **promotional content from influencers**, product placements and brand communication. Such posts by users must, therefore, also be archived and made publicly available. The provider must at least store the content provided by the user and the relevant username. This does not contradict the obligation under Art. 39(1) sent. 2 DSA not to store personal data in the repository. This explicitly refers only to 'personal data of the recipients of the service to whom the advertisement was or could have been presented' – not to the data of the users who themselves placed advertisements or commercial communication on the platform. However, it is unclear whether the information on target group and reach (according to Art. 39(2)(e) and (g) DSA) must also be stored in the case of commercial communications of users. There are good arguments against such an obligation based on the structure of Art. 39 DSA. Point (f) is a sub-item of the enumeration in Art. 39(2) DSA and may therefore be interpreted as an obligation independent of the minimum content for advertisements placed by the provider. Very large services would otherwise have to publish the reach of posts of influencers and companies and their target group(s). Furthermore, it is unclear how to deal with commercial content only made available to a limited group of recipients, for example when posts with commercial content are only visible to friends/followers of an account. The disclosure obligation forces providers to make such content publicly available in the repository. 251

VIII. Data access and research clause (Art. 40 DSA)

For the purposes of regulatory and societal control of the very large services, Art. 40 DSA provides **data access rights for authorities and certain researchers**. The obligation to disclose certain data is intended to reduce the asymmetry of information and thereby provide the basis for an independent evaluation of the positive and negative effects of the very large services, as well as of risk assessment and mitigation carried out by the provider (rec. 96 sent. 1 and 4 DSA). 252

[209] This may lead to the disclosure of highly sensitive competitive information, see Berberich/Seip GRUR-Prax 2021, 4 (6) and GC 27.9.2023 – case T-367/23 R, ECLI:EU:T:2023:589 para. 56 et seqq. – Amazon Services Europe Sàrl v Commission (overturned by ECJ 27.3.2024 – case C-639/23 P(R), ECLI:EU:C:2024:277 – Commission v Amazon Services Europe Sàrl).

1. Data access for authorities (para. 1–3)

253 Art. 40(1) DSA grants the Commission and the competent Digital Services Coordinator[210] the right to inspect the data necessary to monitor compliance with the obligations under the DSA. This includes **access to data and algorithms**. In general, according to Art. 40(3) DSA, information on the design, logic, functioning, accuracy, and testing of algorithmic systems, such as recommender and advertising systems, is considered to be sufficient for supervisory purposes. However, according to the wording of rec. 96 sent. 2 DSA, the authorities can also demand **access to the source code and the training data** used for artificial intelligence systems if necessary. In addition, upon request, providers must disclose statistical and individual case-related data on content moderation and internal complaint-handling systems (rec. 96 sent. 2 DSA). The right of access to data according to Art. 40 DSA does not apply to the data of individual users (rec. 96 sent. 3 DSA). In order to access this data, authorities must issue an information order according to Art. 10 DSA (→ Ch. 3 mn. 110).

2. Data access for vetted researchers (para. 4–11)

254 Art. 40(4) DSA provides a **data access right to enable researchers to identify and assess systemic risks** according to Art. 34 DSA and effective risk mitigation measures according to Art. 35 DSA.[211] This right is limited in scope by restricting the research subjects as well as the eligible researchers. Data access is granted only to **'vetted researchers'** who meet the criteria in Art. 40(8) DSA, in particular the requirement that they do not pursue commercial interests, guarantee the security and confidentiality of the data and make their research available to the public free of charge (open access) within a reasonable period of time. The researchers must also be affiliated to a privileged research organisation as defined in Art. 2(1) DSM Directive, namely a university or other institution conducting scientific research.[212] For the purposes of the DSA, civil society organisations are also considered to be research organisations (rec. 97 sent. 1 DSA).

255 According to Art. 40(8) DSA, data access requests follow a **three-step process**. First, researchers must submit an application to the Digital Services Coordinator of establishment[213] of the very large service describing their research project.[214] Second, the Digital Services Coordinator may recognise them as vetted researchers for the purposes of this research project following consultations of the Commission and the EBDS. Finally, the Digital Services Coordinator obliges the provider to transmit data within a period to be determined.[215]

---

[210] The Digital Services Coordinator at the establishment of the very large service is, in principle, not competent because the Commission has largely exclusive competence for the supervision of very large services according to Art. 56(2) and (3) DSA. Only in exceptional cases set out in Art. 56(4) DSA can the national Digital Services Coordinator take subsidiary action (→ Ch. 5 mn. 18).

[211] For details see Husovec, 'Will the DSA work?'.

[212] Cf. the comments on the national implementation of the DSM Directive, e.g. in German law § 60d(2) German Act on Copyright and Related Rights (*Urheberrechtsgesetz* – UrhG).

[213] According to Art. 3(n) DSA, this is the Digital Services Coordinator of the Member State where the main establishment of the service is located or where its legal representative (→ mn. 29) resides or is established.

[214] According to Art. 40(9) DSA, the application may also be submitted to the Digital Services Coordinator at the place of establishment of the research institution, who shall forward the application to the Digital Services Coordinator of the establishment of the very large service for a decision. In this case, the decision-making power remains with the Digital Services Coordinator of the establishment of the very large service.

[215] The provider may appeal against the data access request according to Art. 40(5) DSA. This adds a fourth step, because the Digital Services Coordinator has to review the decision and amend the request if

The competence of the national Digital Services Coordinator **contradicts the general rule of competence** in Art. 56(2) DSA. In principle, the supervision of very large services is an exclusive competence of the Commission (→ Ch. 5 mn. 12). Art. 40(8) DSA deviates from this general rule for no apparent reason and assigns a single task to the national Digital Services Coordinators (cf. rec. 124 sent. 4 DSA). This bears the risk that Digital Services Coordinators in Member States with many very large services will be overloaded with processing applications for research data access. 256

According to Art. 40(8)(e) DSA, the request for data access must be limited to the data necessary for the purposes of the research. In addition, researchers must **protect the rights and interests of the users concerned and of the service**. The provider should anonymise or pseudonymise user data as far as possible (rec. 98 sent. 5 DSA). The provider cannot deny access to data based on their interest in maintaining secrecy or protecting their trade secrets (rec. 97 sent. 3 DSA). In cases where this is an issue, however, access by researchers may be granted under special technical protection measures, for example in secure data rooms (rec. 97 sent. 4 DSA). The DSA does not provide for reimbursement claims by providers for costs incurred in the provision and transmission of data to researchers. 257

3. Data access for other researchers (para. 12)

Art. 40(12) DSA contains a third data access right, which has a **broader scope of application** and also covers non-vetted researchers. Researchers can invoke this right directly with regard to very large services as long as they do not pursue commercial interests, guarantee the security and confidentiality of the data and their research relates to the identification of systemic risks within the meaning of Art. 34 DSA. 258

The data access right in Art. 40(12) DSA is limited to data that is already publicly accessible via the online interface of the service. This includes, for example, the number of views and the **interactions with content on public pages or in public groups**, such as reactions, shares and comments (rec. 98 sent. 2 DSA). The provider should give researchers access to such data in aggregated form and, if possible, in real time and may not prevent researchers from using data gathered (automatically) from the online interface of the service (rec. 98 DSA).[216] 259

4. Common procedural rules (para. 7 and 13)

According to Art. 40(7) DSA, data access by authorities and vetted researchers must be provided **through appropriate technical interfaces**, such as APIs. Art. 40(13) DSA allows the Commission to adopt delegated acts setting out the conditions and procedures for data access in more detail. 260

IX. Compliance function (Art. 41 DSA)

Art. 41 DSA establishes an obligation to have internal compliance procedures to ensure effective implementation of the DSA at company level. 261

---

necessary as set out in Art. 40(6) DSA. In addition, the provider may seek judicial protection before national courts against the decision to impose the obligation to transmit data (→ Ch. 5 mn. 98).

[216] See the summary of research data access in European Commission, 'Status Report: Mechanisms for Researcher Access to Online Platform Data' (5.4.2024) <https://ec.europa.eu/newsroom/dae/redirection/document/104117> (last accessed: 23.5.2024).

1. Internal compliance department (para. 1–4)

262 Very large services are required to establish a compliance department ('function') consisting of at least one **compliance officer**. According to Art. 41(1) and (2) DSA, this compliance officer must be sufficiently qualified, operationally independent and equipped with the necessary resources and powers to monitor the service's compliance with the DSA. The head of the compliance department shall report to the management body of the provider. In this respect, his position is similar to that of an internal data protection officer. If he identifies systemic risks of the service within the meaning of Art. 34 DSA (→ mn. 225), or if the service does not comply with due diligence obligations set out in the DSA, the compliance officer must have direct access to the management body and issue warnings. However, under the DSA, the compliance officer has no authority to issue binding instructions of his own.

2. Obligations for the provider's management body (para. 5–7)

263 The management body of the provider, for example the **board of directors, must address the risk assessment and mitigation strategies**. The management body must review and approve the risks identified and the measures taken to mitigate the risks at least once a year. In doing so, it must devote sufficient time to the matter and actively participate in the decisions required. This requirement aims to prevent management bodies from delegating compliance with the DSA to the operational level to obtain a blanket exemption. Instead, the management level should be held accountable for sufficient oversight, the allocation of resources and critical decision making with regard to the implementation of the DSA.

X. Extended transparency obligations for very large services (Art. 42 DSA)

264 Very large services are obliged to publish the **transparency reports referred to in Art. 15 DSA every six months** (instead of every 12 months) according to Art. 42(1) DSA. The provider must publish the first report no later than six months after being notified of the decision to be designated as a very large service.

265 For very large online platforms – but not for very large online search engines[217] – the **scope of transparency reports is extended** beyond Art. 15 and 24 DSA. Very large online platforms are required to provide additional data on content moderation, in particular the resources and procedures for removal or blocking of content.[218] Art. 42(2) DSA requires information on the number of staff dedicated for content moderation to be shared, broken down by the relevant official language of the Member State, as well as information on the staff's qualifications, language skills and training, and on indicators

[217] The German language version of Art. 42(2) DSA also refers to 'providers of very large online search engines' being obliged to publish the transparency report with an extended scope. However, this is an editorial mistake. This follows from the wording of Art. 42(2)(a) DSA, which relates only to online platforms. Furthermore, only online platforms (and not online search engines) are obliged to submit a transparency report according to Art. 24(1) DSA which could be extended in scope by Art. 42(2) DSA. The English and French language versions refer only to very large online platforms in Art. 42(2) DSA.

[218] European Commission, 'Impact Assessment', SWD(2020) 348 final, Part 1, p. 26.

of the accuracy of automated systems employed (error rates, broken down by language[219]).

266 In connection with the monitoring of the number of recipients of the service according to Art. 24(2) DSA (→ mn. 151), Art. 42(3) DSA obliges very large online platforms and very large online search engines to indicate the average monthly number of recipients in the transparency report, including a breakdown of recipients per Member State.

267 Art. 42(4) DSA provides for a separate **obligation to publish reports in connection with the audit**. The provider must make available on its website the results of its risk assessment and the risk mitigation measures taken, as well as the audit report and, where applicable (as in the case of an audit opinion that is not only 'positive'), the report on the implementation of the auditor's recommendations. If the report contains confidential information, the sensitive parts may be removed before publication in accordance with Art. 42(5) DSA. This also applies to information that could endanger the security of the service or its users or threaten public safety. If a provider redacts information on this basis, it must provide the full report, including the confidential information and the reasons for removing certain information, to the Commission and the competent Digital Services Coordinator.

XI. Supervisory fee (Art. 43 DSA)

268 In order to finance the costs incurred by the Commission in implementing and enforcing the DSA, Art. 43 DSA provides for an **annual supervisory fee to be paid by very large services**. This fee is intended to ensure that the Commission has the necessary resources in terms of staff and expertise to carry out its tasks in connection with the supervision of very large services (rec. 101(1) sent. 1 DSA).

269 The supervisory fee is **not a digital tax** but an external financial contribution to the activities of the Union which, as earmarked revenue, is not paid into the general budget. The amount of the supervisory fee is equal to the expected costs and generally based on the actual costs of the previous year (rec. 101(1) sent. 3 and (2) sent. 2 DSA). According to Art. 43(2) DSA, the costs for the designation and supervision of very large services and the operation of the content moderation database[220] to be created by the Commission according to Art. 24 DSA shall be allocated to the supervisory fee. Costs for coordination with the Member State authorities can also be included, since it can reasonably be assumed that coordination on a European level will mainly be necessary in the case of very large services (rec. 101(2) sent. 1 DSA). In 2023, the Commission calculated the total supervisory fees to be charged to very large services to be 45 million EUR.

270 The amount of the fee for each very large service shall be determined annually by the Commission by means of an implementing act. On 2.3.2023, the Commission published the Delegated Regulation (EU) 2023/1127 on the detailed methodologies and procedures regarding the supervisory fees charged by the Commission on providers of very large platforms and very large online search engines. According to Art. 43(5)(b) DSA,

---

[219] The breakdown in different languages required by Art. 42(2)(c) DSA is likely to be meaningful only for text-based recognition systems. The information is, therefore, not necessary for automated photo and video filters, unless they are based on linguistic features, such as speech recognition.

[220] The inclusion of costs for the building and maintenance of the content moderation database according to Art. 24 DSA is questionable. All – not only very large – online platforms are required to submit their content moderation decisions to the database. Therefore, the very large services are paying for a general task of the Commission rather than for specific costs incurred by the supervision of very large services. This is particularly striking for very large online search engines which are not subject to the obligation in Art. 24 DSA but are still obliged to pay for the implementation.

the costs shall be shared among the very large services, proportionate to numbers of users. However, Art. 43(5)(c) DSA sets the upper limit for the fee at **0.05 % of worldwide annual net profit** of the very large service. The purpose of this cap is to ensure that the fee never exceeds the economic capacity of the provider, for example in the case of very large non-profit services or loss-making providers (rec. 101(2) sent. 5 DSA).

271 According to Art. 51(6) DSA, supervisory fees may also be **levied for smaller services under national law** (rec. 111 sent. 5 DSA). If necessary, this can be done by means of implementing laws at the Member State level (→ Ch. 5 mn. 10).[221]

H. Self-regulation and standardisation (Art. 44–48 DSA)

272 In order to ensure a uniform application of the due diligence obligations of the DSA, Section 6 provides for **self-regulation measures and comparable soft law instruments**. The latter comprise voluntary standards, codes of conduct and protocols as well as Commission guidelines, all of which have in common that they have no direct legal effect. Compliance with this soft law is not necessarily needed for compliance with the DSA – nor does the implementation of the measures provided in soft law automatically mean that the obligations under the DSA have been fulfilled (rec. 102 sent. 3 and rec. 104 sent. 7 DSA).

I. Standards (Art. 44 DSA)

273 Standards within the meaning of Art. 44 DSA are **technical specifications**, for example for interfaces for reporting illegal content, for the interoperability of databases or for the uniform labelling of advertisements placed on digital services. These standards are set by international or European standardisation bodies, in particular the European Committee for Standardisation (CEN) and the European Telecommunications Standards Institute (ETSI).

II. Codes of conduct (Art. 45–47 DSA)

274 Codes of conduct are an **instrument of self-regulation** whereby a group of companies voluntarily submits to certain self-selected rules. These rules, along with possible self-certification, are usually developed with the participation of the authorities responsible for the regulation in question and the relevant stakeholders. The DSA provides such instruments for the management of online advertising and accessibility for persons with disabilities, and for tackling systemic risks. Rec. 106 DSA highlights in particular the revised code of practice on disinformation published in June 2022,[222] which the major online platforms have signed.[223]

275 The codes of conduct should indicate which public interest they pursue, and which role state authorities will play in evaluating their implementation (rec. 103 sent. 2 DSA).

---

[221] For example, Hungary charges supervisory fees from service providers established in Hungary that exceed a minimum net turnover per year.

[222] The Strengthened Code of Practice on Disinformation, 2022, <https://ec.europa.eu/newsroom/dae/redirection/document/87585> (last accessed: 23.5.2024).

[223] European Commission, 'Disinformation: Commission welcomes the new stronger and more comprehensive Code of Practice on disinformation'. X has since withdrawn from the voluntary code of practice.

Art. 45(4) DSA provides for a baseline of public oversight of the implementation of codes of conduct. In particular, the Commission and the Board may publish conclusions on the effectiveness of the code of conduct or encourage reviews in the case of systematic failure to comply. Against this background, the instrument of codes of conduct has been **criticised because it leaves decisions with significant impact on fundamental rights to private actors**, for example how to tackle illegal content.[224]

III. Crisis protocols (Art. 48 DSA)

The crisis protocol provided for in Art. 48 DSA is a **legally non-binding document of the Commission** that supplements the crisis response mechanism under Art. 36 DSA (→ mn. 234) with a purely voluntary procedure. The crisis protocol shall include measures to be taken by very large services in the event of specific types of crises. This document setting out possible crisis reaction measures is made available before the DSA's formal crisis mechanism is activated. This is intended to speed up the practical and technical implementation of the crisis response. According to Art. 48(2) DSA, the crisis protocols may include measures to highlight official information on the crisis and encourage providers to designate points of contact for crisis management. The crisis protocol – like the crisis response mechanism – is primarily aimed at very large services. However, smaller services and civil society organisations may also participate in the drawing up of the crisis protocol.[225] Like the formal crisis mechanism, the application of the crisis protocol is restricted to specific crises and limited in time (rec. 108 sent. 4 DSA). The specific parameters to determine what is considered a crisis and the procedure to activate the crisis protocol shall be clearly set out in the protocol according to Art. 48(4) DSA. 276

IV. Guidelines

The DSA also provides for Commission guidelines on cooperation with trusted flaggers (Art. 22(8) DSA), the prohibition of dark patterns (Art. 25(3) DSA), the protection of minors (Art. 28(4) DSA), the identification of systemic risks (Art. 34(3) DSA) and the online advertising repository (Art. 39(3) DSA). These guidelines are **legally non-binding statements by the Commission**, intended to provide informal guidance to providers on the application of the due diligence obligations under the DSA. 277

224 Allen/Stockhem, 'Due Diligence in Content Moderation'; Cauffman/Goanta European Journal of Risk Regulation 2021, 758 (767 et seqq.).

225 Spindler GRUR 2021, 653 (661).

CHAPTER 5
ENFORCEMENT

Marvin Bartels

Bibliography: Bertuzzi, 'EU Commission set to cut already strained personnel as inflation bites' (Euractiv, 1.7.2022) <https://www.euractiv.com/section/politics/news/eu-commission-set-to-cut-already-strained-personnel-as-inflation-bites> (last accessed: 23.5.2024); Bodoni, 'Europe's Data Law Is Broken, Departing Privacy Chief Warns' (Bloomberg, 25.6.2021) <https://www.bloomberg.com/news/articles/2021-06-25/eu-s-broken-gdpr-needs-fixing-departing-privacy-chief-warns> (last accessed: 23.5.2024); Brave, 'Europe's Governments are failing the GDPR: Brave's 2020 Report on the Enforcement Capacity of Data Protection Authorities' (Brave, April 2020) <https://brave.com/dpa-report-2020> (last accessed: 23.5.2024); Burgess, 'How GDPR Is Failing' (Wired, 23.5.2022) <https://www.wired.com/story/gdpr-2022> (last accessed: 23.5.2024); Cuthbert, Q&A European Union Law, 10th edn, Abingdon 2015; Degenhart, 'Staatsferne der Medienaufsicht: Zum Entwurf eines Zweiten Gesetzes zur Änderung des Jugendschutzgesetzes – Rechtsgutachten, erstellt im Auftrag der Direktorenkonferenz der Landesmedienanstalten' (2020) <https://www.die-medienanstalten.de/fileadmin/user_upload/die_medienanstalten/Ueber_uns/Positionen/20200909_Staatsferne_der_Medienaufsicht.pdf> (last accessed: 23.5.2024); Eifert et al., 'Taming the Giants: The DMA/DSA Package', CMLR 2021, 987; European Commission, 'Sneak Peek: How the Commission will enforce the DSA & DMA – Blog of Commissioner Thierry Breton' (5.7.2022) <https://ec.europa.eu/commission/presscorner/detail/en/STATEMENT_22_4327> (last accessed: 23.5.2024); German Data Protection Authorities, 'Evaluation of the GDPR under Article 97 – Questions to Data Protection Authorities/European Data Protection Board. Answers from the German Supervisory Authorities' (2020) <https://www.edpb.europa.eu/sites/default/files/de_sas_gdpr_art_97questionnaire.pdf > (last accessed: 23.5.2024); Hartley, The Foundations of European Union Law, 8th edn, Oxford 2014; Jaursch, 'The DSA Draft: Ambitious Rules, Weak Enforcement Mechanisms' (Stiftung Neue Verantwortung, 25.5.2021) <https://www.stiftung-nv.de/en/publication/dsa-draft-ambitious-rules-weak-enforcement-mechanisms> (last accessed: 23.5.2024); Keber, 'Plattformverantwortlichkeit in der Krise – Der neue Crisis Response Mechanism im Digital Services Act' (CR-online.de Blog, 5.7.2022) <https://www.cr-online.de/blog/2022/07/05/plattformverantwortlichkeit-in-der-krise-der-neue-crisis-response-mechanism-im-digital-services-act> (last accessed: 23.5.2024); Kühling, 'Rechtsgutachten zur Unabhängigkeit des Koordinators für digitale Dienste nach dem Gesetz über digitale Dienste der Europäischen Union, erstellt im Auftrag des Bundesministeriums für Digitales und Verkehr' (FragDenStaat, 18.10.2022) <https://fragdenstaat.de/anfrage/rechtsgutachten-zum-deutschen-digital-services-coordinator> (last accessed: 23.5.2024); Monti/De Streel, 'Improving EU institutional design to better supervise digital platforms' (Centre on Regulation in Europe, 17.1.2022) <https://cerre.eu/publications/improving-eu-institutional-design> (last accessed: 23.5.2024); Peukert, 'Five Reasons to be Skeptical About the DSA' (Verfassungsblog, 31.8.2021) <https://verfassungsblog.de/power-dsa-dma-04> (last accessed: 23.5.2024); Picht, 'Private Enforcement for the DSA/DGA/DMA Package' (Verfassungsblog, 3.9.2021) <https://verfassungsblog.de/power-dsa-dma-09> (last accessed: 23.5.2024); Raue, 'Plattformnutzungsverträge im Lichte der gesteigerten Grundrechtsbindung marktstarker sozialer Netze', NJW 2022, 209; Raue/Heesen, 'Der Digital Services Act', NJW 2022, 3537; Ryan/Toner, 'Europe's Enforcement Paralysis: ICCL's 2021 Report on the Enforcement Capacity of Data Protection Authorities' (Irish Council for Civil Liberties, 2021) <https://www.iccl.ie/news/2021-gdpr-report> (last accessed: 23.5.2024); Satariano, 'Europe's Privacy Law Hasn't Shown Its Teeth, Frustrating Advocates' (The New York Times, 27.4.2020) <https://www.nytimes.com/2020/04/27/technology/GDPR-privacy-law-europe.html> (last accessed: 23.5.2024); Schmid/Grewe, 'Digital Services Act: Neues „Grundgesetz für Onlinedienste"? – Auswirkungen des Kommissionsentwurfs für die Digitalwirtschaft', MMR 2021, 279; Spindler, 'Der Vorschlag für ein Neues Haftungsregime für Internetprovider – der EU-Digital Services Act. Teil 2: Large and Particularly Large Platforms', GRUR 2021, 653; Statista, 'Budget of the European data protection authorities (DPAs) in 2020' (Statista, 7.7.2022) <https://www.statista.com/statistics/1174554/data-protection-authorities-budget-eu> (last accessed: 23.5.2024); Van Hoboken, 'European Lessons in Self-Experimentation: From the GDPR to European Platform Regulation' (Centre for International Governance Innovation, 20.6.2022) <https://www.cigionline.org/articles/european-lessons-in-self-experimentation-from-the-gdpr-to-european-platform-regulation> (last accessed: 23.5.2024); Vergnolle, 'Enforcement of the DSA and the DMA: What did we learn from the GDPR?' (Verfassungsblog, 3.9.2021) <https://verfassungsblog.de/power-dsa-dma-10> (last accessed: 23.5.2024); Wagner, 'Prävention und Verhaltenssteuerung durch Privatrecht – Anmaßung oder legitime Aufgabe?', AcP 206 (2006), 352.

Chapter 5 Enforcement

A. Introduction

1 The law is only as good as its enforcement. For many observers from politics and civil society, this has been brought home by their experiences with the GDPR. Although the EU has assumed a global pioneering role in digital regulation, there are complaints that it has failed to live up to its claims. The enforcement of the GDPR has considerable gaps and cannot prevent systematic data protection violations.[1] One reason for this is that the data protection authorities do not always have sufficient financial and personnel resources. In particular, some smaller data protection authorities of Member States have proved to be **bottlenecks of enforcement**, as the authorities of other Member States and the EU are unable to exert sufficient influence.[2] With the DSA, the legislator is keen to avoid repeating these perceived shortcomings of the GDPR enforcement regime.[3] To this end, and further influenced by contributions from the legal academia and the civil society, numerous provisions of the DSA can be understood as a direct response to the **experiences with the GDPR**.[4] Thierry Breton, the EU Commissioner for the Internal Market, who is jointly responsible for the DSA, emphasises: **'Enforcement is key'**.[5] The importance given to the enforcement in the DSA is highlighted by the scope of Chapter IV, which regulates implementation, cooperation, penalties and enforcement: Its Art. 49–88 DSA account for about 43 % of all provisions of the DSA.

---

[1] From the media, e.g. Satariano, 'Europe's Privacy Law Hasn't Shown Its Teeth, Frustrating Advocates'; Bodoni, 'Europe's Data Law Is Broken, Departing Privacy Chief Warns'; Burgess, 'How GDPR Is Failing'. Likewise and with further references and reference to the DSA also Vergnolle, 'Enforcement of the DSA and the DMA: What did we learn from the GDPR?'.

[2] See, for example, Ryan/Toner, 'Europe's Enforcement Paralysis: ICCL's 2021 Report on the Enforcement Capacity of Data Protection Authorities'. In fact, some Member States' data protection supervision costs high tens of millions of euros per year, while the Irish data protection authority has a budget in the low tens of millions, cf. Brave, 'Europe's Governments are failing the GDPR: Brave's 2020 Report on the Enforcement Capacity of Data Protection Authorities', p. 5; Statista, 'Budget of the European data protection authorities (DPAs)'.

[3] Cf. European Commission, 'Impact Assessment', SWD(2020) 348 final, Part 1, p. 25.

[4] See, for example, Monti/De Streel, 'Improving EU institutional design to better supervise digital platforms'; Van Hoboken, 'European Lessons in Self-Experimentation: From the GDPR to European Platform Regulation'. See further Zuboff at the 'Digital Services Act: A Game Changer for our Fundamental Rights?' (event on 7.7.2021) <https://www.youtube.com/watch?v=ZTViF6U4d5Q> (last accessed: 23.5.2024): 'If you design and pass good laws, you must also ensure the funding and capabilities to enforce those laws. My friends, if we have learned anything from the GDPR, it is that great law without committed unrelenting muscular enforcement only strengthens the surveillance empires, their audacity, their lobbyists and their litigators.'

[5] European Commission, 'Sneak Peek: How the Commission will enforce the DSA & DMA – Blog of Commissioner Thierry Breton'. See also European Commission, 'Impact Assessment', SWD(2020) 348 final, Part 1, p. 22 et seq. and 42 et seqq.

In addition to particularly far-reaching powers for national authorities, the **regulatory innovations of the DSA** include the shift of key powers to the European Commission, the introduction of deadlines for action and decision-making by Member State authorities, and the provision for considerable mutual influence among the authorities involved. The effective and timely enforcement of the DSA is also seen as particularly important since illegal digital content can spread very quickly, not only in the platform economy but on the internet in general.[6] 2

In describing the implementation and enforcement of the DSA, this section will first describe the new structure of authorities and the investigative and enforcement powers of Member State authorities and the Commission. This will be followed by an outline of the judicial redress available to providers. The section will conclude with certain criticisms of the enforcement regime and a brief outline of private enforcement by users. 3

B. Enforcement by public authorities

Apart from the notification and complaint procedures of users (→ Ch. 4 mn. 60 et seqq., 106 et seqq.) and possible subsequent private enforcement in court (→ mn. 110 et seqq.), the **enforcement of the DSA is mainly** carried out **by public authorities**. The legislator is particularly ambitious here: In addition to new authority responsibilities and very far-reaching powers of investigation and enforcement, a complex network of possibilities and requirements for cooperation between authorities has been created. 4

I. Authorities

Rather than leaving enforcement of the DSA to the Member States alone and once again running the risk of inconsistent and sometimes cumbersome law enforcement, the DSA provides for a **division of tasks between Member State and European authorities**. 5

1. Member State authorities

In principle, enforcement of the DSA lies with Member State authorities. They apply the DSA in accordance with the respective administrative law of the Member State (cf. Art. 291(1) TFEU). 6

a) Competent authorities and Digital Services Coordinators (DSC)

The Member State authorities responsible for the supervision of providers and the enforcement of the DSA are defined as **competent authorities** (Art. 49(1) DSA). They have far-reaching **powers of investigation and enforcement** (→ mn. 29 et seqq.). The Member States are free to determine the number of competent authorities. They may also assign specific responsibilities to respective competent authorities: for example, to individual sectors of the economy (rec. 109 sent. 2 DSA). In addition, each Member State had to designate one of its competent authorities as its Digital Services Coordinator (**DSC**) by 17.2.2024 (Art. 49(2) subpara. 1 and (3) subpara. 2 DSA). If a Member State designates several competent authorities in addition to its DSC, the respective tasks of the authorities must be clearly differentiated from one another (Art. 49(2) subpara. 3 DSA). 7

---

[6] Cf. also Eifert et al. CMLR 2021, 987 (1018).

8 Contrary to what its name might suggest, the DSC does not only coordinate the work of the other competent authorities. In addition to its supervisory tasks as one of the competent authorities, the DSC is also tasked with ensuring **effective and consistent supervision and enforcement of the DSA** (Art. 49(2) subpara. 1 DSA). This includes receiving complaints from users and possibly forwarding them to the DSC of establishment[7] (Art. 53 DSA), as well as preparing annual activity reports which, in addition to a record of the number of complaints from users, also contain information on orders according to Art. 9 and 10 DSA (→ Ch. 3 mn. 92 et seq.; Art. 55 DSA). In addition, the DSCs cooperate with the authorities at the EU level (Art. 49(2) subpara. 2 DSA) and play an important role in the process of granting vetted researchers data access (Art. 40(8) DSA).

9 Member States may entrust **existing authorities** with roles under the DSA (rec. 109 sent. 2 and rec. 113 sent. 1 DSA). So far, the Member States' implementation confirms a preference for appointing existing authorities which regulate media, though the creation of specific authorities for electronic communications and consumer protection is also a possibility.

b) Requirements

10 The DSA places a wide range of requirements on the Member State authorities, particularly with regard to working methods and equipment. The authorities must **perform** their **duties in an impartial, transparent and timely manner** (Art. 50(1) sent. 1 DSA[8]). In addition, they are to be **completely independent** in exercising their duties and powers, with no outside influence (whether public or private) and without seeking or receiving direct or indirect instructions (Art. 50(2) DSA).[9] Member States must provide the authorities with the necessary human, financial and technical **resources**, including sufficient autonomous budgetary responsibility (Art. 50(1) sent. 2 and 3 DSA).[10] In addition, Member States may transparently levy necessary and proportionate supervisory fees on providers (rec. 111 sent. 5 DSA). Further details are left to the implementing laws of the Member States.

2. European authorities

11 At the European level, the **Commission** and the newly created European Board for Digital Services (**EBDS**) enforce the DSA.

a) European Commission

12 The **Commission** is above all **responsible for the** supervision of providers of **Very Large Online Platforms (VLOP)** and **Very Large Online Search Engines (VLOSE)**. This central role of the Commission is a major difference from the GDPR. In addition to the tasks set out in Chapter III, Section 5 of the DSA (Art. 33–43 DSA, → Ch. 4 mn. 186 et seq.), the Commission also has comprehensive **powers of investigation and**

[7] The DSC of the Member State where the main establishment of a provider of an intermediary service is located or its legal representative resides or is established (Art. 3(n) DSA).

[8] Although Art. 50 DSA only speaks of the DSC, the provision also applies to the other competent authorities (Art. 49(4) DSA). The same applies to Art. 51 DSA (Powers) and Art. 56 DSA (Competences).

[9] These requirements are formulated even more strictly than those according to Art. 30(1) AVMSD, as amended by Directive (EU) 2018/1808.

[10] However, the budgetary right of Member State parliaments, as well as judicial review by Member State courts, remains unaffected (rec. 112 sent. 2 and 3 DSA). This corresponds to the situation regarding Member State data protection authorities (Art. 52 GDPR).

enforcement (→ mn. 55 et seq.) similar to those of the Member State authorities. The Commission's lack of state neutrality is questionable in the context of media and communications supervision (→ mn. 105 et seqq.). It further sets detailed rules through the implementation of acts (Art. 83 DSA).

In addition to supervising the providers of VLOP and VLOSE, the Commission has individual **coordination tasks**, for example within the framework of the EBDS. It can also adopt delegated acts (Art. 87 DSA). When adopting implementing acts, the Commission is assisted by a Digital Services Committee (Art. 88 DSA). 13

b) European Board for Digital Services (EBDS)

The new EBDS is an **independent advisory group** (Art. 61(1) DSA) whose primary role is to assist the Commission in supervising VLOP and VLOSE providers (Art. 61(2) DSA). It is therefore envisaged that, for a whole series of enforcement measures, the Commission turns to the EBDS to obtain **analyses and recommendations**. In addition, the EBDS works towards the uniform application of the DSA and an **effective cooperation between** the DSCs and the Commission. Specifically, the EBDS supports the coordination of joint investigations (→ mn. 25 et seq.), assists competent authorities in **analysing** reports and audit findings, issues **opinions, recommendations and advice** to the DSC, advises the Commission and participates in the development and implementation of **standards, guidelines, reports, templates and codes of conduct** (Art. 63(1) DSA). In doing so, the EBDS should be able to cooperate with other bodies and advisory groups actively, for example, in the fields of non-discrimination, data protection and consumer protection (rec. 134 sent. 2 DSA). The opinions, requests and recommendations of the EBDS should, to some extent, be binding in that the DSC and other competent authorities must give reasons if they do not follow them (Art. 63(2) DSA). 14

The EBDS **consists of the Member State DSCs** (Art. 62(1) sent. 1 DSA). These are represented within the EBDS by high-ranking officials. However, other competent authorities may also participate in the EBDS and other relevant Member State authorities may be invited to its meetings. Decisions are taken by the EBDS by a simple majority, with each Member State having one vote (Art. 62(3) DSA). Despite this prominent role played by the DSCs, in practice the **Commission** is likely to have **considerable influence** within the EBDS, since it both chairs the EBDS and provides it with administrative and analytical support (Art. 62(2) and (4) DSA). It therefore remains to be seen how independent the EBDS will be in practice. Compared to similar cooperation and consultation bodies in other regulatory areas, such as the European Data Protection Board (EDPB, Art. 68 GDPR), the EBDS's lack of any legal personality weakens its position. 15

The EBDS adopts rules of procedure (Art. 62(7) DSA) and builds expertise through the support of internal and external experts (Art. 62(5) DSA). It is welcomed that the EBDS makes public the results of consultations with experts and interested parties (Art. 62(5) sent. 2 and (6) DSA). 16

3. Competence

In principle, the authorities of the Member State in which the **provider** has its **main establishment** are responsible for its supervision (Art. 56(1) DSA).[11] Despite the adverse experiences with the GDPR, the DSA similarly follows the country of origin principle.[12] If the provider does not have an establishment within the EU, the jurisdiction of the au- 17

[11] Rec. 123 sent. 1 DSA simply justifies this with 'clarity, simplicity and effectiveness'.

[12] Concerning the applicability of the DSA, however, it is decisive that the service is offered to recipients that have their place of establishment in or are located in the EU (Art. 2(1) DSA, → Ch. 2 mn. 34 et seqq.).

thorities is based on the place of residence or **establishment of a legal representative** of the provider within the meaning of Art. 13 DSA (→ Ch. 4 mn. 29 et seqq.; Art. 56(6) DSA). If no legal representative is appointed, the authorities of all Member States are competent (Art. 56(7) subpara. 1 DSA).

18 It is the **Commission's role** to supervise **VLOP and VLOSE** providers (Art. 56(2) and (3) DSA) since it ought, in principle, to be in a better position to supervise very large services and take more effective action against systemic and cross-border violations (rec. 125 sent. 2 DSA). However, the authorities of a Member State where the main establishment of the VLOP or VLOSE provider is located may also take investigative and enforcement measures as long as the Commission has not initiated proceedings (Art. 56(4) DSA).

4. Cooperation

19 A number of innovative elements emerge in the DSA's numerous provisions on coordination and cooperation between the authorities involved. These include mutual assistance, cross-border cooperation between DSCs, joint investigation and an information sharing system.

a) Mutual assistance mechanisms

20 In addition to the more specific mutual assistance and information obligations of Member State and European authorities set out in other provisions of the DSA (such as Art. 65–69 DSA), Art. 57 DSA contains general provisions on mutual assistance. According to a proclamation of close cooperation for the purpose of a consistent and efficient application of the DSA (Art. 57(1) sent. 1 DSA), the **DSC of establishment** is obliged to fully **inform** all **DSCs of destination,**[13] as well as the **EBDS** and the **Commission** (Art. 57(1) sent. 2 DSA).

21 In addition, the DSC of establishment can request other DSCs to **provide specific information** and to **carry out investigative measures** (Art. 57(2) DSA). This is likely to be relevant if the providers concerned also carry out activities in other Member States but the DSC of establishment is unable to investigate them. If a DSC receives such a request, it must, in principle, comply with it without delay and no later than two months after receipt (Art. 57(3) subpara. 1 DSA). These rules only do not apply in case of certain narrowly-defined exceptions, such as a resulting violation of the law. In such cases, however, the DSC must give reasons for the refusal without delay, at the latest within two months (Art. 57(3) subpara. 2 DSA). If the DSC complies with the request, it may involve further Member State authorities (Art. 57(2) sent. 2 DSA).

b) Cross-border cooperation between DSCs

22 A striking difference to the GDPR concerns cross-border cooperation between DSCs (Art. 58 and 59 DSA). The term 'cooperation' is used euphemistically, however, since those articles cover the possibility of **forcing idle DSCs to act**. Unless the Commission is already investigating the same infringement by a provider, both the **DSC of destination** and – at the request of at least three DSCs – the **EBDS** may **request** the **DSC of establishment** to take the necessary investigative and enforcement measures (Art. 58(1) and (2) DSA). Provided that this request is duly reasoned and contains the necessary information (Art. 58(3) DSA), the DSC of establishment shall take **'utmost account'** of the request (Art. 58(4) sent. 1 DSA) and provide the requesting DSC and/or the EBDS with

[13] The DSC of a Member State where the intermediary service is provided (Art. 3(o) DSA).

an assessment of the possible infringement and an explanation of any investigation and enforcement measures taken. This must be done without delay, and at the latest two months after receipt of the request. To this end, the DSC of establishment may also request further information (Art. 57 DSA) or initiate a joint investigation (Art. 60 DSA) (→ mn. 25 et seq.), thereby suspending the above-mentioned deadline (Art. 58(4) sent. 2 and 3 DSA).

23 If the DSC of establishment does not comply with the request within the time limit or if the EBDS does not agree with the measures taken or planned, the EBDS may refer the matter to the **Commission** as the next **escalation level** (Art. 59(1) DSA). Within two months of its referral, the Commission assesses the matter (Art. 59(2) DSA). If it agrees that the measures taken by the DSC of establishment are insufficient, it communicates its position to the DSC of establishment and the EBDS and requests the DSC of establishment to review the matter (Art. 59(3) subpara. 1 DSA). The DSC of establishment must then **take** the necessary investigatory and enforcement **measures**, **taking 'utmost account'** of the Commission's views and request for review (Art. 59(3) subpara. 2 sent. 1 DSA). In addition, it must inform the Commission and the requesting DSC or the EBDS of the measures taken within two months of the request for review (Art. 59(3) subpara. 2 sent. 2 DSA).

24 The establishment of an implementation mechanism for these measures should be understood in the light of the experiences with the GDPR. In the interest of effective enforcement of the DSA, it is also to be welcomed that the very existence of the possibility to request is likely to have a motivating effect on inactive DSCs. At the same time, requests according to Art. 58 DSA cannot eliminate capacity and personnel bottlenecks of individual DSCs. **Considerable potential for conflict** therefore exists. It will have to be observed how cross-border cooperation is applied, whether the different views of DSCs involved can be resolved in practice in less conflictual ways or whether legal disputes between Member States and/or the Commission might arise.[14]

c) Joint investigation

25 Another novelty of the DSA is the introduction of joint investigations between several DSCs. On its own initiative or – at the request of at least three DSCs – on the recommendation of the **EBDS**, the **DSC of establishment** may open a joint investigation with the participation **of one or more other DSCs** (Art. 60(1) DSA). A further DSC may request a joint investigation if it has a legitimate interest in participating (Art. 60(2) subpara. 1 sent. 1 DSA). In this case, the joint investigation shall, in principle, be concluded within three months (Art. 60(2) subpara. 1 sent. 2 DSA), and the DSC of establishment shall communicate its initial position on the alleged infringement to all DSCs, the Commission and the EBDS within one further month at the latest (Art. 60(2) subpara. 2 sent. 1 DSA). The initial position shall consider the views of all participating DSCs and set out any enforcement measures envisaged (Art. 60(2) subpara. 2 sent. 2 and 3 DSA).

26 Due to the involvement of several – and potentially many – DSCs, the joint investigation is potentially conflict-prone. One possibility for escalation in the event of disagreement among the DSCs involved or failure of individual DSCs to act promptly is **referral to the Commission by the EBDS**, which is then essentially determined by Art. 59 DSA (Art. 60(3) DSA). The requirement that DSCs cooperate 'in good faith' (Art. 60(4) sent. 1 DSA) is noteworthy. Participating DSCs at the place of destination are further

[14] In particular, infringement procedures for the violation of obligations under the DSA (Art. 258 and 259 TFEU) come into consideration. These can be initiated by the Commission and other Member States (but not by individual Member State authorities such as the DSC), although the latter rarely happens.

entitled to make use of their general investigative powers within their territory (Art. 60(4) sent. 2 DSA).

d) Information sharing system

27 The diverse structure of authorities and their complex cooperation and coordination obligations require an **effective communication system**. To this end, the Commission shall create an information sharing system that must be **reliable and secure** (Art. 85(1) sent. 1 DSA). While the DSC, the Commission and the EBDS must use the information sharing system for all communications (Art. 85(2) DSA), other competent authorities may also have access to the system if necessary for their tasks (Art. 85(1) sent. 2 DSA). Further details are left to implementing acts (Art. 85(3) DSA).

28 Given the large amount of data that is shared, the Commission has a huge responsibility to create a system that is protected from attacks by third parties. This is all the more true as some of this data, such as algorithms and how they work, are commercially very valuable and other data, such as data relating to extensive communications in very large online platforms, is highly sensitive.

II. Powers of the Member State authorities

29 The powers conferred on the Member State authorities for the general supervision of providers (on this competence → mn. 17 et seq.) can be divided into the two categories of **investigation** and **enforcement**. The central provisions are Art. 51 and 52 DSA. Many details, including elements restricting the objective fulfilment of the offence and applicable procedural rules, are governed by the implementing laws of the Member States.

1. Investigative powers

30 The competent authorities, including the DSC,[15] have general investigative powers to the extent necessary for the performance of their duties (Art. 51(1) DSA). Member State authorities may require both providers and any other persons acting in a trade, business, craft or professional capacity who are likely to possess information concerning suspected infringements to **provide** that information without undue delay (Art. 51(1)(a) DSA). Member State authorities may also carry out **inspections** at the premises of the providers and other persons as mentioned above to investigate, seize or make or obtain copies of information concerning an alleged infringement. In addition, where Member State law provides, for example, for judicial review, the Member State authorities may also request judicial authorities (courts) or other authorities of their Member State to issue such inspection orders. The Member State may also request employees or representatives of the providers or other persons to provide **explanations** and record them with their consent. Art. 51(1) DSA does not directly contain any further objective requirements. However, restrictions and details may apply in accordance with Art. 51(6) DSA and the laws of the Member States, in particular their implementing legislation.

31 In addition, a DSC may, under certain conditions, request administrative assistance from other DSCs, request cross-border cooperation from another DSC or initiate a joint investigation (Art. 57–60 DSA; → mn. 19 et seqq.). This is likely to be particularly appropriate in some **cross-border cases**.

[15] Although Art. 51 DSA only refers to the DSC, the same applies to all other competent authorities if there are other competent authorities in addition to the DSC (Art. 49(4) DSA). In the following, the DSC and the other competent authorities are jointly referred to as 'Member State authorities'.

2. Enforcement powers

The enforcement powers of the Member State authorities range from cessation orders to sanctions and interim measures.[16] While Art. 51(2) and (3) DSA, in particular, contain a list of the various powers, the details are specified in Art. 51(6) DSA and Member State law. 32

a) Cessation of infringement and remedy

Member State authorities may order the **cessation** of infringements and impose proportional and necessary **remedies** or request the judicial authorities of their Member State to do so (Art. 51(2)(b) DSA). These are the basic enforcement measures of the Member State authorities. 33

b) Commitment

As in other areas of law, in particular competition law (e.g. Art. 25 DMA and § 32b German Competition Act (*Gesetz gegen Wettbewerbsbeschränkungen* – GWB)), Member State authorities may **make binding any commitments** made by providers (Art. 51(2)(a) DSA). If providers subsequently breach a commitment made with regard to compliance with the DSA which has been declared binding by the Member State authority, the authorities may take further enforcement action. 34

Unlike measures such as a cessation order or the imposition of remedies, commitments can have significant **benefits** for both the provider and the Member State authority. Providers can, for example, pre-empt possible administrative action in advance of formal administrative proceedings and work with the relevant authority to find an appropriate solution. Cooperative adaptation to particular economic and other circumstances can provide considerable scope for flexibility and efficiency. In addition, the provider is spared the stigma of illegality, and both parties avoid a potentially time- and resource-consuming legal dispute. 35

c) Powers in the event of persistent infringements

In addition to stopping and remedying infringements, Member State authorities may, in certain cases, take further **subsidiary** measures. These require that all other powers have been exhausted to no avail and that the continuing infringement is causing serious harm which cannot be avoided by other powers available under EU or national law (Art. 51(3) subpara. 1 DSA). 36

aa) Immediate request for inspection

Firstly, the Member State authorities may require the provider's management body to examine the situation without delay, submit an **action plan** laying out necessary measures, ensure that the measures are taken and subsequently report on them. 37

bb) Temporary access restriction

Secondly, the Member State authorities can request the judicial authorities of their Member State to order the temporary restriction of users' access to the service concerned or to the provider's online interface, i.e. to shut down the service or to block it for users (Art. 51(3) subpara. 1(b) DSA). Due to the **high intensity of such intervention** for 38

[16] These enforcement powers do not include measures under Member State and other EU law, such as orders within the meaning of Art. 9 and 10 DSA. On the latter → Ch. 3 mn. 95 et seqq.

both provider and users and the corresponding high relevance for fundamental rights, the provision contains several further factual and procedural requirements (Art. 51(3) subpara. 2–4 DSA).

(1) Prerequisites for the offence

39 Temporary access restriction further requires that the infringement constitutes a **criminal offence that threatens the life or safety of persons.** The concept of 'safety of persons' may nowadays be understood very broadly as some may refer to it in the context of certain expressions of opinion/hate speech as well. However, in the current context, 'safety' should be interpreted very narrowly due to the potential of profound encroachment on fundamental democratic rights. This position is supported by rec. 56 sent. 1 and 2 DSA which – albeit in respect to Art. 18(1) DSA – cites incitement to terrorism and trafficking in human beings as particularly serious offences that pose a danger to the life and security of persons.

40 Furthermore, the restriction of access imposed must be proportionate to the nature, gravity, recurrence and duration of the infringement and must not unduly restrict the users' access to lawful information (Art. 51(3) subpara. 2 sent. 3 DSA). Due to the particularly high relevance of freedom of information for the functioning of the democratic order, this restrictive condition should also be interpreted narrowly. Temporary restriction of access to services must remain the **absolute exception.**

(2) Addressees of the judicial order

41 In addition to the offending provider, other internet service providers may also be the **addressees of the judicial authority's order** to temporarily restrict users' access to the service in question or the provider's online interface. The wording of the provision contains no restriction to the effect that the judicial order may be addressed only to the offending provider. At the same time, rec. 120 sent. 2 DSA is based on the idea that the order may be directed at other internet service providers and lists other hosting or internet service providers in addition to the provider committing the infringement, including the relevant domain name registry or registrar. In many cases, these additional entities can also effectively restrict access to the provider. This is likely to be particularly helpful if the provider committing the infringement fails to comply with a judicial order or cannot be reached.

(3) Procedural requirements

42 On the procedural side, it should be noted that Member State authorities must allow the **parties involved to submit written observations** on the intended measures and the addressee(s) of the order within two weeks before issuing their request to the judicial authority (Art. 51(3) subpara. 2 sent. 1 DSA). Further, the infringing provider, the addressees of the order and all third parties who can prove a legitimate interest are entitled to **participate in the proceedings before the competent judicial authority** (Art. 51(3) subpara. 2 sent. 2 DSA).

(4) Duration of the access restriction

43 **In principle**, access is **restricted for four weeks** (Art. 51(3) subpara. 3 sent. 1 DSA). The competent judicial authority may allow the Member State authority to **extend** this period for a fixed number of further periods of four weeks, but the extension is subject to additional extended conditions. Taking into account the rights and interests of all par-

ties affected by the access restriction and all relevant circumstances, the Member State authority must believe that the provider has not taken the necessary measures to terminate the infringement and that the temporary restriction does not unduly restrict users' access to lawful information (Art. 51(3) subpara. 3 sent. 2 DSA). The number of users affected and the existence of suitable and easily accessible alternatives to the service must be taken into account.

The Member State authority may additionally send a **new request** to the competent judicial authority to restrict access if the previous period of restriction cannot be extended further (Art. 51(3) subpara. 4 DSA). Because this procedure seems to allow unlimited access restrictions according to the provision's wording, this rule must be interpreted very strictly. **44**

d) Interim measures

To avoid the **risk of serious harm**, Member State authorities may either take interim measures themselves or request the competent Member State judicial authorities to do so (Art. 51(2)(e) DSA). However, these measures should only ensure the prevention of serious harm until a final decision is taken (rec. 114 sent. 3 DSA). **45**

e) Sanctions

In addition, the Member State authorities can impose fines and periodic penalty payments on infringing providers and – in special cases – on third parties. These can reach extreme amounts, at least in theory, but, in line with experience with the GDPR, are not expected to do so in practice for the time being. **46**

aa) Fines

Member State authorities may impose fines on providers for **violations of any DSA provisions** and **non-compliance with investigation orders** (Art. 51(1) DSA, → mn. 30 et seq.) or – depending on the Member State regulation – request the judicial authorities of their Member State to do so (Art. 51(2)(c) DSA). **47**

The maximum amount for fines in the Member States is, in principle, **6 % of the annual worldwide turnover** of the provider concerned in the preceding financial year (Art. 52(3) sent. 1 DSA). Fines of up to **1 % of the annual income or worldwide turnover** of the provider concerned in the preceding financial year may be imposed for the incorrect supply of information and failure to submit to an inspection (Art. 52(3) sent. 2 DSA). This continues the trend of EU legislation towards increasingly draconian maximum fines, in contrast to the German Network Enforcement Act (*Netzwerkdurchsetzungsgesetz* – NetzDG), for example, which provides for a maximum fine of 'only' 5 million EUR (§ 4(2) sent. 1 and 2 German Network Enforcement Act in conjunction with § 30(2) sent. 3 German Act on Regulatory Offences (*Gesetz über Ordnungswidrigkeiten* – OWiG)). **48**

bb) Penalties

To ensure that infringements of cessation orders or failure to take remedial action (Art. 51(2)(b) DSA) and non-compliance with investigation orders (Art. 51(1) DSA) are brought to an end, Member State authorities may impose periodic penalties on providers (Art. 51(2)(d) DSA). The maximum amount is **5 %** of the average **daily worldwide turnover or income** of the provider concerned in the preceding financial year (Art. 52(4) DSA). Periodic penalty payments are due until the infringement has ceased. **49**

cc) Common provisions

50 While the DSA itself contains only rudimentary provisions on the sanctioning powers of the Member State authorities, it requires Member States to fill the gaps and take all necessary measures (Art. 52(1) DSA). **Member States' implementing laws** contain tangible criteria for legal practitioners, particularly regarding the amount of fines and periodic penalty payments, as well as procedural rules. In imposing these measures, Member States must not only ensure that sanctions are **effective, proportionate and dissuasive** (Art. 52(2) sent. 1 DSA), but also they must notify the Commission of relevant Member State rules and measures, as well as report any amendments in this regard to the Commission without delay (Art. 52(2) sent. 2 DSA).

51 Concerning the **level of sanctions**, further indications can be found in the recitals. For example, the authorities should consider whether the provider in question systematically or repeatedly breaches its obligations, how many users are affected, whether the provider is acting intentionally or negligently and in how many Member States it is active (rec. 117 sent. 2 DSA). The maximum sanction amounts may apply with regards to each individual infringement (rec. 117 sent. 3 DSA). However, when calculating the amount of any sanction, it should be taken into account that **extension to a group of companies** is not explicitly provided for (as in rec. 150 sent. 3 GDPR).[17] However, legal uncertainty arises from the fact that the DSA does not define the term 'provider of intermediary services' and that, interpreted very broadly, the term could also include a group of companies.

52 Fines and periodic penalty payments may also be imposed on all **other persons** referred to in Art. 51(1)(a) DSA if they fail to comply with investigation orders (Art. 51(2) subpara. 2 sent. 1 DSA). Before imposing sanctions, however, the Member State authorities must specifically **inform** these other persons about the sanctions and the possibilities for redress (Art. 51(2) subpara. 2 sent. 2 DSA).

3. General provisions

53 The last two paragraphs of Art. 51 DSA contain **general rules covering investigation and enforcement measures** applied by Member State authorities. Those applying the law are first provided with a list of aspects relevant for consideration. For example, the measures taken in the exercise of their powers must be effective, dissuasive and proportionate (Art. 51(5) DSA).[18] In particular, the nature, gravity, recurrence and duration of the (alleged) infringement to which the measures relate, as well as the economic capacity of the provider, must be taken into account (rec. 117 sent. 1 DSA).

54 In addition, Member States are required to lay down **specific rules and procedures for investigative and enforcement powers** (Art. 51(6) DSA). In doing so, they shall provide adequate safeguards in compliance with the Charter of Fundamental Rights and the general principles of EU law. Particular emphasis is placed on the right to respect for private life and the rights of defence, including the right to be heard and the right to access the Commissions' file. Member States are expected to enact comprehensive and detailed **implementing legislation** regulating further details of the exercising of powers and relevant procedures in addition to their respective authority structures. From the providers' point of view and with a view to their legal application costs, it is to be hoped that Member State regulations and their enforcement do not diverge too much.

---

[17] Schmid/Grewe MMR 2021, 279 (281 et seq.); Spindler GRUR 2021, 653 (661).

[18] Given this provision, there would have been no need for Art. 52(2) sent. 1 DSA, which orders the same for the more specific case of sanctions – albeit with a different order of adjectives.

III. Powers of the Commission

55 To enable its supervision of the providers of VLOPs and VLOSEs[19] (on competence → mn. 17 et seq.), the DSA grants the Commission powers of investigation and enforcement that correspond in principle to those of the Member State authorities. Certain deviations are due to the size of the VLOPs and VLOSEs and to the fact that the Commission is not an independent authority.

1. Investigative powers

56 The Commission's investigative powers include requesting information, questioning, conducting inspections and general monitoring measures. In this respect, the DSA – compared to the powers of the Member State authorities, which are also shaped by the implementing laws of the Member States – contains **detailed regulations.** It also clarifies that the Commission may exercise investigative powers even before it has initiated proceedings for non-compliance (Art. 65(1) sent. 1 DSA). However, information obtained may only be used for the purposes of the DSA (Art. 79(5) DSA).

a) Request for information and questioning

57 As a basic investigative power, the Commission may request **the provider** as well as any **other person** acting for purposes related to their trade, business, craft or profession that may be reasonably aware of information relating to the suspected infringement of the DSA to provide such information within a reasonable period (Art. 67(1) DSA).

58 The Commission can act either **by simple request** or **by decision**. While the provider does not need to comply with a simple request for information, it only has a right of legal redress against a decision (→ mn. 93 et seqq.). The efficient simple request procedure is particularly appropriate where the provider or other persons concerned is highly likely to comply. In any case, the Commission shall state the legal basis and purpose of the request for information, specify what information is required, set a reasonable time period for a response and indicate the imposition of a fine in the case of insufficient information being provided (Art. 67(2) and (3) DSA). Only if the Commission acts by decision can it also impose a penalty payment in the case of non-compliance. It must indicate the possibilities of legal redress (Art. 67(3) sent. 2 and 3 DSA).

59 In addition, the Commission may **interview** any consenting person to obtain information about an alleged infringement and record this interview by technical means (Art. 68(1) DSA).

b) Inspection

60 The Commission's power of inspection is regulated in particular detail (Art. 69 DSA). This provision is a further demonstration of how the DSA grants the Commission considerable powers to enable its effective supervision of large tech companies.

aa) General

61 In principle, places of inspection are the **premises** of the provider concerned or of any other person within the meaning of Art. 67(1) DSA (Art. 69(1) DSA). Similarly to within the context of the request for information (→ mn. 58), the Commission does not have to

[19] The text will henceforth refrain from specifying that the Commission's orders concern providers of VLOPs and VLOSEs and use the general term 'provider'.

act by decision. However, the provider or other person concerned is only obliged to **submit to the inspection** if the Commission does act by decision (Art. 69(6) sent. 1 DSA) and only then is there the possibility of legal redress (→ mn. 93 et seqq.). In the case of a decision, the Commission lists the subject matter and the purpose of the inspection, specifies the date on which the inspection is to begin, indicates possible fines and periodic penalty payments and points out the options of legal redress (Art. 69(6) sent. 2 DSA). Before taking a decision, the Commission consults the DSC of the Member State where the inspection takes place (Art. 69(6) sent. 3 DSA).

bb) Concrete powers

62 Within the scope of the inspection, the Commission's staff, as well as accompanying persons authorised by the Commission, are empowered to take **specific actions** (Art. 69(2) DSA). In view of the wording of the provision, which does not contain the phrase 'in particular' or other similar expressions, and considering the severity of some of the intervention measures that might be taken, it can be assumed that the list is exhaustive.

63 The Commission's powers in these circumstances include the **right to enter** all premises, land and means of transport of the provider, examine all relevant books and other records, and take or obtain relevant copies or extracts (Art. 69(2)(a)–(c) DSA). In addition, officials and accompanying persons may request **access to** and record explanations of information on the organisation, its functioning, IT system, algorithms, data-handling and business practices (Art. 69(2)(d) DSA). Officials and accompanying staff may also seal rooms and request representatives to provide explanations on relevant facts or documents and ask questions and record the answers (Art. 69(2)(e)–(g) DSA).

cc) Procedure

64 Not least because of the potential for great technical complexity, the Commission may request the assistance of **auditors**, **experts** and the **DSC** of the Member State in which the inspection takes place, as well as of other **Member State authorities** (Art. 69(3), (5) and (7) DSA). If, in violation of Art. 69(2) DSA, the providers fail to co-operate sufficiently, the Commission officials, and accompanying persons authorised by the Commission, shall act upon presentation of a written authorisation of the Commission stating the subject matter and purpose of the inspection and indicating the possible imposition of fines and periodic penalty payments (Art. 69(4) sent. 1 DSA). The Commission may also adopt implementing measures regarding the modalities of the inspection (Art. 83(1)(a) DSA).

dd) Measures in case of resistance

65 If the provider or other persons concerned oppose an inspection ordered by decision,[20] the Commission staff and accompanying persons authorised by the Commission are entitled to **assistance from other authorities of the relevant Member State** (Art. 69(8) DSA). This may include the application of coercive measures by competent **law enforcement authorities**, in particular, the police.

66 If **authorisations of competent judicial authorities** are required under Member State law – which is likely to be the case given the severity of such measures – the DSC

[20] Although the provision's wording only speaks of 'ordered pursuant to this Article', a decision will be required because, otherwise, the provider would not have to submit to the inspection (Art. 69(6) sent. 1 DSA).

concerned must apply for these authorisations (if necessary, as a precautionary measure) (Art. 69(9) DSA). In its verification, the competent judicial authority of the Member State has only **limited competence**: it may not question the necessity of the review and may not demand information from the Commission's file (Art. 69(10) sent. 3 DSA) since the assessment of the lawfulness of the Commission's decision is exclusively subject to legal redress on the EU level (Art. 69(10) sent. 4 DSA). The judicial authority of the Member State does, however, verify the authenticity of the decision and whether the review is arbitrary or excessive (Art. 69(10) sent. 1 DSA). To this end, it may ask the Commission for explanations on the alleged infringement (Art. 69(10) sent. 2 DSA).

c) Monitoring

In addition to requesting information, questioning and investigating, the Commission may take further necessary measures to monitor the compliance with the DSA (Art. 72(1) sent. 1 DSA). In particular, it may order providers to provide **access to their databases and algorithms** (Art. 72(1) sent. 2 DSA) and require them to retain documents relevant to assessing compliance with the DSA (Art. 72(1) sent. 3 DSA). Furthermore, the Commission may appoint independent external experts and auditors to assist it in its monitoring activities (Art. 72(2) DSA). Concerning these general monitoring measures, the Commission may also determine further details through an implementing act (Art. 83(1)(a) DSA). 67

2. Enforcement powers

The Commission's enforcement powers are similar to those of Member State authorities. They range from measures aimed at stopping infringements to sanctions and interim measures. 68

a) Non-compliance decision

The Commission's basic enforcement measure is the non-compliance decision (Art. 73 DSA). 69

aa) Procedure and facts

The Commission may initiate proceedings regarding the possible adoption of a non-compliance decision where there exists the **suspicion of an infringement** (Art. 66(1) DSA). The decision that may be issued at the end of the proceedings requires the provider to have **breached** DSA provisions, interim measures ordered or binding commitments (Art. 73(1) DSA). Before issuing a non-compliance decision, the Commission shall communicate to the provider its **preliminary findings** and the measures it intends to take or the measures the provider should take (Art. 73(2) DSA). The provider has the right to be heard and to access the Commission's file (Art. 79 DSA, → mn. 88 et seq.). 70

bb) Decision and measures

If, in the course of an investigation, the Commission finds that there is no infringement, it closes the proceedings with immediate effect by decision (Art. 73(5) DSA). However, if the Commission issues a non-compliance decision, it shall require the provider to take **necessary measures** to end the infringement within a reasonable period of time specified by the Commission (Art. 73(3) DSA). The Commission may in addition impose a **fine** (→ mn. 81). The provider is required to provide the Commission with information on the measures planned and/or taken (Art. 73(3) and (4) DSA). 71

cc) Extended supervision

72 In addition, the Commission applies the so-called **extended supervision system** concerning the measures to be taken if the decision of non-compliance is based on a breach by the provider of the obligations under Art. 33–43 DSA (→ Ch. 4 mn. 209 et seq.; Art. 75(1) DSA). These breached obligations concern the management of systemic risks and infringements in such cases can be particularly serious (cf. rec. 145 sent. 1 DSA). Consequently, the requirements imposed by the Commission go beyond the mere provision of information on measures planned and taken. The Commission also requests the provider to submit to the Commission, all DSCs and the EBDS, within a specified period of time, an **action plan** setting out the measures necessary and sufficient to **terminate or remedy the infringement** (Art. 75(2) sent. 1 DSA). Also required is a **commitment** to have the implementation of the required measures monitored by an independent audit, according to Art. 37(3) and (4) DSA (→ Ch. 4 mn. 239 et seq.), specifying the auditors, the methodology, the timeline and the audit follow-up (Art. 75(2) sent. 2 DSA). A commitment[21] by the provider to participate in a **code of conduct** following Art. 45 DSA (→ Ch. 4 mn. 274 et seq.; Art. 75(2) sent. 3 DSA) may additionally be required.

73 Within one month of the Commission receiving the provider's action plan, the **EBDS** sends an opinion to the Commission (Art. 75(3) subpara. 1 sent. 1 DSA). Within one month of receiving the opinion, the Commission decides whether the measures provided for in the action plan are sufficient and sets an appropriate **implementation deadline for the provider**, taking into account a possible commitment and possible participation in a code of conduct (Art. 75(3) subpara. 1 sent. 2 and 3 DSA). As part of the subsequent monitoring of the action plan implementation, the provider sends the audit report as soon as it is available and informs the Commission of the implementation steps taken (Art. 75(3) subpara. 1 sent. 4 and 5 DSA). The Commission may still request the provider to provide additional information within a reasonable time period set by the Commission, insofar as this is necessary for the monitoring (Art. 75(3) subpara. 1 sent. 6 DSA). The Commission shall keep the DSC and the EBDS informed about the implementation of the action plan and its monitoring (Art. 75(3) subpara. 2 DSA).

74 If the provider fails to cooperate sufficiently, for example due to the measures provided in the action plan being insufficient, the Commission can take further necessary measures (Art. 75(4) DSA). These include the imposition of periodic penalty payments (→ mn. 84 et seqq.), as well as other measures in the case of persistent infringements (→ mn. 77 et seqq.).

b) Commitment

75 Like Member State authorities (→ mn. 32 et seq.), the Commission can also, **by decision, declare** commitments made by providers **to be binding** and decide to take no further action (Art. 71(1) DSA). Compared to a possible non-compliance decision, this provides a number of advantages for both the provider and the Commission (→ mn. 34). However, if the Commission considers the provider's commitment to be insufficient to ensure compliance with the provisions of the DSA, it rejects the commitment by way of a reasoned decision (Art. 71(3) DSA).

76 The Commission may, in spite of a binding commitment, reopen the procedure if the relevant facts change, if the provider breaches its commitments, or if the decision is found to have been based on incorrect information provided by the provider or other persons within the meaning of Art. 67(1) DSA (Art. 71(2) DSA).

---

[21] On the commitment → mn. 75 et seq.

c) Powers in the event of persistent infringements

77 Even when all other powers have been exhausted without success and a persistent infringement by a provider continues to cause **serious damage** that other authorities are unable to remedy, the Commission itself cannot, similar to the Member State's power to intervene (→ mn. 33 et seqq.), make a subsidiary request for an immediate inspection or have the service temporarily restricted. The ability to intervene so deeply in fundamental democratic rights would scarcely be compatible with its status as a political authority – in contrast, for example, to an independent media supervisory authority and the Member State authorities under the DSA.

78 However, the Commission may **request** the **DSC of establishment to take** such measures (Art. 82(1) subpara. 1 in conjunction with Art. 51(3) DSA). The reference should be understood to mean that the DSC of establishment examines the elements of Art. 51(3) DSA fully and independently. This way, an independent authority is interposed and acts as the lead authority. In addition, the Commission enables the parties concerned to submit their written **observations** in advance, after describing the measures it intends to request and naming the addressee of the request, within at least 14 working days (Art. 82(1) subpara. 2 DSA). The Commission may also submit observations to the competent judicial authority of the Member State and request that authority to provide **relevant documents** (Art. 82(2) DSA).

d) Interim measures

79 To prevent any **risk of serious damage to users** resulting from an infringement that has been provisionally assessed[22], the Commission may order interim measures against the provider in the context of proceedings that may lead to a non-compliance decision (Art. 70(1) DSA). The order is issued by decision, the duration of which is limited but may be extended if necessary and appropriate (Art. 70(1) and (2) DSA). The Commission should order interim measures primarily in cases where there would otherwise be a threat of damage that could not or could only hardly be reversed at the end of the normal procedure (cf. rec. 142 sent. 2 DSA).

e) Sanctions

80 Like the Member States authorities, the Commission has at its disposal the issuing of fines and periodic penalty payments as possible sanctions.

aa) Fines

81 Firstly, in a **decision for non-compliance** (→ mn. 69 et seqq.), the Commission may impose fines on the provider up to **6 % of the total worldwide annual turnover achieved by the provider in the preceding financial year,**[23] if the provider has intentionally or negligently violated provisions of the DSA, interim measures, or a binding commitment (Art. 74(1) DSA).

82 Secondly, **in the case of a series of further infringements**, the Commission may, by decision, impose fines on the provider or other person within the meaning of Art. 67(1) DSA of up to **1 % of its total annual income or worldwide turnover** in the preceding

[22] The DSA uses the Latin term 'prima facie'. This also applies in the German, French, Spanish and Italian language versions. However, rec. 142 sent. 4 DSA of some versions – including the German version – uses stricter terms.

[23] On the question of whether the turnover of the group of companies can be decisive under the sanctions provisions of the DSA → mn. 51.

financial year. In addition to intent or negligence, the offence requires one of six listed violations. These essentially include: an incorrect or omitted response to a request for information; failure to provide information or the provision of false information; refusal to submit to an inspection; failure to comply with a monitoring measure; and failure to comply with the right to inspect records (Art. 74(2) DSA). Before adopting the decision under Art. 74(2) DSA, the Commission shall communicate its preliminary findings to the provider or the other person referred to in Art. 67(1) DSA (Art. 74(3) DSA).

83 **The criteria** to be applied by the Commission in **determining the amount** of the fine are the nature, gravity, duration and recurrence of the infringement, as well as any delays caused by the provision of incorrect information (Art. 74(4) DSA). In addition to the general principle of proportionality, the prohibition of ne bis in idem must also be observed (rec. 144 sent. 2 DSA). The Commission shall therefore coordinate with other Member State authorities and take into account in its decision any sanctions already imposed on the legal person concerned in respect of the same facts (rec. 144 sent. 3 and 4 DSA).

bb) Penalties

84 The Commission may, by decision, impose on providers or other person referred to in Art. 67(1) DSA a periodic penalty payment per day of up to **5 %** of its average **daily income or its worldwide annual turnover** in the preceding financial year (Art. 76(1) DSA). The Commission may use the penalty payment to enforce one of the five enumerated acts. These include responding to a request for information and submitting to an inspection, insofar as these have been ordered in the form of a decision (Art. 76(1)(a) and (b) DSA). In addition, the Commission may impose periodic penalty payments to ensure that the addressee complies with interim measures, binding commitments, as well as measures and action plans provided for in non-compliance decisions (Art. 76(1)(c)–(e) DSA). Periodic penalty payments are due until the infringement has ceased.

85 A positive incentive to fulfil the obligation enforced by the periodic penalty payment is that the Commission can **subsequently reduce** the periodic penalty payment (Art. 76(2) DSA). However, the DSA does not provide the legal practitioner with the required criteria for this decision. It would make sense for the Commission – as when deciding the amount of a fine – to consider the particular nature of the addressee's transgressive conduct, as well as the nature, gravity and duration of the infringement and whether or not the infringement has been repeated.

cc) Limitation period

86 Both the imposition of fines and periodic penalty payments and their enforcement are subject to a **five-year limitation period** (Art. 77(1) and Art. 78(1) DSA). The limitation period for imposing sanctions begins on the day of the infringement or, in the case of continuous breaches, on the day the violation ceases (Art. 77(2) DSA). The limitation period for enforcing sanctions begins on the day on which the decision to impose them becomes final (Art. 78(2) DSA). Art. 77(3)–(5) DSA and Art. 78(3)–(5) DSA further contain provisions on the interruption and suspension of limitation periods.

3. Special provisions on decisions

87 Following the provisions on the Commission's investigative and enforcement powers, the DSA contains special provisions on decisions, in particular concerning the procedure.

a) Right to be heard and access to the Commission's file

Before the Commission adopts a non-compliance decision (Art. 73 DSA) or imposes sanctions (Art. 74 and 76 DSA), it allows the addressee – i.e. the provider or other person within the meaning of Art. 67(1) DSA – to comment on the Commission's **preliminary findings** and intended measures (Art. 79(1) DSA). The Commission sets the deadline for the submission of written **observations** on its initial evaluation (Art. 79(2) DSA). This is set at 14 days, although longer periods of time are probably required when the facts of the case are complex and the legal situation is unclear. In general, the Commission may base its decisions exclusively on objections on which the parties concerned have been able to comment (Art. 79(3) DSA). 88

Both the addressee of a possible decision and the other parties concerned have the **right to inspect the Commission's file** (Art. 79(4) DSA). This, however, is subject to the legitimate interest of the provider or other persons within the meaning of Art. 67(1) DSA in the protection of business secrets and does not include confidential information and internal documents of the Commission, the EBDS, the DSC, other competent authorities and other public authorities of the Member States (Art. 79(4) sent. 2, 4 and 5 DSA). In a dispute between the parties concerned about the conditions of disclosure of files, the Commission shall decide by decision (Art. 79(4) sent. 3 DSA). 89

b) Publication of decisions

The Commission publishes decisions regarding interim measures, binding commitments, non-compliance, extended supervision, as well as fines and periodic penalty payments (Art. 80(1) DSA). As this includes the parties' names, the main content of the decision and any sanctions imposed, such publications can have a significant **reprimanding effect**. 90

4. Cooperation with DSCs

In addition to the general provisions on cooperation between Member State and European authorities (Art. 57–60 DSA, → mn. 19 et seq.), **numerous** other provisions contain **individual rules on collaboration**. These concern, in particular, cooperation between the Commission and the DSCs within the framework of their investigative powers and the monitoring of implementing measures. Non-exhaustive examples mainly include the information sharing obligations of the Commission towards the DSCs (e.g. Art. 66(2) and (4), Art. 67(6) as well as Art. 69(4) sent. 2 DSA), which are intended to ensure that the DSCs are made aware of relevant Commission procedures. The Commission may also request assistance from DSCs in a number of situations (e.g. Art. 66(3) and Art. 67(5) DSA). The DSCs may in turn request the Commission to investigate possible infringements but must give sufficient reasons for doing so (Art. 65(2) and (3) DSA). 91

IV. Legal redress of providers

Unlike the GDPR (with its Art. 78), the DSA does not contain a provision that governs possibility of legal redress against official measures in more detail. The general principles apply.[24] 92

---

[24] See in particular Cuthbert, p. 67 et seqq.; Rengeling/Middeke/Gellermann Rechtsschutz-HdB §§ 5–10, 34–37.

1. Against decisions of the Commission

93 Providers may bring an **action for annulment** before the Court of Justice of the EU (CJEU)[25] against decisions of the Commission which are addressed to them or affect them directly and individually (Art. 263(4) TFEU).[26] In principle, the CJEU has first-instance jurisdiction for actions for annulment brought by natural and legal persons (Art. 256(1) TFEU in conjunction with Art. 51 CJEU Statute).

94 Concerning decisions to impose fines and periodic penalty payments, the CJEU has the power of **unlimited jurisdiction to review** (Art. 81 sent. 1 DSA in conjunction with Art. 261 TFEU). The CJEU can not only cancel or reduce the fines or periodic penalty payments imposed but can also increase them (Art. 81 sent. 2 DSA). In competition law, the CJEU has already increased fines in the past.[27] Further, actions before the CJEU do **not** have a **suspensory effect** (Art. 278 sent. 1 TFEU) and proceedings before the CJEU sometimes suffer from a very long duration.[28] Possibilities do exist, however, for **interim legal protection**, particularly through the suspension of the challenged legal act (Art. 278 sent. 2 TFEU) and the prescription of interim measures (Art. 279 TFEU).[29]

2. Against other measures by EU authorities

95 Providers cannot use an action for annulment to challenge **simple requests for information** by the Commission (Art. 67(1) and (2) DSA, → mn. 57 et seq.) as these are not legislative or legal acts.[30] Moreover, there exist **no other possibilities of legal redress** before the CJEU, though providers can choose to ignore simple requests for information[31] – albeit at the risk that the Commission will then act by decision.

96 In principle, providers also have no **legal recourse** before the CJEU against **opinions, recommendations, advice and other advisory acts** of the EBDS. Such acts lack the concrete external legal effect required for an action for annulment (cf. Art. 263(1) TFEU).[32] Also in other areas of law, the expert opinions of EU bodies are regarded merely as dependent intermediate acts which do no more than prepare the decisions concluding proceedings.[33] In the context of an action against such a decision, however, the act of the EBDS would implicitly be subject to review.

97 There is a legal remedy by way of an **action for annulment**, however, against the **guidelines** of the Commission (provided for in Art. 22(8), Art. 25(3), Art. 28(4), Art. 35(3) and Art. 39(3) subpara. 2 DSA), according to the prevailing view.[34]

3. Against measures taken by Member State authorities

98 **Legal protection** against measures taken by Member State authorities is also available **before the Member State courts** if they are taken directly based on the DSA (indirect

[25] The CJEU consists of the European Court of Justice (ECJ), the General Court of the EU (GC) and the specialised courts.

[26] Hartley, p. 436 et seqq.

[27] Boß in Grabitz/Hilf/Nettesheim AEUV Art. 251 mn. 15.

[28] Cf. Mayer in Grabitz/Hilf/Nettesheim EUV Art. 19 mn. 105; Huber in Streinz EUV Art. 19 mn. 9–11; Wegener in Calliess/Ruffert EUV Art. 19 mn. 15–17.

[29] Classen/Nettesheim in Oppermann/Classen/Nettesheim EuropaR § 13 mn. 87.

[30] Cf. Classen/Nettesheim in Oppermann/Classen/Nettesheim EuropaR § 13 mn. 44.

[31] Cf. Hennig in Immenga/Mestmäcker VO 1/2003 Art. 18 mn. 70–75 and 78.

[32] On this admissibility requirement, see Ehricke in Streinz AEUV Art. 263 mn. 21–24.

[33] Dörr in Grabitz/Hilf/Nettesheim AEUV Art. 263 mn. 39.

[34] Cremer in Calliess/Ruffert AEUV Art. 263 mn. 17.

enforcement of EU law).[35] According to general principles of EU law, legal protection must be effective.[36] Moreover, decisions of Member State courts may not counter decisions the Commission has already taken in the matter, or intends to take in proceedings that have already been initiated (Art. 82(3) sent. 1 and 2 DSA). In such cases, the Member State court may stay the proceedings pending before it (Art. 82(3) sent. 3 DSA).

Insofar as there exist ambiguities about the interpretation of the DSA that would be relevant for the decision, the appointed Member State court may or – in the case of courts of the last instance – must refer the question to the CJEU[37] by way of **preliminary ruling proceedings** (Art. 267 TFEU). This may be the case particularly if it is unclear whether a Member States' implementing law – e.g. concerning the structure of the authorities or the form of the enforcement measures – meets the requirements of the DSA. 99

The appointed Member State court can – and in the prevailing opinion must – also refer to the CJEU if it considers parts of the DSA to be contrary to primary law.[38] However, if a provider challenges parts of implementing laws that are not determined by the DSA or other EU law, only national jurisdiction is considered competent.[39] 100

V. Problems

Given the extremely high relevance of the DSA to fundamental rights and the complex interplay of different authorities, it is not surprising that the enforcement regime of the DSA faces a number of challenges. Two aspects in particular are addressed below. The first arises from the fact that there is no guarantee that all authorities are able to build up sufficient **capabilities** to fulfil their tasks to an adequate standard. The second revolves around concerns over enforcement from the perspective of **fundamental rights** as well as the **rule of law** and the **principle of democracy**, especially in view of the role of the Commission. 101

1. Questionable capabilities

Having seen deficits in these areas become apparent within the context of the GDPR (→ mn. 1 et seq.), the DSA sets out very high requirements in the realms of equipment, competence and cooperation from the authorities. However, it remains to be seen whether these **requirements** will always be met, especially since the DSA is breaking new regulatory ground with its particularly complex authority structure. For one thing, it is not yet possible to estimate how many **staff the DSA** actually requires across all authorities. Enforcement of the German Network Enforcement Act alone is said to have employed 40 people at the German Ministry of Justice, although it contained far fewer obligations and was applicable only in Germany.[40] 102

---

35 Reimer in BeckOK VwGO § 40 mn. 22; Pache in HK-UnionsR AEUV Art. 267 mn. 4. On the indirect enforcement of EU law, see von Alemann/Scheffczyk in BeckOK VwVfG § 35 mn. 103.

36 Wegener in Calliess/Ruffert EUV Art. 19 mn. 64–79.

37 In contrast to actions for annulment brought by natural or legal persons, the CJEU has direct jurisdiction for preliminary ruling proceedings. Although the General Court of the CJEU may have jurisdiction to determine questions referred for preliminary rulings in specific areas laid down by the Statute (Art. 256(3) TFEU), the Statute of the CJEU has so far not defined any subject matter.

38 Wegener in Calliess/Ruffert EUV Art. 19 mn. 67. On the obligation to also refer to courts of instance in the case of an invalid EU provision relevant to the decision, see Karpenstein in Grabitz/Hilf/Nettesheim AEUV Art. 267 mn. 62; Pache in HK-UnionsR AEUV Art. 267 mn. 33.

39 On the subject of the questions referred for a preliminary ruling, see Karpenstein in Grabitz/Hilf/Nettesheim AEUV Art. 267 mn. 19–24.

40 Cf. German Parliament, 'Entwurf eines Gesetzes zur Verbesserung der Rechtsdurchsetzung in sozialen Netzwerken' (16.5.2017), BT-Drs. 18/12356, 3 et seq.

103 It is also questionable, for example, what the actual **consequences** might be if, contrary to Art. 50(1) DSA (→ mn. 10), individual **Member State authorities** fail to adequately equip themselves with resources necessary to carry out their tasks or are unable to meet deadlines due to staff shortages, and cooperation with other Member State or European authorities does not work (contrary to Art. 57 or 58 DSA). It would be possible for the Commission or other Member States to initiate **infringement procedures** (Art. 258 and 259 TFEU). This would not go down well, and was therefore not even seriously discussed in the context of the GDPR implementation deficits, although violations of Art. 54(4) GDPR were close to evident.

104 It is also by no means certain that the **Commission** has sufficient capacity to comprehensively supervise all VLOP and VLOSE providers and not be forced to limit itself to initiating proceedings against only a few infringements. The Commission apparently plans to have around 100 full-time positions in the Directorates-General for Competition and for Communications Networks, Content and Technology for both the DMA and the DSA from 2024.[41] However, it will probably be several **years** before the Commission attains real power. In addition to recruiting sufficient staff members, it will also be necessary to build up **special expertise**, including first-class data scientists and other technical experts. The EBDS (→ mn. 14 et seqq.) and cooperation with Member State authorities are particularly helpful in this regard. The Commission can also draw on staff and expertise from Member States and other EU institutions (Art. 64(1), (3) and (4) DSA) and consult external experts, user associations, civil society organisations and other stakeholders (rec. 137 sent. 6 DSA). Incidentally, the Commission also sometimes suffers from budgetary constraints.[42] It can, however, recoup some of its costs through supervisory fees (→ Ch. 4 mn. 268 et seqq.).

2. Lack of independence from the state

105 **Media supervision** has so far been organised **independently from the state**, due to the rules on **freedom of reporting** (Art. 5(1) sent. 2 German Constitution (*Grundgesetz* – GG)).[43] The DSA also places strict requirements for the safeguarding of the **independence of Member State authorities** (→ mn. 10). From this perspective, it is surprising that it is the role of the **Commission** to supervise the very large platforms that are hugely important the formation of public opinion. After all, the Commission is very much not an independent authority but the **politically elected executive body** of the EU.

106 This should not necessarily result in an **infringement of primary law** (recognised as such by the CJEU). However, the massive influence of the Commission on media and communication is questionable both from a democratic perspective and from the perspective of the rule of law.[44] Only media supervision independent of the state can guarantee a democratic media order based on the rule of law, so it is not surprising

---

[41] European Commission, 'Sneak Peek: How the Commission will enforce the DSA & DMA – Blog of Commissioner Thierry Breton'.

[42] See Bertuzzi, 'EU Commission set to cut already strained personnel as inflation bites'.

[43] Instructive on the principle of state neutrality Kühling in BeckOK InfoMedienR GG Art. 5 mn. 45–59, 74 et seq.; Kühling, 'Rechtsgutachten zur Unabhängigkeit des Koordinators für digitale Dienste nach dem Gesetz über digitale Dienste der Europäischen Union', p. 33 et seqq. On state-remote supervision by media institutions, see, for example, Degenhart, 'Staatsferne der Medienaufsicht', p. 16 et seqq.

[44] On the rule of law principle within the EU, cf. Hilf/Schorkopf in Grabitz/Hilf/Nettesheim EUV Art. 2 mn. 34 et seq.; Calliess in Calliess/Ruffert EUV Art. 2 mn. 26 et seq. General discussions on possible democratic and constitutional deficiencies of the EU itself, for example, due to a not yet fully developed separation of powers, democratic legitimacy and individual legal redress possibilities, should not be addressed here.

that even voices from politics and civil society highly sympathetic to European platform regulation are **critical** of the Commission's role.[45]

107 In addition, a number of other complicating factors should be considered. First, there are no rules in the DSA to safeguard the independence of Commission officials from **political influence**. On the contrary, the Commission has **discretionary powers** concerning the initiation of proceedings,[46] and it has already been shown in the context of infringement procedures (Art. 258 TFEU) that the Commission is not free of political considerations when exercising its discretionary powers. Moreover, it cannot be ruled out that the Commission, in particular through its chairmanship, also influences the **EBDS** (→ mn. 15). It remains to be seen whether the EDBS – in line with the EDPB, which has its own legal personality (Art. 68(1) GDPR) – will not shy away from necessary criticism of the DSA and its implementation.

108 Overall, it would have been desirable for the DSA to create an **independent European digital authority.**[47] The European Central Bank (ECB), for example, is also independent and cooperates successfully with Member State authorities.

3. Further criticism

109 Beyond the lack of state neutrality, there is further criticism of the history and content of the DSA from the perspective of fundamental rights and the principles of democracy and the rule of law. For example, within the framework of the non-transparent **trilogue procedure**, amendments that could not be discussed in the European Parliament beforehand were inserted into the DSA.[48] Furthermore, the DSA exacerbates **increasing surveillance tendencies** of citizens' online communication behaviour with its **far-reaching transparency and information obligations**, such as the notification of any orders due to allegedly unlawful content via the information sharing system (Art. 9(3) and (4) and Art. 10(3) and (4) DSA) and the database of all decisions to remove or moderate content and their justification (Art. 24(5) DSA, → Ch. 4 mn. 154 et seqq.).[49] Civil society, legal experts and other observers should, therefore, closely monitor the application of the DSA, especially insofar as it is carried out by the Commission.

C. Private enforcement

110 **Private enforcement** of the DSA also plays a role parallel to the official investigation and enforcement measures (→ mn. 29 et seqq.). This section will briefly address the (ul-

[45] For example, MEP Patrick Breyer, who participated in the negotiations on the DSA as rapporteur of the European Parliament's Committee on Civil Liberties, Justice and Home Affairs (LIBE), commented on Twitter on 5.7.2022: 'Unfortunately, the Commission is not an independent authority, and its track record for enforcing the law is poor (see infringement procedures).' (available at <https://twitter.com/echo_pbreyer/status/1544422540319379456> (last accessed: 23.5.2024)). Vergnolle, 'Enforcement of the DSA and the DMA: What did we learn from the GDPR?'.

[46] Art. 67(1) DSA contains the verb 'may'. Also clearly in favour of a margin of discretion is rec. 139 sent. 1 DSA.

[47] See also Jaursch, 'The DSA Draft: Ambitious Rules, Weak Enforcement Mechanisms'. Although the Commission's latest draft of a European Media Freedom Act (16.9.2022), COM(2022) 457 final, seeks to create a European media authority, it faces even stronger criticism from the press.

[48] These amendments concern, among other things, the crisis response mechanism (Art. 36 DSA, → Ch. 4 mn. 234 et seqq.), which Keber, 'Plattformverantwortlichkeit in der Krise – Der neue Crisis Response Mechanism im Digital Services Act', criticises.

[49] Peukert, 'Five Reasons to be Skeptical About the DSA', criticises this: 'Such a panoptical position creates new risks of manipulation and misuse'.

timately judicial) enforcement of private claims by users against providers for their violation of **obligations under the DSA** (in particular, Art. 11–48 DSA).

111 There are points of contact between liability for illegal third-party content (**intermediary liability**, see Ch. 3) and the **reporting and complaint-handling system** (→ Ch. 4 mn. 60 et seqq., 106 et seqq.) which can also be understood under private law enforcement in a broader sense. For example, incorrect review decisions under the complaint-handling system (Art. 20 DSA) can also lead to further civil claims.[50] In addition, civil claims for unlawful third-party content may arise if the provider's liability privilege has lapsed due to violations of the obligation to remove or disable access to the illegal content (Art. 6(1)(b) DSA).

I. General rule

112 When private parties violate EU regulations, individuals may be entitled **to injunctive relief and damages** under the applicable civil law of the Member States, subject to the relevant conditions.[51] Private enforcement has recently gained importance, for example in competition and data protection law, due to the fact that supervisory authorities sometimes proceed only selectively because of limited resources. Private parties are additionally motivated by the prospect of damages and may possess superior knowledge.

113 Accordingly, when providers have violated obligations under the DSA (in particular Art. 11–48), for example because they have not properly implemented the notification and complaints procedure, **applications for injunction or removal and claims for damages** by users are in principle possible, for example under § 1004(1), § 823(2) German Civil Code (*Bürgerliches Gesetzbuch* – BGB).

II. Particularities of the DSA

114 However, certain particularities result from Art. 54 DSA.

1. Content of Art. 54 DSA

115 According to Art. 54 DSA, users 'have the right to seek, in accordance with Union and national law, **compensation** from providers [for] any damage or loss suffered due to an infringement by those providers of their obligations under this Regulation'. The exact legal effect of Art. 54 DSA is not immediately apparent, also because the provision was added late in the legislative process and little further guidance can be found in the relevant rec. 121 DSA. The resulting **legal uncertainty** must be resolved by case law. Ultimately, only decisions by the CJEU will provide clarity on the individual questions outlined below.

116 Art. 54 DSA **does not constitute a separate basis for a claim**. The provision does contain the essential requirements of a claim, namely damage based on a provider's breach of its DSA obligations. However, unlike Art. 82 GDPR, it contains no further rules (e.g. on burden of proof, competent courts or possibilities of exculpation) but opens itself up to other bases for claims, in particular Member State law, with its use of

[50] This applies even where the user pursues an out-of-court dispute settlement (Art. 21(1) subpara. 3 DSA; rec. 59 sent. 6 and 7 DSA).

[51] Wagner in MüKoBGB § 823 mn. 539–547; Picht, 'Private Enforcement for the DSA/DGA/DMA Package'.

the wording 'in accordance with [...]'. The question is, therefore, to what extent Art. 54 DSA influences the interpretation of Member State claims.

2. Interpretation of § 823(2) German Civil Code

In German civil law, for example, applications for injunction and removal are often based on **§ 1004(1) German Civil Code in analogy** in conjunction with the respective regulation. Common claims for damages follow contractually from **§§ 280 et seqq. German Civil Code** as well as in tort from **§ 823(2) German Civil Code** (in conjunction with the respective regulation as a protective law) and **§ 9(1) (competitors) and (2) (consumers) German Act against Unfair Competition** (*Gesetz gegen den unlauteren Wettbewerb* – UWG) (in each case in conjunction with the respective regulation as a rule of market conduct). It must be taken into account that a claim for damages by way of in rem restitution (*Naturalrestitution*) can also include the restoration of the previous situation, e.g. the reversal of a deletion of content.[52] Whether these claims exist in the individual case depends largely on the regulations violated – for example, whether they represent protective laws or rules of market conduct. 117

At the very least, § 823(2) German Civil Code, **interpreted in conformity with EU law**, should be **applicable in the event of a breach of any obligations under the DSA**. In principle, § 823(2) German Civil Code requires the violation of a 'statute that is intended to protect another person' (protective law – *Schutzgesetz*), meaning that it is at least also intended to protect the individual financial interests of the claimant.[53] Although the protective nature of some DSA provisions is obvious (e.g. consumer-protective obligations under Art. 25–32), there is much room for debate around numerous other provisions. However, § 823(2) German Civil Code has already been interpreted more broadly in conformity with EU law to the effect that the infringed provision need not be intended to protect the infringed party when no other sanction mechanisms are available.[54] The same can be applied to the case where a provision of Union law requires a basis for a claim in the Member States and extends liability to the infringement of further provisions, irrespective of whether these would be protective laws within the meaning of § 823(2) of the German Civil Code. By referring to 'obligations under this Regulation' but not narrowing them down further, this is exactly what Art. 54 DSA is likely to do. The **protective law requirement** should therefore **not apply** in the context of a violation of DSA obligations. 118

In addition, the question arises whether § 823(2) German Civil Code is to be interpreted in **conformity with EU law** in such a way that the provision does not require **fault on the part of the provider** (negligence or intent). It can be argued that Art. 54 DSA directly contains neither a fault requirement nor a possibility of exculpation. It could also be concluded from the title of Art. 54 DSA ('Compensation') that the provision does not refer to ordinary claims for damages that require fault. Moreover, rec. 121 DSA does not speak of fault on the part of the provider but essentially only repeats the wording of Art. 54 DSA. However, Art. 54 DSA does not necessarily imply that Member State claims must not require fault but, via its wording 'in accordance with', partially opens the compensation claim to the requirements of the relevant Member State claim as long as they do not contradict the wording of Art. 54 DSA. 119

---

[52] Raue NJW 2022, 209 (214).
[53] Förster in BeckOK BGB § 823 mn. 276–280.
[54] Wagner in MüKoBGB § 823 mn. 540.

120 All in all, there are better reasons for **not dropping the fault requirement** in the context of § 823(2) German Civil Code.[55] A contrary interpretation of Art. 54 DSA in conformity with EU law would only be necessary if the fault requirement prevented an effective, proportionate and dissuasive enforcement of rights.[56] However, this is not the case. The fault requirement need not lead to a disproportionate restriction of the claim but instead simply filter out cases for which liability is not necessary anyway. Besides, the parallel enforcement powers of the authorities already result in effective and deterrent enforcement of the DSA. Moreover, in most cases, providers will have acted negligently when breaching their obligations under Art. 11–48 DSA. After all, these companies are subject to the corresponding due diligence requirements. In addition, claimants can already benefit from considerable **relief from the burden of proof** under German case law.[57]

3. Further questions

121 Since Art. 54 DSA does not contain any further provisions – e.g. on the burden of presentation and proof – the provisions of the Member State standards apply in principle. The DSA also contains no special provisions on jurisdiction and applicable civil law (Art. 2(4) DSA; cf. rec. 126 sent. 1 DSA). Therefore, in this respect, the **general rules** of international civil procedure law and private international law apply. Art. 54 DSA is similarly not exhaustive (cf. rec. 121 sent. 2 DSA) and users may also be entitled to further claims and remedies in addition to claims for damages and compensation modified under EU law.

122 It is also open to question why Art. 54 DSA is located in **Section 1** of Chapter IV, which governs the Member State authorities and their powers, and not as Art. 86 DSA in the more general Section 5. This may suggest that a claim for damages/compensation should only exist in the event of a breach of such obligations which in turn are enforced by the Member State authorities. However, given the wording 'obligations under this Regulation', which does not contain such a restriction, and to ensure effective private enforcement, Art. 54 DSA should not be understood in a correspondingly restricted way. Rather, it must be assumed that the legislator simply did not give sufficient thought to this point.

III. Representation

123 A useful addition to the possibilities of private enforcement is found in the representation provision of Art. 86 DSA. In part to prevent rational apathy on the part of individuals entitled to damages, for whom the effort of suing for comparatively small amounts will often not be worthwhile, users can mandate **bodies, organisations and associations** to exercise their rights (Art. 86 DSA). These representatives must not pursue a profit-making objective, must have been properly constituted and must have a legitimate interest in ensuring compliance with the DSA according to their statutory objectives.

124 According to Art. 86 DSA, this is without prejudice to the recent **Directive on Representative Actions** and the corresponding recent or upcoming provisions of the Member States. Therefore more general possibilities for the employment of collective efforts may also be considered. An additional advantage of Art. 86 DSA lies in its second paragraph,

---

[55] Likewise Raue/Heesen NJW 2022, 3537 (3542 et seq.).

[56] This is the formula of the CJEU, see Wagner AcP 206 (2006), 352 (413).

[57] For example, when proving negligent conduct in violation of administrative regulations. Cf. Wagner in MüKoBGB § 823 mn. 619.

according to which the providers must ensure through necessary organisational and technical measures that the bodies entrusted with representation can also exercise **other rights of users provided for in the DSA**, such as rights in connection with the submission of notifications, the challenging of providers' decisions and the filing of complaints (→ Ch. 4 mn. 60 et seq., 106 et seq.).[58] Providers must process these matters as a priority and reach a decision without delay.

D. Conclusion

The highly ambitious enforcement regime of the DSA represents a **major step in developing EU secondary law**. In light of the experience with previous legal acts, first and foremost the GDPR (→ mn. 1 et seq.), the DSA creates a new type of close and complex interaction between Member State and European authorities, which, in conjunction with private enforcement, is geared towards maximum enforcement power. In this respect, the DSA could be a model for future regulations – even beyond Europe. 125

Nevertheless, a degree of **scepticism** is indicated for the time being. It remains to be seen whether the aims of this major step can be achieved in practice – and whether it is actually a step in the right direction. It presents the Member State and European authorities with considerable **challenges** – including financial ones – when it comes to actually enforcing the numerous strict obligations of the providers, and cooperating effectively while doing so. There is a risk of particularly high **enforcement costs**, which would result in corresponding opportunity costs in view of limited public budgets. That the German data protection authorities, which have by far the largest budget among the authorities of the Member States,[59] still consider that budget too small for effective fulfilment of the task[60] should also give pause for thought. No regulatory act should be issued whose enforcement either does not work or would be prohibitively costly. In this context, it is to be welcomed that Art. 54 and 86 DSA open up the possibility of private enforcement. 126

The authoritative **role of the Commission** is also **ambivalent**. From the perspective of effective enforcement, it is probably to be welcomed that responsibility for many large platforms is being transferred from smaller and sometimes inadequately resourced authorities in the Member States to the Commission. On the other hand, such an abundance of power in the hands of a politically elected executive authority in the context of media regulation raises concerns of its compatibility with our fundamental rights and the rule of law. It is also not yet certain how quickly the Commission acquires broad supervisory powers and that it will actually be more resistant to lobbying attempts than a decentralised supervisory system. 127

The success of the DSA enforcement regime – and thus of the DSA as a whole – not only depends on the Member States and the Commission **taking the necessary steps and initiating processes** to effectively supervise providers from the date of application of the DSA (Art. 92 and Art. 93(2) DSA). Given the complexities of cooperation between 128

[58] Art. 86(2) DSA only refers to Art. 20(1) DSA, which directly regulates only user complaints. However, the provision refers not only to complaints in this context but to 'mechanisms' in the plural. In addition, rec. 149 sent. 1 and 2 DSA also list further rights.

[59] Brave, 'Europe's Governments are failing the GDPR: Brave's 2020 Report on the Enforcement Capacity of Data Protection Authorities', p. 5; Statista, 'Budget of the European data protection authorities (DPAs) in 2020'.

[60] See German Data Protection Authorities, 'Evaluation of the GDPR under Article 97 – Questions to Data Protection Authorities/European Data Protection Board. Answers from the German Supervisory Authorities', p. 15.

authorities and the particular relevance of fundamental rights associated with the DSA, the authorities should also remain **flexible and willing to learn**. That way they should continue to receive the support of the civil society and legal scholars, as well as practical input from the industry. The regular reviews of the DSA provided for in Art. 91 DSA should offer an appropriate forum.

Annex: Digital Services Act

REGULATION (EU) 2022/2065 OF THE EUROPEAN PARLIAMENT AND OF THE COUNCIL

of 19 October 2022

on a Single Market For Digital Services and amending Directive 2000/31/EC (Digital Services Act)

(Text with EEA relevance)

THE EUROPEAN PARLIAMENT AND THE COUNCIL OF THE EUROPEAN UNION,

Having regard to the Treaty on the Functioning of the European Union, and in particular Article 114 thereof,

Having regard to the proposal from the European Commission,

After transmission of the draft legislative act to the national parliaments,

Having regard to the opinion of the European Economic and Social Committee[1],

Having regard to the opinion of the Committee of the Regions[2],

Acting in accordance with the ordinary legislative procedure[3],

Whereas:

(1) Information society services and especially intermediary services have become an important part of the Union's economy and the daily life of Union citizens. Twenty years after the adoption of the existing legal framework applicable to such services laid down in Directive 2000/31/EC of the European Parliament and of the Council[4], new and innovative business models and services, such as online social networks and online platforms allowing consumers to conclude distance contracts with traders, have allowed business users and consumers to impart and access information and engage in transactions in novel ways. A majority of Union citizens now uses those services on a daily basis. However, the digital transformation and increased use of those services has also resulted in new risks and challenges for individual recipients of the relevant service, companies and society as a whole.

(2) Member States are increasingly introducing, or are considering introducing, national laws on the matters covered by this Regulation, imposing, in particular, diligence requirements for providers of intermediary services as regards the way they should tackle illegal content, online disinformation or other societal risks. Those diverging national laws negatively affect the internal market, which, pursuant to Article 26 of the Treaty on the Functioning of the European Union (TFEU), comprises an area without internal frontiers in which the free movement of goods and services and freedom of establishment are ensured, taking into

---

[1] OJ C 286, 16.7.2021, p. 70.

[2] OJ C 440, 29.10.2021, p. 67.

[3] Position of the European Parliament of 5 July 2022 (not yet published in the Official Journal) and decision of the Council of 4 October 2022.

[4] Directive 2000/31/EC of the European Parliament and of the Council of 8 June 2000 on certain legal aspects of information society services, in particular electronic commerce, in the Internal Market ('Directive on electronic commerce') (OJ L 178, 17.7.2000, p. 1).

account the inherently cross-border nature of the internet, which is generally used to provide those services. The conditions for the provision of intermediary services across the internal market should be harmonised, so as to provide businesses with access to new markets and opportunities to exploit the benefits of the internal market, while allowing consumers and other recipients of the services to have increased choice. Business users, consumers and other users are considered to be 'recipients of the service' for the purpose of this Regulation.

(3) Responsible and diligent behaviour by providers of intermediary services is essential for a safe, predictable and trustworthy online environment and for allowing Union citizens and other persons to exercise their fundamental rights guaranteed in the Charter of Fundamental Rights of the European Union (the 'Charter'), in particular the freedom of expression and of information, the freedom to conduct a business, the right to non-discrimination and the attainment of a high level of consumer protection.

(4) Therefore, in order to safeguard and improve the functioning of the internal market, a targeted set of uniform, effective and proportionate mandatory rules should be established at Union level. This Regulation provides the conditions for innovative digital services to emerge and to scale up in the internal market. The approximation of national regulatory measures at Union level concerning the requirements for providers of intermediary services is necessary to avoid and put an end to fragmentation of the internal market and to ensure legal certainty, thus reducing uncertainty for developers and fostering interoperability. By using requirements that are technology neutral, innovation should not be hampered but instead be stimulated.

(5) This Regulation should apply to providers of certain information society services as defined in Directive (EU) 2015/1535 of the European Parliament and of the Council[5], that is, any service normally provided for remuneration, at a distance, by electronic means and at the individual request of a recipient. Specifically, this Regulation should apply to providers of intermediary services, and in particular intermediary services consisting of services known as 'mere conduit', 'caching' and 'hosting' services, given that the exponential growth of the use made of those services, mainly for legitimate and socially beneficial purposes of all kinds, has also increased their role in the intermediation and spread of unlawful or otherwise harmful information and activities.

(6) In practice, certain providers of intermediary services intermediate in relation to services that may or may not be provided by electronic means, such as remote information technology services, transport, accommodation or delivery services. This Regulation should apply only to intermediary services and not affect requirements set out in Union or national law relating to products or services intermediated through intermediary services, including in situations where the intermediary service constitutes an integral part of another service which is not an intermediary service as recognised in the case-law of the Court of Justice of the European Union.

(7) In order to ensure the effectiveness of the rules laid down in this Regulation and a level playing field within the internal market, those rules should apply to

[5] Directive (EU) 2015/1535 of the European Parliament and of the Council of 9 September 2015 laying down a procedure for the provision of information in the field of technical regulations and of rules on Information Society services (OJ L 241, 17.9.2015, p. 1).

providers of intermediary services irrespective of their place of establishment or their location, in so far as they offer services in the Union, as evidenced by a substantial connection to the Union.

(8) Such a substantial connection to the Union should be considered to exist where the service provider has an establishment in the Union or, in the absence of such an establishment, where the number of recipients of the service in one or more Member States is significant in relation to the population thereof, or on the basis of the targeting of activities towards one or more Member States. The targeting of activities towards one or more Member States can be determined on the basis of all relevant circumstances, including factors such as the use of a language or a currency generally used in that Member State, or the possibility of ordering products or services, or the use of a relevant top-level domain. The targeting of activities towards a Member State could also be derived from the availability of an application in the relevant national application store, from the provision of local advertising or advertising in a language used in that Member State, or from the handling of customer relations such as by providing customer service in a language generally used in that Member State. A substantial connection should also be assumed where a service provider directs its activities to one or more Member States within the meaning of Article 17(1), point (c), of Regulation (EU) No 1215/2012 of the European Parliament and of the Council[6]. In contrast, mere technical accessibility of a website from the Union cannot, on that ground alone, be considered as establishing a substantial connection to the Union.

(9) This Regulation fully harmonises the rules applicable to intermediary services in the internal market with the objective of ensuring a safe, predictable and trusted online environment, addressing the dissemination of illegal content online and the societal risks that the dissemination of disinformation or other content may generate, and within which fundamental rights enshrined in the Charter are effectively protected and innovation is facilitated. Accordingly, Member States should not adopt or maintain additional national requirements relating to the matters falling within the scope of this Regulation, unless explicitly provided for in this Regulation, since this would affect the direct and uniform application of the fully harmonised rules applicable to providers of intermediary services in accordance with the objectives of this Regulation. This should not preclude the possibility of applying other national legislation applicable to providers of intermediary services, in compliance with Union law, including Directive 2000/31/EC, in particular its Article 3, where the provisions of national law pursue other legitimate public interest objectives than those pursued by this Regulation.

(10) This Regulation should be without prejudice to other acts of Union law regulating the provision of information society services in general, regulating other aspects of the provision of intermediary services in the internal market or specifying and complementing the harmonised rules set out in this Regulation, such as Directive 2010/13/EU of the European Parliament and of the Council[7] including the provi-

[6] Regulation (EU) No 1215/2012 of the European Parliament and of the Council of 12 December 2012 on jurisdiction and the recognition and enforcement of judgments in civil and commercial matters (OJ L 351, 20.12.2012, p. 1).

[7] Directive 2010/13/EU of the European Parliament and of the Council of 10 March 2010 on the coordination of certain provisions laid down by law, regulation or administrative action in Member States concerning the provision of audiovisual media services (Audiovisual Media Services Directive) (OJ L 95, 15.4.2010, p. 1).

sions thereof regarding video-sharing platforms, Regulations (EU) 2019/1148[8], (EU) 2019/1150[9], (EU) 2021/784[10] and (EU) 2021/1232[11] of the European Parliament and of the Council and Directive 2002/58/EC of the European Parliament and of the Council[12], and provisions of Union law set out in a Regulation on European Production and Preservation Orders for electronic evidence in criminal matters and in a Directive laying down harmonised rules on the appointment of legal representatives for the purpose of gathering evidence in criminal proceedings.

Similarly, for reasons of clarity, this Regulation should be without prejudice to Union law on consumer protection, in particular Regulations (EU) 2017/2394[13] and (EU) 2019/1020[14] of the European Parliament and of the Council, Directives 2001/95/EC[15], 2005/29/EC[16], 2011/83/EU[17] and 2013/11/EU[18] of the European Parliament and of the Council, and Council Directive 93/13/EEC[19], and on the protection of personal data, in particular Regulation (EU) 2016/679 of the European Parliament and of the Council[20].

---

[8] Regulation (EU) 2019/1148 of the European Parliament and of the Council of 20 June 2019 on the marketing and use of explosives precursors, amending Regulation (EC) No 1907/2006 and repealing Regulation (EU) No 98/2013 (OJ L 186, 11.7.2019, p. 1).

[9] Regulation (EU) 2019/1150 of the European Parliament and of the Council of 20 June 2019 on promoting fairness and transparency for business users of online intermediation services (OJ L 186, 11.7.2019, p. 57).

[10] Regulation (EU) 2021/784 of the European Parliament and of the Council of 29 April 2021 on addressing the dissemination of the terrorist content online (OJ L 172, 17.5.2021, p. 79).

[11] Regulation (EU) 2021/1232 of the European Parliament and of the Council of 14 July 2021 on temporary derogation from certain provisions of Directive 2002/58/EC as regards the use of technologies by providers of number-independent interpersonal communications services for the processing of personal and other data for the purpose of combating online child sexual abuse (OJ L 274, 30.7.2021, p. 41).

[12] Directive 2002/58/EC of the European Parliament and of the Council of 12 July 2002 concerning the processing of personal data and the protection of privacy in the electronic communications sector (Directive on privacy and electronic communications) (OJ L 201, 31.7.2002, p. 37).

[13] Regulation (EU) 2017/2394 of the European Parliament and of the Council of 12 December 2017 on cooperation between national authorities responsible for the enforcement of consumer protection laws and repealing Regulation (EC) No 2006/2004 (OJ L 345, 27.12.2017, p. 1).

[14] Regulation (EU) 2019/1020 of the European Parliament and of the Council of 20 June 2019 on market surveillance and compliance of products and amending Directive 2004/42/EC and Regulations (EC) No 765/2008 and (EU) No 305/2011 (OJ L 169, 25.6.2019, p. 1).

[15] Directive 2001/95/EC of the European Parliament and of the Council of 3 December 2001 on general product safety (OJ L 11, 15.1.2002, p. 4).

[16] Directive 2005/29/EC of the European Parliament and of the Council of 11 May 2005 concerning unfair business-to-consumer commercial practices in the internal market and amending Council Directive 84/450/EEC, Directives 97/7/EC, 98/27/EC and 2002/65/EC of the European Parliament and of the Council and Regulation (EC) No 2006/2004 of the European Parliament and of the Council ('Unfair Commercial Practices Directive') (OJ L 149, 11.6.2005, p. 22).

[17] Directive 2011/83/EU of the European Parliament and of the Council of 25 October 2011 on consumer rights, amending Council Directive 93/13/EEC and Directive 1999/44/EC of the European Parliament and of the Council and repealing Council Directive 85/577/EEC and Directive 97/7/EC of the European Parliament and of the Council (OJ L 304, 22.11.2011, p. 64).

[18] Directive 2013/11/EU of the European Parliament and of the Council of 21 May 2013 on alternative dispute resolution for consumer disputes and amending Regulation (EC) No 2006/2004 and Directive 2009/22/EC (OJ L 165, 18.6.2013, p. 63).

[19] Council Directive 93/13/EEC of 5 April 1993 on unfair terms in consumer contracts (OJ L 95, 21.4.1993, p. 29).

[20] Regulation (EU) 2016/679 of the European Parliament and of the Council of 27 April 2016 on the protection of natural persons with regard to the processing of personal data and on the free movement of such data, and repealing Directive 95/46/EC (General Data Protection Regulation) (OJ L 119, 4.5.2016, p. 1).

This Regulation should also be without prejudice to Union rules on private international law, in particular rules regarding jurisdiction and the recognition and enforcement of judgments in civil and commercial matters, as Regulation (EU) No 1215/2012, and rules on the law applicable to contractual and non-contractual obligations. The protection of individuals with regard to the processing of personal data is governed solely by the rules of Union law on that subject, in particular Regulation (EU) 2016/679 and Directive 2002/58/EC. This Regulation should also be without prejudice to Union law on working conditions and Union law in the field of judicial cooperation in civil and criminal matters. However, to the extent that those Union legal acts pursue the same objectives as those laid down in this Regulation, the rules of this Regulation should apply in respect of issues that are not addressed or not fully addressed by those other legal acts as well as issues on which those other legal acts leave Member States the possibility of adopting certain measures at national level.

(11) It should be clarified that this Regulation is without prejudice to Union law on copyright and related rights, including Directives 2001/29/EC[21], 2004/48/EC[22] and (EU) 2019/790[23] of the European Parliament and of the Council, which establish specific rules and procedures that should remain unaffected.

(12) In order to achieve the objective of ensuring a safe, predictable and trustworthy online environment, for the purpose of this Regulation the concept of 'illegal content' should broadly reflect the existing rules in the offline environment. In particular, the concept of 'illegal content' should be defined broadly to cover information relating to illegal content, products, services and activities. In particular, that concept should be understood to refer to information, irrespective of its form, that under the applicable law is either itself illegal, such as illegal hate speech or terrorist content and unlawful discriminatory content, or that the applicable rules render illegal in view of the fact that it relates to illegal activities. Illustrative examples include the sharing of images depicting child sexual abuse, the unlawful non-consensual sharing of private images, online stalking, the sale of non-compliant or counterfeit products, the sale of products or the provision of services in infringement of consumer protection law, the non-authorised use of copyright protected material, the illegal offer of accommodation services or the illegal sale of live animals. In contrast, an eyewitness video of a potential crime should not be considered to constitute illegal content, merely because it depicts an illegal act, where recording or disseminating such a video to the public is not illegal under national or Union law. In this regard, it is immaterial whether the illegality of the information or activity results from Union law or from national law that is in compliance with Union law and what the precise nature or subject matter is of the law in question.

(13) Considering the particular characteristics of the services concerned and the corresponding need to make the providers thereof subject to certain specific obligations, it is necessary to distinguish, within the broader category of providers

---

[21] Directive 2001/29/EC of the European Parliament and of the Council of 22 May 2001 on the harmonisation of certain aspects of copyright and related rights in the information society (OJ L 167, 22.6.2001, p. 10).

[22] Directive 2004/48/EC of the European Parliament and of the Council of 29 April 2004 on the enforcement of intellectual property rights (OJ L 157, 30.4.2004, p. 45).

[23] Directive (EU) 2019/790 of the European Parliament and of the Council of 17 April 2019 on copyright and related rights in the Digital Single Market and amending Directives 96/9/EC and 2001/29/EC (OJ L 130, 17.5.2019, p. 92).

of hosting services as defined in this Regulation, the subcategory of online platforms. Online platforms, such as social networks or online platforms allowing consumers to conclude distance contracts with traders, should be defined as providers of hosting services that not only store information provided by the recipients of the service at their request, but that also disseminate that information to the public at the request of the recipients of the service. However, in order to avoid imposing overly broad obligations, providers of hosting services should not be considered as online platforms where the dissemination to the public is merely a minor and purely ancillary feature that is intrinsically linked to another service, or a minor functionality of the principal service, and that feature or functionality cannot, for objective technical reasons, be used without that other or principal service, and the integration of that feature or functionality is not a means to circumvent the applicability of the rules of this Regulation applicable to online platforms. For example, the comments section in an online newspaper could constitute such a feature, where it is clear that it is ancillary to the main service represented by the publication of news under the editorial responsibility of the publisher. In contrast, the storage of comments in a social network should be considered an online platform service where it is clear that it is not a minor feature of the service offered, even if it is ancillary to publishing the posts of recipients of the service. For the purposes of this Regulation, cloud computing or web-hosting services should not be considered to be an online platform where dissemination of specific information to the public constitutes a minor and ancillary feature or a minor functionality of such services.

Moreover, cloud computing services and web-hosting services, when serving as infrastructure, such as the underlying infrastructural storage and computing services of an internet-based application, website or online platform, should not in themselves be considered as disseminating to the public information stored or processed at the request of a recipient of the application, website or online platform which they host.

(14) The concept of 'dissemination to the public', as used in this Regulation, should entail the making available of information to a potentially unlimited number of persons, meaning making the information easily accessible to recipients of the service in general without further action by the recipient of the service providing the information being required, irrespective of whether those persons actually access the information in question. Accordingly, where access to information requires registration or admittance to a group of recipients of the service, that information should be considered to be disseminated to the public only where recipients of the service seeking to access the information are automatically registered or admitted without a human decision or selection of whom to grant access. Interpersonal communication services, as defined in Directive (EU) 2018/1972 of the European Parliament and of the Council[24], such as emails or private messaging services, fall outside the scope of the definition of online platforms as they are used for interpersonal communication between a finite number of persons determined by the sender of the communication. However, the obligations set out in this Regulation for providers of online platforms may apply to services that allow the making available of information to a potentially unlimited number of recipients, not determined by the sender of the communication, such as through

[24] Directive (EU) 2018/1972 of the European Parliament and of the Council of 11 December 2018 establishing the European Electronic Communications Code (OJ L 321, 17.12.2018, p. 36).

public groups or open channels. Information should be considered disseminated to the public within the meaning of this Regulation only where that dissemination occurs upon the direct request by the recipient of the service that provided the information.

(15) Where some of the services provided by a provider are covered by this Regulation whilst others are not, or where the services provided by a provider are covered by different sections of this Regulation, the relevant provisions of this Regulation should apply only in respect of those services that fall within their scope.

(16) The legal certainty provided by the horizontal framework of conditional exemptions from liability for providers of intermediary services, laid down in Directive 2000/31/EC, has allowed many novel services to emerge and scale up across the internal market. That framework should therefore be preserved. However, in view of the divergences when transposing and applying the relevant rules at national level, and for reasons of clarity and coherence, that framework should be incorporated in this Regulation. It is also necessary to clarify certain elements of that framework, having regard to the case-law of the Court of Justice of the European Union.

(17) The rules on liability of providers of intermediary services set out in this Regulation should only establish when the provider of intermediary services concerned cannot be held liable in relation to illegal content provided by the recipients of the service. Those rules should not be understood to provide a positive basis for establishing when a provider can be held liable, which is for the applicable rules of Union or national law to determine. Furthermore, the exemptions from liability established in this Regulation should apply in respect of any type of liability as regards any type of illegal content, irrespective of the precise subject matter or nature of those laws.

(18) The exemptions from liability established in this Regulation should not apply where, instead of confining itself to providing the services neutrally by a merely technical and automatic processing of the information provided by the recipient of the service, the provider of intermediary services plays an active role of such a kind as to give it knowledge of, or control over, that information. Those exemptions should accordingly not be available in respect of liability relating to information provided not by the recipient of the service but by the provider of the intermediary service itself, including where the information has been developed under the editorial responsibility of that provider.

(19) In view of the different nature of the activities of 'mere conduit', 'caching' and 'hosting' and the different position and abilities of the providers of the services in question, it is necessary to distinguish the rules applicable to those activities, in so far as under this Regulation they are subject to different requirements and conditions and their scope differs, as interpreted by the Court of Justice of the European Union.

(20) Where a provider of intermediary services deliberately collaborates with a recipient of the services in order to undertake illegal activities, the services should not be deemed to have been provided neutrally and the provider should therefore not be able to benefit from the exemptions from liability provided for in this Regulation. This should be the case, for instance, where the provider offers its service with the main purpose of facilitating illegal activities, for example by making explicit that its purpose is to facilitate illegal activities or that its services

are suited for that purpose. The fact alone that a service offers encrypted transmissions or any other system that makes the identification of the user impossible should not in itself qualify as facilitating illegal activities.

(21) A provider should be able to benefit from the exemptions from liability for 'mere conduit' and for 'caching' services when it is in no way involved with the information transmitted or accessed. This requires, among other things, that the provider does not modify the information that it transmits or to which it provides access. However, this requirement should not be understood to cover manipulations of a technical nature which take place in the course of the transmission or access, as long as those manipulations do not alter the integrity of the information transmitted or to which access is provided.

(22) In order to benefit from the exemption from liability for hosting services, the provider should, upon obtaining actual knowledge or awareness of illegal activities or illegal content, act expeditiously to remove or to disable access to that content. The removal or disabling of access should be undertaken in the observance of the fundamental rights of the recipients of the service, including the right to freedom of expression and of information. The provider can obtain such actual knowledge or awareness of the illegal nature of the content, inter alia through its own-initiative investigations or through notices submitted to it by individuals or entities in accordance with this Regulation in so far as such notices are sufficiently precise and adequately substantiated to allow a diligent economic operator to reasonably identify, assess and, where appropriate, act against the allegedly illegal content. However, such actual knowledge or awareness cannot be considered to be obtained solely on the ground that that provider is aware, in a general sense, of the fact that its service is also used to store illegal content. Furthermore, the fact that the provider automatically indexes information uploaded to its service, that it has a search function or that it recommends information on the basis of the profiles or preferences of the recipients of the service is not a sufficient ground for considering that provider to have 'specific' knowledge of illegal activities carried out on that platform or of illegal content stored on it.

(23) The exemption of liability should not apply where the recipient of the service is acting under the authority or the control of the provider of a hosting service. For example, where the provider of an online platform that allows consumers to conclude distance contracts with traders determines the price of the goods or services offered by the trader, it could be considered that the trader acts under the authority or control of that online platform.

(24) In order to ensure the effective protection of consumers when engaging in intermediated commercial transactions online, certain providers of hosting services, namely online platforms that allow consumers to conclude distance contracts with traders, should not be able to benefit from the exemption from liability for hosting service providers established in this Regulation, in so far as those online platforms present the relevant information relating to the transactions at issue in such a way as to lead consumers to believe that that information was provided by those online platforms themselves or by traders acting under their authority or control, and that those online platforms thus have knowledge of or control over the information, even if that may in reality not be the case. Examples of such behaviour could be where an online platform fails to display clearly the identity of the trader, as required by this Regulation, where an online platform withholds the identity or contact details of the trader until after the conclusion of

the contract concluded between the trader and the consumer, or where an online platform markets the product or service in its own name rather than in the name of the trader who will supply that product or service. In that regard, it should be determined objectively, on the basis of all relevant circumstances, whether the presentation could lead an average consumer to believe that the information in question was provided by the online platform itself or by traders acting under its authority or control.

(25) The exemptions from liability established in this Regulation should not affect the possibility of injunctions of different kinds against providers of intermediary services, even where they meet the conditions set out as part of those exemptions. Such injunctions could, in particular, consist of orders by courts or administrative authorities, issued in compliance with Union law, requiring the termination or prevention of any infringement, including the removal of illegal content specified in such orders, or the disabling of access to it.

(26) In order to create legal certainty, and not to discourage activities that aim to detect, identify and act against illegal content that providers of all categories of intermediary services undertake on a voluntary basis, it should be clarified that the mere fact that providers undertake such activities does not render unavailable the exemptions from liability set out in this Regulation, provided those activities are carried out in good faith and in a diligent manner. The condition of acting in good faith and in a diligent manner should include acting in an objective, non-discriminatory and proportionate manner, with due regard to the rights and legitimate interests of all parties involved, and providing the necessary safeguards against unjustified removal of legal content, in accordance with the objective and requirements of this Regulation. To that aim, the providers concerned should, for example, take reasonable measures to ensure that, where automated tools are used to conduct such activities, the relevant technology is sufficiently reliable to limit to the maximum extent possible the rate of errors. In addition, it is appropriate to clarify that the mere fact that the providers take measures, in good faith, to comply with the requirements of Union law, including those set out in this Regulation as regards the implementation of their terms and conditions, should not render unavailable the exemptions from liability set out in this Regulation. Therefore, any such activities and measures that a provider may have taken should not be taken into account when determining whether the provider can rely on an exemption from liability, in particular as regards whether the provider provides its service neutrally and can therefore fall within the scope of the relevant provision, without this rule however implying that the provider can necessarily rely thereon. Voluntary actions should not be used to circumvent the obligations of providers of intermediary services under this Regulation.

(27) Whilst the rules on liability of providers of intermediary services set out in this Regulation concentrate on the exemption from liability of providers of intermediary services, it is important to recall that, despite the generally important role played by such providers, the problem of illegal content and activities online should not be dealt with by solely focusing on their liability and responsibilities. Where possible, third parties affected by illegal content transmitted or stored online should attempt to resolve conflicts relating to such content without involving the providers of intermediary services in question. Recipients of the service should be held liable, where the applicable rules of Union and national law determining such liability so provide, for the illegal content that they provide and

may disseminate to the public through intermediary services. Where appropriate, other actors, such as group moderators in closed online environments, in particular in the case of large groups, should also help to avoid the spread of illegal content online, in accordance with the applicable law. Furthermore, where it is necessary to involve information society services providers, including providers of intermediary services, any requests or orders for such involvement should, as a general rule, be directed to the specific provider that has the technical and operational ability to act against specific items of illegal content, so as to prevent and minimise any possible negative effects on the availability and accessibility of information that is not illegal content.

(28) Since 2000, new technologies have emerged that improve the availability, efficiency, speed, reliability, capacity and security of systems for the transmission, 'findability' and storage of data online, leading to an increasingly complex online ecosystem. In this regard, it should be recalled that providers of services establishing and facilitating the underlying logical architecture and proper functioning of the internet, including technical auxiliary functions, can also benefit from the exemptions from liability set out in this Regulation, to the extent that their services qualify as 'mere conduit', 'caching' or 'hosting' services. Such services include, as the case may be, wireless local area networks, domain name system (DNS) services, top-level domain name registries, registrars, certificate authorities that issue digital certificates, virtual private networks, online search engines, cloud infrastructure services, or content delivery networks, that enable, locate or improve the functions of other providers of intermediary services. Likewise, services used for communications purposes, and the technical means of their delivery, have also evolved considerably, giving rise to online services such as Voice over IP, messaging services and web-based email services, where the communication is delivered via an internet access service. Those services, too, can benefit from the exemptions from liability, to the extent that they qualify as 'mere conduit', 'caching' or 'hosting' services.

(29) Intermediary services span a wide range of economic activities which take place online and that develop continually to provide for transmission of information that is swift, safe and secure, and to ensure convenience of all participants of the online ecosystem. For example, 'mere conduit' intermediary services include generic categories of services, such as internet exchange points, wireless access points, virtual private networks, DNS services and resolvers, top-level domain name registries, registrars, certificate authorities that issue digital certificates, voice over IP and other interpersonal communication services, while generic examples of 'caching' intermediary services include the sole provision of content delivery networks, reverse proxies or content adaptation proxies. Such services are crucial to ensure the smooth and efficient transmission of information delivered on the internet. Examples of 'hosting services' include categories of services such as cloud computing, web hosting, paid referencing services or services enabling sharing information and content online, including file storage and sharing. Intermediary services may be provided in isolation, as a part of another type of intermediary service, or simultaneously with other intermediary services. Whether a specific service constitutes a 'mere conduit', 'caching' or 'hosting' service depends solely on its technical functionalities, which might evolve in time, and should be assessed on a case-by-case basis.

(30) Providers of intermediary services should not be, neither de jure, nor de facto, subject to a monitoring obligation with respect to obligations of a general nature. This does not concern monitoring obligations in a specific case and, in particular, does not affect orders by national authorities in accordance with national legislation, in compliance with Union law, as interpreted by the Court of Justice of the European Union, and in accordance with the conditions established in this Regulation. Nothing in this Regulation should be construed as an imposition of a general monitoring obligation or a general active fact-finding obligation, or as a general obligation for providers to take proactive measures in relation to illegal content.

(31) Depending on the legal system of each Member State and the field of law at issue, national judicial or administrative authorities, including law enforcement authorities, may order providers of intermediary services to act against one or more specific items of illegal content or to provide certain specific information. The national laws on the basis of which such orders are issued differ considerably and the orders are increasingly addressed in cross-border situations. In order to ensure that those orders can be complied with in an effective and efficient manner, in particular in a cross-border context, so that the public authorities concerned can carry out their tasks and the providers are not subject to any disproportionate burdens, without unduly affecting the rights and legitimate interests of any third parties, it is necessary to set certain conditions that those orders should meet and certain complementary requirements relating to the processing of those orders. Consequently, this Regulation should harmonise only certain specific minimum conditions that such orders should fulfil in order to give rise to the obligation of providers of intermediary services to inform the relevant authorities about the effect given to those orders. Therefore, this Regulation does not provide the legal basis for the issuing of such orders, nor does it regulate their territorial scope or cross-border enforcement.

(32) The applicable Union or national law on the basis of which those orders are issued might require additional conditions and should be the basis for the enforcement of the respective orders. In the event of non-compliance with such orders, the issuing Member State should be able to enforce them in accordance with its national law. The applicable national law should be in compliance with Union law, including the Charter and the TFEU provisions on the freedom of establishment and the freedom to provide services within the Union, in particular with regard to online gambling and betting services. Similarly, the application of such national laws for the enforcement of the respective orders is without prejudice to applicable Union legal acts or international agreements concluded by the Union or by Member States relating to the cross-border recognition, execution and enforcement of those orders, in particular in civil and criminal matters. On the other hand, the enforcement of the obligation to inform the relevant authorities about the effect given to those orders, as opposed to the enforcement of the orders themselves, should be subject to the rules set out in this Regulation.

(33) The provider of intermediary services should inform the issuing authority about any follow-up given to such orders without undue delay, in compliance with the time limits set out in relevant Union or national law.

(34) Relevant national authorities should be able to issue such orders against content considered illegal or orders to provide information on the basis of Union law or national law in compliance with Union law, in particular the Charter, and to

address them to providers of intermediary services, including those established in another Member State. However, this Regulation should be without prejudice to Union law in the field of judicial cooperation in civil or criminal matters, including Regulation (EU) No 1215/2012 and a Regulation on European production and preservation orders for electronic evidence in criminal matters, and to national criminal or civil procedural law. Therefore, where those laws in the context of criminal or civil proceedings provide for conditions that are additional to or incompatible with the conditions provided for in this Regulation in relation to orders to act against illegal content or to provide information, the conditions provided for in this Regulation might not apply or might be adapted. In particular, the obligation on the Digital Services Coordinator from the Member State of the issuing authority to transmit a copy of the orders to all other Digital Services Coordinators might not apply in the context of criminal proceedings or might be adapted, where the applicable national criminal procedural law so provides.

Furthermore, the obligation for the orders to contain a statement of reasons explaining why the information is illegal content should be adapted, where necessary, under the applicable national criminal procedural law for the prevention, investigation, detection and prosecution of criminal offences. Finally, the obligation on the providers of intermediary services to inform the recipient of the service might be delayed in accordance with applicable Union or national law, in particular in the context of criminal, civil or administrative proceedings. In addition, the orders should be issued in compliance with Regulation (EU) 2016/679 and the prohibition of general obligations to monitor information or to actively seek facts or circumstances indicating illegal activity laid down in this Regulation. The conditions and requirements laid down in this Regulation which apply to orders to act against illegal content are without prejudice to other Union acts providing for similar systems for acting against specific types of illegal content, such as Regulation (EU) 2021/784, Regulation (EU) 2019/1020, or Regulation (EU) 2017/2394 that confers specific powers to order the provision of information to Member State consumer law enforcement authorities, whilst the conditions and requirements that apply to orders to provide information are without prejudice to other Union acts providing for similar relevant rules for specific sectors. Those conditions and requirements should be without prejudice to retention and preservation rules under applicable national law, in compliance with Union law and confidentiality requests by law enforcement authorities related to the non-disclosure of information. Those conditions and requirements should not affect the possibility for Member States to require a provider of intermediary services to prevent an infringement, in compliance with Union law including this Regulation, and in particular with the prohibition of general monitoring obligations.

(35) The conditions and requirements laid down in this Regulation should be fulfilled at the latest when the order is transmitted to the provider concerned. Therefore, the order may be issued in one of the official languages of the issuing authority of the Member State concerned. However, where that language is different from the language declared by the provider of intermediary services, or from another official language of the Member States agreed between the authority issuing the order and the provider of intermediary services, the transmission of the order should be accompanied by a translation of at least the elements of the order which are set out in this Regulation. Where a provider of intermediary services has agreed with the authorities of a Member State to use a certain language, it

should be encouraged to accept orders in the same language issued by authorities in other Member States. The orders should include elements that enable the addressee to identify the issuing authority, including the contact details of a contact point within that authority where appropriate, and to verify the authenticity of the order.

(36) The territorial scope of such orders to act against illegal content should be clearly set out on the basis of the applicable Union or national law enabling the issuance of the order and should not exceed what is strictly necessary to achieve its objectives. In that regard, the national judicial or administrative authority, which might be a law enforcement authority, issuing the order should balance the objective that the order seeks to achieve, in accordance with the legal basis enabling its issuance, with the rights and legitimate interests of all third parties that may be affected by the order, in particular their fundamental rights under the Charter. In particular in a cross-border context, the effect of the order should in principle be limited to the territory of the issuing Member State, unless the illegality of the content derives directly from Union law or the issuing authority considers that the rights at stake require a wider territorial scope, in accordance with Union and international law, while taking into account the interests of international comity.

(37) The orders to provide information regulated by this Regulation concern the production of specific information about individual recipients of the intermediary service concerned who are identified in those orders for the purposes of determining compliance by the recipients of the service with applicable Union or national rules. Such orders should request information with the aim of enabling the identification of the recipients of the service concerned. Therefore, orders regarding information on a group of recipients of the service who are not specifically identified, including orders to provide aggregate information required for statistical purposes or evidence-based policy-making, are not covered by the requirements of this Regulation on the provision of information.

(38) Orders to act against illegal content and to provide information are subject to the rules safeguarding the competence of the Member State in which the service provider addressed is established and the rules laying down possible derogations from that competence in certain cases, set out in Article 3 of Directive 2000/31/EC, only if the conditions of that Article are met. Given that the orders in question relate to specific items of illegal content and information, respectively, where they are addressed to providers of intermediary services established in another Member State they do not in principle restrict those providers' freedom to provide their services across borders. Therefore, the rules set out in Article 3 of Directive 2000/31/EC, including those regarding the need to justify measures derogating from the competence of the Member State in which the service provider is established on certain specified grounds and regarding the notification of such measures, do not apply in respect of those orders.

(39) The requirements to provide information on redress mechanisms available to the provider of the intermediary service and to the recipient of the service who provided the content include a requirement to provide information about administrative complaint-handling mechanisms and judicial redress including appeals against orders issued by judicial authorities. Moreover, Digital Services Coordinators could develop national tools and guidance as regards complaint and redress mechanisms applicable in their respective territory, in order to facilitate access to such mechanisms by recipients of the service. Finally, when applying this

Regulation Member States should respect the fundamental right to an effective judicial remedy and to a fair trial as provided for in Article 47 of the Charter. This Regulation should therefore not prevent the relevant national judicial or administrative authorities from issuing, on the basis of the applicable Union or national law, an order to restore content, where such content was in compliance with the terms and conditions of the provider of the intermediary service but has been erroneously considered as illegal by that provider and has been removed.

(40) In order to achieve the objectives of this Regulation, and in particular to improve the functioning of the internal market and ensure a safe and transparent online environment, it is necessary to establish a clear, effective, predictable and balanced set of harmonised due diligence obligations for providers of intermediary services. Those obligations should aim in particular to guarantee different public policy objectives such as the safety and trust of the recipients of the service, including consumers, minors and users at particular risk of being subject to hate speech, sexual harassment or other discriminatory actions, the protection of relevant fundamental rights enshrined in the Charter, the meaningful accountability of those providers and the empowerment of recipients and other affected parties, whilst facilitating the necessary oversight by competent authorities.

(41) In that regard, it is important that the due diligence obligations are adapted to the type, size and nature of the intermediary service concerned. This Regulation therefore sets out basic obligations applicable to all providers of intermediary services, as well as additional obligations for providers of hosting services and, more specifically, providers of online platforms and of very large online platforms and of very large online search engines. To the extent that providers of intermediary services fall within a number of different categories in view of the nature of their services and their size, they should comply with all the corresponding obligations of this Regulation in relation to those services. Those harmonised due diligence obligations, which should be reasonable and non-arbitrary, are needed to address the identified public policy concerns, such as safeguarding the legitimate interests of the recipients of the service, addressing illegal practices and protecting the fundamental rights enshrined in the Charter. The due diligence obligations are independent from the question of liability of providers of intermediary services which need therefore to be assessed separately.

(42) In order to facilitate smooth and efficient two-way communications, including, where relevant, by acknowledging the receipt of such communications, relating to matters covered by this Regulation, providers of intermediary services should be required to designate a single electronic point of contact and to publish and update relevant information relating to that point of contact, including the languages to be used in such communications. The electronic point of contact can also be used by trusted flaggers and by professional entities which are under a specific relationship with the provider of intermediary services. In contrast to the legal representative, the electronic point of contact should serve operational purposes and should not be required to have a physical location. Providers of intermediary services can designate the same single point of contact for the requirements of this Regulation as well as for the purposes of other acts of Union law. When specifying the languages of communication, providers of intermediary services are encouraged to ensure that the languages chosen do not in themselves constitute an obstacle to communication. Where necessary, it should be possible for providers of intermediary services and Member States' authorities to reach

a separate agreement on the language of communication, or to seek alternative means to overcome the language barrier, including by using all available technological means or internal and external human resources.

(43) Providers of intermediary services should also be required to designate a single point of contact for recipients of services, enabling rapid, direct and efficient communication in particular by easily accessible means such as telephone numbers, email addresses, electronic contact forms, chatbots or instant messaging. It should be explicitly indicated when a recipient of the service communicates with chatbots. Providers of intermediary services should allow recipients of services to choose means of direct and efficient communication which do not solely rely on automated tools. Providers of intermediary services should make all reasonable efforts to guarantee that sufficient human and financial resources are allocated to ensure that this communication is performed in a timely and efficient manner.

(44) Providers of intermediary services that are established in a third country and that offer services in the Union should designate a sufficiently mandated legal representative in the Union and provide information relating to their legal representatives to the relevant authorities and make it publicly available. In order to comply with that obligation, such providers of intermediary services should ensure that the designated legal representative has the necessary powers and resources to cooperate with the relevant authorities. This could be the case, for example, where a provider of intermediary services appoints a subsidiary undertaking of the same group as the provider, or its parent undertaking, if that subsidiary or parent undertaking is established in the Union. However, it might not be the case, for instance, when the legal representative is subject to reconstruction proceedings, bankruptcy, or personal or corporate insolvency. That obligation should allow for the effective oversight and, where necessary, enforcement of this Regulation in relation to those providers. It should be possible for a legal representative to be mandated, in accordance with national law, by more than one provider of intermediary services. It should be possible for the legal representative to also function as a point of contact, provided the relevant requirements of this Regulation are complied with.

(45) Whilst the freedom of contract of providers of intermediary services should in principle be respected, it is appropriate to set certain rules on the content, application and enforcement of the terms and conditions of those providers in the interests of transparency, the protection of recipients of the service and the avoidance of unfair or arbitrary outcomes. Providers of the intermediary services should clearly indicate and maintain up-to-date in their terms and conditions the information as to the grounds on the basis of which they may restrict the provision of their services. In particular, they should include information on any policies, procedures, measures and tools used for the purpose of content moderation, including algorithmic decision-making and human review, as well as the rules of procedure of their internal complaint-handling system. They should also provide easily accessible information on the right to terminate the use of the service. Providers of intermediary services may use graphical elements in their terms of service, such as icons or images, to illustrate the main elements of the information requirements set out in this Regulation. Providers should inform recipients of their service through appropriate means of significant changes made to terms and conditions, for instance when they modify the rules on information

that is permitted on their service, or other such changes which could directly impact the ability of the recipients to make use of the service.

(46) Providers of intermediary services that are primarily directed at minors, for example through the design or marketing of the service, or which are used predominantly by minors, should make particular efforts to render the explanation of their terms and conditions easily understandable to minors.

(47) When designing, applying and enforcing those restrictions, providers of intermediary services should act in a non-arbitrary and non-discriminatory manner and take into account the rights and legitimate interests of the recipients of the service, including fundamental rights as enshrined in the Charter. For example, providers of very large online platforms should in particular pay due regard to freedom of expression and of information, including media freedom and pluralism. All providers of intermediary services should also pay due regard to relevant international standards for the protection of human rights, such as the United Nations Guiding Principles on Business and Human Rights.

(48) Given their special role and reach, it is appropriate to impose on very large online platforms and very large online search engines additional requirements regarding information and transparency of their terms and conditions. Consequently, providers of very large online platforms and very large online search engines should provide their terms and conditions in the official languages of all Member States in which they offer their services and should also provide recipients of the services with a concise and easily readable summary of the main elements of the terms and conditions. Such summaries should identify the main elements of the information requirements, including the possibility of easily opting out from optional clauses.

(49) To ensure an adequate level of transparency and accountability, providers of intermediary services should make publicly available an annual report in a machine-readable format, in accordance with the harmonised requirements contained in this Regulation, on the content moderation in which they engage, including the measures taken as a result of the application and enforcement of their terms and conditions. However, in order to avoid disproportionate burdens, those transparency reporting obligations should not apply to providers that are micro or small enterprises as defined in Commission Recommendation 2003/361/EC[25] and which are not very large online platforms within the meaning of this Regulation.

(50) Providers of hosting services play a particularly important role in tackling illegal content online, as they store information provided by and at the request of the recipients of the service and typically give other recipients access thereto, sometimes on a large scale. It is important that all providers of hosting services, regardless of their size, put in place easily accessible and user-friendly notice and action mechanisms that facilitate the notification of specific items of information that the notifying party considers to be illegal content to the provider of hosting services concerned ('notice'), pursuant to which that provider can decide whether or not it agrees with that assessment and wishes to remove or disable access to that content ('action'). Such mechanisms should be clearly identifiable, located close to the information in question and at least as easy to find and use as notification mechanisms for content that violates the terms and conditions of the

[25] Commission Recommendation 2003/361/EC of 6 May 2003 concerning the definition of micro, small and medium-sized enterprises (OJ L 124, 20.5.2003, p. 36).

hosting service provider. Provided the requirements on notices are met, it should be possible for individuals or entities to notify multiple specific items of allegedly illegal content through a single notice in order to ensure the effective operation of notice and action mechanisms. The notification mechanism should allow, but not require, the identification of the individual or the entity submitting a notice. For some types of items of information notified, the identity of the individual or the entity submitting a notice might be necessary to determine whether the information in question constitutes illegal content, as alleged. The obligation to put in place notice and action mechanisms should apply, for instance, to file storage and sharing services, web hosting services, advertising servers and paste bins, in so far as they qualify as hosting services covered by this Regulation.

(51) Having regard to the need to take due account of the fundamental rights guaranteed under the Charter of all parties concerned, any action taken by a provider of hosting services pursuant to receiving a notice should be strictly targeted, in the sense that it should serve to remove or disable access to the specific items of information considered to constitute illegal content, without unduly affecting the freedom of expression and of information of recipients of the service. Notices should therefore, as a general rule, be directed to the providers of hosting services that can reasonably be expected to have the technical and operational ability to act against such specific items. The providers of hosting services who receive a notice for which they cannot, for technical or operational reasons, remove the specific item of information should inform the person or entity who submitted the notice.

(52) The rules on such notice and action mechanisms should be harmonised at Union level, so as to provide for the timely, diligent and non-arbitrary processing of notices on the basis of rules that are uniform, transparent and clear and that provide for robust safeguards to protect the right and legitimate interests of all affected parties, in particular their fundamental rights guaranteed by the Charter, irrespective of the Member State in which those parties are established or reside and of the field of law at issue. Those fundamental rights include but are not limited to: for the recipients of the service, the right to freedom of expression and of information, the right to respect for private and family life, the right to protection of personal data, the right to non-discrimination and the right to an effective remedy; for the service providers, the freedom to conduct a business, including the freedom of contract; for parties affected by illegal content, the right to human dignity, the rights of the child, the right to protection of property, including intellectual property, and the right to non-discrimination. Providers of hosting services should act upon notices in a timely manner, in particular by taking into account the type of illegal content being notified and the urgency of taking action. For instance, such providers can be expected to act without delay when allegedly illegal content involving a threat to life or safety of persons is being notified. The provider of hosting services should inform the individual or entity notifying the specific content without undue delay after taking a decision whether or not to act upon the notice.

(53) The notice and action mechanisms should allow for the submission of notices which are sufficiently precise and adequately substantiated to enable the provider of hosting services concerned to take an informed and diligent decision, compatible with the freedom of expression and of information, in respect of the content to which the notice relates, in particular whether or not that content is to be

considered illegal content and is to be removed or access thereto is to be disabled. Those mechanisms should be such as to facilitate the provision of notices that contain an explanation of the reasons why the individual or the entity submitting a notice considers that content to be illegal content, and a clear indication of the location of that content. Where a notice contains sufficient information to enable a diligent provider of hosting services to identify, without a detailed legal examination, that it is clear that the content is illegal, the notice should be considered to give rise to actual knowledge or awareness of illegality. Except for the submission of notices relating to offences referred to in Articles 3 to 7 of Directive 2011/93/EU of the European Parliament and of the Council[26], those mechanisms should ask the individual or the entity submitting a notice to disclose its identity in order to avoid misuse.

(54) Where a provider of hosting services decides, on the ground that the information provided by the recipients is illegal content or is incompatible with its terms and conditions, to remove or disable access to information provided by a recipient of the service or to otherwise restrict its visibility or monetisation, for instance following receipt of a notice or acting on its own initiative, including exclusively by automated means, that provider should inform in a clear and easily comprehensible way the recipient of its decision, the reasons for its decision and the available possibilities for redress to contest the decision, in view of the negative consequences that such decisions may have for the recipient, including as regards the exercise of its fundamental right to freedom of expression. That obligation should apply irrespective of the reasons for the decision, in particular whether the action has been taken because the information notified is considered to be illegal content or incompatible with the applicable terms and conditions. Where the decision was taken following receipt of a notice, the provider of hosting services should only reveal the identity of the person or entity who submitted the notice to the recipient of the service where this information is necessary to identify the illegality of the content, such as in cases of infringements of intellectual property rights.

(55) Restriction of visibility may consist in demotion in ranking or in recommender systems, as well as in limiting accessibility by one or more recipients of the service or blocking the user from an online community without the user being aware ('shadow banning'). The monetisation via advertising revenue of information provided by the recipient of the service can be restricted by suspending or terminating the monetary payment or revenue associated to that information. The obligation to provide a statement of reasons should however not apply with respect to deceptive high-volume commercial content disseminated through intentional manipulation of the service, in particular inauthentic use of the service such as the use of bots or fake accounts or other deceptive uses of the service. Irrespective of other possibilities to challenge the decision of the provider of hosting services, the recipient of the service should always have a right to effective remedy before a court in accordance with the national law.

(56) A provider of hosting services may in some instances become aware, such as through a notice by a notifying party or through its own voluntary measures, of information relating to certain activity of a recipient of the service, such as

[26] Directive 2011/93/EU of the European Parliament and of the Council of 13 December 2011 on combating the sexual abuse and sexual exploitation of children and child pornography, and replacing Council Framework Decision 2004/68/JHA (OJ L 335, 17.12.2011, p. 1).

the provision of certain types of illegal content, that reasonably justify, having regard to all relevant circumstances of which the provider of hosting services is aware, the suspicion that that recipient may have committed, may be committing or is likely to commit a criminal offence involving a threat to the life or safety of person or persons, such as offences specified in Directive 2011/36/EU of the European Parliament and of the Council[27], Directive 2011/93/EU or Directive (EU) 2017/541 of the European Parliament and of the Council[28]. For example, specific items of content could give rise to a suspicion of a threat to the public, such as incitement to terrorism within the meaning of Article 21 of Directive (EU) 2017/541. In such instances, the provider of hosting services should inform without delay the competent law enforcement authorities of such suspicion. The provider of hosting services should provide all relevant information available to it, including, where relevant, the content in question and, if available, the time when the content was published, including the designated time zone, an explanation of its suspicion and the information necessary to locate and identify the relevant recipient of the service. This Regulation does not provide the legal basis for profiling of recipients of the services with a view to the possible identification of criminal offences by providers of hosting services. Providers of hosting services should also respect other applicable rules of Union or national law for the protection of the rights and freedoms of individuals when informing law enforcement authorities.

(57) To avoid disproportionate burdens, the additional obligations imposed under this Regulation on providers of online platforms, including platforms allowing consumers to conclude distance contracts with traders, should not apply to providers that qualify as micro or small enterprises as defined in Recommendation 2003/361/EC. For the same reason, those additional obligations should also not apply to providers of online platforms that previously qualified as micro or small enterprises during a period of 12 months after they lose that status. Such providers should not be excluded from the obligation to provide information on the average monthly active recipients of the service at the request of the Digital Services Coordinator of establishment or the Commission. However, considering that very large online platforms or very large online search engines have a larger reach and a greater impact in influencing how recipients of the service obtain information and communicate online, such providers should not benefit from that exclusion, irrespective of whether they qualify or recently qualified as micro or small enterprises. The consolidation rules laid down in Recommendation 2003/361/EC help ensure that any circumvention of those additional obligations is prevented. Nothing in this Regulation precludes providers of online platforms that are covered by that exclusion from setting up, on a voluntary basis, a system that complies with one or more of those obligations.

(58) Recipients of the service should be able to easily and effectively contest certain decisions of providers of online platforms concerning the illegality of content or its incompatibility with the terms and conditions that negatively affect them. Therefore, providers of online platforms should be required to provide for internal

[27] Directive 2011/36/EU of the European Parliament and of the Council of 5 April 2011 on preventing and combating trafficking in human beings and protecting its victims, and replacing Council Framework Decision 2002/629/JHA (OJ L 101, 15.4.2011, p. 1).

[28] Directive (EU) 2017/541 of the European Parliament and of the Council of 15 March 2017 on combating terrorism and replacing Council Framework Decision 2002/475/JHA and amending Council Decision 2005/671/JHA (OJ L 88, 31.3.2017, p. 6).

complaint-handling systems, which meet certain conditions that aim to ensure that the systems are easily accessible and lead to swift, non-discriminatory, non-arbitrary and fair outcomes, and are subject to human review where automated means are used. Such systems should enable all recipients of the service to lodge a complaint and should not set formal requirements, such as referral to specific, relevant legal provisions or elaborate legal explanations. Recipients of the service who submitted a notice through the notice and action mechanism provided for in this Regulation or through the notification mechanism for content that violate the terms and conditions of the provider of online platforms should be entitled to use the complaint mechanism to contest the decision of the provider of online platforms on their notices, including when they consider that the action taken by that provider was not adequate. The possibility to lodge a complaint for the reversal of the contested decisions should be available for at least six months, to be calculated from the moment at which the provider of online platforms informed the recipient of the service of the decision.

(59) In addition, provision should be made for the possibility of engaging, in good faith, in the out-of-court dispute settlement of such disputes, including those that could not be resolved in a satisfactory manner through the internal complaint-handling systems, by certified bodies that have the requisite independence, means and expertise to carry out their activities in a fair, swift and cost-effective manner. The independence of the out-of-court dispute settlement bodies should be ensured also at the level of the natural persons in charge of resolving disputes, including through rules on conflict of interest. The fees charged by the out-of-court dispute settlement bodies should be reasonable, accessible, attractive, inexpensive for consumers and proportionate, and assessed on a case-by-case basis. Where an out-of-court dispute settlement body is certified by the competent Digital Services Coordinator, that certification should be valid in all Member States. Providers of online platforms should be able to refuse to engage in out-of-court dispute settlement procedures under this Regulation when the same dispute, in particular as regards the information concerned and the grounds for taking the contested decision, the effects of the decision and the grounds raised for contesting the decision, has already been resolved by or is already subject to an ongoing procedure before the competent court or before another competent out-of-court dispute settlement body. Recipients of the service should be able to choose between the internal complaint mechanism, an out-of-court dispute settlement and the possibility to initiate, at any stage, judicial proceedings. Since the outcome of the out-of-court dispute settlement procedure is not binding, the parties should not be prevented from initiating judicial proceedings in relation to the same dispute. The possibilities to contest decisions of providers of online platforms thus created should leave unaffected in all respects the possibility to seek judicial redress in accordance with the laws of the Member State concerned, and therefore should not affect the exercise of the right to an effective judicial remedy under Article 47 of the Charter. The provisions in this Regulation on out-of-court dispute settlement should not require Member States to establish such out-of-court settlement bodies.

(60) For contractual consumer-to-business disputes regarding the purchase of goods or services, Directive 2013/11/EU ensures that Union consumers and businesses in the Union have access to quality-certified alternative dispute resolution entities. In this regard, it should be clarified that the rules of this Regulation on

out-of-court dispute settlement are without prejudice to that Directive, including the right of consumers under that Directive to withdraw from the procedure at any stage if they are dissatisfied with the performance or the operation of the procedure.

(61) Action against illegal content can be taken more quickly and reliably where providers of online platforms take the necessary measures to ensure that notices submitted by trusted flaggers, acting within their designated area of expertise, through the notice and action mechanisms required by this Regulation are treated with priority, without prejudice to the requirement to process and decide upon all notices submitted under those mechanisms in a timely, diligent and non-arbitrary manner. Such trusted flagger status should be awarded by the Digital Services Coordinator of the Member State in which the applicant is established and should be recognised by all providers of online platforms within the scope of this Regulation. Such trusted flagger status should only be awarded to entities, and not individuals, that have demonstrated, among other things, that they have particular expertise and competence in tackling illegal content and that they work in a diligent, accurate and objective manner. Such entities can be public in nature, such as, for terrorist content, internet referral units of national law enforcement authorities or of the European Union Agency for Law Enforcement Cooperation ('Europol') or they can be non-governmental organisations and private or semi-public bodies such as the organisations part of the INHOPE network of hotlines for reporting child sexual abuse material and organisations committed to notifying illegal racist and xenophobic expressions online. To avoid diminishing the added value of such mechanism, the overall number of trusted flaggers awarded in accordance with this Regulation should be limited. In particular, industry associations representing their members' interests are encouraged to apply for the status of trusted flaggers, without prejudice to the right of private entities or individuals to enter into bilateral agreements with the providers of online platforms.

(62) Trusted flaggers should publish easily comprehensible and detailed reports on notices submitted in accordance with this Regulation. Those reports should indicate information such as the number of notices categorised by the provider of hosting services, the type of content, and the action taken by the provider. Given that trusted flaggers have demonstrated expertise and competence, the processing of notices submitted by trusted flaggers can be expected to be less burdensome and therefore faster compared to notices submitted by other recipients of the service. However, the average time taken to process may still vary depending on factors including the type of illegal content, the quality of notices, and the actual technical procedures put in place for the submission of such notices.

For example, while the Code of conduct on countering illegal hate speech online of 2016 sets a benchmark for the participating companies with respect to the time needed to process valid notifications for removal of illegal hate speech, other types of illegal content may take considerably different timelines for processing, depending on the specific facts and circumstances and types of illegal content at stake. In order to avoid abuses of the trusted flagger status, it should be possible to suspend such status when a Digital Services Coordinator of establishment opened an investigation based on legitimate reasons. The rules of this Regulation on trusted flaggers should not be understood to prevent providers of online platforms from giving similar treatment to notices submitted by entities or individuals that have not been awarded trusted flagger status under this Regulation, from otherwise cooperating with other entities, in accordance with the applicable law, including this Regulation and Regulation (EU) 2016/794 of the European Parliament and of the Council[29]. The rules of this Regulation should not prevent the providers of online platforms from making use of such trusted flagger or similar mechanisms to take quick and reliable action against content that is incompatible with their terms and conditions, in particular against content that is harmful for vulnerable recipients of the service, such as minors.

(63) The misuse of online platforms by frequently providing manifestly illegal content or by frequently submitting manifestly unfounded notices or complaints under the mechanisms and systems, respectively, established under this Regulation undermines trust and harms the rights and legitimate interests of the parties concerned. Therefore, there is a need to put in place appropriate, proportionate and effective safeguards against such misuse, that need to respect the rights and legitimate interests of all parties involved, including the applicable fundamental rights and freedoms as enshrined in the Charter, in particular the freedom of expression. Information should be considered to be manifestly illegal content and notices or complaints should be considered manifestly unfounded where it is evident to a layperson, without any substantive analysis, that the content is illegal or, respectively, that the notices or complaints are unfounded.

(64) Under certain conditions, providers of online platforms should temporarily suspend their relevant activities in respect of the person engaged in abusive behaviour. This is without prejudice to the freedom by providers of online platforms to determine their terms and conditions and establish stricter measures in the case of manifestly illegal content related to serious crimes, such as child sexual abuse material. For reasons of transparency, this possibility should be set out, clearly and in sufficient detail, in the terms and conditions of the online platforms. Redress should always be open to the decisions taken in this regard by providers of online platforms and they should be subject to oversight by the competent Digital Services Coordinator. Providers of online platforms should send a prior warning before deciding on the suspension, which should include the reasons for the possible suspension and the means of redress against the decision of the providers of the online platform. When deciding on the suspension, providers of online platforms should send the statement of reasons in accordance with the rules set out in this Regulation. The rules of this Regulation on misuse should not prevent providers of online platforms from taking other measures to address the provision of illegal content by recipients of their service or other misuse of their services, including through the violation of their terms and conditions, in accordance with the applicable Union and national law. Those rules are without prejudice to any possibility to hold the persons engaged in misuse liable, including for damages, provided for in Union or national law.

(65) In view of the particular responsibilities and obligations of providers of online platforms, they should be made subject to transparency reporting obligations, which apply in addition to the transparency reporting obligations applicable to all providers of intermediary services under this Regulation. For the purposes of

[29] Regulation (EU) 2016/794 of the European Parliament and of the Council of 11 May 2016 on the European Union Agency for Law Enforcement Cooperation (Europol) and replacing and repealing Council Decisions 2009/371/JHA, 2009/934/JHA, 2009/935/JHA, 2009/936/JHA and 2009/968/JHA (OJ L 135, 24.5.2016, p. 53).

determining whether online platforms and online search engines may be very large online platforms or very large online search engines, respectively, that are subject to certain additional obligations under this Regulation, the transparency reporting obligations for online platforms and online search engines should include certain obligations relating to the publication and communication of information on the average monthly active recipients of the service in the Union.

(66) In order to ensure transparency and to enable scrutiny over the content moderation decisions of the providers of online platforms and monitoring the spread of illegal content online, the Commission should maintain and publish a database which contains the decisions and statements of reasons of the providers of online platforms when they remove or otherwise restrict availability of and access to information. In order to keep the database continuously updated, the providers of online platforms should submit, in a standard format, the decisions and statement of reasons without undue delay after taking a decision, to allow for real-time updates where technically possible and proportionate to the means of the online platform in question. The structured database should allow access to, and queries for, the relevant information, in particular as regards the type of alleged illegal content at stake.

(67) Dark patterns on online interfaces of online platforms are practices that materially distort or impair, either on purpose or in effect, the ability of recipients of the service to make autonomous and informed choices or decisions. Those practices can be used to persuade the recipients of the service to engage in unwanted behaviours or into undesired decisions which have negative consequences for them. Providers of online platforms should therefore be prohibited from deceiving or nudging recipients of the service and from distorting or impairing the autonomy, decision-making, or choice of the recipients of the service via the structure, design or functionalities of an online interface or a part thereof. This should include, but not be limited to, exploitative design choices to direct the recipient to actions that benefit the provider of online platforms, but which may not be in the recipients' interests, presenting choices in a non-neutral manner, such as giving more prominence to certain choices through visual, auditory, or other components, when asking the recipient of the service for a decision.

It should also include repeatedly requesting a recipient of the service to make a choice where such a choice has already been made, making the procedure of cancelling a service significantly more cumbersome than signing up to it, or making certain choices more difficult or time-consuming than others, making it unreasonably difficult to discontinue purchases or to sign out from a given online platform allowing consumers to conclude distance contracts with traders, and deceiving the recipients of the service by nudging them into decisions on transactions, or by default settings that are very difficult to change, and so unreasonably bias the decision making of the recipient of the service, in a way that distorts and impairs their autonomy, decision-making and choice. However, rules preventing dark patterns should not be understood as preventing providers to interact directly with recipients of the service and to offer new or additional services to them. Legitimate practices, for example in advertising, that are in compliance with Union law should not in themselves be regarded as constituting dark patterns. Those rules on dark patterns should be interpreted as covering prohibited practices falling within the scope of this Regulation to the extent that those practices are not already covered under Directive 2005/29/EC or Regulation (EU) 2016/679.

(68) Online advertising plays an important role in the online environment, including in relation to the provision of online platforms, where the provision of the service is sometimes in whole or in part remunerated directly or indirectly, through advertising revenues. Online advertising can contribute to significant risks, ranging from advertisements that are themselves illegal content, to contributing to financial incentives for the publication or amplification of illegal or otherwise harmful content and activities online, or the discriminatory presentation of advertisements with an impact on the equal treatment and opportunities of citizens. In addition to the requirements resulting from Article 6 of Directive 2000/31/EC, providers of online platforms should therefore be required to ensure that the recipients of the service have certain individualised information necessary for them to understand when and on whose behalf the advertisement is presented. They should ensure that the information is salient, including through standardised visual or audio marks, clearly identifiable and unambiguous for the average recipient of the service, and should be adapted to the nature of the individual service's online interface. In addition, recipients of the service should have information directly accessible from the online interface where the advertisement is presented, on the main parameters used for determining that a specific advertisement is presented to them, providing meaningful explanations of the logic used to that end, including when this is based on profiling.

Such explanations should include information on the method used for presenting the advertisement, for example whether it is contextual or other type of advertising, and, where applicable, the main profiling criteria used; it should also inform the recipient about any means available for them to change such criteria. The requirements of this Regulation on the provision of information relating to advertising is without prejudice to the application of the relevant provisions of Regulation (EU) 2016/679, in particular those regarding the right to object, automated individual decision-making, including profiling, and specifically the need to obtain consent of the data subject prior to the processing of personal data for targeted advertising. Similarly, it is without prejudice to the provisions laid down in Directive 2002/58/EC in particular those regarding the storage of information in terminal equipment and the access to information stored therein. Finally, this Regulation complements the application of the Directive 2010/13/EU which imposes measures to enable users to declare audiovisual commercial communications in user-generated videos. It also complements the obligations for traders regarding the disclosure of commercial communications deriving from Directive 2005/29/EC.

(69) When recipients of the service are presented with advertisements based on targeting techniques optimised to match their interests and potentially appeal to their vulnerabilities, this can have particularly serious negative effects. In certain cases, manipulative techniques can negatively impact entire groups and amplify societal harms, for example by contributing to disinformation campaigns or by discriminating against certain groups. Online platforms are particularly sensitive environments for such practices and they present a higher societal risk. Consequently, providers of online platforms should not present advertisements based on profiling as defined in Article 4, point (4), of Regulation (EU) 2016/679, using special categories of personal data referred to in Article 9(1) of that Regu-

lation, including by using profiling categories based on those special categories. This prohibition is without prejudice to the obligations applicable to providers of online platforms or any other service provider or advertiser involved in the dissemination of the advertisements under Union law on protection of personal data.

(70) A core part of the online platform's business is the manner in which information is prioritised and presented on its online interface to facilitate and optimise access to information for the recipients of the service. This is done, for example, by algorithmically suggesting, ranking and prioritising information, distinguishing through text or other visual representations, or otherwise curating information provided by recipients. Such recommender systems can have a significant impact on the ability of recipients to retrieve and interact with information online, including to facilitate the search of relevant information for recipients of the service and contribute to an improved user experience. They also play an important role in the amplification of certain messages, the viral dissemination of information and the stimulation of online behaviour. Consequently, online platforms should consistently ensure that recipients of their service are appropriately informed about how recommender systems impact the way information is displayed, and can influence how information is presented to them. They should clearly present the parameters for such recommender systems in an easily comprehensible manner to ensure that the recipients of the service understand how information is prioritised for them. Those parameters should include at least the most important criteria in determining the information suggested to the recipient of the service and the reasons for their respective importance, including where information is prioritised based on profiling and their online behaviour.

(71) The protection of minors is an important policy objective of the Union. An online platform can be considered to be accessible to minors when its terms and conditions permit minors to use the service, when its service is directed at or predominantly used by minors, or where the provider is otherwise aware that some of the recipients of its service are minors, for example because it already processes personal data of the recipients of its service revealing their age for other purposes. Providers of online platforms used by minors should take appropriate and proportionate measures to protect minors, for example by designing their online interfaces or parts thereof with the highest level of privacy, safety and security for minors by default where appropriate or adopting standards for protection of minors, or participating in codes of conduct for protecting minors. They should consider best practices and available guidance, such as that provided by the communication of the Commission on A Digital Decade for children and youth: the new European strategy for a better internet for kids (BIK+). Providers of online platforms should not present advertisements based on profiling using personal data of the recipient of the service when they are aware with reasonable certainty that the recipient of the service is a minor. In accordance with Regulation (EU) 2016/679, notably the principle of data minimisation as provided for in Article 5(1), point (c), thereof, this prohibition should not lead the provider of the online platform to maintain, acquire or process more personal data than it already has in order to assess if the recipient of the service is a minor. Thus, this obligation should not incentivize providers of online platforms to collect the age of the recipient of the service prior to their use. It should be without prejudice to Union law on protection of personal data.

(72) In order to contribute to a safe, trustworthy and transparent online environment for consumers, as well as for other interested parties such as competing traders and holders of intellectual property rights, and to deter traders from selling products or services in violation of the applicable rules, online platforms allowing consumers to conclude distance contracts with traders should ensure that such traders are traceable. The trader should therefore be required to provide certain essential information to the providers of online platforms allowing consumers to conclude distance contracts with traders, including for purposes of promoting messages on or offering products. That requirement should also be applicable to traders that promote messages on products or services on behalf of brands, based on underlying agreements. Those providers of online platforms should store all information in a secure manner for the duration of their contractual relationship with the trader and 6 months thereafter, to allow any claims to be filed against the trader or orders related to the trader to be complied with.

This obligation is necessary and proportionate, so that the information can be accessed, in accordance with the applicable law, including on the protection of personal data, by public authorities and private parties with a legitimate interest, including through the orders to provide information referred to in this Regulation. This obligation leaves unaffected potential obligations to preserve certain content for longer periods of time, on the basis of other Union law or national laws, in compliance with Union law. Without prejudice to the definition provided for in this Regulation, any trader, irrespective of whether it is a natural or legal person, identified on the basis of Article 6a(1), point (b), of Directive 2011/83/EU and Article 7(4), point (f), of Directive 2005/29/EC should be traceable when offering a product or service through an online platform. Directive 2000/31/EC obliges all information society services providers to render easily, directly and permanently accessible to the recipients of the service and competent authorities certain information allowing the identification of all providers. The traceability requirements for providers of online platforms allowing consumers to conclude distance contracts with traders set out in this Regulation do not affect the application of Council Directive (EU) 2021/514[30], which pursues other legitimate public interest objectives.

(73) To ensure an efficient and adequate application of that obligation, without imposing any disproportionate burdens, providers of online platforms allowing consumers to conclude distance contracts with traders should make best efforts to assess the reliability of the information provided by the traders concerned, in particular by using freely available official online databases and online interfaces, such as national trade registers and the VAT Information Exchange System, or request the traders concerned to provide trustworthy supporting documents, such as copies of identity documents, certified payment accounts' statements, company certificates and trade register certificates. They may also use other sources, available for use at a distance, which offer a similar degree of reliability for the purpose of complying with this obligation. However, the providers of online platforms concerned should not be required to engage in excessive or costly online fact-finding exercises or to carry out disproportionate verifications on the spot. Nor should such providers, which have made the best efforts required by

[30] Council Directive (EU) 2021/514 of 22 March 2021 amending Directive 2011/16/EU on administrative cooperation in the field of taxation (OJ L 104, 25.3.2021, p. 1).

this Regulation, be understood as guaranteeing the reliability of the information towards consumer or other interested parties.

(74) Providers of online platforms allowing consumers to conclude distance contracts with traders should design and organise their online interface in a way that enables traders to comply with their obligations under relevant Union law, in particular the requirements set out in Articles 6 and 8 of Directive 2011/83/EU, Article 7 of Directive 2005/29/EC, Articles 5 and 6 of Directive 2000/31/EC and Article 3 of Directive 98/6/EC of the European Parliament and of the Council[31]. For that purpose, the providers of online platforms concerned should make best efforts to assess whether the traders using their services have uploaded complete information on their online interfaces, in line with relevant applicable Union law. The providers of online platforms should ensure that products or services are not offered as long as such information is not complete. This should not amount to an obligation for the providers of online platforms concerned to generally monitor the products or services offered by traders through their services nor a general fact-finding obligation, in particular to assess the accuracy of the information provided by traders. The online interfaces should be user-friendly and easily accessible for traders and consumers. Additionally and after allowing the offering of the product or service by the trader, the providers of online platforms concerned should make reasonable efforts to randomly check whether the products or services offered have been identified as being illegal in any official, freely accessible and machine-readable online databases or online interfaces available in a Member State or in the Union. The Commission should also encourage traceability of products through technology solutions such as digitally signed Quick Response codes (or 'QR codes') or non-fungible tokens. The Commission should promote the development of standards and, in the absence of them, of market led solutions which can be acceptable to the parties concerned.

(75) Given the importance of very large online platforms, due to their reach, in particular as expressed in the number of recipients of the service, in facilitating public debate, economic transactions and the dissemination to the public of information, opinions and ideas and in influencing how recipients obtain and communicate information online, it is necessary to impose specific obligations on the providers of those platforms, in addition to the obligations applicable to all online platforms. Due to their critical role in locating and making information retrievable online, it is also necessary to impose those obligations, to the extent they are applicable, on the providers of very large online search engines. Those additional obligations on providers of very large online platforms and of very large online search engines are necessary to address those public policy concerns, there being no alternative and less restrictive measures that would effectively achieve the same result.

(76) Very large online platforms and very large online search engines may cause societal risks, different in scope and impact from those caused by smaller platforms. Providers of such very large online platforms and of very large online search engines should therefore bear the highest standard of due diligence obligations, proportionate to their societal impact. Once the number of active recipients of an online platform or of active recipients of an online search engine, calculated as an

[31] Directive 98/6/EC of the European Parliament and of the Council of 16 February 1998 on consumer protection in the indication of the prices of products offered to consumers (OJ L 80, 18.3.1998, p. 27).

average over a period of six months, reaches a significant share of the Union population, the systemic risks the online platform or online search engine poses may have a disproportionate impact in the Union. Such significant reach should be considered to exist where such number exceeds an operational threshold set at 45 million, that is, a number equivalent to 10 % of the Union population. This operational threshold should be kept up to date and therefore the Commission should be empowered to supplement the provisions of this Regulation by adopting delegated acts, where necessary.

(77) In order to determine the reach of a given online platform or online search engine, it is necessary to establish the average number of active recipients of each service individually. Accordingly, the number of average monthly active recipients of an online platform should reflect all the recipients actually engaging with the service at least once in a given period of time, by being exposed to information disseminated on the online interface of the online platform, such as viewing it or listening to it, or by providing information, such as traders on an online platforms allowing consumers to conclude distance contracts with traders.

For the purposes of this Regulation, engagement is not limited to interacting with information by clicking on, commenting, linking, sharing, purchasing or carrying out transactions on an online platform. Consequently, the concept of active recipient of the service does not necessarily coincide with that of a registered user of a service. As regards online search engines, the concept of active recipients of the service should cover those who view information on their online interface, but not, for example, the owners of the websites indexed by an online search engine, as they do not actively engage with the service. The number of active recipients of a service should include all unique recipients of the service that engage with the specific service. To this effect, a recipient of the service that uses different online interfaces, such as websites or applications, including where the services are accessed through different uniform resource locators (URLs) or domain names, should, where possible, be counted only once. However, the concept of active recipient of the service should not include incidental use of the service by recipients of other providers of intermediary services that indirectly make available information hosted by the provider of online platforms through linking or indexing by a provider of online search engine. Further, this Regulation does not require providers of online platforms or of online search engines to perform specific tracking of individuals online. Where such providers are able to discount automated users such as bots or scrapers without further processing of personal data and tracking, they may do so. The determination of the number of active recipients of the service can be impacted by market and technical developments and therefore the Commission should be empowered to supplement the provisions of this Regulation by adopting delegated acts laying down the methodology to determine the active recipients of an online platform or of an online search engine, where necessary, reflecting the nature of the service and the way recipients of the service interact with it.

(78) In view of the network effects characterising the platform economy, the user base of an online platform or an online search engine may quickly expand and reach the dimension of a very large online platform or a very large online search engine, with the related impact on the internal market. This may be the case in the event of exponential growth experienced in short periods of time, or by a large global presence and turnover allowing the online platform or the online search engine

to fully exploit network effects and economies of scale and of scope. A high annual turnover or market capitalisation can in particular be an indication of fast scalability in terms of user reach. In those cases, the Digital Services Coordinator of establishment or the Commission should be able to request more frequent reporting from the provider of the online platform or of the online search engine on the number of active recipients of the service to be able to timely identify the moment at which that platform or that search engine should be designated as a very large online platform or very large online search engine, respectively, for the purposes of this Regulation.

(79) Very large online platforms and very large online search engines can be used in a way that strongly influences safety online, the shaping of public opinion and discourse, as well as online trade. The way they design their services is generally optimised to benefit their often advertising-driven business models and can cause societal concerns. Effective regulation and enforcement is necessary in order to effectively identify and mitigate the risks and the societal and economic harm that may arise. Under this Regulation, providers of very large online platforms and of very large online search engines should therefore assess the systemic risks stemming from the design, functioning and use of their services, as well as from potential misuses by the recipients of the service, and should take appropriate mitigating measures in observance of fundamental rights. In determining the significance of potential negative effects and impacts, providers should consider the severity of the potential impact and the probability of all such systemic risks. For example, they could assess whether the potential negative impact can affect a large number of persons, its potential irreversibility, or how difficult it is to remedy and restore the situation prevailing prior to the potential impact.

(80) Four categories of systemic risks should be assessed in-depth by the providers of very large online platforms and of very large online search engines. A first category concerns the risks associated with the dissemination of illegal content, such as the dissemination of child sexual abuse material or illegal hate speech or other types of misuse of their services for criminal offences, and the conduct of illegal activities, such as the sale of products or services prohibited by Union or national law, including dangerous or counterfeit products, or illegally-traded animals. For example, such dissemination or activities may constitute a significant systemic risk where access to illegal content may spread rapidly and widely through accounts with a particularly wide reach or other means of amplification. Providers of very large online platforms and of very large online search engines should assess the risk of dissemination of illegal content irrespective of whether or not the information is also incompatible with their terms and conditions. This assessment is without prejudice to the personal responsibility of the recipient of the service of very large online platforms or of the owners of websites indexed by very large online search engines for possible illegality of their activity under the applicable law.

(81) A second category concerns the actual or foreseeable impact of the service on the exercise of fundamental rights, as protected by the Charter, including but not limited to human dignity, freedom of expression and of information, including media freedom and pluralism, the right to private life, data protection, the right to non-discrimination, the rights of the child and consumer protection. Such risks may arise, for example, in relation to the design of the algorithmic systems used by the very large online platform or by the very large online search engine or

the misuse of their service through the submission of abusive notices or other methods for silencing speech or hampering competition. When assessing risks to the rights of the child, providers of very large online platforms and of very large online search engines should consider for example how easy it is for minors to understand the design and functioning of the service, as well as how minors can be exposed through their service to content that may impair minors' health, physical, mental and moral development. Such risks may arise, for example, in relation to the design of online interfaces which intentionally or unintentionally exploit the weaknesses and inexperience of minors or which may cause addictive behaviour.

(82) A third category of risks concerns the actual or foreseeable negative effects on democratic processes, civic discourse and electoral processes, as well as public security.

(83) A fourth category of risks stems from similar concerns relating to the design, functioning or use, including through manipulation, of very large online platforms and of very large online search engines with an actual or foreseeable negative effect on the protection of public health, minors and serious negative consequences to a person's physical and mental well-being, or on gender-based violence. Such risks may also stem from coordinated disinformation campaigns related to public health, or from online interface design that may stimulate behavioural addictions of recipients of the service.

(84) When assessing such systemic risks, providers of very large online platforms and of very large online search engines should focus on the systems or other elements that may contribute to the risks, including all the algorithmic systems that may be relevant, in particular their recommender systems and advertising systems, paying attention to the related data collection and use practices. They should also assess whether their terms and conditions and the enforcement thereof are appropriate, as well as their content moderation processes, technical tools and allocated resources. When assessing the systemic risks identified in this Regulation, those providers should also focus on the information which is not illegal, but contributes to the systemic risks identified in this Regulation. Such providers should therefore pay particular attention on how their services are used to disseminate or amplify misleading or deceptive content, including disinformation. Where the algorithmic amplification of information contributes to the systemic risks, those providers should duly reflect this in their risk assessments. Where risks are localised or there are linguistic differences, those providers should also account for this in their risk assessments. Providers of very large online platforms and of very large online search engines should, in particular, assess how the design and functioning of their service, as well as the intentional and, oftentimes, coordinated manipulation and use of their services, or the systemic infringement of their terms of service, contribute to such risks. Such risks may arise, for example, through the inauthentic use of the service, such as the creation of fake accounts, the use of bots or deceptive use of a service, and other automated or partially automated behaviours, which may lead to the rapid and widespread dissemination to the public of information that is illegal content or incompatible with an online platform's or online search engine's terms and conditions and that contributes to disinformation campaigns.

(85) In order to make it possible that subsequent risk assessments build on each other and show the evolution of the risks identified, as well as to facilitate investigations

and enforcement actions, providers of very large online platforms and of very large online search engines should preserve all supporting documents relating to the risk assessments that they carried out, such as information regarding the preparation thereof, underlying data and data on the testing of their algorithmic systems.

(86) Providers of very large online platforms and of very large online search engines should deploy the necessary means to diligently mitigate the systemic risks identified in the risk assessments, in observance of fundamental rights. Any measures adopted should respect the due diligence requirements of this Regulation and be reasonable and effective in mitigating the specific systemic risks identified. They should be proportionate in light of the economic capacity of the provider of the very large online platform or of the very large online search engine and the need to avoid unnecessary restrictions on the use of their service, taking due account of potential negative effects on those fundamental rights. Those providers should give particular consideration to the impact on freedom of expression.

(87) Providers of very large online platforms and of very large online search engines should consider under such mitigating measures, for example, adapting any necessary design, feature or functioning of their service, such as the online interface design. They should adapt and apply their terms and conditions, as necessary, and in accordance with the rules of this Regulation on terms and conditions. Other appropriate measures could include adapting their content moderation systems and internal processes or adapting their decision-making processes and resources, including the content moderation personnel, their training and local expertise. This concerns in particular the speed and quality of processing of notices. In this regard, for example, the Code of conduct on countering illegal hate speech online of 2016 sets a benchmark to process valid notifications for removal of illegal hate speech in less than 24 hours. Providers of very large online platforms, in particular those primarily used for the dissemination to the public of pornographic content, should diligently meet all their obligations under this Regulation in respect of illegal content constituting cyber violence, including illegal pornographic content, especially with regard to ensuring that victims can effectively exercise their rights in relation to content representing non-consensual sharing of intimate or manipulated material through the rapid processing of notices and removal of such content without undue delay. Other types of illegal content may require longer or shorter timelines for processing of notices, which will depend on the facts, circumstances and types of illegal content at hand. Those providers may also initiate or increase cooperation with trusted flaggers and organise training sessions and exchanges with trusted flagger organisations.

(88) Providers of very large online platforms and of very large online search engines should also be diligent in the measures they take to test and, where necessary, adapt their algorithmic systems, not least their recommender systems. They may need to mitigate the negative effects of personalised recommendations and correct the criteria used in their recommendations. The advertising systems used by providers of very large online platforms and of very large online search engines can also be a catalyser for the systemic risks. Those providers should consider corrective measures, such as discontinuing advertising revenue for specific information, or other actions, such as improving the visibility of authoritative information sources, or more structurally adapting their advertising systems. Providers of very large online platforms and of very large online search engines may need

to reinforce their internal processes or supervision of any of their activities, in particular as regards the detection of systemic risks, and conduct more frequent or targeted risk assessments related to new functionalities. In particular, where risks are shared across different online platforms or online search engines, they should cooperate with other service providers, including by initiating or joining existing codes of conduct or other self-regulatory measures. They should also consider awareness-raising actions, in particular where risks relate to disinformation campaigns.

(89) Providers of very large online platforms and of very large online search engines should take into account the best interests of minors in taking measures such as adapting the design of their service and their online interface, especially when their services are aimed at minors or predominantly used by them. They should ensure that their services are organised in a way that allows minors to access easily mechanisms provided for in this Regulation, where applicable, including notice and action and complaint mechanisms. They should also take measures to protect minors from content that may impair their physical, mental or moral development and provide tools that enable conditional access to such information. In selecting the appropriate mitigation measures, providers can consider, where appropriate, industry best practices, including as established through self-regulatory cooperation, such as codes of conduct, and should take into account the guidelines from the Commission.

(90) Providers of very large online platforms and of very large online search engines should ensure that their approach to risk assessment and mitigation is based on the best available information and scientific insights and that they test their assumptions with the groups most impacted by the risks and the measures they take. To this end, they should, where appropriate, conduct their risk assessments and design their risk mitigation measures with the involvement of representatives of the recipients of the service, representatives of groups potentially impacted by their services, independent experts and civil society organisations. They should seek to embed such consultations into their methodologies for assessing the risks and designing mitigation measures, including, as appropriate, surveys, focus groups, round tables, and other consultation and design methods. In the assessment on whether a measure is reasonable, proportionate and effective, special consideration should be given to the right to freedom of expression.

(91) In times of crisis, there might be a need for certain specific measures to be taken urgently by providers of very large online platforms, in addition to measures they would be taking in view of their other obligations under this Regulation. In that regard, a crisis should be considered to occur when extraordinary circumstances occur that can lead to a serious threat to public security or public health in the Union or significant parts thereof. Such crises could result from armed conflicts or acts of terrorism, including emerging conflicts or acts of terrorism, natural disasters such as earthquakes and hurricanes, as well as from pandemics and other serious cross-border threats to public health. The Commission should be able to require, upon recommendation by the European Board for Digital Services ('the Board'), providers of very large online platforms and providers of very large search engines to initiate a crisis response as a matter of urgency. Measures that those providers may identify and consider applying may include, for example, adapting content moderation processes and increasing the resources dedicated to content moderation, adapting terms and conditions, relevant algorithmic

systems and advertising systems, further intensifying cooperation with trusted flaggers, taking awareness-raising measures and promoting trusted information and adapting the design of their online interfaces. The necessary requirements should be provided for to ensure that such measures are taken within a very short time frame and that the crisis response mechanism is only used where, and to the extent that, this is strictly necessary and any measures taken under this mechanism are effective and proportionate, taking due account of the rights and legitimate interests of all parties concerned. The use of the mechanism should be without prejudice to the other provisions of this Regulation, such as those on risk assessments and mitigation measures and the enforcement thereof and those on crisis protocols.

(92) Given the need to ensure verification by independent experts, providers of very large online platforms and of very large online search engines should be accountable, through independent auditing, for their compliance with the obligations laid down by this Regulation and, where relevant, any complementary commitments undertaken pursuant to codes of conduct and crises protocols. In order to ensure that audits are carried out in an effective, efficient and timely manner, providers of very large online platforms and of very large online search engines should provide the necessary cooperation and assistance to the organisations carrying out the audits, including by giving the auditor access to all relevant data and premises necessary to perform the audit properly, including, where appropriate, to data related to algorithmic systems, and by answering oral or written questions. Auditors should also be able to make use of other sources of objective information, including studies by vetted researchers. Providers of very large online platforms and of very large online search engines should not undermine the performance of the audit. Audits should be performed according to best industry practices and high professional ethics and objectivity, with due regard, as appropriate, to auditing standards and codes of practice. Auditors should guarantee the confidentiality, security and integrity of the information, such as trade secrets, that they obtain when performing their tasks. This guarantee should not be a means to circumvent the applicability of audit obligations in this Regulation. Auditors should have the necessary expertise in the area of risk management and technical competence to audit algorithms. They should be independent, in order to be able to perform their tasks in an adequate and trustworthy manner. They should comply with core independence requirements for prohibited non-auditing services, firm rotation and non-contingent fees. If their independence and technical competence is not beyond doubt, they should resign or abstain from the audit engagement.

(93) The audit report should be substantiated, in order to give a meaningful account of the activities undertaken and the conclusions reached. It should help inform, and where appropriate suggest improvements to the measures taken by the providers of the very large online platform and of the very large online search engine to comply with their obligations under this Regulation. The audit report should be transmitted to the Digital Services Coordinator of establishment, the Commission and the Board following the receipt of the audit report. Providers should also transmit upon completion without undue delay each of the reports on the risk assessment and the mitigation measures, as well as the audit implementation report of the provider of the very large online platform or of the very large online search engine showing how they have addressed the audit's recommendations. The audit report should include an audit opinion based on the conclusions drawn from the

audit evidence obtained. A 'positive opinion' should be given where all evidence shows that the provider of the very large online platform or of the very large online search engine complies with the obligations laid down by this Regulation or, where applicable, any commitments it has undertaken pursuant to a code of conduct or crisis protocol, in particular by identifying, evaluating and mitigating the systemic risks posed by its system and services. A 'positive opinion' should be accompanied by comments where the auditor wishes to include remarks that do not have a substantial effect on the outcome of the audit. A 'negative opinion' should be given where the auditor considers that the provider of the very large online platform or of the very large online search engine does not comply with this Regulation or the commitments undertaken. Where the audit opinion could not reach a conclusion for specific elements that fall within the scope of the audit, an explanation of reasons for the failure to reach such a conclusion should be included in the audit opinion. Where applicable, the report should include a description of specific elements that could not be audited, and an explanation of why these could not be audited.

(94) The obligations on assessment and mitigation of risks should trigger, on a case-by-case basis, the need for providers of very large online platforms and of very large online search engines to assess and, where necessary, adjust the design of their recommender systems, for example by taking measures to prevent or minimise biases that lead to the discrimination of persons in vulnerable situations, in particular where such adjustment is in accordance with data protection law and when the information is personalised on the basis of special categories of personal data referred to in Article 9 of the Regulation (EU) 2016/679. In addition, and complementing the transparency obligations applicable to online platforms as regards their recommender systems, providers of very large online platforms and of very large online search engines should consistently ensure that recipients of their service enjoy alternative options which are not based on profiling, within the meaning of Regulation (EU) 2016/679, for the main parameters of their recommender systems. Such choices should be directly accessible from the online interface where the recommendations are presented.

(95) Advertising systems used by very large online platforms and very large online search engines pose particular risks and require further public and regulatory supervision on account of their scale and ability to target and reach recipients of the service based on their behaviour within and outside that platform's or search engine's online interface. Very large online platforms or very large online search engines should ensure public access to repositories of advertisements presented on their online interfaces to facilitate supervision and research into emerging risks brought about by the distribution of advertising online, for example in relation to illegal advertisements or manipulative techniques and disinformation with a real and foreseeable negative impact on public health, public security, civil discourse, political participation and equality. Repositories should include the content of advertisements, including the name of the product, service or brand and the subject matter of the advertisement, and related data on the advertiser, and, if different, the natural or legal person who paid for the advertisement, and the delivery of the advertisement, in particular where targeted advertising is concerned. This information should include both information about targeting criteria and delivery criteria, in particular when advertisements are delivered to persons in vulnerable situations, such as minors.

(96) In order to appropriately monitor and assess the compliance of very large online platforms and of very large online search engines with the obligations laid down by this Regulation, the Digital Services Coordinator of establishment or the Commission may require access to or reporting of specific data, including data related to algorithms. Such a requirement may include, for example, the data necessary to assess the risks and possible harms brought about by the very large online platform's or the very large online search engine's systems, data on the accuracy, functioning and testing of algorithmic systems for content moderation, recommender systems or advertising systems, including, where appropriate, training data and algorithms, or data on processes and outputs of content moderation or of internal complaint-handling systems within the meaning of this Regulation. Such data access requests should not include requests to produce specific information about individual recipients of the service for the purpose of determining compliance of such recipients with other applicable Union or national law. Investigations by researchers on the evolution and severity of online systemic risks are particularly important for bridging information asymmetries and establishing a resilient system of risk mitigation, informing providers of online platforms, providers of online search engines, Digital Services Coordinators, other competent authorities, the Commission and the public.

(97) This Regulation therefore provides a framework for compelling access to data from very large online platforms and very large online search engines to vetted researchers affiliated to a research organisation within the meaning of Article 2 of Directive (EU) 2019/790, which may include, for the purpose of this Regulation, civil society organisations that are conducting scientific research with the primary goal of supporting their public interest mission. All requests for access to data under that framework should be proportionate and appropriately protect the rights and legitimate interests, including the protection of personal data, trade secrets and other confidential information, of the very large online platform or of the very large online search engine and any other parties concerned, including the recipients of the service. However, to ensure that the objective of this Regulation is achieved, consideration of the commercial interests of providers should not lead to a refusal to provide access to data necessary for the specific research objective pursuant to a request under this Regulation. In this regard, whilst without prejudice to Directive (EU) 2016/943 of the European Parliament and of the Council[32], providers should ensure appropriate access for researchers, including, where necessary, by taking technical protections such as through data vaults. Data access requests could cover, for example, the number of views or, where relevant, other types of access to content by recipients of the service prior to its removal by the providers of very large online platforms or of very large online search engines.

(98) In addition, where data is publicly accessible, such providers should not prevent researchers meeting an appropriate subset of criteria from using this data for research purposes that contribute to the detection, identification and understanding of systemic risks. They should provide access to such researchers including, where technically possible, in real-time, to the publicly accessible data, for example on aggregated interactions with content from public pages, public groups, or public figures, including impression and engagement data such as the number of

[32] Directive (EU) 2016/943 of the European Parliament and of the Council of 8 June 2016 on the protection of undisclosed know-how and business information (trade secrets) against their unlawful acquisition, use and disclosure (OJ L 157, 15.6.2016, p. 1).

reactions, shares, comments from recipients of the service. Providers of very large online platforms or of very large online search engines should be encouraged to cooperate with researchers and provide broader access to data for monitoring societal concerns through voluntary efforts, including through commitments and procedures agreed under codes of conduct or crisis protocols. Those providers and researchers should pay particular attention to the protection of personal data, and ensure that any processing of personal data complies with Regulation (EU) 2016/679. Providers should anonymise or pseudonymise personal data except in those cases that would render impossible the research purpose pursued.

(99) Given the complexity of the functioning of the systems deployed and the systemic risks they present to society, providers of very large online platforms and of very large online search engines should establish a compliance function, which should be independent from the operational functions of those providers. The head of the compliance function should report directly to the management of those providers, including for concerns of non-compliance with this Regulation. The compliance officers that are part of the compliance function should have the necessary qualifications, knowledge, experience and ability to operationalise measures and monitor the compliance with this Regulation within the organisation of the providers of very large online platform or of very large online search engine. Providers of very large online platforms and of very large online search engines should ensure that the compliance function is involved, properly and in a timely manner, in all issues which relate to this Regulation including in the risk assessment and mitigation strategy and specific measures, as well as assessing compliance, where applicable, with commitments made by those providers under the codes of conduct and crisis protocols they subscribe to.

(100) In view of the additional risks relating to their activities and their additional obligations under this Regulation, additional transparency requirements should apply specifically to very large online platforms and very large online search engines, notably to report comprehensively on the risk assessments performed and subsequent measures adopted as provided by this Regulation.

(101) The Commission should be in possession of all the necessary resources, in terms of staffing, expertise, and financial means, for the performance of its tasks under this Regulation. In order to ensure the availability of the resources necessary for the adequate supervision at Union level under this Regulation, and considering that Member States should be entitled to charge providers established in their territory a supervisory fee to in respect of the supervisory and enforcement tasks exercised by their authorities, the Commission should charge a supervisory fee, the level of which should be established on an annual basis, on very large online platforms and very large online search engines. The overall amount of the annual supervisory fee charged should be established on the basis of the overall amount of the costs incurred by the Commission to exercise its supervisory tasks under this Regulation, as reasonably estimated beforehand. Such amount should include costs relating to the exercise of the specific powers and tasks of supervision, investigation, enforcement and monitoring in respect of providers of very large online platforms and of very large online search engines, including costs related to the designation of very large online platforms and of very large online search engines or to the set up, maintenance and operation of the databases envisaged under this Regulation.

It should also include costs relating to the set-up, maintenance and operation of the basic information and institutional infrastructure for the cooperation among Digital Services Coordinators, the Board and the Commission, taking into account the fact that in view of their size and reach very large online platforms and very large online search engines have a significant impact on the resources needed to support such infrastructure. The estimation of the overall costs should take into account the supervisory costs incurred in the previous year including, where applicable, those costs exceeding the individual annual supervisory fee charged in the previous year. The external assigned revenues resulting from the annual supervisory fee could be used to finance additional human resources, such as contractual agents and seconded national experts, and other expenditure related to the fulfilment of the tasks entrusted to the Commission by this Regulation. The annual supervisory fee to be charged on providers of very large online platforms and of very large online search engines should be proportionate to the size of the service as reflected by the number of its active recipients of the service in the Union. Moreover, the individual annual supervisory fee should not exceed an overall ceiling for each provider of very large online platforms or of very large online search engines taking into account the economic capacity of the provider of the designated service or services.

(102) To facilitate the effective and consistent application of the obligations in this Regulation that may require implementation through technological means, it is important to promote voluntary standards covering certain technical procedures, where the industry can help develop standardised means to support providers of intermediary services in complying with this Regulation, such as allowing the submission of notices, including through application programming interfaces, or standards related to terms and conditions or standards relating to audits, or standards related to the interoperability of advertisement repositories. In addition, such standards could include standards related to online advertising, recommender systems, accessibility and the protection of minors online. Providers of intermediary services are free to adopt the standards, but their adoption does not presume compliance with this Regulation. At the same time, by providing best practices, such standards could in particular be useful for relatively small providers of intermediary services. The standards could distinguish between different types of illegal content or different types of intermediary services, as appropriate.

(103) The Commission and the Board should encourage the drawing-up of voluntary codes of conduct, as well as the implementation of the provisions of those codes in order to contribute to the application of this Regulation. The Commission and the Board should aim that the codes of conduct clearly define the nature of the public interest objectives being addressed, that they contain mechanisms for independent evaluation of the achievement of those objectives and that the role of relevant authorities is clearly defined. Particular attention should be given to avoiding negative effects on security, the protection of privacy and personal data, as well as to the prohibition on imposing general monitoring obligations. While the implementation of codes of conduct should be measurable and subject to public oversight, this should not impair the voluntary nature of such codes and the freedom of interested parties to decide whether to participate. In certain circumstances, it is important that very large online platforms cooperate in the drawing-up and adhere to specific codes of conduct. Nothing in this Regulation

prevents other service providers from adhering to the same standards of due diligence, adopting best practices and benefitting from the guidelines provided by the Commission and the Board, by participating in the same codes of conduct.

(104) It is appropriate that this Regulation identify certain areas of consideration for such codes of conduct. In particular, risk mitigation measures concerning specific types of illegal content should be explored via self- and co-regulatory agreements. Another area for consideration is the possible negative impacts of systemic risks on society and democracy, such as disinformation or manipulative and abusive activities or any adverse effects on minors. This includes coordinated operations aimed at amplifying information, including disinformation, such as the use of bots or fake accounts for the creation of intentionally inaccurate or misleading information, sometimes with a purpose of obtaining economic gain, which are particularly harmful for vulnerable recipients of the service, such as minors. In relation to such areas, adherence to and compliance with a given code of conduct by a very large online platform or a very large online search engine may be considered as an appropriate risk mitigating measure. The refusal without proper explanations by a provider of an online platform or of an online search engine of the Commission's invitation to participate in the application of such a code of conduct could be taken into account, where relevant, when determining whether the online platform or the online search engine has infringed the obligations laid down by this Regulation. The mere fact of participating in and implementing a given code of conduct should not in itself presume compliance with this Regulation.

(105) The codes of conduct should facilitate the accessibility of very large online platforms and very large online search engines, in compliance with Union and national law, in order to facilitate their foreseeable use by persons with disabilities. In particular, the codes of conduct could ensure that the information is presented in a perceivable, operable, understandable and robust way and that forms and measures provided pursuant to this Regulation are made available in a manner that is easy to find and accessible to persons with disabilities.

(106) The rules on codes of conduct under this Regulation could serve as a basis for already established self-regulatory efforts at Union level, including the Product Safety Pledge, the Memorandum of understanding on the sale of counterfeit goods on the internet, the Code of conduct on countering illegal hate speech online, as well as the Code of Practice on Disinformation. In particular for the latter, following the Commission's guidance, the Code of Practice on Disinformation has been strengthened as announced in the European Democracy Action Plan.

(107) The provision of online advertising generally involves several actors, including intermediary services that connect publishers of advertisements with advertisers. Codes of conduct should support and complement the transparency obligations relating to advertising for providers of online platforms, of very large online platforms and of very large online search engines set out in this Regulation in order to provide for flexible and effective mechanisms to facilitate and enhance the compliance with those obligations, notably as concerns the modalities of the transmission of the relevant information. This should include facilitating the transmission of the information on the advertiser who pays for the advertisement when they differ from the natural or legal person on whose behalf the advertisement is presented on the online interface of an online platform. The codes of conduct should also include measures to ensure that meaningful information about

the monetisation of data is appropriately shared throughout the value chain. The involvement of a wide range of stakeholders should ensure that those codes of conduct are widely supported, technically sound, effective and offer the highest levels of user-friendliness to ensure that the transparency obligations achieve their objectives. In order to ensure the effectiveness of codes of conduct, the Commission should include evaluation mechanisms in drawing up the codes of conduct. Where appropriate, the Commission may invite the Fundamental Rights Agency or the European Data Protection Supervisor to express their opinions on the respective code of conduct.

(108) In addition to the crisis response mechanism for very large online platforms and very large online search engines, the Commission may initiate the drawing up of voluntary crisis protocols to coordinate a rapid, collective and cross-border response in the online environment. Such can be the case, for example, where online platforms are misused for the rapid spread of illegal content or disinformation or where the need arises for rapid dissemination of reliable information. In light of the important role of very large online platforms in disseminating information in our societies and across borders, providers of such platforms should be encouraged in drawing up and applying specific crisis protocols. Such crisis protocols should be activated only for a limited period of time and the measures adopted should also be limited to what is strictly necessary to address the extraordinary circumstance. Those measures should be consistent with this Regulation, and should not amount to a general obligation for the participating providers of very large online platforms and of very large online search engines to monitor the information which they transmit or store, nor actively to seek facts or circumstances indicating illegal content.

(109) In order to ensure adequate oversight and enforcement of the obligations laid down in this Regulation, Member States should designate at least one authority with the task to supervise the application and enforce this Regulation, without prejudice to the possibility to designate an existing authority and to its legal form in accordance with national law. Member States should, however, be able to entrust more than one competent authority, with specific supervisory or enforcement tasks and competences concerning the application of this Regulation, for example for specific sectors where existing authorities may also be empowered, such as electronic communications' regulators, media regulators or consumer protection authorities, reflecting their domestic constitutional, organisational and administrative structure. In the exercise of their tasks, all competent authorities should contribute to the achievement of the objectives of this Regulation, namely to the proper functioning of the internal market for intermediary services where the harmonised rules for a safe, predictable and trusted online environment that facilitates innovation, and in particular the due diligence obligations applicable to different categories of providers of intermediary services, are effectively supervised and enforced, with a view to ensure that fundamental rights, as enshrined in the Charter, including the principle of consumer protection, are effectively protected. This Regulation does not require Member States to confer on competent authorities the task to adjudicate on the lawfulness of specific items of content.

(110) Given the cross-border nature of the services at stake and the horizontal range of obligations introduced by this Regulation, one authority appointed with the task of supervising the application and, where necessary, enforcing this Regulation should be identified as a Digital Services Coordinator in each Member State.

Where more than one competent authority is appointed to supervise the application of, and enforce, this Regulation, only one authority in that Member State should be designated as a Digital Services Coordinator. The Digital Services Coordinator should act as the single contact point with regard to all matters related to the application of this Regulation for the Commission, the Board, the Digital Services Coordinators of other Member States, as well as for other competent authorities of the Member State in question. In particular, where several competent authorities are entrusted with tasks under this Regulation in a given Member State, the Digital Services Coordinator should coordinate and cooperate with those authorities in accordance with the national law setting their respective tasks and without prejudice to the independent assessment of the other competent authorities. While not entailing any hierarchical supraordination over other competent authorities in the exercise of their tasks, the Digital Services Coordinator should ensure effective involvement of all relevant competent authorities and should timely report their assessment in the context of cooperation on supervision and enforcement at Union level. Moreover, in addition to the specific mechanisms provided for in this Regulation as regards cooperation at Union level, Member State should also ensure cooperation among the Digital Services Coordinator and other competent authorities designated at national level, where applicable, through appropriate tools, such as by pooling of resources, joint task forces, joint investigations and mutual assistance mechanisms.

(111) The Digital Services Coordinator, as well as other competent authorities designated under this Regulation, play a crucial role in ensuring the effectiveness of the rights and obligations laid down in this Regulation and the achievement of its objectives. Accordingly, it is necessary to ensure that those authorities have the necessary means, including financial and human resources, to supervise all the providers of intermediary services falling within their competence, in the interest of all Union citizens. Given the variety of providers of intermediary services and their use of advanced technology in providing their services, it is also essential that the Digital Services Coordinator and the relevant competent authorities are equipped with the necessary number of staff and experts with specialised skills and advanced technical means, and that they autonomously manage financial resources to carry out their tasks. Furthermore, the level of resources should take into account the size, complexity and potential societal impact of the providers of intermediary services falling within their competence, as well as the reach of their services across the Union. This Regulation is without prejudice to the possibility for Member States to establish funding mechanisms based on a supervisory fee charged to providers of intermediary services under national law in compliance with Union law, to the extent that it is levied on providers of intermediary services having their main establishment in the Member State in question, that it is strictly limited to what is necessary and proportionate to cover the costs for the fulfilment of the tasks conferred upon the competent authorities pursuant to this Regulation, with the exclusion of the tasks conferred upon the Commission, and that adequate transparency is ensured regarding the levying and the use of such a supervisory fee.

(112) The competent authorities designated under this Regulation should also act in complete independence from private and public bodies, without the obligation or possibility to seek or receive instructions, including from the government, and without prejudice to the specific duties to cooperate with other competent

authorities, the Digital Services Coordinators, the Board and the Commission. On the other hand, the independence of those authorities should not mean that they cannot be subject, in accordance with national constitutions and without endangering the achievement of the objectives of this Regulation, to proportionate accountability mechanisms regarding the general activities of the Digital Services Coordinators, such as their financial expenditure or reporting to the national parliaments. The requirement of independence should also not prevent the exercise of judicial review, or the possibility to consult or regularly exchange views with other national authorities, including law enforcement authorities, crisis management authorities or consumer protection authorities, where appropriate, in order to inform each other about ongoing investigations, without affecting the exercise of their respective powers.

(113) Member States can designate an existing national authority with the function of the Digital Services Coordinator, or with specific tasks to supervise the application and enforce this Regulation, provided that any such appointed authority complies with the requirements laid down in this Regulation, such as in relation to its independence. Moreover, Member States are in principle not precluded from merging functions within an existing authority, in accordance with Union law. The measures to that effect may include, inter alia, the preclusion to dismiss the president or a board member of a collegiate body of an existing authority before the expiry of their terms of office, on the sole ground that an institutional reform has taken place involving the merger of different functions within one authority, in the absence of any rules guaranteeing that such dismissals do not jeopardise the independence and impartiality of such members.

(114) Member States should provide the Digital Services Coordinator, and any other competent authority designated under this Regulation, with sufficient powers and means to ensure effective investigation and enforcement, in accordance with the tasks conferred on them. This includes the power of competent authorities to adopt interim measures in accordance with national law in case of risk of serious harm. Such interim measures, which may include orders to terminate or remedy a given alleged infringement, should not go beyond what is necessary to ensure that serious harm is prevented pending the final decision. The Digital Services Coordinators should in particular be able to search for and obtain information which is located in its territory, including in the context of joint investigations, with due regard to the fact that oversight and enforcement measures concerning a provider under the jurisdiction of another Member State or the Commission should be adopted by the Digital Services Coordinator of that other Member State, where relevant in accordance with the procedures relating to cross-border cooperation, or, where applicable, by the Commission.

(115) Member States should set out in their national law, in accordance with Union law and in particular this Regulation and the Charter, the detailed conditions and limits for the exercise of the investigatory and enforcement powers of their Digital Services Coordinators, and other competent authorities where relevant, under this Regulation.

(116) In the course of the exercise of those powers, the competent authorities should comply with the applicable national rules regarding procedures and matters such as the need for a prior judicial authorisation to enter certain premises and legal professional privilege. Those provisions should in particular ensure respect for the fundamental rights to an effective remedy and to a fair trial, including the rights

of defence, and, the right to respect for private life. In this regard, the guarantees provided for in relation to the proceedings of the Commission pursuant to this Regulation could serve as an appropriate point of reference. A prior, fair and impartial procedure should be guaranteed before taking any final decision, including the right to be heard of the persons concerned, and the right to have access to the file, while respecting confidentiality and professional and business secrecy, as well as the obligation to give meaningful reasons for the decisions. This should not preclude the taking of measures, however, in duly substantiated cases of urgency and subject to appropriate conditions and procedural arrangements. The exercise of powers should also be proportionate to, inter alia the nature and the overall actual or potential harm caused by the infringement or suspected infringement. The competent authorities should take all relevant facts and circumstances of the case into account, including information gathered by competent authorities in other Member States.

(117) Member States should ensure that violations of the obligations laid down in this Regulation can be sanctioned in a manner that is effective, proportionate and dissuasive, taking into account the nature, gravity, recurrence and duration of the violation, in view of the public interest pursued, the scope and kind of activities carried out, as well as the economic capacity of the infringer. In particular, penalties should take into account whether the provider of intermediary services concerned systematically or recurrently fails to comply with its obligations stemming from this Regulation, as well as, where relevant, the number of recipients of the service affected, the intentional or negligent character of the infringement and whether the provider is active in several Member States. Where this Regulation provides for a maximum amount of fines or of a periodic penalty payment, this maximum amount should apply per infringement of this Regulation and without prejudice to the modulation of the fines or periodic penalty payments for specific infringements. Member States should ensure that the imposition of fines or periodic penalty payments in respect of infringements should in each individual case be effective, proportionate and dissuasive by setting up national rules and procedures in accordance with this Regulation, taking into account all the criteria concerning the general conditions for imposing the fines or periodic penalty payments.

(118) In order to ensure effective enforcement of the obligations laid down in this Regulation, individuals or representative organisations should be able to lodge any complaint related to compliance with those obligations with the Digital Services Coordinator in the territory where they received the service, without prejudice to this Regulation's rules on allocation of competences and to the applicable rules on handling of complaints in accordance with national principles of good administration. Complaints could provide a faithful overview of concerns related to a particular intermediary service provider's compliance and could also inform the Digital Services Coordinator of any more cross-cutting issues. The Digital Services Coordinator should involve other national competent authorities as well as the Digital Services Coordinator of another Member State, and in particular the one of the Member State where the provider of intermediary services concerned is established, if the issue requires cross-border cooperation.

(119) Member States should ensure that Digital Services Coordinators can take measures that are effective in addressing and proportionate to certain particularly serious and persistent infringements of this Regulation. Especially where those

measures can affect the rights and interests of third parties, as may be the case in particular where the access to online interfaces is restricted, it is appropriate to require that the measures are subject to additional safeguards. In particular, third parties potentially affected should be afforded the opportunity to be heard and such orders should only be issued when powers to take such measures as provided by other acts of Union law or by national law, for instance to protect collective interests of consumers, to ensure the prompt removal of web pages containing or disseminating child pornography, or to disable access to services that are being used by a third party to infringe an intellectual property right, are not reasonably available.

(120) Such an order to restrict access should not go beyond what is necessary to achieve its objective. For that purpose, it should be temporary and be addressed in principle to a provider of intermediary services, such as the relevant hosting service provider, internet service provider or domain registry or registrar, which is in a reasonable position to achieve that objective without unduly restricting access to lawful information.

(121) Without prejudice to the provisions on the exemption from liability provided for in this Regulation as regards the information transmitted or stored at the request of a recipient of the service, a provider of intermediary services should be liable for the damages suffered by recipients of the service that are caused by an infringement of the obligations set out in this Regulation by that provider. Such compensation should be in accordance with the rules and procedures set out in the applicable national law and without prejudice to other possibilities for redress available under consumer protection rules.

(122) The Digital Services Coordinator should regularly publish, for example on its website, a report on the activities carried out under this Regulation. In particular, the report should be published in a machine-readable format and include an overview of complaints received and of their follow-up, such as the overall number of complaints received and the number of complaints that led to the opening of a formal investigation or to the transmission to other Digital Services Coordinators, without referring to any personal data. Given that the Digital Services Coordinator is also made aware of orders to take action against illegal content or to provide information regulated by this Regulation through the information sharing system, the Digital Services Coordinator should include in its annual report the number and categories of such orders addressed to providers of intermediary services issued by judicial and administrative authorities in its Member State.

(123) In the interest of clarity, simplicity and effectiveness, the powers to supervise and enforce the obligations under this Regulation should be conferred to the competent authorities in the Member State where the main establishment of the provider of intermediary services is located, that is, where the provider has its head office or registered office within which the principal financial functions and operational control are exercised. In respect of providers that are not established in the Union, but that offer services in the Union and therefore fall within the scope of this Regulation, the Member State where those providers appointed their legal representative should have competence, considering the function of legal representatives under this Regulation. In the interest of the effective application of this Regulation, all Member States or the Commission, where applicable, should, however, have competence in respect of providers that failed to designate

a legal representative. That competence may be exercised by any of the competent authorities or the Commission, provided that the provider is not subject to enforcement proceedings for the same facts by another competent authority or the Commission. In order to ensure that the principle of ne bis in idem is respected, and in particular to avoid that the same infringement of the obligations laid down in this Regulation is sanctioned more than once, each Member State that intends to exercise its competence in respect of such providers should, without undue delay, inform all other authorities, including the Commission, through the information sharing system established for the purpose of this Regulation.

(124) In view of their potential impact and the challenges involved in effectively supervising them, special rules are needed regarding the supervision and enforcement in respect of providers of very large online platforms and of very large online search engines. The Commission should be responsible, with the support of national competent authorities where relevant, for oversight and public enforcement of systemic issues, such as issues with a wide impact on collective interests of recipients of the service. Therefore, the Commission should have exclusive powers of supervision and enforcement of the additional obligations to manage systemic risks imposed on providers of very large online platforms and of very large online search engines by this Regulation. The exclusive powers of the Commission should be without prejudice to certain administrative tasks assigned by this Regulation to the competent authorities of the Member State of establishment, such as the vetting of researchers.

(125) The powers of supervision and enforcement of due diligence obligations, other than the additional obligations to manage systemic risks imposed on providers of very large online platforms and of very large online search engines by this Regulation, should be shared by the Commission and by the national competent authorities. On the one hand, the Commission could in many instances be better placed to address systemic infringements committed by those providers, such as those affecting multiple Member States or serious repeated infringements or concerning a failure to establish effective mechanisms required by this Regulation. On the other hand, the competent authorities in the Member State where the main establishment of a provider of very large online platform or of very large online search engine is located could be better placed to address individual infringements committed by those providers, that do not raise any systemic or cross-border issues. In the interest of efficiency, to avoid duplication and to ensure compliance with the principle of ne bis in idem, it should be for the Commission to assess whether it deems it appropriate to exercise those shared competences in a given case and, once it has initiated proceedings, Member States should no longer have the ability to do so. Member States should cooperate closely both with each other and with the Commission, and the Commission should cooperate closely with the Member States, in order to ensure that the system of supervision and enforcement set up by this Regulation functions smoothly and effectively.

(126) The rules of this Regulation on the allocation of competence should be without prejudice to the provisions of Union law and national rules on private international law concerning jurisdiction and applicable law in civil and commercial matters, such as proceedings brought by consumers in the courts of the Member State where they are domiciled in accordance with relevant provisions of Union law. Regarding the obligations imposed by this Regulation on providers of inter-

mediary services to inform the issuing authority of the effect given to the orders to act against illegal content and orders to provide information, the rules on allocation of competence should only apply to the supervision of enforcement of those obligations, but not to other matters related to the order, such as the competence to issue the order.

(127) Given the cross-border and cross-sectoral relevance of intermediary services, a high level of cooperation is necessary to ensure the consistent application of this Regulation and the availability of relevant information for the exercise of enforcement tasks through the information sharing system. Cooperation may take different forms depending on the issues at stake, without prejudice to specific joint investigation exercises. It is in any case necessary that the Digital Services Coordinator of establishment of a provider of intermediary services informs other Digital Services Coordinators about issues, investigations and actions which are going to be taken vis à vis such a provider. Moreover, when a competent authority in a Member State holds relevant information for an investigation carried out by the competent authorities in the Member State of establishment, or is able to gather such information located in its territory to which the competent authorities in the Member State of establishment do not have access, the Digital Services Coordinator of destination should assist the Digital Services Coordinator of establishment in a timely manner, including through the exercise of its powers of investigation in accordance with the applicable national procedures and the Charter. The addressee of such investigatory measures should comply with them and be liable in case of failure to comply, and the competent authorities in the Member State of establishment should be able to rely on the information gathered through mutual assistance, in order to ensure compliance with this Regulation.

(128) The Digital Services Coordinator of destination, in particular on the basis of complaints received or of the input of other national competent authorities where appropriate, or the Board in case of issues involving at least three Member States, should be able to ask the Digital Services Coordinator of establishment to take investigatory or enforcement actions with regard to a provider under its competence. Such requests for action should be based on well-substantiated evidence showing the existence of an alleged infringement with negative impact on collective interests of the recipients of the service in its Member State or having a negative societal impact. The Digital Services Coordinator of establishment should be able to rely on mutual assistance or invite the requesting Digital Services Coordinator to a joint investigation in case further information is needed to take a decision, without prejudice to the possibility to request the Commission to assess the matter if it has reason to suspect that a systemic infringement by a very large online platform or a very large online search engine may be at stake.

(129) The Board should be able to refer the matter to the Commission in case of any disagreement as to the assessments or the measures taken or proposed or of a failure to adopt any measures in accordance with this Regulation following a cross-border cooperation request or a joint investigation. Where the Commission, on the basis of the information made available by the concerned authorities, considers that the proposed measures, including the proposed level of fines, cannot ensure the effective enforcement of the obligations laid down in this Regulation, it should accordingly be able to express its serious doubts and request the competent Digital Services Coordinator to re-assess the matter and take the necessary measures to ensure compliance with this Regulation within a defined

period. This possibility is without prejudice to the Commission's general duty to oversee the application of, and where necessary enforce, Union law under the control of the Court of Justice of the European Union in accordance with the Treaties.

(130) In order to facilitate cross-border supervision and investigations of obligations laid down in this Regulation involving several Member States, the Digital Services Coordinators of establishment should be able, through the information sharing system, to invite other Digital Services Coordinators to a joint investigation concerning an alleged infringement of this Regulation. Other Digital Services Coordinators, and other competent authorities, where appropriate, should be able to join the investigation proposed by the Digital Services Coordinator of establishment, unless the latter considers that an excessive number of participating authorities may affect the effectiveness of the investigation taking into account the features of the alleged infringement and the lack of direct effects on the recipients of the service in those Member States. Joint investigation activities may include a variety of actions to be coordinated by the Digital Services Coordinator of establishment in accordance with the availabilities of the participating authorities, such as coordinated data gathering exercises, pooling of resources, task forces, coordinated requests for information or common inspections of premises. All competent authorities participating in a joint investigation should cooperate with the Digital Services Coordinator of establishment, including by exercising their powers of investigation within their territory, in accordance with the applicable national procedures. The joint investigation should be concluded within a given timeframe with a final report taking into account the contribution of all participating competent authorities. Also the Board, where this is requested by at least three Digital Services Coordinators of destination, may recommend to a Digital Services Coordinator of establishment to launch such joint investigation and give indications on its organisation. In order to avoid deadlocks, the Board should be able to refer the matter to the Commission in specific cases, including where the Digital Services Coordinator of establishment refuses to launch the investigation and the Board does not agree with the justification given.

(131) In order to ensure a consistent application of this Regulation, it is necessary to set up an independent advisory group at Union level, a European Board for Digital Services, which should support the Commission and help coordinate the actions of Digital Services Coordinators. The Board should consist of the Digital Services Coordinators, where these have been appointed, without prejudice to the possibility for Digital Services Coordinators to invite in its meetings or appoint ad hoc delegates from other competent authorities entrusted with specific tasks under this Regulation, where that is required pursuant to their national allocation of tasks and competences. In case of multiple participants from one Member State, the voting right should remain limited to one representative per Member State.

(132) The Board should contribute to achieving a common Union perspective on the consistent application of this Regulation and to the cooperation among competent authorities, including by advising the Commission and the Digital Services Coordinators about appropriate investigation and enforcement measures, in particular vis à vis the providers of very large online platforms or of very large online search engines and having regard, in particular, to the freedom of the providers of intermediary services to provide services across the Union. The Board should also

contribute to the drafting of relevant templates and codes of conduct and to the analysis of emerging general trends in the development of digital services in the Union, including by issuing opinions or recommendations on matters related to standards.

(133) For that purpose, the Board should be able to adopt opinions, requests and recommendations addressed to Digital Services Coordinators or other competent national authorities. While not legally binding, the decision to deviate therefrom should be properly explained and could be taken into account by the Commission in assessing the compliance of the Member State concerned with this Regulation.

(134) The Board should bring together the representatives of the Digital Services Coordinators and possible other competent authorities under the chairmanship of the Commission, with a view to ensuring an assessment of matters submitted to it in a fully European dimension. In view of possible cross-cutting elements that may be of relevance for other regulatory frameworks at Union level, the Board should be allowed to cooperate with other Union bodies, offices, agencies and advisory groups with responsibilities in fields such as equality, including gender equality, and non-discrimination, data protection, electronic communications, audiovisual services, detection and investigation of frauds against the Union budget as regards custom duties, consumer protection, or competition law, as necessary for the performance of its tasks.

(135) The Commission, through the Chair, should participate in the Board without voting rights. Through the Chair, the Commission should ensure that the agenda of the meetings is set in accordance with the requests of the members of the Board as laid down in the rules of procedure and in compliance with the duties of the Board laid down in this Regulation.

(136) In view of the need to ensure support for the Board's activities, the Board should be able to rely on the expertise and human resources of the Commission and of the competent national authorities. The specific operational arrangements for the internal functioning of the Board should be further specified in the rules of procedure of the Board.

(137) Given the importance of very large online platforms or very large online search engines, in view of their reach and impact, their failure to comply with the specific obligations applicable to them may affect a substantial number of recipients of the services across different Member States and may cause large societal harms, while such failures may also be particularly complex to identify and address. For this reason the Commission, in cooperation with the Digital Services Coordinators and the Board, should develop the Union expertise and capabilities as regards the supervision of very large online platforms or very large online search engines. The Commission should therefore be able to coordinate and rely on the expertise and resources of such authorities, for example by analysing, on a permanent or temporary basis, specific trends or issues emerging with regard to one or more very large online platforms or very large online search engines. Member States should cooperate with the Commission in developing such capabilities, including through secondment of personnel where appropriate, and contributing to the creation of a common Union supervisory capacity. In order to develop the Union expertise and capabilities, the Commission may also draw on the expertise and capabilities of the Observatory on the Online Platform Economy as set up in Commission Decision of 26 April 2018 on setting up the group of experts for the Observatory on the Online Platform Economy, relevant expert bodies, as

well as centres of excellence. The Commission may invite experts with specific expertise, including in particular vetted researchers, representatives of Union agencies and bodies, industry representatives, associations representing users or civil society, international organisations, experts from the private sector, as well as other stakeholders.

(138) The Commission should be able to investigate infringements on its own initiative in accordance with the powers provided for in this Regulation, including by asking access to data, by requesting information or by performing inspections, as well as by relying on the support of the Digital Services Coordinators. Where supervision by the competent national authorities of individual alleged infringements by providers of very large online platforms or very large online search engines points to systemic issues, such as issues with a wide impact on collective interests of recipients of the service, the Digital Services Coordinators should be able to, on the basis of a duly reasoned request, refer such issues to the Commission. Such a request should contain, at least, all the necessary facts and circumstances supporting the alleged infringement and its systemic nature. Depending on the outcome of its own assessment, the Commission should be able to take the necessary investigative and enforcement measures pursuant to this Regulation, including, where relevant, launching an investigation or adopting interim measures.

(139) In order to effectively perform its tasks, the Commission should maintain a margin of discretion as to the decision to initiate proceedings against providers of very large online platforms or of very large online search engine. Once the Commission initiated the proceedings, the Digital Services Coordinators of establishment concerned should be precluded from exercising their investigative and enforcement powers in respect of the concerned conduct of the provider of the very large online platform or of very large online search engine, so as to avoid duplication, inconsistencies and risks from the viewpoint of the principle of ne bis in idem. The Commission, however, should be able to ask for the individual or joint contribution of the Digital Services Coordinators to the investigation. In accordance with the duty of sincere cooperation, the Digital Services Coordinator should make its best efforts in fulfilling justified and proportionate requests by the Commission in the context of an investigation. Moreover, the Digital Services Coordinator of establishment, as well as the Board and any other Digital Services Coordinators where relevant, should provide the Commission with all necessary information and assistance to allow it to perform its tasks effectively, including information gathered in the context of data gathering or data access exercises, to the extent that this is not precluded by the legal basis according to which the information has been gathered. Conversely, the Commission should keep the Digital Services Coordinator of establishment and the Board informed on the exercise of its powers and in particular when it intends to initiate the proceeding and exercise its investigatory powers. Moreover, when the Commission communicates its preliminary findings, including any matter to which it objects, to providers of very large online platforms or of very large online search engines concerned, it should also communicate them to the Board. The Board should provide its views on the objections and assessment made by the Commission, which should take this opinion into account in the reasoning underpinning Commission's final decision.

(140) In view of both the particular challenges that may arise in seeking to ensure compliance by providers of very large online platforms or of very large online search engines and the importance of doing so effectively, considering their size and impact and the harms that they may cause, the Commission should have strong investigative and enforcement powers to allow it to investigate, enforce and monitor compliance with the rules laid down in this Regulation, in full respect of the fundamental right to be heard and to have access to the file in the context of enforcement proceedings, the principle of proportionality and the rights and interests of the affected parties.

(141) The Commission should be able to request information necessary for the purpose of ensuring the effective implementation of and compliance with the obligations laid down in this Regulation, throughout the Union. In particular, the Commission should have access to any relevant documents, data and information necessary to open and conduct investigations and to monitor the compliance with the relevant obligations laid down in this Regulation, irrespective of who possesses the documents, data or information in question, and regardless of their form or format, their storage medium, or the precise place where they are stored. The Commission should be able to directly require by means of a duly substantiated request for information that the provider of the very large online platform or of the very large online search engine concerned as well as any other natural or legal persons acting for purposes related to their trade, business, craft or profession that may be reasonably aware of information relating to the suspected infringement or the infringement, as applicable, provide any relevant evidence, data and information. In addition, the Commission should be able to request any relevant information from any public authority, body or agency within the Member State for the purpose of this Regulation. The Commission should be able to require access to, and explanations by means of exercise of investigatory powers, such as requests for information or interviews, relating to documents, data, information, data-bases and algorithms of relevant persons, and to interview, with their consent, any natural or legal persons who may be in possession of useful information and to record the statements made by any technical means. The Commission should also be empowered to undertake such inspections as are necessary to enforce the relevant provisions of this Regulation. Those investigatory powers aim to complement the Commission's possibility to ask Digital Services Coordinators and other Member States' authorities for assistance, for instance by providing information or in the exercise of those powers.

(142) Interim measures can be an important tool to ensure that, while an investigation is ongoing, the infringement being investigated does not lead to the risk of serious damage for the recipients of the service. This tool is important to avoid developments that could be very difficult to reverse by a decision taken by the Commission at the end of the proceedings. The Commission should therefore have the power to impose interim measures by decision in the context of proceedings opened in view of the possible adoption of a decision of non-compliance. This power should apply in cases where the Commission has made a prima facie finding of infringement of obligations under this Regulation by the provider of very large online platform or of very large online search engine. A decision imposing interim measures should only apply for a specified period, either one ending with the conclusion of the proceedings by the Commission, or for a fixed period which can be renewed insofar as it is necessary and appropriate.

(143) The Commission should be able to take the necessary actions to monitor the effective implementation of and compliance with the obligations laid down in this Regulation. Such actions should include the ability to appoint independent external experts and auditors to assist the Commission in this process, including where applicable from competent authorities of the Member States, such as data or consumer protection authorities. When appointing auditors, the Commission should ensure sufficient rotation.

(144) Compliance with the relevant obligations imposed under this Regulation should be enforceable by means of fines and periodic penalty payments. To that end, appropriate levels of fines and periodic penalty payments should also be laid down for non-compliance with the obligations and breach of the procedural rules, subject to appropriate limitation periods in accordance with the principles of proportionality and ne bis in idem. The Commission and the relevant national authorities should coordinate their enforcement efforts in order to ensure that those principles are respected. In particular, the Commission should take into account any fines and penalties imposed on the same legal person for the same facts through a final decision in proceedings relating to an infringement of other Union or national rules, so as to ensure that the overall fines and penalties imposed are proportionate and correspond to the seriousness of the infringements committed. All decisions taken by the Commission under this Regulation are subject to review by the Court of Justice of the European Union in accordance with the TFEU. The Court of Justice of the European Union should have unlimited jurisdiction in respect of fines and penalty payments in accordance with Article 261 TFEU.

(145) Given the potential significant societal effects of an infringement of the additional obligations to manage systemic risks that solely apply to very large online platforms and very large online search engines and in order to address those public policy concerns, it is necessary to provide for a system of enhanced supervision of any action undertaken to effectively terminate and remedy infringements of this Regulation. Therefore, once an infringement of one of the provisions of this Regulation that solely apply to very large online platforms or very large online search engines has been ascertained and, where necessary, sanctioned, the Commission should request the provider of such platform or of such search engine to draw a detailed action plan to remedy any effect of the infringement for the future and communicate such action plan within a timeline set by the Commission, to the Digital Services Coordinators, the Commission and the Board. The Commission, taking into account the opinion of the Board, should establish whether the measures included in the action plan are sufficient to address the infringement, taking also into account whether adherence to relevant code of conduct is included among the measures proposed. The Commission should also monitor any subsequent measure taken by the provider of a very large online platform or of a very large online search engine concerned as set out in its action plan, taking into account also an independent audit of the provider. If following the implementation of the action plan the Commission still considers that the infringement has not been fully remedied, or if the action plan has not been provided or is not considered suitable, it should be able to use any investigative or enforcement powers pursuant to this Regulation, including the power to impose periodic penalty payments and initiating the procedure to disable access to the infringing service.

(146) The provider of the very large online platform or of the very large online search engine concerned and other persons subject to the exercise of the Commission's powers whose interests may be affected by a decision should be given the opportunity of submitting their observations beforehand, and the decisions taken should be widely publicised. While ensuring the rights of defence of the parties concerned, in particular, the right of access to the file, it is essential that confidential information be protected. Furthermore, while respecting the confidentiality of the information, the Commission should ensure that any information relied on for the purpose of its decision is disclosed to an extent that allows the addressee of the decision to understand the facts and considerations that led up to the decision.

(147) In order to safeguard the harmonised application and enforcement of this Regulation, it is important to ensure that national authorities, including national courts, have all necessary information to ensure that their decisions do not run counter to a decision adopted by the Commission under this Regulation. This is without prejudice to Article 267 TFEU.

(148) The effective enforcement and monitoring of this Regulation requires a seamless and real-time exchange of information among the Digital Services Coordinators, the Board and the Commission, based on the information flows and procedures set out in this Regulation. This may also warrant access to this system by other competent authorities, where appropriate. At the same time, given that the information exchanged may be confidential or involving personal data, it should remain protected from unauthorised access, in accordance with the purposes for which the information has been gathered. For this reason, all communications between those authorities should take place on the basis of a reliable and secure information sharing system, whose details should be laid down in an implementing act. The information sharing system may be based on existing internal market tools, to the extent that they can meet the objectives of this Regulation in a cost-effective manner.

(149) Without prejudice to the rights of recipients of services to turn to a representative in accordance with the Directive (EU) 2020/1828 of the European Parliament and of the Council[33] or to any other type of representation under national law, recipients of the services should also have the right to mandate a legal person or a public body to exercise their rights provided for in this Regulation. Such rights may include the rights related to the submission of notices, the challenging of the decisions taken by providers of intermediary services, and the lodging of complaints against the providers for infringing this Regulation. Certain bodies, organisations and associations have particular expertise and competence in detecting and flagging erroneous or unjustified content moderation decisions, and their complaints on behalf of recipients of the service may have a positive impact on freedom of expression and of information in general, therefore, providers of online platforms should treat those complaints without undue delay.

(150) In the interest of effectiveness and efficiency, the Commission should carry out a general evaluation of this Regulation. In particular, that general evaluation should address, inter alia, the scope of the services covered by this Regulation, the

[33] Directive (EU) 2020/1828 of the European Parliament and of the Council of 25 November 2020 on representative actions for the protection of the collective interests of consumers and repealing Directive 2009/22/EC (OJ L 409, 4.12.2020, p. 1).

interplay with other legal acts, the impact of this Regulation on the functioning of the internal market, in particular regarding digital services, the implementation of codes of conduct, the obligation to designate a legal representative established in the Union, the effect of the obligations on small and micro enterprises, the effectiveness of the supervision and enforcement mechanism and the impact on the right to freedom of expression and of information. In addition, to avoid disproportionate burdens and ensure the continued effectiveness of this Regulation, the Commission should perform an evaluation of the impact of the obligations set out in this Regulation on small and medium-sized enterprises within three years from the start of its application and an evaluation on the scope of the services covered by this Regulation, particularly for very large online platforms and for very large online search engines, and the interplay with other legal acts within three years from its entry into force.

(151) In order to ensure uniform conditions for the implementation of this Regulation, implementing powers should be conferred on the Commission to lay down templates concerning the form, content and other details of reports on content moderation, to establish the amount of the annual supervisory fee charged on providers of very large online platforms and of very large online search engines, to lay down the practical arrangements for the proceedings, the hearings and the negotiated disclosure of information carried out in the context of supervision, investigation, enforcement and monitoring in respect of providers of very large online platforms and of very large online search engines, as well as to lay down the practical and operational arrangements for the functioning of the information sharing system and its interoperability with other relevant systems. Those powers should be exercised in accordance with Regulation (EU) No 182/2011 of the European Parliament and of the Council[34].

(152) In order to fulfil the objectives of this Regulation, the power to adopt acts in accordance with Article 290 TFEU should be delegated to the Commission to supplement this Regulation, in respect of criteria for the identification of very large online platforms and of very large online search engines, the procedural steps, methodologies and reporting templates for the audits, the technical specifications for access requests and the detailed methodology and procedures for setting the supervisory fee. It is of particular importance that the Commission carry out appropriate consultations during its preparatory work, including at expert level, and that those consultations be conducted in accordance with the principles laid down in the Interinstitutional Agreement of 13 April 2016 on Better Law-Making[35]. In particular, to ensure equal participation in the preparation of delegated acts, the European Parliament and the Council receive all documents at the same time as Member States' experts, and their experts systematically have access to meetings of Commission expert groups dealing with the preparation of delegated acts.

(153) This Regulation respects the fundamental rights recognised by the Charter and the fundamental rights constituting general principles of Union law. Accordingly, this Regulation should be interpreted and applied in accordance with those fundamental rights, including the freedom of expression and of information, as well

[34] Regulation (EU) No 182/2011 of the European Parliament and of the Council of 16 February 2011 laying down the rules and general principles concerning mechanisms for control by Member States of the Commission's exercise of implementing powers (OJ L 55, 28.2.2011, p. 13).

[35] OJ L 123, 12.5.2016, p. 1.

as the freedom and pluralism of the media. When exercising the powers set out in this Regulation, all public authorities involved should achieve, in situations where the relevant fundamental rights conflict, a fair balance between the rights concerned, in accordance with the principle of proportionality.

(154) Given the scope and impact of societal risks that may be caused by very large online platforms and very large online search engines, the need to address those risks as a matter of priority and the capacity to take the necessary measures, it is justified to limit the period after which this Regulation starts to apply to the providers of those services.

(155) Since the objectives of this Regulation, namely to contribute to the proper functioning of the internal market and to ensure a safe, predictable and trusted online environment in which the fundamental rights enshrined in the Charter are duly protected, cannot be sufficiently achieved by the Member States because they cannot achieve the necessary harmonisation and cooperation by acting alone, but can rather, by reason of territorial and personal scope, be better achieved at the Union level, the Union may adopt measures, in accordance with the principle of subsidiarity as set out in Article 5 of the Treaty on European Union. In accordance with the principle of proportionality as set out in that Article, this Regulation does not go beyond what is necessary in order to achieve those objectives.

(156) The European Data Protection Supervisor was consulted in accordance with Article 42(1) of Regulation (EU) 2018/1725 of the European Parliament and of the Council[36] and delivered an opinion on 10 February 2021[37],

HAVE ADOPTED THIS REGULATION:

CHAPTER I
GENERAL PROVISIONS

Article 1
Subject matter

1. The aim of this Regulation is to contribute to the proper functioning of the internal market for intermediary services by setting out harmonised rules for a safe, predictable and trusted online environment that facilitates innovation and in which fundamental rights enshrined in the Charter, including the principle of consumer protection, are effectively protected.

2. This Regulation lays down harmonised rules on the provision of intermediary services in the internal market. In particular, it establishes:

(a) a framework for the conditional exemption from liability of providers of intermediary services;
(b) rules on specific due diligence obligations tailored to certain specific categories of providers of intermediary services;

[36] Regulation (EU) 2018/1725 of the European Parliament and of the Council of 23 October 2018 on the protection of natural persons with regard to the processing of personal data by the Union institutions, bodies, offices and agencies and on the free movement of such data, and repealing Regulation (EC) No 45/2001 and Decision No 1247/2002/EC (OJ L 295, 21.11.2018, p. 39).

[37] OJ C 149, 27.4.2021, p. 3.

(c) rules on the implementation and enforcement of this Regulation, including as regards the cooperation of and coordination between the competent authorities.

Article 2
Scope

1. This Regulation shall apply to intermediary services offered to recipients of the service that have their place of establishment or are located in the Union, irrespective of where the providers of those intermediary services have their place of establishment.

2. This Regulation shall not apply to any service that is not an intermediary service or to any requirements imposed in respect of such a service, irrespective of whether the service is provided through the use of an intermediary service.

3. This Regulation shall not affect the application of Directive 2000/31/EC.

4. This Regulation is without prejudice to the rules laid down by other Union legal acts regulating other aspects of the provision of intermediary services in the internal market or specifying and complementing this Regulation, in particular, the following:

(a) Directive 2010/13/EU;
(b) Union law on copyright and related rights;
(c) Regulation (EU) 2021/784;
(d) Regulation (EU) 2019/1148;
(e) Regulation (EU) 2019/1150;
(f) Union law on consumer protection and product safety, including Regulations (EU) 2017/2394 and (EU) 2019/1020 and Directives 2001/95/EC and 2013/11/EU;
(g) Union law on the protection of personal data, in particular Regulation (EU) 2016/679 and Directive 2002/58/EC;
(h) Union law in the field of judicial cooperation in civil matters, in particular Regulation (EU) No 1215/2012 or any Union legal act laying down the rules on law applicable to contractual and non-contractual obligations;
(i) Union law in the field of judicial cooperation in criminal matters, in particular a Regulation on European Production and Preservation Orders for electronic evidence in criminal matters;
(j) a Directive laying down harmonised rules on the appointment of legal representatives for the purpose of gathering evidence in criminal proceedings.

Article 3
Definitions

For the purpose of this Regulation, the following definitions shall apply:

(a) 'information society service' means a 'service' as defined in Article 1(1), point (b), of Directive (EU) 2015/1535;
(b) 'recipient of the service' means any natural or legal person who uses an intermediary service, in particular for the purposes of seeking information or making it accessible;
(c) 'consumer' means any natural person who is acting for purposes which are outside his or her trade, business, craft, or profession;

(d) 'to offer services in the Union' means enabling natural or legal persons in one or more Member States to use the services of a provider of intermediary services that has a substantial connection to the Union;

(e) 'substantial connection to the Union' means a connection of a provider of intermediary services with the Union resulting either from its establishment in the Union or from specific factual criteria, such as:
   - a significant number of recipients of the service in one or more Member States in relation to its or their population; or
   - the targeting of activities towards one or more Member States;

(f) 'trader' means any natural person, or any legal person irrespective of whether it is privately or publicly owned, who is acting, including through any person acting in his or her name or on his or her behalf, for purposes relating to his or her trade, business, craft or profession;

(g) 'intermediary service' means one of the following information society services:
   (i) a 'mere conduit' service, consisting of the transmission in a communication network of information provided by a recipient of the service, or the provision of access to a communication network;
   (ii) a 'caching' service, consisting of the transmission in a communication network of information provided by a recipient of the service, involving the automatic, intermediate and temporary storage of that information, performed for the sole purpose of making more efficient the information's onward transmission to other recipients upon their request;
   (iii) a 'hosting' service, consisting of the storage of information provided by, and at the request of, a recipient of the service;

(h) 'illegal content' means any information that, in itself or in relation to an activity, including the sale of products or the provision of services, is not in compliance with Union law or the law of any Member State which is in compliance with Union law, irrespective of the precise subject matter or nature of that law;

(i) 'online platform' means a hosting service that, at the request of a recipient of the service, stores and disseminates information to the public, unless that activity is a minor and purely ancillary feature of another service or a minor functionality of the principal service and, for objective and technical reasons, cannot be used without that other service, and the integration of the feature or functionality into the other service is not a means to circumvent the applicability of this Regulation;

(j) 'online search engine' means an intermediary service that allows users to input queries in order to perform searches of, in principle, all websites, or all websites in a particular language, on the basis of a query on any subject in the form of a keyword, voice request, phrase or other input, and returns results in any format in which information related to the requested content can be found;

(k) 'dissemination to the public' means making information available, at the request of the recipient of the service who provided the information, to a potentially unlimited number of third parties;

(l) 'distance contract' means 'distance contract' as defined in Article 2, point (7), of Directive 2011/83/EU;

(m) 'online interface' means any software, including a website or a part thereof, and applications, including mobile applications;

(n) 'Digital Services Coordinator of establishment' means the Digital Services Coordinator of the Member State where the main establishment of a provider of an intermediary service is located or its legal representative resides or is established;

(o) 'Digital Services Coordinator of destination' means the Digital Services Coordinator of a Member State where the intermediary service is provided;
(p) 'active recipient of an online platform' means a recipient of the service that has engaged with an online platform by either requesting the online platform to host information or being exposed to information hosted by the online platform and disseminated through its online interface;
(q) 'active recipient of an online search engine' means a recipient of the service that has submitted a query to an online search engine and been exposed to information indexed and presented on its online interface;
(r) 'advertisement' means information designed to promote the message of a legal or natural person, irrespective of whether to achieve commercial or non-commercial purposes, and presented by an online platform on its online interface against remuneration specifically for promoting that information;
(s) 'recommender system' means a fully or partially automated system used by an online platform to suggest in its online interface specific information to recipients of the service or prioritise that information, including as a result of a search initiated by the recipient of the service or otherwise determining the relative order or prominence of information displayed;
(t) 'content moderation' means the activities, whether automated or not, undertaken by providers of intermediary services, that are aimed, in particular, at detecting, identifying and addressing illegal content or information incompatible with their terms and conditions, provided by recipients of the service, including measures taken that affect the availability, visibility, and accessibility of that illegal content or that information, such as demotion, demonetisation, disabling of access to, or removal thereof, or that affect the ability of the recipients of the service to provide that information, such as the termination or suspension of a recipient's account;
(u) 'terms and conditions' means all clauses, irrespective of their name or form, which govern the contractual relationship between the provider of intermediary services and the recipients of the service;
(v) 'persons with disabilities' means 'persons with disabilities' as referred to in Article 3, point (1), of Directive (EU) 2019/882 of the European Parliament and of the Council[38];
(w) 'commercial communication' means 'commercial communication' as defined in Article 2, point (f), of Directive 2000/31/EC;
(x) 'turnover' means the amount derived by an undertaking within the meaning of Article 5(1) of Council Regulation (EC) No 139/2004[39].

CHAPTER II
LIABILITY OF PROVIDERS OF INTERMEDIARY SERVICES

Article 4
'Mere conduit'

1. Where an information society service is provided that consists of the transmission in a communication network of information provided by a recipient of the service, or

[38] Directive (EU) 2019/882 of the European Parliament and of the Council of 17 April 2019 on the accessibility requirements for products and services (OJ L 151, 7.6.2019, p. 70).
[39] Council Regulation (EC) No 139/2004 of 20 January 2004 on the control of concentrations between undertakings (OJ L 24, 29.1.2004, p. 1).

the provision of access to a communication network, the service provider shall not be liable for the information transmitted or accessed, on condition that the provider:

(a) does not initiate the transmission;
(b) does not select the receiver of the transmission; and
(c) does not select or modify the information contained in the transmission.

2. The acts of transmission and of provision of access referred to in paragraph 1 shall include the automatic, intermediate and transient storage of the information transmitted in so far as this takes place for the sole purpose of carrying out the transmission in the communication network, and provided that the information is not stored for any period longer than is reasonably necessary for the transmission.

3. This Article shall not affect the possibility for a judicial or administrative authority, in accordance with a Member State's legal system, to require the service provider to terminate or prevent an infringement.

Article 5
'Caching'

1. Where an information society service is provided that consists of the transmission in a communication network of information provided by a recipient of the service, the service provider shall not be liable for the automatic, intermediate and temporary storage of that information, performed for the sole purpose of making more efficient or more secure the information's onward transmission to other recipients of the service upon their request, on condition that the provider:

(a) does not modify the information;
(b) complies with conditions on access to the information;
(c) complies with rules regarding the updating of the information, specified in a manner widely recognised and used by industry;
(d) does not interfere with the lawful use of technology, widely recognised and used by industry, to obtain data on the use of the information; and
(e) acts expeditiously to remove or to disable access to the information it has stored upon obtaining actual knowledge of the fact that the information at the initial source of the transmission has been removed from the network, or access to it has been disabled, or that a judicial or an administrative authority has ordered such removal or disablement.

2. This Article shall not affect the possibility for a judicial or administrative authority, in accordance with a Member State's legal system, to require the service provider to terminate or prevent an infringement.

Article 6
Hosting

1. Where an information society service is provided that consists of the storage of information provided by a recipient of the service, the service provider shall not be liable for the information stored at the request of a recipient of the service, on condition that the provider:

(a) does not have actual knowledge of illegal activity or illegal content and, as regards claims for damages, is not aware of facts or circumstances from which the illegal activity or illegal content is apparent; or
(b) upon obtaining such knowledge or awareness, acts expeditiously to remove or to disable access to the illegal content.

2. Paragraph 1 shall not apply where the recipient of the service is acting under the authority or the control of the provider.

3. Paragraph 1 shall not apply with respect to the liability under consumer protection law of online platforms that allow consumers to conclude distance contracts with traders, where such an online platform presents the specific item of information or otherwise enables the specific transaction at issue in a way that would lead an average consumer to believe that the information, or the product or service that is the object of the transaction, is provided either by the online platform itself or by a recipient of the service who is acting under its authority or control.

4. This Article shall not affect the possibility for a judicial or administrative authority, in accordance with a Member State's legal system, to require the service provider to terminate or prevent an infringement.

Article 7
Voluntary own-initiative investigations and legal compliance

Providers of intermediary services shall not be deemed ineligible for the exemptions from liability referred to in Articles 4, 5 and 6 solely because they, in good faith and in a diligent manner, carry out voluntary own-initiative investigations into, or take other measures aimed at detecting, identifying and removing, or disabling access to, illegal content, or take the necessary measures to comply with the requirements of Union law and national law in compliance with Union law, including the requirements set out in this Regulation.

Article 8
No general monitoring or active fact-finding obligations

No general obligation to monitor the information which providers of intermediary services transmit or store, nor actively to seek facts or circumstances indicating illegal activity shall be imposed on those providers.

Article 9
Orders to act against illegal content

1. Upon the receipt of an order to act against one or more specific items of illegal content, issued by the relevant national judicial or administrative authorities, on the basis of the applicable Union law or national law in compliance with Union law, providers of intermediary services shall inform the authority issuing the order, or any other authority specified in the order, of any effect given to the order without undue delay, specifying if and when effect was given to the order.

2. Member States shall ensure that when an order referred to in paragraph 1 is transmitted to the provider, it meets at least the following conditions:

(a) that order contains the following elements:
  (i) a reference to the legal basis under Union or national law for the order;
  (ii) a statement of reasons explaining why the information is illegal content, by reference to one or more specific provisions of Union law or national law in compliance with Union law;
  (iii) information identifying the issuing authority;
  (iv) clear information enabling the provider of intermediary services to identify and locate the illegal content concerned, such as one or more exact URL and, where necessary, additional information;
  (v) information about redress mechanisms available to the provider of intermediary services and to the recipient of the service who provided the content;
  (vi) where applicable, information about which authority is to receive the information about the effect given to the orders;

(b) the territorial scope of that order, on the basis of the applicable rules of Union and national law, including the Charter, and, where relevant, general principles of international law, is limited to what is strictly necessary to achieve its objective;

(c) that order is transmitted in one of the languages declared by the provider of intermediary services pursuant to Article 11(3) or in another official language of the Member States, agreed between the authority issuing the order and that provider, and is sent to the electronic point of contact designated by that provider, in accordance with Article 11; where the order is not drafted in the language declared by the provider of intermediary services or in another bilaterally agreed language, the order may be transmitted in the language of the authority issuing the order, provided that it is accompanied by a translation into such declared or bilaterally agreed language of at least the elements set out in points (a) and (b) of this paragraph.

3. The authority issuing the order or, where applicable, the authority specified therein, shall transmit it, along with any information received from the provider of intermediary services concerning the effect given to that order to the Digital Services Coordinator from the Member State of the issuing authority.

4. After receiving the order from the judicial or administrative authority, the Digital Services Coordinator of the Member State concerned shall, without undue delay, transmit a copy of the order referred to in paragraph 1 of this Article to all other Digital Services Coordinators through the system established in accordance with Article 85.

5. At the latest when effect is given to the order or, where applicable, at the time provided by the issuing authority in its order, providers of intermediary services shall inform the recipient of the service concerned of the order received and to the effect given to it. Such information provided to the recipient of the service shall include a statement of reasons, the possibilities for redress that exist, and a description of the territorial scope of the order, in accordance with paragraph 2.

6. The conditions and requirements laid down in this Article shall be without prejudice to national civil and criminal procedural law.

Article 10
Orders to provide information

1. Upon receipt of an order to provide specific information about one or more specific individual recipients of the service, issued by the relevant national judicial or adminis-

trative authorities on the basis of the applicable Union law or national law in compliance with Union law, providers of intermediary services shall, without undue delay inform the authority issuing the order, or any other authority specified in the order, of its receipt and of the effect given to the order, specifying if and when effect was given to the order.

2. Member States shall ensure that when an order referred to in paragraph 1 is transmitted to the provider, it meets at least the following conditions:

(a) that order contains the following elements:
   (i) a reference to the legal basis under Union or national law for the order;
   (ii) information identifying the issuing authority;
   (iii) clear information enabling the provider of intermediary services to identify the specific recipient or recipients on whom information is sought, such as one or more account names or unique identifiers;
   (iv) a statement of reasons explaining the objective for which the information is required and why the requirement to provide the information is necessary and proportionate to determine compliance by the recipients of the intermediary services with applicable Union law or national law in compliance with Union law, unless such a statement cannot be provided for reasons related to the prevention, investigation, detection and prosecution of criminal offences;
   (v) information about redress mechanisms available to the provider and to the recipients of the service concerned;
   (vi) where applicable, information about which authority is to receive the information about the effect given to the orders;
(b) that order only requires the provider to provide information already collected for the purposes of providing the service and which lies within its control;
(c) that order is transmitted in one of the languages declared by the provider of intermediary services pursuant to Article 11(3) or in another official language of the Member States, agreed between the authority issuing the order and the provider, and is sent to the electronic point of contact designated by that provider, in accordance with Article 11; where the order is not drafted in the language declared by the provider of intermediary services or in another bilaterally agreed language, the order may be transmitted in the language of the authority issuing the order, provided that it is accompanied by a translation into such declared or bilaterally agreed language of at least the elements set out in points (a) and (b) of this paragraph.

3. The authority issuing the order or, where applicable, the authority specified therein, shall transmit it, along with any information received from the provider of intermediary services concerning the effect given to that order to the Digital Services Coordinator from the Member State of the issuing authority.

4. After receiving the order from the judicial or administrative authority, the Digital Services Coordinator of the Member State concerned shall, without undue delay, transmit a copy of the order referred to in paragraph 1 of this Article to all Digital Services Coordinators through the system established in accordance with Article 85.

5. At the latest when effect is given to the order, or, where applicable, at the time provided by the issuing authority in its order, providers of intermediary services shall inform the recipient of the service concerned of the order received and the effect given to it. Such information provided to the recipient of the service shall include a statement of reasons and the possibilities for redress that exist, in accordance with paragraph 2.

6. The conditions and requirements laid down in this Article shall be without prejudice to national civil and criminal procedural law.

CHAPTER III
DUE DILIGENCE OBLIGATIONS FOR A TRANSPARENT AND SAFE ONLINE ENVIRONMENT

SECTION 1
Provisions applicable to all providers of intermediary services

Article 11
Points of contact for Member States' authorities, the Commission and the Board

1. Providers of intermediary services shall designate a single point of contact to enable them to communicate directly, by electronic means, with Member States' authorities, the Commission and the Board referred to in Article 61 for the application of this Regulation.

2. Providers of intermediary services shall make public the information necessary to easily identify and communicate with their single points of contact. That information shall be easily accessible, and shall be kept up to date.

3. Providers of intermediary services shall specify in the information referred to in paragraph 2 the official language or languages of the Member States which, in addition to a language broadly understood by the largest possible number of Union citizens, can be used to communicate with their points of contact, and which shall include at least one of the official languages of the Member State in which the provider of intermediary services has its main establishment or where its legal representative resides or is established.

Article 12
Points of contact for recipients of the service

1. Providers of intermediary services shall designate a single point of contact to enable recipients of the service to communicate directly and rapidly with them, by electronic means and in a user-friendly manner, including by allowing recipients of the service to choose the means of communication, which shall not solely rely on automated tools.

2. In addition to the obligations provided under Directive 2000/31/EC, providers of intermediary services shall make public the information necessary for the recipients of the service in order to easily identify and communicate with their single points of contact. That information shall be easily accessible, and shall be kept up to date.

Article 13
Legal representatives

1. Providers of intermediary services which do not have an establishment in the Union but which offer services in the Union shall designate, in writing, a legal or natural person to act as their legal representative in one of the Member States where the provider offers its services.

2. Providers of intermediary services shall mandate their legal representatives for the purpose of being addressed in addition to or instead of such providers, by the Member States' competent authorities, the Commission and the Board, on all issues necessary for

the receipt of, compliance with and enforcement of decisions issued in relation to this Regulation. Providers of intermediary services shall provide their legal representative with necessary powers and sufficient resources to guarantee their efficient and timely cooperation with the Member States' competent authorities, the Commission and the Board, and to comply with such decisions.

3. It shall be possible for the designated legal representative to be held liable for non-compliance with obligations under this Regulation, without prejudice to the liability and legal actions that could be initiated against the provider of intermediary services.

4. Providers of intermediary services shall notify the name, postal address, email address and telephone number of their legal representative to the Digital Services Coordinator in the Member State where that legal representative resides or is established. They shall ensure that that information is publicly available, easily accessible, accurate and kept up to date.

5. The designation of a legal representative within the Union pursuant to paragraph 1 shall not constitute an establishment in the Union.

Article 14
Terms and conditions

1. Providers of intermediary services shall include information on any restrictions that they impose in relation to the use of their service in respect of information provided by the recipients of the service, in their terms and conditions. That information shall include information on any policies, procedures, measures and tools used for the purpose of content moderation, including algorithmic decision-making and human review, as well as the rules of procedure of their internal complaint handling system. It shall be set out in clear, plain, intelligible, user-friendly and unambiguous language, and shall be publicly available in an easily accessible and machine-readable format.

2. Providers of intermediary services shall inform the recipients of the service of any significant change to the terms and conditions.

3. Where an intermediary service is primarily directed at minors or is predominantly used by them, the provider of that intermediary service shall explain the conditions for, and any restrictions on, the use of the service in a way that minors can understand.

4. Providers of intermediary services shall act in a diligent, objective and proportionate manner in applying and enforcing the restrictions referred to in paragraph 1, with due regard to the rights and legitimate interests of all parties involved, including the fundamental rights of the recipients of the service, such as the freedom of expression, freedom and pluralism of the media, and other fundamental rights and freedoms as enshrined in the Charter.

5. Providers of very large online platforms and of very large online search engines shall provide recipients of services with a concise, easily-accessible and machine-readable summary of the terms and conditions, including the available remedies and redress mechanisms, in clear and unambiguous language.

6. Very large online platforms and very large online search engines within the meaning of Article 33 shall publish their terms and conditions in the official languages of all the Member States in which they offer their services.

Article 15
Transparency reporting obligations for providers of intermediary services

1. Providers of intermediary services shall make publicly available, in a machine-readable format and in an easily accessible manner, at least once a year, clear, easily comprehensible reports on any content moderation that they engaged in during the relevant period. Those reports shall include, in particular, information on the following, as applicable:

(a) for providers of intermediary services, the number of orders received from Member States' authorities including orders issued in accordance with Articles 9 and 10, categorised by the type of illegal content concerned, the Member State issuing the order, and the median time needed to inform the authority issuing the order, or any other authority specified in the order, of its receipt, and to give effect to the order;
(b) for providers of hosting services, the number of notices submitted in accordance with Article 16, categorised by the type of alleged illegal content concerned, the number of notices submitted by trusted flaggers, any action taken pursuant to the notices by differentiating whether the action was taken on the basis of the law or the terms and conditions of the provider, the number of notices processed by using automated means and the median time needed for taking the action;
(c) for providers of intermediary services, meaningful and comprehensible information about the content moderation engaged in at the providers' own initiative, including the use of automated tools, the measures taken to provide training and assistance to persons in charge of content moderation, the number and type of measures taken that affect the availability, visibility and accessibility of information provided by the recipients of the service and the recipients' ability to provide information through the service, and other related restrictions of the service; the information reported shall be categorised by the type of illegal content or violation of the terms and conditions of the service provider, by the detection method and by the type of restriction applied;
(d) for providers of intermediary services, the number of complaints received through the internal complaint-handling systems in accordance with the provider's terms and conditions and additionally, for providers of online platforms, in accordance with Article 20, the basis for those complaints, decisions taken in respect of those complaints, the median time needed for taking those decisions and the number of instances where those decisions were reversed;
(e) any use made of automated means for the purpose of content moderation, including a qualitative description, a specification of the precise purposes, indicators of the accuracy and the possible rate of error of the automated means used in fulfilling those purposes, and any safeguards applied.

2. Paragraph 1 of this Article shall not apply to providers of intermediary services that qualify as micro or small enterprises as defined in Recommendation 2003/361/EC and which are not very large online platforms within the meaning of Article 33 of this Regulation.

3. The Commission may adopt implementing acts to lay down templates concerning the form, content and other details of reports pursuant to paragraph 1 of this Article, including harmonised reporting periods. Those implementing acts shall be adopted in accordance with the advisory procedure referred to in Article 88.

SECTION 2
Additional provisions applicable to providers of hosting services, including online platforms

Article 16
Notice and action mechanisms

1. Providers of hosting services shall put mechanisms in place to allow any individual or entity to notify them of the presence on their service of specific items of information that the individual or entity considers to be illegal content. Those mechanisms shall be easy to access and user-friendly, and shall allow for the submission of notices exclusively by electronic means.

2. The mechanisms referred to in paragraph 1 shall be such as to facilitate the submission of sufficiently precise and adequately substantiated notices. To that end, the providers of hosting services shall take the necessary measures to enable and to facilitate the submission of notices containing all of the following elements:

(a) a sufficiently substantiated explanation of the reasons why the individual or entity alleges the information in question to be illegal content;
(b) a clear indication of the exact electronic location of that information, such as the exact URL or URLs, and, where necessary, additional information enabling the identification of the illegal content adapted to the type of content and to the specific type of hosting service;
(c) the name and email address of the individual or entity submitting the notice, except in the case of information considered to involve one of the offences referred to in Articles 3 to 7 of Directive 2011/93/EU;
(d) a statement confirming the bona fide belief of the individual or entity submitting the notice that the information and allegations contained therein are accurate and complete.

3. Notices referred to in this Article shall be considered to give rise to actual knowledge or awareness for the purposes of Article 6 in respect of the specific item of information concerned where they allow a diligent provider of hosting services to identify the illegality of the relevant activity or information without a detailed legal examination.

4. Where the notice contains the electronic contact information of the individual or entity that submitted it, the provider of hosting services shall, without undue delay, send a confirmation of receipt of the notice to that individual or entity.

5. The provider shall also, without undue delay, notify that individual or entity of its decision in respect of the information to which the notice relates, providing information on the possibilities for redress in respect of that decision.

6. Providers of hosting services shall process any notices that they receive under the mechanisms referred to in paragraph 1 and take their decisions in respect of the information to which the notices relate, in a timely, diligent, non-arbitrary and objective manner. Where they use automated means for that processing or decision-making, they shall include information on such use in the notification referred to in paragraph 5.

Article 17
Statement of reasons

1. Providers of hosting services shall provide a clear and specific statement of reasons to any affected recipients of the service for any of the following restrictions imposed on the ground that the information provided by the recipient of the service is illegal content or incompatible with their terms and conditions:

(a) any restrictions of the visibility of specific items of information provided by the recipient of the service, including removal of content, disabling access to content, or demoting content;
(b) suspension, termination or other restriction of monetary payments;
(c) suspension or termination of the provision of the service in whole or in part;
(d) suspension or termination of the recipient of the service's account.

2. Paragraph 1 shall only apply where the relevant electronic contact details are known to the provider. It shall apply at the latest from the date that the restriction is imposed, regardless of why or how it was imposed.

Paragraph 1 shall not apply where the information is deceptive high-volume commercial content.

3. The statement of reasons referred to in paragraph 1 shall at least contain the following information:

(a) information on whether the decision entails either the removal of, the disabling of access to, the demotion of or the restriction of the visibility of the information, or the suspension or termination of monetary payments related to that information, or imposes other measures referred to in paragraph 1 with regard to the information, and, where relevant, the territorial scope of the decision and its duration;
(b) the facts and circumstances relied on in taking the decision, including, where relevant, information on whether the decision was taken pursuant to a notice submitted in accordance with Article 16 or based on voluntary own-initiative investigations and, where strictly necessary, the identity of the notifier;
(c) where applicable, information on the use made of automated means in taking the decision, including information on whether the decision was taken in respect of content detected or identified using automated means;
(d) where the decision concerns allegedly illegal content, a reference to the legal ground relied on and explanations as to why the information is considered to be illegal content on that ground;
(e) where the decision is based on the alleged incompatibility of the information with the terms and conditions of the provider of hosting services, a reference to the contractual ground relied on and explanations as to why the information is considered to be incompatible with that ground;
(f) clear and user-friendly information on the possibilities for redress available to the recipient of the service in respect of the decision, in particular, where applicable through internal complaint-handling mechanisms, out-of-court dispute settlement and judicial redress.

4. The information provided by the providers of hosting services in accordance with this Article shall be clear and easily comprehensible and as precise and specific as reasonably possible under the given circumstances. The information shall, in particular, be

such as to reasonably allow the recipient of the service concerned to effectively exercise the possibilities for redress referred to in of paragraph 3, point (f).

5. This Article shall not apply to any orders referred to in Article 9.

Article 18
Notification of suspicions of criminal offences

1. Where a provider of hosting services becomes aware of any information giving rise to a suspicion that a criminal offence involving a threat to the life or safety of a person or persons has taken place, is taking place or is likely to take place, it shall promptly inform the law enforcement or judicial authorities of the Member State or Member States concerned of its suspicion and provide all relevant information available.

2. Where the provider of hosting services cannot identify with reasonable certainty the Member State concerned, it shall inform the law enforcement authorities of the Member State in which it is established or where its legal representative resides or is established or inform Europol, or both.

For the purpose of this Article, the Member State concerned shall be the Member State in which the offence is suspected to have taken place, to be taking place or to be likely to take place, or the Member State where the suspected offender resides or is located, or the Member State where the victim of the suspected offence resides or is located.

SECTION 3
Additional provisions applicable to providers of online platforms

Article 19
Exclusion for micro and small enterprises

1. This Section, with the exception of Article 24(3) thereof, shall not apply to providers of online platforms that qualify as micro or small enterprises as defined in Recommendation 2003/361/EC.

This Section, with the exception of Article 24(3) thereof, shall not apply to providers of online platforms that previously qualified for the status of a micro or small enterprise as defined in Recommendation 2003/361/EC during the 12 months following their loss of that status pursuant to Article 4(2) thereof, except when they are very large online platforms in accordance with Article 33.

2. By derogation from paragraph 1 of this Article, this Section shall apply to providers of online platforms that have been designated as very large online platforms in accordance with Article 33, irrespective of whether they qualify as micro or small enterprises.

Article 20
Internal complaint-handling system

1. Providers of online platforms shall provide recipients of the service, including individuals or entities that have submitted a notice, for a period of at least six months following the decision referred to in this paragraph, with access to an effective internal complaint-handling system that enables them to lodge complaints, electronically and free of charge, against the decision taken by the provider of the online platform upon the re-

ceipt of a notice or against the following decisions taken by the provider of the online platform on the grounds that the information provided by the recipients constitutes illegal content or is incompatible with its terms and conditions:

(a) decisions whether or not to remove or disable access to or restrict visibility of the information;
(b) decisions whether or not to suspend or terminate the provision of the service, in whole or in part, to the recipients;
(c) decisions whether or not to suspend or terminate the recipients' account;
(d) decisions whether or not to suspend, terminate or otherwise restrict the ability to monetise information provided by the recipients.

2. The period of at least six months referred to in paragraph 1 of this Article shall start on the day on which the recipient of the service is informed about the decision in accordance with Article 16(5) or Article 17.

3. Providers of online platforms shall ensure that their internal complaint-handling systems are easy to access, user-friendly and enable and facilitate the submission of sufficiently precise and adequately substantiated complaints.

4. Providers of online platforms shall handle complaints submitted through their internal complaint-handling system in a timely, non-discriminatory, diligent and non-arbitrary manner. Where a complaint contains sufficient grounds for the provider of the online platform to consider that its decision not to act upon the notice is unfounded or that the information to which the complaint relates is not illegal and is not incompatible with its terms and conditions, or contains information indicating that the complainant's conduct does not warrant the measure taken, it shall reverse its decision referred to in paragraph 1 without undue delay.

5. Providers of online platforms shall inform complainants without undue delay of their reasoned decision in respect of the information to which the complaint relates and of the possibility of out-of-court dispute settlement provided for in Article 21 and other available possibilities for redress.

6. Providers of online platforms shall ensure that the decisions, referred to in paragraph 5, are taken under the supervision of appropriately qualified staff, and not solely on the basis of automated means.

Article 21
Out-of-court dispute settlement

1. Recipients of the service, including individuals or entities that have submitted notices, addressed by the decisions referred to in Article 20(1) shall be entitled to select any out-of-court dispute settlement body that has been certified in accordance with paragraph 3 of this Article in order to resolve disputes relating to those decisions, including complaints that have not been resolved by means of the internal complaint-handling system referred to in that Article.

Providers of online platforms shall ensure that information about the possibility for recipients of the service to have access to an out-of-court dispute settlement, as referred to in the first subparagraph, is easily accessible on their online interface, clear and user-friendly.

The first subparagraph is without prejudice to the right of the recipient of the service concerned to initiate, at any stage, proceedings to contest those decisions by the providers of online platforms before a court in accordance with the applicable law.

2. Both parties shall engage, in good faith, with the selected certified out-of-court dispute settlement body with a view to resolving the dispute.

Providers of online platforms may refuse to engage with such out-of-court dispute settlement body if a dispute has already been resolved concerning the same information and the same grounds of alleged illegality or incompatibility of content.

The certified out-of-court dispute settlement body shall not have the power to impose a binding settlement of the dispute on the parties.

3. The Digital Services Coordinator of the Member State where the out-of-court dispute settlement body is established shall, for a maximum period of five years, which may be renewed, certify the body, at its request, where the body has demonstrated that it meets all of the following conditions:

(a) it is impartial and independent, including financially independent, of providers of online platforms and of recipients of the service provided by providers of online platforms, including of individuals or entities that have submitted notices;
(b) it has the necessary expertise in relation to the issues arising in one or more particular areas of illegal content, or in relation to the application and enforcement of terms and conditions of one or more types of online platform, allowing the body to contribute effectively to the settlement of a dispute;
(c) its members are remunerated in a way that is not linked to the outcome of the procedure;
(d) the out-of-court dispute settlement that it offers is easily accessible, through electronic communications technology and provides for the possibility to initiate the dispute settlement and to submit the requisite supporting documents online;
(e) it is capable of settling disputes in a swift, efficient and cost-effective manner and in at least one of the official languages of the institutions of the Union;
(f) the out-of-court dispute settlement that it offers takes place in accordance with clear and fair rules of procedure that are easily and publicly accessible, and that comply with applicable law, including this Article.

The Digital Services Coordinator shall, where applicable, specify in the certificate:

(a) the particular issues to which the body's expertise relates, as referred to in point (b) of the first subparagraph; and
(b) the official language or languages of the institutions of the Union in which the body is capable of settling disputes, as referred to in point (e) of the first subparagraph.

4. Certified out-of-court dispute settlement bodies shall report to the Digital Services Coordinator that certified them, on an annual basis, on their functioning, specifying at least the number of disputes they received, the information about the outcomes of those disputes, the average time taken to resolve them and any shortcomings or difficulties encountered. They shall provide additional information at the request of that Digital Services Coordinator.

Digital Services Coordinators shall, every two years, draw up a report on the functioning of the out-of-court dispute settlement bodies that they certified. That report shall in particular:

(a) list the number of disputes that each certified out-of-court dispute settlement body has received annually;
(b) indicate the outcomes of the procedures brought before those bodies and the average time taken to resolve the disputes;
(c) identify and explain any systematic or sectoral shortcomings or difficulties encountered in relation to the functioning of those bodies;
(d) identify best practices concerning that functioning;
(e) make recommendations as to how to improve that functioning, where appropriate.

Certified out-of-court dispute settlement bodies shall make their decisions available to the parties within a reasonable period of time and no later than 90 calendar days after the receipt of the complaint. In the case of highly complex disputes, the certified out-of-court dispute settlement body may, at its own discretion, extend the 90 calendar day period for an additional period that shall not exceed 90 days, resulting in a maximum total duration of 180 days.

5. If the out-of-court dispute settlement body decides the dispute in favour of the recipient of the service, including the individual or entity that has submitted a notice, the provider of the online platform shall bear all the fees charged by the out-of-court dispute settlement body, and shall reimburse that recipient, including the individual or entity, for any other reasonable expenses that it has paid in relation to the dispute settlement. If the out-of-court dispute settlement body decides the dispute in favour of the provider of the online platform, the recipient of the service, including the individual or entity, shall not be required to reimburse any fees or other expenses that the provider of the online platform paid or is to pay in relation to the dispute settlement, unless the out-of-court dispute settlement body finds that that recipient manifestly acted in bad faith.

The fees charged by the out-of-court dispute settlement body to the providers of online platforms for the dispute settlement shall be reasonable and shall in any event not exceed the costs incurred by the body. For recipients of the service, the dispute settlement shall be available free of charge or at a nominal fee.

Certified out-of-court dispute settlement bodies shall make the fees, or the mechanisms used to determine the fees, known to the recipient of the service, including to the individuals or entities that have submitted a notice, and to the provider of the online platform concerned, before engaging in the dispute settlement.

6. Member States may establish out-of-court dispute settlement bodies for the purposes of paragraph 1 or support the activities of some or all out-of-court dispute settlement bodies that they have certified in accordance with paragraph 3.

Member States shall ensure that any of their activities undertaken under the first subparagraph do not affect the ability of their Digital Services Coordinators to certify the bodies concerned in accordance with paragraph 3.

7. A Digital Services Coordinator that has certified an out-of-court dispute settlement body shall revoke that certification if it determines, following an investigation either on its own initiative or on the basis of the information received by third parties, that the out-of-court dispute settlement body no longer meets the conditions set out in paragraph 3. Before revoking that certification, the Digital Services Coordinator shall afford that body an opportunity to react to the findings of its investigation and its intention to revoke the out-of-court dispute settlement body's certification.

8. Digital Services Coordinators shall notify to the Commission the out-of-court dispute settlement bodies that they have certified in accordance with paragraph 3, including where applicable the specifications referred to in the second subparagraph of that

paragraph, as well as the out-of-court dispute settlement bodies the certification of which they have revoked. The Commission shall publish a list of those bodies, including those specifications, on a dedicated website that is easily accessible, and keep it up to date.

9. This Article is without prejudice to Directive 2013/11/EU and alternative dispute resolution procedures and entities for consumers established under that Directive.

Article 22
Trusted flaggers

1. Providers of online platforms shall take the necessary technical and organisational measures to ensure that notices submitted by trusted flaggers, acting within their designated area of expertise, through the mechanisms referred to in Article 16, are given priority and are processed and decided upon without undue delay.

2. The status of 'trusted flagger' under this Regulation shall be awarded, upon application by any entity, by the Digital Services Coordinator of the Member State in which the applicant is established, to an applicant that has demonstrated that it meets all of the following conditions:

(a) it has particular expertise and competence for the purposes of detecting, identifying and notifying illegal content;
(b) it is independent from any provider of online platforms;
(c) it carries out its activities for the purposes of submitting notices diligently, accurately and objectively.

3. Trusted flaggers shall publish, at least once a year easily comprehensible and detailed reports on notices submitted in accordance with Article 16 during the relevant period. The report shall list at least the number of notices categorised by:

(a) the identity of the provider of hosting services,
(b) the type of allegedly illegal content notified,
(c) the action taken by the provider.

Those reports shall include an explanation of the procedures in place to ensure that the trusted flagger retains its independence.

Trusted flaggers shall send those reports to the awarding Digital Services Coordinator, and shall make them publicly available. The information in those reports shall not contain personal data.

4. Digital Services Coordinators shall communicate to the Commission and the Board the names, addresses and email addresses of the entities to which they have awarded the status of the trusted flagger in accordance with paragraph 2 or whose trusted flagger status they have suspended in accordance with paragraph 6 or revoked in accordance with paragraph 7.

5. The Commission shall publish the information referred to in paragraph 4 in a publicly available database, in an easily accessible and machine-readable format, and shall keep the database up to date.

6. Where a provider of online platforms has information indicating that a trusted flagger has submitted a significant number of insufficiently precise, inaccurate or inadequately substantiated notices through the mechanisms referred to in Article 16, including information gathered in connection to the processing of complaints through the in-

ternal complaint-handling systems referred to in Article 20(4), it shall communicate that information to the Digital Services Coordinator that awarded the status of trusted flagger to the entity concerned, providing the necessary explanations and supporting documents. Upon receiving the information from the provider of online platforms, and if the Digital Services Coordinator considers that there are legitimate reasons to open an investigation, the status of trusted flagger shall be suspended during the period of the investigation. That investigation shall be carried out without undue delay.

7. The Digital Services Coordinator that awarded the status of trusted flagger to an entity shall revoke that status if it determines, following an investigation either on its own initiative or on the basis information received from third parties, including the information provided by a provider of online platforms pursuant to paragraph 6, that the entity no longer meets the conditions set out in paragraph 2. Before revoking that status, the Digital Services Coordinator shall afford the entity an opportunity to react to the findings of its investigation and its intention to revoke the entity's status as trusted flagger.

8. The Commission, after consulting the Board, shall, where necessary, issue guidelines to assist providers of online platforms and Digital Services Coordinators in the application of paragraphs 2, 6 and 7.

Article 23
Measures and protection against misuse

1. Providers of online platforms shall suspend, for a reasonable period of time and after having issued a prior warning, the provision of their services to recipients of the service that frequently provide manifestly illegal content.

2. Providers of online platforms shall suspend, for a reasonable period of time and after having issued a prior warning, the processing of notices and complaints submitted through the notice and action mechanisms and internal complaints-handling systems referred to in Articles 16 and 20, respectively, by individuals or entities or by complainants that frequently submit notices or complaints that are manifestly unfounded.

3. When deciding on suspension, providers of online platforms shall assess, on a case-by-case basis and in a timely, diligent and objective manner, whether the recipient of the service, the individual, the entity or the complainant engages in the misuse referred to in paragraphs 1 and 2, taking into account all relevant facts and circumstances apparent from the information available to the provider of online platforms. Those circumstances shall include at least the following:

(a) the absolute numbers of items of manifestly illegal content or manifestly unfounded notices or complaints, submitted within a given time frame;
(b) the relative proportion thereof in relation to the total number of items of information provided or notices submitted within a given time frame;
(c) the gravity of the misuses, including the nature of illegal content, and of its consequences;
(d) where it is possible to identify it, the intention of the recipient of the service, the individual, the entity or the complainant.

4. Providers of online platforms shall set out, in a clear and detailed manner, in their terms and conditions their policy in respect of the misuse referred to in paragraphs 1 and 2, and shall give examples of the facts and circumstances that they take into account

when assessing whether certain behaviour constitutes misuse and the duration of the suspension.

Article 24
Transparency reporting obligations for providers of online platforms

1. In addition to the information referred to in Article 15, providers of online platforms shall include in the reports referred to in that Article information on the following:

(a) the number of disputes submitted to the out-of-court dispute settlement bodies referred to in Article 21, the outcomes of the dispute settlement, and the median time needed for completing the dispute settlement procedures, as well as the share of disputes where the provider of the online platform implemented the decisions of the body;

(b) the number of suspensions imposed pursuant to Article 23, distinguishing between suspensions enacted for the provision of manifestly illegal content, the submission of manifestly unfounded notices and the submission of manifestly unfounded complaints.

2. By 17 February 2023 and at least once every six months thereafter, providers shall publish for each online platform or online search engine, in a publicly available section of their online interface, information on the average monthly active recipients of the service in the Union, calculated as an average over the period of the past six months and in accordance with the methodology laid down in the delegated acts referred to in Article 33(3), where those delegated acts have been adopted.

3. Providers of online platforms or of online search engines shall communicate to the Digital Services Coordinator of establishment and the Commission, upon their request and without undue delay, the information referred to in paragraph 2, updated to the moment of such request. That Digital Services Coordinator or the Commission may require the provider of the online platform or of the online search engine to provide additional information as regards the calculation referred to in that paragraph, including explanations and substantiation in respect of the data used. That information shall not include personal data.

4. When the Digital Services Coordinator of establishment has reasons to consider, based the information received pursuant to paragraphs 2 and 3 of this Article, that a provider of online platforms or of online search engines meets the threshold of average monthly active recipients of the service in the Union laid down in Article 33(1), it shall inform the Commission thereof.

5. Providers of online platforms shall, without undue delay, submit to the Commission the decisions and the statements of reasons referred to in Article 17(1) for the inclusion in a publicly accessible machine-readable database managed by the Commission. Providers of online platforms shall ensure that the information submitted does not contain personal data.

6. The Commission may adopt implementing acts to lay down templates concerning the form, content and other details of reports pursuant to paragraph 1 of this Article. Those implementing acts shall be adopted in accordance with the advisory procedure referred to in Article 88.

Article 25
Online interface design and organisation

1. Providers of online platforms shall not design, organise or operate their online interfaces in a way that deceives or manipulates the recipients of their service or in a way that otherwise materially distorts or impairs the ability of the recipients of their service to make free and informed decisions.

2. The prohibition in paragraph 1 shall not apply to practices covered by Directive 2005/29/EC or Regulation (EU) 2016/679.

3. The Commission may issue guidelines on how paragraph 1 applies to specific practices, notably:

(a) giving more prominence to certain choices when asking the recipient of the service for a decision;
(b) repeatedly requesting that the recipient of the service make a choice where that choice has already been made, especially by presenting pop-ups that interfere with the user experience;
(c) making the procedure for terminating a service more difficult than subscribing to it.

Article 26
Advertising on online platforms

1. Providers of online platforms that present advertisements on their online interfaces shall ensure that, for each specific advertisement presented to each individual recipient, the recipients of the service are able to identify, in a clear, concise and unambiguous manner and in real time, the following:

(a) that the information is an advertisement, including through prominent markings, which might follow standards pursuant to Article 44;
(b) the natural or legal person on whose behalf the advertisement is presented;
(c) the natural or legal person who paid for the advertisement if that person is different from the natural or legal person referred to in point (b);
(d) meaningful information directly and easily accessible from the advertisement about the main parameters used to determine the recipient to whom the advertisement is presented and, where applicable, about how to change those parameters.

2. Providers of online platforms shall provide recipients of the service with a functionality to declare whether the content they provide is or contains commercial communications.

When the recipient of the service submits a declaration pursuant to this paragraph, the provider of online platforms shall ensure that other recipients of the service can identify in a clear and unambiguous manner and in real time, including through prominent markings, which might follow standards pursuant to Article 44, that the content provided by the recipient of the service is or contains commercial communications, as described in that declaration.

3. Providers of online platforms shall not present advertisements to recipients of the service based on profiling as defined in Article 4, point (4), of Regulation (EU) 2016/679 using special categories of personal data referred to in Article 9(1) of Regulation (EU) 2016/679.

Article 27
Recommender system transparency

1. Providers of online platforms that use recommender systems shall set out in their terms and conditions, in plain and intelligible language, the main parameters used in their recommender systems, as well as any options for the recipients of the service to modify or influence those main parameters.

2. The main parameters referred to in paragraph 1 shall explain why certain information is suggested to the recipient of the service. They shall include, at least:

(a) the criteria which are most significant in determining the information suggested to the recipient of the service;
(b) the reasons for the relative importance of those parameters.

3. Where several options are available pursuant to paragraph 1 for recommender systems that determine the relative order of information presented to recipients of the service, providers of online platforms shall also make available a functionality that allows the recipient of the service to select and to modify at any time their preferred option. That functionality shall be directly and easily accessible from the specific section of the online platform's online interface where the information is being prioritised.

Article 28
Online protection of minors

1. Providers of online platforms accessible to minors shall put in place appropriate and proportionate measures to ensure a high level of privacy, safety, and security of minors, on their service.

2. Providers of online platform shall not present advertisements on their interface based on profiling as defined in Article 4, point (4), of Regulation (EU) 2016/679 using personal data of the recipient of the service when they are aware with reasonable certainty that the recipient of the service is a minor.

3. Compliance with the obligations set out in this Article shall not oblige providers of online platforms to process additional personal data in order to assess whether the recipient of the service is a minor.

4. The Commission, after consulting the Board, may issue guidelines to assist providers of online platforms in the application of paragraph 1.

SECTION 4
Additional provisions applicable to providers of online platforms allowing consumers to conclude distance contracts with traders

Article 29
Exclusion for micro and small enterprises

1. This Section shall not apply to providers of online platforms allowing consumers to conclude distance contracts with traders that qualify as micro or small enterprises as defined in Recommendation 2003/361/EC.

This Section shall not apply to providers of online platforms allowing consumers to conclude distance contracts with traders that previously qualified for the status of a micro or small enterprise as defined in Recommendation 2003/361/EC during the 12 months following their loss of that status pursuant to Article 4(2) thereof, except when they are very large online platforms in accordance with Article 33.

2. By derogation from paragraph 1 of this Article, this Section shall apply to providers of online platforms allowing consumers to conclude distance contracts with traders that have been designated as very large online platforms in accordance with Article 33, irrespective of whether they qualify as micro or small enterprises.

Article 30
Traceability of traders

1. Providers of online platforms allowing consumers to conclude distance contracts with traders shall ensure that traders can only use those online platforms to promote messages on or to offer products or services to consumers located in the Union if, prior to the use of their services for those purposes, they have obtained the following information, where applicable to the trader:

(a) the name, address, telephone number and email address of the trader;
(b) a copy of the identification document of the trader or any other electronic identification as defined by Article 3 of Regulation (EU) No 910/2014 of the European Parliament and of the Council[40];
(c) the payment account details of the trader;
(d) where the trader is registered in a trade register or similar public register, the trade register in which the trader is registered and its registration number or equivalent means of identification in that register;
(e) a self-certification by the trader committing to only offer products or services that comply with the applicable rules of Union law.

2. Upon receiving the information referred to in paragraph 1 and prior to allowing the trader concerned to use its services, the provider of the online platform allowing consumers to conclude distance contracts with traders shall, through the use of any freely accessible official online database or online interface made available by a Member State or the Union or through requests to the trader to provide supporting documents from reliable sources, make best efforts to assess whether the information referred to in paragraph 1, points (a) to (e), is reliable and complete. For the purpose of this Regulation, traders shall be liable for the accuracy of the information provided.

As regards traders that are already using the services of providers of online platforms allowing consumers to conclude distance contracts with traders for the purposes referred to in paragraph 1 on 17 February 2024, the providers shall make best efforts to obtain the information listed from the traders concerned within 12 months. Where the traders concerned fail to provide the information within that period, the providers shall suspend the provision of their services to those traders until they have provided all information.

3. Where the provider of the online platform allowing consumers to conclude distance contracts with traders obtains sufficient indications or has reason to believe that any item of information referred to in paragraph 1 obtained from the trader concerned is

[40] Regulation (EU) No 910/2014 of the European Parliament and of the Council of 23 July 2014 on electronic identification and trust services for electronic transactions in the internal market and repealing Directive 1999/93/EC (OJ L 257, 28.8.2014, p. 73).

inaccurate, incomplete or not up-to-date, that provider shall request that the trader remedy that situation without delay or within the period set by Union and national law.

Where the trader fails to correct or complete that information, the provider of the online platform allowing consumers to conclude distance contracts with traders shall swiftly suspend the provision of its service to that trader in relation to the offering of products or services to consumers located in the Union until the request has been fully complied with.

4. Without prejudice to Article 4 of Regulation (EU) 2019/1150, if a provider of an online platform allowing consumers to conclude distance contracts with traders refuses to allow a trader to use its service pursuant to paragraph 1, or suspends the provision of its service pursuant to paragraph 3 of this Article, the trader concerned shall have the right to lodge a complaint as provided for in Articles 20 and 21 of this Regulation.

5. Providers of online platforms allowing consumers to conclude distance contracts with traders shall store the information obtained pursuant to paragraphs 1 and 2 in a secure manner for a period of six months after the end of the contractual relationship with the trader concerned. They shall subsequently delete the information.

6. Without prejudice to paragraph 2 of this Article, the provider of the online platform allowing consumers to conclude distance contracts with traders shall only disclose the information to third parties where so required in accordance with the applicable law, including the orders referred to in Article 10 and any orders issued by Member States' competent authorities or the Commission for the performance of their tasks under this Regulation.

7. The provider of the online platform allowing consumers to conclude distance contracts with traders shall make the information referred to in paragraph 1, points (a), (d) and (e) available on its online platform to the recipients of the service in a clear, easily accessible and comprehensible manner. That information shall be available at least on the online platform's online interface where the information on the product or service is presented.

Article 31
Compliance by design

1. Providers of online platforms allowing consumers to conclude distance contracts with traders shall ensure that its online interface is designed and organised in a way that enables traders to comply with their obligations regarding pre-contractual information, compliance and product safety information under applicable Union law.

In particular, the provider concerned shall ensure that its online interface enables traders to provide information on the name, address, telephone number and email address of the economic operator, as defined in Article 3, point (13), of Regulation (EU) 2019/1020 and other Union law.

2. Providers of online platforms allowing consumers to conclude distance contracts with traders shall ensure that its online interface is designed and organised in a way that it allows traders to provide at least the following:

(a) the information necessary for the clear and unambiguous identification of the products or the services promoted or offered to consumers located in the Union through the services of the providers;
(b) any sign identifying the trader such as the trademark, symbol or logo; and,

(c) where applicable, the information concerning the labelling and marking in compliance with rules of applicable Union law on product safety and product compliance.

3. Providers of online platforms allowing consumers to conclude distance contracts with traders shall make best efforts to assess whether such traders have provided the information referred to in paragraphs 1 and 2 prior to allowing them to offer their products or services on those platforms. After allowing the trader to offer products or services on its online platform that allows consumers to conclude distance contracts with traders, the provider shall make reasonable efforts to randomly check in any official, freely accessible and machine-readable online database or online interface whether the products or services offered have been identified as illegal.

Article 32
Right to information

1. Where a provider of an online platform allowing consumers to conclude distance contracts with traders becomes aware, irrespective of the means used, that an illegal product or service has been offered by a trader to consumers located in the Union through its services, that provider shall inform, insofar as it has their contact details, consumers who purchased the illegal product or service through its services of the following:

(a) the fact that the product or service is illegal;
(b) the identity of the trader; and
(c) any relevant means of redress.

The obligation laid down in the first subparagraph shall be limited to purchases of illegal products or services made within the six months preceding the moment that the provider became aware of the illegality.

2. Where, in the situation referred to in paragraph 1, the provider of the online platform allowing consumers to conclude distance contracts with traders does not have the contact details of all consumers concerned, that provider shall make publicly available and easily accessible on its online interface the information concerning the illegal product or service, the identity of the trader and any relevant means of redress.

SECTION 5
Additional obligations for providers of very large online platforms and of very large online search engines to manage systemic risks

Article 33
Very large online platforms and very large online search engines

1. This Section shall apply to online platforms and online search engines which have a number of average monthly active recipients of the service in the Union equal to or higher than 45 million, and which are designated as very large online platforms or very large online search engines pursuant to paragraph 4.

2. The Commission shall adopt delegated acts in accordance with Article 87 to adjust the number of average monthly active recipients of the service in the Union referred to in paragraph 1, where the Union's population increases or decreases at least by 5 % in relation to its population in 2020 or its population after adjustment by means of a dele-

gated act in the year in which the latest delegated act was adopted. In such a case, it shall adjust the number so that it corresponds to 10 % of the Union's population in the year in which it adopts the delegated act, rounded up or down to allow the number to be expressed in millions.

3. The Commission may adopt delegated acts in accordance with Article 87, after consulting the Board, to supplement the provisions of this Regulation by laying down the methodology for calculating the number of average monthly active recipients of the service in the Union, for the purposes of paragraph 1 of this Article and Article 24(2), ensuring that the methodology takes account of market and technological developments.

4. The Commission shall, after having consulted the Member State of establishment or after taking into account the information provided by the Digital Services Coordinator of establishment pursuant to Article 24(4), adopt a decision designating as a very large online platform or a very large online search engine for the purposes of this Regulation the online platform or the online search engine which has a number of average monthly active recipients of the service equal to or higher than the number referred to in paragraph 1 of this Article. The Commission shall take its decision on the basis of data reported by the provider of the online platform or of the online search engine pursuant to Article 24(2), or information requested pursuant to Article 24(3) or any other information available to the Commission.

The failure by the provider of the online platform or of the online search engine to comply with Article 24(2) or to comply with the request by the Digital Services Coordinator of establishment or by the Commission pursuant to Article 24(3) shall not prevent the Commission from designating that provider as a provider of a very large online platform or of a very large online search engine pursuant to this paragraph.

Where the Commission bases its decision on other information available to the Commission pursuant to the first subparagraph of this paragraph or on the basis of additional information requested pursuant to Article 24(3), the Commission shall give the provider of the online platform or of the online search engine concerned 10 working days in which to submit its views on the Commission's preliminary findings and on its intention to designate the online platform or the online search engine as a very large online platform or as a very large online search engine, respectively. The Commission shall take due account of the views submitted by the provider concerned.

The failure of the provider of the online platform or of the online search engine concerned to submit its views pursuant to the third subparagraph shall not prevent the Commission from designating that online platform or that online search engine as a very large online platform or as a very large online search engine, respectively, based on other information available to it.

5. The Commission shall terminate the designation if, during an uninterrupted period of one year, the online platform or the online search engine does not have a number of average monthly active recipients of the service equal to or higher than the number referred to in paragraph 1.

6. The Commission shall notify its decisions pursuant to paragraphs 4 and 5, without undue delay, to the provider of the online platform or of the online search engine concerned, to the Board and to the Digital Services Coordinator of establishment.

The Commission shall ensure that the list of designated very large online platforms and very large online search engines is published in the Official Journal of the European Union, and shall keep that list up to date. The obligations set out in this Section shall apply, or cease to apply, to the very large online platforms and very large online search engines concerned from four months after the notification to the provider concerned referred to in the first subparagraph.

Article 34
Risk assessment

1. Providers of very large online platforms and of very large online search engines shall diligently identify, analyse and assess any systemic risks in the Union stemming from the design or functioning of their service and its related systems, including algorithmic systems, or from the use made of their services.

They shall carry out the risk assessments by the date of application referred to in Article 33(6), second subparagraph, and at least once every year thereafter, and in any event prior to deploying functionalities that are likely to have a critical impact on the risks identified pursuant to this Article. This risk assessment shall be specific to their services and proportionate to the systemic risks, taking into consideration their severity and probability, and shall include the following systemic risks:

(a) the dissemination of illegal content through their services;
(b) any actual or foreseeable negative effects for the exercise of fundamental rights, in particular the fundamental rights to human dignity enshrined in Article 1 of the Charter, to respect for private and family life enshrined in Article 7 of the Charter, to the protection of personal data enshrined in Article 8 of the Charter, to freedom of expression and information, including the freedom and pluralism of the media, enshrined in Article 11 of the Charter, to non-discrimination enshrined in Article 21 of the Charter, to respect for the rights of the child enshrined in Article 24 of the Charter and to a high-level of consumer protection enshrined in Article 38 of the Charter;
(c) any actual or foreseeable negative effects on civic discourse and electoral processes, and public security;
(d) any actual or foreseeable negative effects in relation to gender-based violence, the protection of public health and minors and serious negative consequences to the person's physical and mental well-being.

2. When conducting risk assessments, providers of very large online platforms and of very large online search engines shall take into account, in particular, whether and how the following factors influence any of the systemic risks referred to in paragraph 1:

(a) the design of their recommender systems and any other relevant algorithmic system;
(b) their content moderation systems;
(c) the applicable terms and conditions and their enforcement;
(d) systems for selecting and presenting advertisements;
(e) data related practices of the provider.

The assessments shall also analyse whether and how the risks pursuant to paragraph 1 are influenced by intentional manipulation of their service, including by inauthentic use or automated exploitation of the service, as well as the amplification and potentially rapid and wide dissemination of illegal content and of information that is incompatible with their terms and conditions.

The assessment shall take into account specific regional or linguistic aspects, including when specific to a Member State.

3. Providers of very large online platforms and of very large online search engines shall preserve the supporting documents of the risk assessments for at least three years after the performance of risk assessments, and shall, upon request, communicate them to the Commission and to the Digital Services Coordinator of establishment.

Article 35
Mitigation of risks

1. Providers of very large online platforms and of very large online search engines shall put in place reasonable, proportionate and effective mitigation measures, tailored to the specific systemic risks identified pursuant to Article 34, with particular consideration to the impacts of such measures on fundamental rights. Such measures may include, where applicable:

(a) adapting the design, features or functioning of their services, including their online interfaces;
(b) adapting their terms and conditions and their enforcement;
(c) adapting content moderation processes, including the speed and quality of processing notices related to specific types of illegal content and, where appropriate, the expeditious removal of, or the disabling of access to, the content notified, in particular in respect of illegal hate speech or cyber violence, as well as adapting any relevant decision-making processes and dedicated resources for content moderation;
(d) testing and adapting their algorithmic systems, including their recommender systems;
(e) adapting their advertising systems and adopting targeted measures aimed at limiting or adjusting the presentation of advertisements in association with the service they provide;
(f) reinforcing the internal processes, resources, testing, documentation, or supervision of any of their activities in particular as regards detection of systemic risk;
(g) initiating or adjusting cooperation with trusted flaggers in accordance with Article 22 and the implementation of the decisions of out-of-court dispute settlement bodies pursuant to Article 21;
(h) initiating or adjusting cooperation with other providers of online platforms or of online search engines through the codes of conduct and the crisis protocols referred to in Articles 45 and 48 respectively;
(i) taking awareness-raising measures and adapting their online interface in order to give recipients of the service more information;
(j) taking targeted measures to protect the rights of the child, including age verification and parental control tools, tools aimed at helping minors signal abuse or obtain support, as appropriate;
(k) ensuring that an item of information, whether it constitutes a generated or manipulated image, audio or video that appreciably resembles existing persons, objects, places or other entities or events and falsely appears to a person to be authentic or truthful is distinguishable through prominent markings when presented on their online interfaces, and, in addition, providing an easy to use functionality which enables recipients of the service to indicate such information.

2. The Board, in cooperation with the Commission, shall publish comprehensive reports, once a year. The reports shall include the following:

(a) identification and assessment of the most prominent and recurrent systemic risks reported by providers of very large online platforms and of very large online search engines or identified through other information sources, in particular those provided in compliance with Articles 39, 40 and 42;
(b) best practices for providers of very large online platforms and of very large online search engines to mitigate the systemic risks identified.

Those reports shall present systemic risks broken down by the Member States in which they occurred and in the Union as a whole, as applicable.

3. The Commission, in cooperation with the Digital Services Coordinators, may issue guidelines on the application of paragraph 1 in relation to specific risks, in particular to present best practices and recommend possible measures, having due regard to the possible consequences of the measures on fundamental rights enshrined in the Charter of all parties involved. When preparing those guidelines the Commission shall organise public consultations.

Article 36
Crisis response mechanism

1. Where a crisis occurs, the Commission, acting upon a recommendation of the Board may adopt a decision, requiring one or more providers of very large online platforms or of very large online search engines to take one or more of the following actions:

(a) assess whether, and if so to what extent and how, the functioning and use of their services significantly contribute to a serious threat as referred to in paragraph 2, or are likely to do so;
(b) identify and apply specific, effective and proportionate measures, such as any of those provided for in Article 35(1) or Article 48(2), to prevent, eliminate or limit any such contribution to the serious threat identified pursuant to point (a) of this paragraph;
(c) report to the Commission by a certain date or at regular intervals specified in the decision, on the assessments referred to in point (a), on the precise content, implementation and qualitative and quantitative impact of the specific measures taken pursuant to point (b) and on any other issue related to those assessments or those measures, as specified in the decision.

When identifying and applying measures pursuant to point (b) of this paragraph, the service provider or providers shall take due account of the gravity of the serious threat referred to in paragraph 2, of the urgency of the measures and of the actual or potential implications for the rights and legitimate interests of all parties concerned, including the possible failure of the measures to respect the fundamental rights enshrined in the Charter.

2. For the purpose of this Article, a crisis shall be deemed to have occurred where extraordinary circumstances lead to a serious threat to public security or public health in the Union or in significant parts of it.

3. When taking the decision referred to in paragraph 1, the Commission shall ensure that all of the following requirements are met:

(a) the actions required by the decision are strictly necessary, justified and proportionate, having regard in particular to the gravity of the serious threat referred to in paragraph 2, the urgency of the measures and the actual or potential implications

for the rights and legitimate interests of all parties concerned, including the possible failure of the measures to respect the fundamental rights enshrined in the Charter;
(b) the decision specifies a reasonable period within which specific measures referred to in paragraph 1, point (b), are to be taken, having regard, in particular, to the urgency of those measures and the time needed to prepare and implement them;
(c) the actions required by the decision are limited to a period not exceeding three months.

4. After adopting the decision referred to in paragraph 1, the Commission shall, without undue delay, take the following steps:

(a) notify the decision to the provider or providers to which the decision is addressed;
(b) make the decision publicly available; and
(c) inform the Board of the decision, invite it to submit its views thereon, and keep it informed of any subsequent developments relating to the decision.

5. The choice of specific measures to be taken pursuant to paragraph 1, point (b), and to paragraph 7, second subparagraph, shall remain with the provider or providers addressed by the Commission's decision.

6. The Commission may on its own initiative or at the request of the provider, engage in a dialogue with the provider to determine whether, in light of the provider's specific circumstances, the intended or implemented measures referred to in paragraph 1, point (b), are effective and proportionate in achieving the objectives pursued. In particular, the Commission shall ensure that the measures taken by the service provider under paragraph 1, point (b), meet the requirements referred to in paragraph 3, points (a) and (c).

7. The Commission shall monitor the application of the specific measures taken pursuant to the decision referred to in paragraph 1 of this Article on the basis of the reports referred to in point (c) of that paragraph and any other relevant information, including information it may request pursuant to Article 40 or 67, taking into account the evolution of the crisis. The Commission shall report regularly to the Board on that monitoring, at least on a monthly basis.

Where the Commission considers that the intended or implemented specific measures pursuant to paragraph 1, point (b), are not effective or proportionate it may, after consulting the Board, adopt a decision requiring the provider to review the identification or application of those specific measures.

8. Where appropriate in view of the evolution of the crisis, the Commission, acting on the Board's recommendation, may amend the decision referred to in paragraph 1 or in paragraph 7, second subparagraph, by:

(a) revoking the decision and, where appropriate, requiring the very large online platform or very large online search engine to cease to apply the measures identified and implemented pursuant to paragraph 1, point (b), or paragraph 7, second subparagraph, in particular where the grounds for such measures do not exist anymore;
(b) extending the period referred to paragraph 3, point (c), by a period of no more than three months;
(c) taking account of experience gained in applying the measures, in particular the possible failure of the measures to respect the fundamental rights enshrined in the Charter.

9. The requirements of paragraphs 1 to 6 shall apply to the decision and to the amendment thereof referred to in this Article.

10. The Commission shall take utmost account of the recommendation of the Board issued pursuant to this Article.

11. The Commission shall report to the European Parliament and to the Council on a yearly basis following the adoption of decisions in accordance with this Article, and, in any event, three months after the end of the crisis, on the application of the specific measures taken pursuant to those decisions.

Article 37
Independent audit

1. Providers of very large online platforms and of very large online search engines shall be subject, at their own expense and at least once a year, to independent audits to assess compliance with the following:

(a) the obligations set out in Chapter III;
(b) any commitments undertaken pursuant to the codes of conduct referred to in Articles 45 and 46 and the crisis protocols referred to in Article 48.

2. Providers of very large online platforms and of very large online search engines shall afford the organisations carrying out the audits pursuant to this Article the cooperation and assistance necessary to enable them to conduct those audits in an effective, efficient and timely manner, including by giving them access to all relevant data and premises and by answering oral or written questions. They shall refrain from hampering, unduly influencing or undermining the performance of the audit.

Such audits shall ensure an adequate level of confidentiality and professional secrecy in respect of the information obtained from the providers of very large online platforms and of very large online search engines and third parties in the context of the audits, including after the termination of the audits. However, complying with that requirement shall not adversely affect the performance of the audits and other provisions of this Regulation, in particular those on transparency, supervision and enforcement. Where necessary for the purpose of the transparency reporting pursuant to Article 42(4), the audit report and the audit implementation report referred to in paragraphs 4 and 6 of this Article shall be accompanied with versions that do not contain any information that could reasonably be considered to be confidential.

3. Audits performed pursuant to paragraph 1 shall be performed by organisations which:

(a) are independent from, and do not have any conflicts of interest with, the provider of very large online platforms or of very large online search engines concerned and any legal person connected to that provider; in particular:
    (i) have not provided non-audit services related to the matters audited to the provider of very large online platform or of very large online search engine concerned and to any legal person connected to that provider in the 12 months' period before the beginning of the audit and have committed to not providing them with such services in the 12 months' period after the completion of the audit;
    (ii) have not provided auditing services pursuant to this Article to the provider of very large online platform or of very large online search engine concerned and

any legal person connected to that provider during a period longer than 10 consecutive years;
(iii) are not performing the audit in return for fees which are contingent on the result of the audit;

(b) have proven expertise in the area of risk management, technical competence and capabilities;
(c) have proven objectivity and professional ethics, based in particular on adherence to codes of practice or appropriate standards.

4. Providers of very large online platforms and of very large online search engines shall ensure that the organisations that perform the audits establish an audit report for each audit. That report shall be substantiated, in writing, and shall include at least the following:

(a) the name, address and the point of contact of the provider of the very large online platform or of the very large online search engine subject to the audit and the period covered;
(b) the name and address of the organisation or organisations performing the audit;
(c) a declaration of interests;
(d) a description of the specific elements audited, and the methodology applied;
(e) a description and a summary of the main findings drawn from the audit;
(f) a list of the third parties consulted as part of the audit;
(g) an audit opinion on whether the provider of the very large online platform or of the very large online search engine subject to the audit complied with the obligations and with the commitments referred to in paragraph 1, namely 'positive', 'positive with comments' or 'negative';
(h) where the audit opinion is not 'positive', operational recommendations on specific measures to achieve compliance and the recommended timeframe to achieve compliance.

5. Where the organisation performing the audit was unable to audit certain specific elements or to express an audit opinion based on its investigations, the audit report shall include an explanation of the circumstances and the reasons why those elements could not be audited.

6. Providers of very large online platforms or of very large online search engines receiving an audit report that is not 'positive' shall take due account of the operational recommendations addressed to them with a view to take the necessary measures to implement them. They shall, within one month from receiving those recommendations, adopt an audit implementation report setting out those measures. Where they do not implement the operational recommendations, they shall justify in the audit implementation report the reasons for not doing so and set out any alternative measures that they have taken to address any instances of non-compliance identified.

7. The Commission is empowered to adopt delegated acts in accordance with Article 87 to supplement this Regulation by laying down the necessary rules for the performance of the audits pursuant to this Article, in particular as regards the necessary rules on the procedural steps, auditing methodologies and reporting templates for the audits performed pursuant to this Article. Those delegated acts shall take into account any voluntary auditing standards referred to in Article 44(1), point (e).

Article 38
Recommender systems

In addition to the requirements set out in Article 27, providers of very large online platforms and of very large online search engines that use recommender systems shall provide at least one option for each of their recommender systems which is not based on profiling as defined in Article 4, point (4), of Regulation (EU) 2016/679.

Article 39
Additional online advertising transparency

1. Providers of very large online platforms or of very large online search engines that present advertisements on their online interfaces shall compile and make publicly available in a specific section of their online interface, through a searchable and reliable tool that allows multicriteria queries and through application programming interfaces, a repository containing the information referred to in paragraph 2, for the entire period during which they present an advertisement and until one year after the advertisement was presented for the last time on their online interfaces. They shall ensure that the repository does not contain any personal data of the recipients of the service to whom the advertisement was or could have been presented, and shall make reasonable efforts to ensure that the information is accurate and complete.

2. The repository shall include at least all of the following information:

(a) the content of the advertisement, including the name of the product, service or brand and the subject matter of the advertisement;
(b) the natural or legal person on whose behalf the advertisement is presented;
(c) the natural or legal person who paid for the advertisement, if that person is different from the person referred to in point (b);
(d) the period during which the advertisement was presented;
(e) whether the advertisement was intended to be presented specifically to one or more particular groups of recipients of the service and if so, the main parameters used for that purpose including where applicable the main parameters used to exclude one or more of such particular groups;
(f) the commercial communications published on the very large online platforms and identified pursuant to Article 26(2);
(g) the total number of recipients of the service reached and, where applicable, aggregate numbers broken down by Member State for the group or groups of recipients that the advertisement specifically targeted.

3. As regards paragraph 2, points (a), (b) and (c), where a provider of very large online platform or of very large online search engine has removed or disabled access to a specific advertisement based on alleged illegality or incompatibility with its terms and conditions, the repository shall not include the information referred to in those points. In such case, the repository shall include, for the specific advertisement concerned, the information referred to in Article 17(3), points (a) to (e), or Article 9(2), point (a)(i), as applicable.

The Commission may, after consultation of the Board, the relevant vetted researchers referred to in Article 40 and the public, issue guidelines on the structure, organisation and functionalities of the repositories referred to in this Article.

Article 40
Data access and scrutiny

1. Providers of very large online platforms or of very large online search engines shall provide the Digital Services Coordinator of establishment or the Commission, at their reasoned request and within a reasonable period specified in that request, access to data that are necessary to monitor and assess compliance with this Regulation.

2. Digital Services Coordinators and the Commission shall use the data accessed pursuant to paragraph 1 only for the purpose of monitoring and assessing compliance with this Regulation and shall take due account of the rights and interests of the providers of very large online platforms or of very large online search engines and the recipients of the service concerned, including the protection of personal data, the protection of confidential information, in particular trade secrets, and maintaining the security of their service.

3. For the purposes of paragraph 1, providers of very large online platforms or of very large online search engines shall, at the request of either the Digital Service Coordinator of establishment or of the Commission, explain the design, the logic, the functioning and the testing of their algorithmic systems, including their recommender systems.

4. Upon a reasoned request from the Digital Services Coordinator of establishment, providers of very large online platforms or of very large online search engines shall, within a reasonable period, as specified in the request, provide access to data to vetted researchers who meet the requirements in paragraph 8 of this Article, for the sole purpose of conducting research that contributes to the detection, identification and understanding of systemic risks in the Union, as set out pursuant to Article 34(1), and to the assessment of the adequacy, efficiency and impacts of the risk mitigation measures pursuant to Article 35.

5. Within 15 days following receipt of a request as referred to in paragraph 4, providers of very large online platforms or of very large online search engines may request the Digital Services Coordinator of establishment, to amend the request, where they consider that they are unable to give access to the data requested because one of following two reasons:

(a) they do not have access to the data;
(b) giving access to the data will lead to significant vulnerabilities in the security of their service or the protection of confidential information, in particular trade secrets.

6. Requests for amendment pursuant to paragraph 5 shall contain proposals for one or more alternative means through which access may be provided to the requested data or other data which are appropriate and sufficient for the purpose of the request.

The Digital Services Coordinator of establishment shall decide on the request for amendment within 15 days and communicate to the provider of the very large online platform or of the very large online search engine its decision and, where relevant, the amended request and the new period to comply with the request.

7. Providers of very large online platforms or of very large online search engines shall facilitate and provide access to data pursuant to paragraphs 1 and 4 through appropriate interfaces specified in the request, including online databases or application programming interfaces.

8. Upon a duly substantiated application from researchers, the Digital Services Coordinator of establishment shall grant such researchers the status of 'vetted researchers' for

the specific research referred to in the application and issue a reasoned request for data access to a provider of very large online platform or of very large online search engine a pursuant to paragraph 4, where the researchers demonstrate that they meet all of the following conditions:

(a) they are affiliated to a research organisation as defined in Article 2, point (1), of Directive (EU) 2019/790;
(b) they are independent from commercial interests;
(c) their application discloses the funding of the research;
(d) they are capable of fulfilling the specific data security and confidentiality requirements corresponding to each request and to protect personal data, and they describe in their request the appropriate technical and organisational measures that they have put in place to this end;
(e) their application demonstrates that their access to the data and the time frames requested are necessary for, and proportionate to, the purposes of their research, and that the expected results of that research will contribute to the purposes laid down in paragraph 4;
(f) the planned research activities will be carried out for the purposes laid down in paragraph 4;
(g) they have committed themselves to making their research results publicly available free of charge, within a reasonable period after the completion of the research, subject to the rights and interests of the recipients of the service concerned, in accordance with Regulation (EU) 2016/679.

Upon receipt of the application pursuant to this paragraph, the Digital Services Coordinator of establishment shall inform the Commission and the Board.

9. Researchers may also submit their application to the Digital Services Coordinator of the Member State of the research organisation to which they are affiliated. Upon receipt of the application pursuant to this paragraph the Digital Services Coordinator shall conduct an initial assessment as to whether the respective researchers meet all of the conditions set out in paragraph 8. The respective Digital Services Coordinator shall subsequently send the application, together with the supporting documents submitted by the respective researchers and the initial assessment, to the Digital Services Coordinator of establishment. The Digital Services Coordinator of establishment shall take a decision whether to award a researcher the status of 'vetted researcher' without undue delay.

While taking due account of the initial assessment provided, the final decision to award a researcher the status of 'vetted researcher' lies within the competence of Digital Services Coordinator of establishment, pursuant to paragraph 8.

10. The Digital Services Coordinator that awarded the status of vetted researcher and issued the reasoned request for data access to the providers of very large online platforms or of very large online search engines in favour of a vetted researcher shall issue a decision terminating the access if it determines, following an investigation either on its own initiative or on the basis of information received from third parties, that the vetted researcher no longer meets the conditions set out in paragraph 8, and shall inform the provider of the very large online platform or of the very large online search engine concerned of the decision. Before terminating the access, the Digital Services Coordinator shall allow the vetted researcher to react to the findings of its investigation and to its intention to terminate the access.

11. Digital Services Coordinators of establishment shall communicate to the Board the names and contact information of the natural persons or entities to which they have

awarded the status of 'vetted researcher' in accordance with paragraph 8, as well as the purpose of the research in respect of which the application was made or, where they have terminated the access to the data in accordance with paragraph 10, communicate that information to the Board.

12. Providers of very large online platforms or of very large online search engines shall give access without undue delay to data, including, where technically possible, to real-time data, provided that the data is publicly accessible in their online interface by researchers, including those affiliated to not for profit bodies, organisations and associations, who comply with the conditions set out in paragraph 8, points (b), (c), (d) and (e), and who use the data solely for performing research that contributes to the detection, identification and understanding of systemic risks in the Union pursuant to Article 34(1).

13. The Commission shall, after consulting the Board, adopt delegated acts supplementing this Regulation by laying down the technical conditions under which providers of very large online platforms or of very large online search engines are to share data pursuant to paragraphs 1 and 4 and the purposes for which the data may be used. Those delegated acts shall lay down the specific conditions under which such sharing of data with researchers can take place in compliance with Regulation (EU) 2016/679, as well as relevant objective indicators, procedures and, where necessary, independent advisory mechanisms in support of sharing of data, taking into account the rights and interests of the providers of very large online platforms or of very large online search engines and the recipients of the service concerned, including the protection of confidential information, in particular trade secrets, and maintaining the security of their service.

Article 41
Compliance function

1. Providers of very large online platforms or of very large online search engines shall establish a compliance function, which is independent from their operational functions and composed of one or more compliance officers, including the head of the compliance function. That compliance function shall have sufficient authority, stature and resources, as well as access to the management body of the provider of the very large online platform or of the very large online search engine to monitor the compliance of that provider with this Regulation.

2. The management body of the provider of the very large online platform or of the very large online search engine shall ensure that compliance officers have the professional qualifications, knowledge, experience and ability necessary to fulfil the tasks referred to in paragraph 3.

The management body of the provider of the very large online platform or of the very large online search engine shall ensure that the head of the compliance function is an independent senior manager with distinct responsibility for the compliance function.

The head of the compliance function shall report directly to the management body of the provider of the very large online platform or of the very large online search engine, and may raise concerns and warn that body where risks referred to in Article 34 or non-compliance with this Regulation affect or may affect the provider of the very large online platform or of the very large online search engine concerned, without prejudice to the responsibilities of the management body in its supervisory and managerial functions.

The head of the compliance function shall not be removed without prior approval of the management body of the provider of the very large online platform or of the very large online search engine.

3. Compliance officers shall have the following tasks:

(a) cooperating with the Digital Services Coordinator of establishment and the Commission for the purpose of this Regulation;
(b) ensuring that all risks referred to in Article 34 are identified and properly reported on and that reasonable, proportionate and effective risk-mitigation measures are taken pursuant to Article 35;
(c) organising and supervising the activities of the provider of the very large online platform or of the very large online search engine relating to the independent audit pursuant to Article 37;
(d) informing and advising the management and employees of the provider of the very large online platform or of the very large online search engine about relevant obligations under this Regulation;
(e) monitoring the compliance of the provider of the very large online platform or of the very large online search engine with its obligations under this Regulation;
(f) where applicable, monitoring the compliance of the provider of the very large online platform or of the very large online search engine with commitments made under the codes of conduct pursuant to Articles 45 and 46 or the crisis protocols pursuant to Article 48.

4. Providers of very large online platforms or of very large online search engines shall communicate the name and contact details of the head of the compliance function to the Digital Services Coordinator of establishment and to the Commission.

5. The management body of the provider of the very large online platform or of the very large online search engine shall define, oversee and be accountable for the implementation of the provider's governance arrangements that ensure the independence of the compliance function, including the division of responsibilities within the organisation of the provider of very large online platform or of very large online search engine, the prevention of conflicts of interest, and sound management of systemic risks identified pursuant to Article 34.

6. The management body shall approve and review periodically, at least once a year, the strategies and policies for taking up, managing, monitoring and mitigating the risks identified pursuant to Article 34 to which the very large online platform or the very large online search engine is or might be exposed to.

7. The management body shall devote sufficient time to the consideration of the measures related to risk management. It shall be actively involved in the decisions related to risk management, and shall ensure that adequate resources are allocated to the management of the risks identified in accordance with Article 34.

Article 42
Transparency reporting obligations

1. Providers of very large online platforms or of very large online search engines shall publish the reports referred to in Article 15 at the latest by two months from the date of application referred to in Article 33(6), second subparagraph, and thereafter at least every six months.

2. The reports referred to in paragraph 1 of this Article published by providers of very large online platforms shall, in addition to the information referred to in Article 15 and Article 24(1), specify:

(a) the human resources that the provider of very large online platforms dedicates to content moderation in respect of the service offered in the Union, broken down by each applicable official language of the Member States, including for compliance with the obligations set out in Articles 16 and 22, as well as for compliance with the obligations set out in Article 20;
(b) the qualifications and linguistic expertise of the persons carrying out the activities referred to in point (a), as well as the training and support given to such staff;
(c) the indicators of accuracy and related information referred to in Article 15(1), point (e), broken down by each official language of the Member States.

The reports shall be published in at least one of the official languages of the Member States.

3. In addition to the information referred to in Articles 24(2), the providers of very large online platforms or of very large online search engines shall include in the reports referred to in paragraph 1 of this Article the information on the average monthly recipients of the service for each Member State.

4. Providers of very large online platforms or of very large online search engines shall transmit to the Digital Services Coordinator of establishment and the Commission, without undue delay upon completion, and make publicly available at the latest three months after the receipt of each audit report pursuant to Article 37(4):

(a) a report setting out the results of the risk assessment pursuant to Article 34;
(b) the specific mitigation measures put in place pursuant to Article 35(1);
(c) the audit report provided for in Article 37(4);
(d) the audit implementation report provided for in Article 37(6);
(e) where applicable, information about the consultations conducted by the provider in support of the risk assessments and design of the risk mitigation measures.

5. Where a provider of very large online platform or of very large online search engine considers that the publication of information pursuant to paragraph 4 might result in the disclosure of confidential information of that provider or of the recipients of the service, cause significant vulnerabilities for the security of its service, undermine public security or harm recipients, the provider may remove such information from the publicly available reports. In that case, the provider shall transmit the complete reports to the Digital Services Coordinator of establishment and the Commission, accompanied by a statement of the reasons for removing the information from the publicly available reports.

Article 43
Supervisory fee

1. The Commission shall charge providers of very large online platforms and of very large online search engines an annual supervisory fee upon their designation pursuant to Article 33.

2. The overall amount of the annual supervisory fees shall cover the estimated costs that the Commission incurs in relation to its supervisory tasks under this Regulation, in particular costs related to the designation pursuant to Article 33, to the set-up, mainte-

nance and operation of the database pursuant to Article 24(5) and to the information sharing system pursuant to Article 85, to referrals pursuant to Article 59, to supporting the Board pursuant to Article 62 and to the supervisory tasks pursuant to Article 56 and Section 4 of Chapter IV.

3. The providers of very large online platforms and of very large online search engines shall be charged annually a supervisory fee for each service for which they have been designated pursuant to Article 33.

The Commission shall adopt implementing acts establishing the amount of the annual supervisory fee in respect of each provider of very large online platform or of very large online search engine. When adopting those implementing acts, the Commission shall apply the methodology laid down in the delegated act referred to in paragraph 4 of this Article and shall respect the principles set out in paragraph 5 of this Article. Those implementing acts shall be adopted in accordance with the advisory procedure referred to in Article 88.

4. The Commission shall adopt delegated acts, in accordance with Article 87, laying down the detailed methodology and procedures for:

(a) the determination of the estimated costs referred to in paragraph 2;
(b) the determination of the individual annual supervisory fees referred to in paragraph 5, points (b) and (c);
(c) the determination of the maximum overall limit defined in paragraph 5, point (c); and
(d) the detailed arrangements necessary to make payments.

When adopting those delegated acts, the Commission shall respect the principles set out in paragraph 5 of this Article.

5. The implementing act referred to in paragraph 3 and the delegated act referred to in paragraph 4 shall respect the following principles:

(a) the estimation of the overall amount of the annual supervisory fee takes into account the costs incurred in the previous year;
(b) the annual supervisory fee is proportionate to the number of average monthly active recipients in the Union of each very large online platform or each very large online search engine designated pursuant to Article 33;
(c) the overall amount of the annual supervisory fee charged on a given provider of very large online platform or very large search engine does not, in any case, exceed 0,05 % of its worldwide annual net income in the preceding financial year.

6. The individual annual supervisory fees charged pursuant to paragraph 1 of this Article shall constitute external assigned revenue in accordance with Article 21(5) of Regulation (EU, Euratom) 2018/1046 of the European Parliament and of the Council[41].

7. The Commission shall report annually to the European Parliament and to the Council on the overall amount of the costs incurred for the fulfilment of the tasks under this Regulation and the total amount of the individual annual supervisory fees charged in the preceding year.

---

[41] Regulation (EU, Euratom) 2018/1046 of the European Parliament and of the Council of 18 July 2018 on the financial rules applicable to the general budget of the Union, amending Regulations (EU) No 1296/2013, (EU) No 1301/2013, (EU) No 1303/2013, (EU) No 1304/2013, (EU) No 1309/2013, (EU) No 1316/2013, (EU) No 223/2014, (EU) No 283/2014, and Decision No 541/2014/EU and repealing Regulation (EU, Euratom) No 966/2012 (OJ L 193, 30.7.2018, p. 1).

SECTION 6
Other provisions concerning due diligence obligations

Article 44
Standards

1. The Commission shall consult the Board, and shall support and promote the development and implementation of voluntary standards set by relevant European and international standardisation bodies, at least in respect of the following:

(a) electronic submission of notices under Article 16;
(b) templates, design and process standards for communicating with the recipients of the service in a user-friendly manner on restrictions resulting from terms and conditions and changes thereto;
(c) electronic submission of notices by trusted flaggers under Article 22, including through application programming interfaces;
(d) specific interfaces, including application programming interfaces, to facilitate compliance with the obligations set out in Articles 39 and 40;
(e) auditing of very large online platforms and of very large online search engines pursuant to Article 37;
(f) interoperability of the advertisement repositories referred to in Article 39(2);
(g) transmission of data between advertising intermediaries in support of transparency obligations pursuant to Article 26(1), points (b), (c) and (d);
(h) technical measures to enable compliance with obligations relating to advertising contained in this Regulation, including the obligations regarding prominent markings for advertisements and commercial communications referred to in Article 26;
(i) choice interfaces and presentation of information on the main parameters of different types of recommender systems, in accordance with Articles 27 and 38;
(j) standards for targeted measures to protect minors online.

2. The Commission shall support the update of the standards in the light of technological developments and the behaviour of the recipients of the services in question. The relevant information regarding the update of the standards shall be publicly available and easily accessible.

Article 45
Codes of conduct

1. The Commission and the Board shall encourage and facilitate the drawing up of voluntary codes of conduct at Union level to contribute to the proper application of this Regulation, taking into account in particular the specific challenges of tackling different types of illegal content and systemic risks, in accordance with Union law in particular on competition and the protection of personal data.

2. Where significant systemic risk within the meaning of Article 34(1) emerge and concern several very large online platforms or very large online search engines, the Commission may invite the providers of very large online platforms concerned or the providers of very large online search engines concerned, and other providers of very large online platforms, of very large online search engines, of online platforms and of other intermediary services, as appropriate, as well as relevant competent authorities, civil society organisations and other relevant stakeholders, to participate in the drawing

up of codes of conduct, including by setting out commitments to take specific risk mitigation measures, as well as a regular reporting framework on any measures taken and their outcomes.

3. When giving effect to paragraphs 1 and 2, the Commission and the Board, and where relevant other bodies, shall aim to ensure that the codes of conduct clearly set out their specific objectives, contain key performance indicators to measure the achievement of those objectives and take due account of the needs and interests of all interested parties, and in particular citizens, at Union level. The Commission and the Board shall also aim to ensure that participants report regularly to the Commission and their respective Digital Services Coordinators of establishment on any measures taken and their outcomes, as measured against the key performance indicators that they contain. Key performance indicators and reporting commitments shall take into account differences in size and capacity between different participants.

4. The Commission and the Board shall assess whether the codes of conduct meet the aims specified in paragraphs 1 and 3, and shall regularly monitor and evaluate the achievement of their objectives, having regard to the key performance indicators that they might contain. They shall publish their conclusions.

The Commission and the Board shall also encourage and facilitate regular review and adaptation of the codes of conduct.

In the case of systematic failure to comply with the codes of conduct, the Commission and the Board may invite the signatories to the codes of conduct to take the necessary action.

Article 46
Codes of conduct for online advertising

1. The Commission shall encourage and facilitate the drawing up of voluntary codes of conduct at Union level by providers of online platforms and other relevant service providers, such as providers of online advertising intermediary services, other actors involved in the programmatic advertising value chain, or organisations representing recipients of the service and civil society organisations or relevant authorities to contribute to further transparency for actors in the online advertising value chain beyond the requirements of Articles 26 and 39.

2. The Commission shall aim to ensure that the codes of conduct pursue an effective transmission of information that fully respects the rights and interests of all parties involved, as well as a competitive, transparent and fair environment in online advertising, in accordance with Union and national law, in particular on competition and the protection of privacy and personal data. The Commission shall aim to ensure that the codes of conduct at least address the following:

(a) the transmission of information held by providers of online advertising intermediaries to recipients of the service concerning the requirements set in Article 26(1), points (b), (c) and (d);
(b) the transmission of information held by providers of online advertising intermediaries to the repositories pursuant to Article 39;
(c) meaningful information on data monetisation.

3. The Commission shall encourage the development of the codes of conduct by 18 February 2025 and their application by 18 August 2025.

4. The Commission shall encourage all the actors in the online advertising value chain referred to in paragraph 1 to endorse the commitments stated in the codes of conduct, and to comply with them.

Article 47
Codes of conduct for accessibility

1. The Commission shall encourage and facilitate the drawing up of codes of conduct at Union level with the involvement of providers of online platforms and other relevant service providers, organisations representing recipients of the service and civil society organisations or relevant authorities to promote full and effective, equal participation, by improving access to online services that, through their initial design or subsequent adaptation, address the particular needs of persons with disabilities.

2. The Commission shall aim to ensure that the codes of conduct pursue the objective of ensuring that those services are accessible in compliance with Union and national law, in order to maximise their foreseeable use by persons with disabilities. The Commission shall aim to ensure that the codes of conduct address at least the following objectives:

(a) designing and adapting services to make them accessible to persons with disabilities by making them perceivable, operable, understandable and robust;
(b) explaining how the services meet the applicable accessibility requirements and making this information available to the public in an accessible manner for persons with disabilities;
(c) making information, forms and measures provided pursuant to this Regulation available in such a manner that they are easy to find, easy to understand, and accessible to persons with disabilities.

3. The Commission shall encourage the development of the codes of conduct by 18 February 2025 and their application by 18 August 2025.

Article 48
Crisis protocols

1. The Board may recommend that the Commission initiate the drawing up, in accordance with paragraphs 2, 3 and 4, of voluntary crisis protocols for addressing crisis situations. Those situations shall be strictly limited to extraordinary circumstances affecting public security or public health.

2. The Commission shall encourage and facilitate the providers of very large online platforms, of very large online search engines and, where appropriate, the providers of other online platforms or of other online search engines, to participate in the drawing up, testing and application of those crisis protocols. The Commission shall aim to ensure that those crisis protocols include one or more of the following measures:

(a) prominently displaying information on the crisis situation provided by Member States' authorities or at Union level, or, depending on the context of the crisis, by other relevant reliable bodies;
(b) ensuring that the provider of intermediary services designates a specific point of contact for crisis management; where relevant, this may be the electronic point of contact referred to in Article 11 or, in the case of providers of very large online

platforms or of very large online search engines, the compliance officer referred to in Article 41;
(c) where applicable, adapt the resources dedicated to compliance with the obligations set out in Articles 16, 20, 22, 23 and 35 to the needs arising from the crisis situation.

3. The Commission shall, as appropriate, involve Member States' authorities, and may also involve Union bodies, offices and agencies in drawing up, testing and supervising the application of the crisis protocols. The Commission may, where necessary and appropriate, also involve civil society organisations or other relevant organisations in drawing up the crisis protocols.

4. The Commission shall aim to ensure that the crisis protocols set out clearly all of the following:

(a) the specific parameters to determine what constitutes the specific extraordinary circumstance the crisis protocol seeks to address and the objectives it pursues;
(b) the role of each participant and the measures they are to put in place in preparation and once the crisis protocol has been activated;
(c) a clear procedure for determining when the crisis protocol is to be activated;
(d) a clear procedure for determining the period during which the measures to be taken once the crisis protocol has been activated are to be taken, which is strictly limited to what is necessary for addressing the specific extraordinary circumstances concerned;
(e) safeguards to address any negative effects on the exercise of the fundamental rights enshrined in the Charter, in particular the freedom of expression and information and the right to non-discrimination;
(f) a process to publicly report on any measures taken, their duration and their outcomes, upon the termination of the crisis situation.

5. If the Commission considers that a crisis protocol fails to effectively address the crisis situation, or to safeguard the exercise of fundamental rights as referred to in paragraph 4, point (e), it shall request the participants to revise the crisis protocol, including by taking additional measures.

CHAPTER IV
IMPLEMENTATION, COOPERATION, PENALTIES AND ENFORCEMENT

SECTION 1
Competent authorities and national Digital Services Coordinators

Article 49
Competent authorities and Digital Services Coordinators

1. Member States shall designate one or more competent authorities to be responsible for the supervision of providers of intermediary services and enforcement of this Regulation ('competent authorities').

2. Member States shall designate one of the competent authorities as their Digital Services Coordinator. The Digital Services Coordinator shall be responsible for all matters relating to supervision and enforcement of this Regulation in that Member State, unless the Member State concerned has assigned certain specific tasks or sectors to other com-

petent authorities. The Digital Services Coordinator shall in any event be responsible for ensuring coordination at national level in respect of those matters and for contributing to the effective and consistent supervision and enforcement of this Regulation throughout the Union.

For that purpose, Digital Services Coordinators shall cooperate with each other, other national competent authorities, the Board and the Commission, without prejudice to the possibility for Member States to provide for cooperation mechanisms and regular exchanges of views between the Digital Services Coordinator and other national authorities where relevant for the performance of their respective tasks.

Where a Member State designates one or more competent authorities in addition to the Digital Services Coordinator, it shall ensure that the respective tasks of those authorities and of the Digital Services Coordinator are clearly defined and that they cooperate closely and effectively when performing their tasks.

3. Member States shall designate the Digital Services Coordinators by 17 February 2024.

Member States shall make publicly available, and communicate to the Commission and the Board, the name of their competent authority designated as Digital Services Coordinator and information on how it can be contacted. The Member State concerned shall communicate to the Commission and the Board the name of the other competent authorities referred to in paragraph 2, as well as their respective tasks.

4. The provisions applicable to Digital Services Coordinators set out in Articles 50, 51 and 56 shall also apply to any other competent authorities that the Member States designate pursuant to paragraph 1 of this Article.

Article 50
Requirements for Digital Services Coordinators

1. Member States shall ensure that their Digital Services Coordinators perform their tasks under this Regulation in an impartial, transparent and timely manner. Member States shall ensure that their Digital Services Coordinators have all necessary resources to carry out their tasks, including sufficient technical, financial and human resources to adequately supervise all providers of intermediary services falling within their competence. Each Member State shall ensure that its Digital Services Coordinator has sufficient autonomy in managing its budget within the budget's overall limits, in order not to adversely affect the independence of the Digital Services Coordinator.

2. When carrying out their tasks and exercising their powers in accordance with this Regulation, the Digital Services Coordinators shall act with complete independence. They shall remain free from any external influence, whether direct or indirect, and shall neither seek nor take instructions from any other public authority or any private party.

3. Paragraph 2 of this Article is without prejudice to the tasks of Digital Services Coordinators within the system of supervision and enforcement provided for in this Regulation and the cooperation with other competent authorities in accordance with Article 49(2). Paragraph 2 of this Article shall not prevent the exercise of judicial review and shall also be without prejudice to proportionate accountability requirements regarding the general activities of the Digital Services Coordinators, such as financial expenditure or reporting to national parliaments, provided that those requirements do not undermine the achievement of the objectives of this Regulation.

Article 51
Powers of Digital Services Coordinators

1. Where needed in order to carry out their tasks under this Regulation, Digital Services Coordinators shall have the following powers of investigation, in respect of conduct by providers of intermediary services falling within the competence of their Member State:

(a) the power to require those providers, as well as any other persons acting for purposes related to their trade, business, craft or profession that may reasonably be aware of information relating to a suspected infringement of this Regulation, including organisations performing the audits referred to in Article 37 and Article 75(2), to provide such information without undue delay;
(b) the power to carry out, or to request a judicial authority in their Member State to order, inspections of any premises that those providers or those persons use for purposes related to their trade, business, craft or profession, or to request other public authorities to do so, in order to examine, seize, take or obtain copies of information relating to a suspected infringement in any form, irrespective of the storage medium;
(c) the power to ask any member of staff or representative of those providers or those persons to give explanations in respect of any information relating to a suspected infringement and to record the answers with their consent by any technical means.

2. Where needed for carrying out their tasks under this Regulation, Digital Services Coordinators shall have the following enforcement powers, in respect of providers of intermediary services falling within the competence of their Member State:

(a) the power to accept the commitments offered by those providers in relation to their compliance with this Regulation and to make those commitments binding;
(b) the power to order the cessation of infringements and, where appropriate, to impose remedies proportionate to the infringement and necessary to bring the infringement effectively to an end, or to request a judicial authority in their Member State to do so;
(c) the power to impose fines, or to request a judicial authority in their Member State to do so, in accordance with Article 52 for failure to comply with this Regulation, including with any of the investigative orders issued pursuant to paragraph 1 of this Article;
(d) the power to impose a periodic penalty payment, or to request a judicial authority in their Member State to do so, in accordance with Article 52 to ensure that an infringement is terminated in compliance with an order issued pursuant to point (b) of this subparagraph or for failure to comply with any of the investigative orders issued pursuant to paragraph 1 of this Article;
(e) the power to adopt interim measures or to request the competent national judicial authority in their Member State to do so, to avoid the risk of serious harm.

As regards the first subparagraph, points (c) and (d), Digital Services Coordinators shall also have the enforcement powers set out in those points in respect of the other persons referred to in paragraph 1 for failure to comply with any of the orders issued to them pursuant to that paragraph. They shall only exercise those enforcement powers after providing those other persons in good time with all relevant information relating to such orders, including the applicable period, the fines or periodic payments that may be imposed for failure to comply and the possibilities for redress.

3. Where needed for carrying out their tasks under this Regulation, Digital Services Coordinators shall, in respect of providers of intermediary services falling within the competence of their Member State, where all other powers pursuant to this Article to bring about the cessation of an infringement have been exhausted and the infringement has not been remedied or is continuing and is causing serious harm which cannot be avoided through the exercise of other powers available under Union or national law, also have the power to take the following measures:

(a) to require the management body of those providers, without undue delay, to examine the situation, adopt and submit an action plan setting out the necessary measures to terminate the infringement, ensure that the provider takes those measures, and report on the measures taken;
(b) where the Digital Services Coordinator considers that a provider of intermediary services has not sufficiently complied with the requirements referred to in point (a), that the infringement has not been remedied or is continuing and is causing serious harm, and that that infringement entails a criminal offence involving a threat to the life or safety of persons, to request that the competent judicial authority of its Member State order the temporary restriction of access of recipients to the service concerned by the infringement or, only where that is not technically feasible, to the online interface of the provider of intermediary services on which the infringement takes place.

The Digital Services Coordinator shall, except where it acts upon the Commission's request referred to in Article 82, prior to submitting the request referred to in the first subparagraph, point (b), of this paragraph invite interested parties to submit written observations within a period that shall not be less than two weeks, describing the measures that it intends to request and identifying the intended addressee or addressees thereof. The provider of intermediary services, the intended addressee or addressees and any other third party demonstrating a legitimate interest shall be entitled to participate in the proceedings before the competent judicial authority. Any measure ordered shall be proportionate to the nature, gravity, recurrence and duration of the infringement, without unduly restricting access to lawful information by recipients of the service concerned.

The restriction of access shall be for a period of four weeks, subject to the possibility for the competent judicial authority, in its order, to allow the Digital Services Coordinator to extend that period for further periods of the same lengths, subject to a maximum number of extensions set by that judicial authority. The Digital Services Coordinator shall only extend the period where, having regard to the rights and interests of all parties affected by that restriction and all relevant circumstances, including any information that the provider of intermediary services, the addressee or addressees and any other third party that demonstrated a legitimate interest may provide to it, it considers that both of the following conditions have been met:

(a) the provider of intermediary services has failed to take the necessary measures to terminate the infringement;
(b) the temporary restriction does not unduly restrict access to lawful information by recipients of the service, having regard to the number of recipients affected and whether any adequate and readily accessible alternatives exist.

Where the Digital Services Coordinator considers that the conditions set out in the third subparagraph, points (a) and (b), have been met but it cannot further extend the period pursuant to the third subparagraph, it shall submit a new request to the competent judicial authority, as referred to in the first subparagraph, point (b).

4. The powers listed in paragraphs 1, 2 and 3 shall be without prejudice to Section 3.

5. The measures taken by the Digital Services Coordinators in the exercise of their powers listed in paragraphs 1, 2 and 3 shall be effective, dissuasive and proportionate, having regard, in particular, to the nature, gravity, recurrence and duration of the infringement or suspected infringement to which those measures relate, as well as the economic, technical and operational capacity of the provider of the intermediary services concerned where relevant.

6. Member States shall lay down specific rules and procedures for the exercise of the powers pursuant to paragraphs 1, 2 and 3 and shall ensure that any exercise of those powers is subject to adequate safeguards laid down in the applicable national law in compliance with the Charter and with the general principles of Union law. In particular, those measures shall only be taken in accordance with the right to respect for private life and the rights of defence, including the rights to be heard and of access to the file, and subject to the right to an effective judicial remedy of all affected parties.

Article 52
Penalties

1. Member States shall lay down the rules on penalties applicable to infringements of this Regulation by providers of intermediary services within their competence and shall take all the necessary measures to ensure that they are implemented in accordance with Article 51.

2. Penalties shall be effective, proportionate and dissuasive. Member States shall notify the Commission of those rules and of those measures and shall notify it, without delay, of any subsequent amendments affecting them.

3. Member States shall ensure that the maximum amount of fines that may be imposed for a failure to comply with an obligation laid down in this Regulation shall be 6 % of the annual worldwide turnover of the provider of intermediary services concerned in the preceding financial year. Member States shall ensure that the maximum amount of the fine that may be imposed for the supply of incorrect, incomplete or misleading information, failure to reply or rectify incorrect, incomplete or misleading information and failure to submit to an inspection shall be 1 % of the annual income or worldwide turnover of the provider of intermediary services or person concerned in the preceding financial year.

4. Member States shall ensure that the maximum amount of a periodic penalty payment shall be 5 % of the average daily worldwide turnover or income of the provider of intermediary services concerned in the preceding financial year per day, calculated from the date specified in the decision concerned.

Article 53
Right to lodge a complaint

Recipients of the service and any body, organisation or association mandated to exercise the rights conferred by this Regulation on their behalf shall have the right to lodge a complaint against providers of intermediary services alleging an infringement of this

Regulation with the Digital Services Coordinator of the Member State where the recipient of the service is located or established. The Digital Services Coordinator shall assess the complaint and, where appropriate, transmit it to the Digital Services Coordinator of establishment, accompanied, where considered appropriate, by an opinion. Where the complaint falls under the responsibility of another competent authority in its Member State, the Digital Services Coordinator receiving the complaint shall transmit it to that authority. During these proceedings, both parties shall have the right to be heard and receive appropriate information about the status of the complaint, in accordance with national law.

Article 54
Compensation

Recipients of the service shall have the right to seek, in accordance with Union and national law, compensation from providers of intermediary services, in respect of any damage or loss suffered due to an infringement by those providers of their obligations under this Regulation.

Article 55
Activity reports

1. Digital Services Coordinators shall draw up annual reports on their activities under this Regulation, including the number of complaints received pursuant to Article 53 and an overview of their follow-up. The Digital Services Coordinators shall make the annual reports available to the public in a machine-readable format, subject to the applicable rules on the confidentiality of information pursuant to Article 84, and shall communicate them to the Commission and to the Board.

2. The annual report shall also include the following information:

(a) the number and subject matter of orders to act against illegal content and orders to provide information issued in accordance with Articles 9 and 10 by any national judicial or administrative authority of the Member State of the Digital Services Coordinator concerned;
(b) the effects given to those orders, as communicated to the Digital Services Coordinator pursuant to Articles 9 and 10.

3. Where a Member State has designated several competent authorities pursuant to Article 49, it shall ensure that the Digital Services Coordinator draws up a single report covering the activities of all competent authorities and that the Digital Services Coordinator receives all relevant information and support needed to that effect from the other competent authorities concerned.

SECTION 2
Competences, coordinated investigation and consistency mechanisms

Article 56
Competences

1. The Member State in which the main establishment of the provider of intermediary services is located shall have exclusive powers to supervise and enforce this Regulation, except for the powers provided for in paragraphs 2, 3 and 4.

2. The Commission shall have exclusive powers to supervise and enforce Section 5 of Chapter III.

3. The Commission shall have powers to supervise and enforce this Regulation, other than those laid down in Section 5 of Chapter III thereof, against providers of very large online platforms and of very large online search engines.

4. Where the Commission has not initiated proceedings for the same infringement, the Member State in which the main establishment of the provider of very large online platform or of very large online search engine is located shall have powers to supervise and enforce the obligations under this Regulation, other than those laid down in Section 5 of Chapter III, with respect to those providers.

5. Member States and the Commission shall supervise and enforce the provisions of this Regulation in close cooperation.

6. Where a provider of intermediary services does not have an establishment in the Union, the Member State where its legal representative resides or is established or the Commission shall have powers, as applicable, in accordance with paragraphs 1 and 4 of this Article, to supervise and enforce the relevant obligations under this Regulation.

7. Where a provider of intermediary services fails to appoint a legal representative in accordance with Article 13, all Member States and, in case of a provider of a very large online platform or very large online search engine, the Commission shall have powers to supervise and enforce in accordance with this Article.

Where a Digital Services Coordinator intends to exercise its powers under this paragraph, it shall notify all other Digital Services Coordinators and the Commission, and ensure that the applicable safeguards afforded by the Charter are respected, in particular to avoid that the same conduct is sanctioned more than once for the infringement of the obligations laid down in this Regulation. Where the Commission intends to exercise its powers under this paragraph, it shall notify all other Digital Services Coordinators of that intention. Following the notification pursuant to this paragraph, other Member States shall not initiate proceedings for the same infringement as that referred to in the notification.

Article 57
Mutual assistance

1. Digital Services Coordinators and the Commission shall cooperate closely and provide each other with mutual assistance in order to apply this Regulation in a consistent and efficient manner. Mutual assistance shall include, in particular, exchange of information in accordance with this Article and the duty of the Digital Services Coordinator

of establishment to inform all Digital Services Coordinators of destination, the Board and the Commission about the opening of an investigation and the intention to take a final decision, including its assessment, in respect of a specific provider of intermediary services.

2. For the purpose of an investigation, the Digital Services Coordinator of establishment may request other Digital Services Coordinators to provide specific information in their possession as regards a specific provider of intermediary services or to exercise their investigative powers referred to in Article 51(1) with regard to specific information located in their Member State. Where appropriate, the Digital Services Coordinator receiving the request may involve other competent authorities or other public authorities of the Member State in question.

3. The Digital Services Coordinator receiving the request pursuant to paragraph 2 shall comply with such request and inform the Digital Services Coordinator of establishment about the action taken, without undue delay and no later than two months after its receipt, unless:

(a) the scope or the subject matter of the request is not sufficiently specified, justified or proportionate in view of the investigative purposes; or
(b) neither the requested Digital Service Coordinator nor other competent authority or other public authority of that Member State is in possession of the requested information nor can have access to it; or
(c) the request cannot be complied with without infringing Union or national law.

The Digital Services Coordinator receiving the request shall justify its refusal by submitting a reasoned reply, within the period set out in the first subparagraph.

Article 58
Cross-border cooperation among Digital Services Coordinators

1. Unless the Commission has initiated an investigation for the same alleged infringement, where a Digital Services Coordinator of destination has reason to suspect that a provider of an intermediary service has infringed this Regulation in a manner negatively affecting the recipients of the service in the Member State of that Digital Services Coordinator, it may request the Digital Services Coordinator of establishment to assess the matter and to take the necessary investigatory and enforcement measures to ensure compliance with this Regulation.

2. Unless the Commission has initiated an investigation for the same alleged infringement, and at the request of at least three Digital Services Coordinators of destination that have reason to suspect that a specific provider of intermediary services infringed this Regulation in a manner negatively affecting recipients of the service in their Member States, the Board may request the Digital Services Coordinator of establishment to assess the matter and take the necessary investigatory and enforcement measures to ensure compliance with this Regulation.

3. A request pursuant to paragraph 1 or 2 shall be duly reasoned, and shall at least indicate:

(a) the point of contact of the provider of the intermediary services concerned as provided for in Article 11;
(b) a description of the relevant facts, the provisions of this Regulation concerned and the reasons why the Digital Services Coordinator that sent the request, or the Board,

suspects that the provider infringed this Regulation, including the description of the negative effects of the alleged infringement;

(c) any other information that the Digital Services Coordinator that sent the request, or the Board, considers relevant, including, where appropriate, information gathered on its own initiative or suggestions for specific investigatory or enforcement measures to be taken, including interim measures.

4. The Digital Services Coordinator of establishment shall take utmost account of the request pursuant to paragraphs 1 or 2 of this Article. Where it considers that it has insufficient information to act upon the request and has reasons to consider that the Digital Services Coordinator that sent the request, or the Board, could provide additional information, the Digital Services Coordinator of establishment may either request such information in accordance with Article 57 or, alternatively, may launch a joint investigation pursuant to Article 60(1) involving at least the requesting Digital Services Coordinator. The period laid down in paragraph 5 of this Article shall be suspended until that additional information is provided or until the invitation to participate in the joint investigation is refused.

5. The Digital Services Coordinator of establishment shall, without undue delay and in any event not later than two months following receipt of the request pursuant to paragraph 1 or 2, communicate to the Digital Services Coordinator that sent the request, and the Board, the assessment of the suspected infringement and an explanation of any investigatory or enforcement measures taken or envisaged in relation thereto to ensure compliance with this Regulation.

Article 59
Referral to the Commission

1. In the absence of a communication within the period laid down in Article 58(5), in the case of a disagreement of the Board with the assessment or the measures taken or envisaged pursuant to Article 58(5) or in the cases referred to in Article 60(3), the Board may refer the matter to the Commission, providing all relevant information. That information shall include at least the request or recommendation sent to the Digital Services Coordinator of establishment, the assessment by that Digital Services Coordinator, the reasons for the disagreement and any additional information supporting the referral.

2. The Commission shall assess the matter within two months following the referral of the matter pursuant to paragraph 1, after having consulted the Digital Services Coordinator of establishment.

3. Where, pursuant to paragraph 2 of this Article, the Commission considers that the assessment or the investigatory or enforcement measures taken or envisaged pursuant to Article 58(5) are insufficient to ensure effective enforcement or otherwise incompatible with this Regulation, it shall communicate its views to the Digital Services Coordinator of establishment and the Board and request the Digital Services Coordinator of establishment to review the matter.

The Digital Services Coordinator of establishment shall take the necessary investigatory or enforcement measures to ensure compliance with this Regulation, taking utmost account of the views and request for review by the Commission. The Digital Services Coordinator of establishment shall inform the Commission, as well as the requesting Digital Services Coordinator or the Board that took action pursuant to Article 58(1) or (2), about the measures taken within two months from that request for review.

Article 60
Joint investigations

1. The Digital Services Coordinator of establishment may launch and lead joint investigations with the participation of one or more other Digital Services Coordinators concerned:

(a) at its own initiative, to investigate an alleged infringement of this Regulation by a given provider of intermediary services in several Member States; or
(b) upon recommendation of the Board, acting on the request of at least three Digital Services Coordinators alleging, based on a reasonable suspicion, an infringement by a given provider of intermediary services affecting recipients of the service in their Member States.

2. Any Digital Services Coordinator that proves that it has a legitimate interest in participating in a joint investigation pursuant to paragraph 1 may request to do so. The joint investigation shall be concluded within three months from its launch, unless otherwise agreed amongst the participants.

The Digital Services Coordinator of establishment shall communicate its preliminary position on the alleged infringement no later than one month after the end of the deadline referred to in the first subparagraph to all Digital Services Coordinators, the Commission and the Board. The preliminary position shall take into account the views of all other Digital Services Coordinators participating in the joint investigation. Where applicable, this preliminary position shall also set out the enforcement measures envisaged.

3. The Board may refer the matter to the Commission pursuant to Article 59, where:

(a) the Digital Services Coordinator of establishment failed to communicate its preliminary position within the deadline set out in paragraph 2;
(b) the Board substantially disagrees with the preliminary position communicated by the Digital Services Coordinator of establishment; or
(c) the Digital Services Coordinator of establishment failed to initiate the joint investigation promptly following the recommendation by the Board pursuant to paragraph 1, point (b).

4. In carrying out the joint investigation, the participating Digital Services Coordinators shall cooperate in good faith, taking into account, where applicable, the indications of the Digital Services Coordinator of establishment and the Board's recommendation. The Digital Services Coordinators of destination participating in the joint investigation shall be entitled, at the request of or after having consulted the Digital Services Coordinator of establishment, to exercise their investigative powers referred to in Article 51(1) in respect of the providers of intermediary services concerned by the alleged infringement, with regard to information and premises located within their territory.

SECTION 3
European Board for Digital Services

Article 61
European Board for Digital Services

1. An independent advisory group of Digital Services Coordinators on the supervision of providers of intermediary services named 'European Board for Digital Services' (the 'Board') is established.

2. The Board shall advise the Digital Services Coordinators and the Commission in accordance with this Regulation to achieve the following objectives:

(a) contributing to the consistent application of this Regulation and effective cooperation of the Digital Services Coordinators and the Commission with regard to matters covered by this Regulation;
(b) coordinating and contributing to guidelines and analysis of the Commission and Digital Services Coordinators and other competent authorities on emerging issues across the internal market with regard to matters covered by this Regulation;
(c) assisting the Digital Services Coordinators and the Commission in the supervision of very large online platforms.

Article 62
Structure of the Board

1. The Board shall be composed of Digital Services Coordinators who shall be represented by high-level officials. The failure by one or more Member States to designate a Digital Services Coordinator shall not prevent the Board from performing its tasks under this Regulation. Where provided for by national law, other competent authorities entrusted with specific operational responsibilities for the application and enforcement of this Regulation alongside the Digital Services Coordinator may participate in the Board. Other national authorities may be invited to the meetings, where the issues discussed are of relevance for them.

2. The Board shall be chaired by the Commission. The Commission shall convene the meetings and prepare the agenda in accordance with the tasks of the Board pursuant to this Regulation and in line with its rules of procedure. When the Board is requested to adopt a recommendation pursuant to this Regulation, it shall immediately make the request available to other Digital Services Coordinators through the information sharing system set out in Article 85.

3. Each Member State shall have one vote. The Commission shall not have voting rights.

The Board shall adopt its acts by simple majority. When adopting a recommendation to the Commission referred to in Article 36(1), first subparagraph, the Board shall vote within 48 hours after the request of the Chair of the Board.

4. The Commission shall provide administrative and analytical support for the activities of the Board pursuant to this Regulation.

5. The Board may invite experts and observers to attend its meetings, and may cooperate with other Union bodies, offices, agencies and advisory groups, as well as external

experts as appropriate. The Board shall make the results of this cooperation publicly available.

6. The Board may consult interested parties, and shall make the results of such consultation publicly available.

7. The Board shall adopt its rules of procedure, following the consent of the Commission.

Article 63
Tasks of the Board

1. Where necessary to meet the objectives set out in Article 61(2), the Board shall in particular:

(a) support the coordination of joint investigations;
(b) support the competent authorities in the analysis of reports and results of audits of very large online platforms or of very large online search engines to be transmitted pursuant to this Regulation;
(c) issue opinions, recommendations or advice to Digital Services Coordinators in accordance with this Regulation, taking into account, in particular, the freedom to provide services of the providers of intermediary service;
(d) advise the Commission on the measures referred to in Article 66 and, adopt opinions concerning very large online platforms or very large online search engines in accordance with this Regulation;
(e) support and promote the development and implementation of European standards, guidelines, reports, templates and code of conducts in cooperation with relevant stakeholders as provided for in this Regulation, including by issuing opinions or recommendations on matters related to Article 44, as well as the identification of emerging issues, with regard to matters covered by this Regulation.

2. Digital Services Coordinators and, where applicable, other competent authorities that do not follow the opinions, requests or recommendations addressed to them adopted by the Board shall provide the reasons for this choice, including an explanation on the investigations, actions and the measures that they have implemented, when reporting pursuant to this Regulation or when adopting their relevant decisions, as appropriate.

SECTION 4
Supervision, investigation, enforcement and monitoring in respect of providers of very large online platforms and of very large online search engines

Article 64
Development of expertise and capabilities

1. The Commission, in cooperation with the Digital Services Coordinators and the Board, shall develop Union expertise and capabilities, including, where appropriate, through the secondment of Member States' personnel.

2. In addition, the Commission, in cooperation with the Digital Services Coordinators and the Board, shall coordinate the assessment of systemic and emerging issues across

the Union in relation to very large online platforms or very large online search engines with regard to matters covered by this Regulation.

3. The Commission may ask the Digital Services Coordinators, the Board and other Union bodies, offices and agencies with relevant expertise to support the assessment of systemic and emerging issues across the Union under this Regulation.

4. Member States shall cooperate with the Commission, in particular through their respective Digital Services Coordinators and other competent authorities, where applicable, including by making available their expertise and capabilities.

Article 65
Enforcement of obligations of providers of very large online platforms and of very large online search engines

1. For the purposes of investigating compliance of providers of very large online platforms and of very large online search engines with the obligations laid down in this Regulation, the Commission may exercise the investigatory powers laid down in this Section even before initiating proceedings pursuant to Article 66(2). It may exercise those powers on its own initiative or following a request pursuant to paragraph 2 of this Article.

2. Where a Digital Services Coordinator has reason to suspect that a provider of a very large online platform or of a very large online search engine has infringed the provisions of Section 5 of Chapter III or has systemically infringed any of the provisions of this Regulation in a manner that seriously affects recipients of the service in its Member State, it may send, through the information sharing system referred to in Article 85, a request to the Commission to assess the matter.

3. A request pursuant to paragraph 2 shall be duly reasoned and at least indicate:

(a) the point of contact of the provider of the very large online platform or of the very large online search engine concerned as provided for in Article 11;
(b) a description of the relevant facts, the provisions of this Regulation concerned and the reasons why the Digital Services Coordinator that sent the request suspects that the provider of the very large online platforms or of the very large online search engine concerned infringed this Regulation, including a description of the facts that show that the suspected infringement is of a systemic nature;
(c) any other information that the Digital Services Coordinator that sent the request considers relevant, including, where appropriate, information gathered on its own initiative.

Article 66
Initiation of proceedings by the Commission and cooperation in investigation

1. The Commission may initiate proceedings in view of the possible adoption of decisions pursuant to Articles 73 and 74 in respect of the relevant conduct by the provider of the very large online platform or of the very large online search engine that the Commission suspect of having infringed any of the provisions of this Regulation.

2. Where the Commission decides to initiate proceedings pursuant to paragraph 1 of this Article, it shall notify all Digital Services Coordinators and the Board through the

information sharing system referred to in Article 85, as well as the provider of the very large online platform or of the very large online search engine concerned.

The Digital Services Coordinators shall, without undue delay after being informed of initiation of the proceedings, transmit to the Commission any information they hold about the infringement at stake.

The initiation of proceedings pursuant to paragraph 1 of this Article by the Commission shall relieve the Digital Services Coordinator, or any competent authority where applicable, of its powers to supervise and enforce provided for in this Regulation pursuant to Article 56(4).

3. In the exercise of its powers of investigation under this Regulation the Commission may request the individual or joint support of any Digital Services Coordinators concerned by the suspected infringement, including the Digital Services Coordinator of establishment. The Digital Services Coordinators that have received such a request, and, where involved by the Digital Services Coordinator, any other competent authority, shall cooperate sincerely and in a timely manner with the Commission and shall be entitled to exercise their investigative powers referred to in Article 51(1) in respect of the provider of the very large online platform or of the very large online search engine at stake, with regard to information, persons and premises located within the territory of their Member State and in accordance with the request.

4. The Commission shall provide the Digital Services Coordinator of establishment and the Board with all relevant information about the exercise of the powers referred to in Articles 67 to 72 and its preliminary findings referred to in Article 79(1). The Board shall submit its views on those preliminary findings to the Commission within the period set pursuant to Article 79(2). The Commission shall take utmost account of any views of the Board in its decision.

Article 67
Requests for information

1. In order to carry out the tasks assigned to it under this Section, the Commission may, by simple request or by decision, require the provider of the very large online platform or of the very large online search engine concerned, as well as any other natural or legal person acting for purposes related to their trade, business, craft or profession that may be reasonably aware of information relating to the suspected infringement, including organisations performing the audits referred to in Article 37 and Article 75(2), to provide such information within a reasonable period.

2. When sending a simple request for information to the provider of the very large online platform or of the very large online search engine concerned or other person referred to in paragraph 1 of this Article, the Commission shall state the legal basis and the purpose of the request, specify what information is required and set the period within which the information is to be provided, and the fines provided for in Article 74 for supplying incorrect, incomplete or misleading information.

3. Where the Commission requires the provider of the very large online platform or of the very large online search engine concerned or other person referred to in paragraph 1 of this Article to supply information by decision, it shall state the legal basis and the purpose of the request, specify what information is required and set the period within which it is to be provided. It shall also indicate the fines provided for in Article 74 and indicate or impose the periodic penalty payments provided for in Article 76. It shall fur-

ther indicate the right to have the decision reviewed by the Court of Justice of the European Union.

4. The providers of the very large online platform or of the very large online search engine concerned or other person referred to in paragraph 1 or their representatives and, in the case of legal persons, companies or firms, or where they have no legal personality, the persons authorised to represent them by law or by their constitution shall supply the information requested on behalf of the provider of the very large online platform or of the very large online search engine concerned or other person referred to in paragraph 1. Lawyers duly authorised to act may supply the information on behalf of their clients. The latter shall remain fully responsible if the information supplied is incomplete, incorrect or misleading.

5. At the request of the Commission, the Digital Services Coordinators and other competent authorities shall provide the Commission with all necessary information to carry out the tasks assigned to it under this Section.

6. The Commission shall, without undue delay after sending the simple request or the decision referred to in paragraph 1 of this Article, send a copy thereof to the Digital Services Coordinators, through the information sharing system referred to in Article 85.

Article 68
Power to take interviews and statements

1. In order to carry out the tasks assigned to it under this Section, the Commission may interview any natural or legal person who consents to being interviewed for the purpose of collecting information, relating to the subject-matter of an investigation, in relation to the suspected infringement. The Commission shall be entitled to record such interview by appropriate technical means.

2. If the interview referred to in paragraph 1 is conducted on other premises than those of the Commission, the Commission shall inform the Digital Services Coordinator of the Member State in the territory of which the interview takes place. If so requested by that Digital Services Coordinator, its officials may assist the officials and other accompanying persons authorised by the Commission to conduct the interview.

Article 69
Power to conduct inspections

1. In order to carry out the tasks assigned to it under this Section, the Commission may conduct all necessary inspections at the premises of the provider of the very large online platform or of the very large online search engine concerned or of another person referred to in Article 67(1).

2. The officials and other accompanying persons authorised by the Commission to conduct an inspection shall be empowered to:

(a) enter any premises, land and means of transport of the provider of the very large online platform or of the very large online search engine concerned or of the other person concerned;
(b) examine the books and other records related to the provision of the service concerned, irrespective of the medium on which they are stored;
(c) take or obtain in any form copies of or extracts from such books or other records;

(d) require the provider of the very large online platform or of the very large online search engine or the other person concerned to provide access to and explanations on its organisation, functioning, IT system, algorithms, data-handling and business practices and to record or document the explanations given;
(e) seal any premises used for purposes related to the trade, business, craft or profession of the provider of the very large online platform or of the very large online search engine or of the other person concerned, as well as books or other records, for the period and to the extent necessary for the inspection;
(f) ask any representative or member of staff of the provider of the very large online platform or of the very large online search engine or the other person concerned for explanations on facts or documents relating to the subject-matter and purpose of the inspection and to record the answers;
(g) address questions to any such representative or member of staff relating to the subject-matter and purpose of the inspection and to record the answers.

3. Inspections may be carried out with the assistance of auditors or experts appointed by the Commission pursuant to Article 72(2), and of Digital Services Coordinator or other competent national authorities of the Member State in the territory of which the inspection is conducted.

4. Where the production of required books or other records related to the provision of the service concerned is incomplete or where the answers to questions asked under paragraph 2 of this Article are incorrect, incomplete or misleading, the officials and other accompanying persons authorised by the Commission to conduct an inspection shall exercise their powers upon production of a written authorisation specifying the subject matter and purpose of the inspection and the penalties provided for in Articles 74 and 76. In good time before the inspection, the Commission shall inform the Digital Services Coordinator of the Member State in the territory in which the inspection is to be conducted thereof.

5. During inspections, the officials and other accompanying persons authorised by the Commission, the auditors and experts appointed by the Commission, the Digital Services Coordinator or the other competent authorities of the Member State in the territory of which the inspection is conducted may require the provider of the very large online platform or of the very large online search engine or other person concerned to provide explanations on its organisation, functioning, IT system, algorithms, data-handling and business conducts, and may address questions to its key personnel.

6. The provider of the very large online platform or of the very large online search engine or other natural or legal person concerned shall be required to submit to an inspection ordered by decision of the Commission. The decision shall specify the subject matter and purpose of the inspection, set the date on which it is to begin and indicate the penalties provided for in Articles 74 and 76 and the right to have the decision reviewed by the Court of Justice of the European Union. The Commission shall consult the Digital Services Coordinator of the Member State on territory of which the inspection is to be conducted prior to taking that decision.

7. Officials of, and other persons authorised or appointed by, the Digital Services Coordinator of the Member State on the territory of which the inspection is to be conducted shall, at the request of that Digital Services Coordinator or of the Commission, actively assist the officials and other accompanying persons authorised by the Commission in relation to the inspection. To this end, they shall have the powers listed in paragraph 2.

8. Where the officials and other accompanying persons authorised by the Commission find that the provider of the very large online platform or of the very large online search engine or the other person concerned opposes an inspection ordered pursuant to this Article, the Member State in the territory of which the inspection is to be conducted shall, at the request of those officials or other accompanying persons and in accordance with the national law of the Member State, afford them necessary assistance, including, where appropriate under that national law, in the form of coercive measures taken by a competent law enforcement authority, so as to enable them to conduct the inspection.

9. If the assistance provided for in paragraph 8 requires authorisation from a national judicial authority in accordance with the national law of the Member State concerned, such authorisation shall be applied for by the Digital Services Coordinator of that Member State at the request of the officials and other accompanying persons authorised by the Commission. Such authorisation may also be applied for as a precautionary measure.

10. Where the authorisation referred to in paragraph 9 is applied for, the national judicial authority before which a case has been brought shall verify that the Commission decision ordering the inspection is authentic and that the coercive measures envisaged are neither arbitrary nor excessive having regard to the subject matter of the inspection. When conducting such verification, the national judicial authority may ask the Commission, directly or through the Digital Services Coordinators of the Member State concerned, for detailed explanations, in particular those concerning the grounds on which the Commission suspects an infringement of this Regulation, concerning the seriousness of the suspected infringement and concerning the nature of the involvement of the provider of the very large online platform or of the very large online search engine or of the other person concerned. However, the national judicial authority shall not call into question the necessity for the inspection nor demand information from the case file of the Commission. The lawfulness of the Commission decision shall be subject to review only by the Court of Justice of the European Union.

Article 70
Interim measures

1. In the context of proceedings which may lead to the adoption of a decision of non-compliance pursuant to Article 73(1), where there is an urgency due to the risk of serious damage for the recipients of the service, the Commission may, by decision, order interim measures against the provider of the very large online platform or of the very large online search engine concerned on the basis of a prima facie finding of an infringement.

2. A decision under paragraph 1 shall apply for a specified period of time and may be renewed in so far this is necessary and appropriate.

Article 71
Commitments

1. If, during proceedings under this Section, the provider of the very large online platform or of the very large online search engine concerned offers commitments to ensure compliance with the relevant provisions of this Regulation, the Commission may by decision make those commitments binding on the provider of the very large online plat-

form or of the very large online search engine concerned and declare that there are no further grounds for action.

2. The Commission may, upon request or on its own initiative, reopen the proceedings:

(a) where there has been a material change in any of the facts on which the decision was based;
(b) where the provider of the very large online platform or of the very large online search engine concerned acts contrary to its commitments; or
(c) where the decision was based on incomplete, incorrect or misleading information provided by the provider of the very large online platform or of the very large online search engine concerned or other person referred to in Article 67(1).

3. Where the Commission considers that the commitments offered by the provider of the very large online platform or of the very large online search engine concerned are unable to ensure effective compliance with the relevant provisions of this Regulation, it shall reject those commitments in a reasoned decision when concluding the proceedings.

Article 72
Monitoring actions

1. For the purposes of carrying out the tasks assigned to it under this Section, the Commission may take the necessary actions to monitor the effective implementation and compliance with this Regulation by providers of the very large online platform and of the very large online search engines. The Commission may order them to provide access to, and explanations relating to, its databases and algorithms. Such actions may include, imposing an obligation on the provider of the very large online platform or of the very large online search engine to retain all documents deemed to be necessary to assess the implementation of and compliance with the obligations under this Regulation.

2. The actions pursuant to paragraph 1 may include the appointment of independent external experts and auditors, as well as experts and auditors from competent national authorities with the agreement of the authority concerned, to assist the Commission in monitoring the effective implementation and compliance with the relevant provisions of this Regulation and to provide specific expertise or knowledge to the Commission.

Article 73
Non-compliance

1. The Commission shall adopt a non-compliance decision where it finds that the provider of the very large online platform or of the very large online search engine concerned does not comply with one or more of the following:

(a) the relevant provisions of this Regulation;
(b) interim measures ordered pursuant to Article 70;
(c) commitments made binding pursuant to Article 71.

2. Before adopting the decision pursuant to paragraph 1, the Commission shall communicate its preliminary findings to the provider of the very large online platform or of the very large online search engine concerned. In the preliminary findings, the Commis-

sion shall explain the measures that it considers taking, or that it considers that the provider of the very large online platform or of the very large online search engine concerned should take, in order to effectively address the preliminary findings.

3. In the decision adopted pursuant to paragraph 1 the Commission shall order the provider of the very large online platform or of the very large online search engine concerned to take the necessary measures to ensure compliance with the decision pursuant to paragraph 1 within a reasonable period specified therein and to provide information on the measures that that provider intends to take to comply with the decision.

4. The provider of the very large online platform or of the very large online search engine concerned shall provide the Commission with a description of the measures it has taken to ensure compliance with the decision pursuant to paragraph 1 upon their implementation.

5. Where the Commission finds that the conditions of paragraph 1 are not met, it shall close the investigation by a decision. The decision shall apply with immediate effect.

Article 74
Fines

1. In the decision referred to in Article 73, the Commission may impose on the provider of the very large online platform or of the very large online search engine concerned fines not exceeding 6 % of its total worldwide annual turnover in the preceding financial year where it finds that the provider, intentionally or negligently:

(a) infringes the relevant provisions of this Regulation;
(b) fails to comply with a decision ordering interim measures under Article 70; or
(c) fails to comply with a commitment made binding by a decision pursuant to Article 71.

2. The Commission may adopt a decision imposing on the provider of the very large online platform or of the very large online search engine concerned or on another natural or legal person referred to in Article 67(1) fines not exceeding 1 % of the total annual income or worldwide turnover in the preceding financial year, where they intentionally or negligently:

(a) supply incorrect, incomplete or misleading information in response to a simple request or request by a decision pursuant to Article 67;
(b) fail to reply to the request for information by decision within the set period;
(c) fail to rectify within the period set by the Commission, incorrect, incomplete or misleading information given by a member of staff, or fail or refuse to provide complete information;
(d) refuse to submit to an inspection pursuant to Article 69;
(e) fail to comply with the measures adopted by the Commission pursuant to Article 72; or
(f) fail to comply with the conditions for access to the Commission's file pursuant to Article 79(4).

3. Before adopting the decision pursuant to paragraph 2 of this Article, the Commission shall communicate its preliminary findings to the provider of the very large online platform or of the very large online search engine concerned or to another person referred to in Article 67(1).

4. In fixing the amount of the fine, the Commission shall have regard to the nature, gravity, duration and recurrence of the infringement and, for fines imposed pursuant to paragraph 2, the delay caused to the proceedings.

Article 75
Enhanced supervision of remedies to address infringements of obligations laid down in Section 5 of Chapter III

1. When adopting a decision pursuant to Article 73 in relation to an infringement by a provider of a very large online platform or of a very large online search engine of any of the provisions of Section 5 of Chapter III, the Commission shall make use of the enhanced supervision system laid down in this Article. When doing so, it shall take utmost account of any opinion of the Board pursuant to this Article.

2. In the decision referred to in Article 73, the Commission shall require the provider of a very large online platform or of a very large online search engine concerned to draw up and communicate, within a reasonable period specified in the decision, to the Digital Services Coordinators, the Commission and the Board an action plan setting out the necessary measures which are sufficient to terminate or remedy the infringement. Those measures shall include a commitment to perform an independent audit in accordance with Article 37(3) and (4) on the implementation of the other measures, and shall specify the identity of the auditors, as well as the methodology, timing and follow-up of the audit. The measures may also include, where appropriate, a commitment to participate in a relevant code of conduct, as provided for in Article 45.

3. Within one month following receipt of the action plan, the Board shall communicate its opinion on the action plan to the Commission. Within one month following receipt of that opinion, the Commission shall decide whether the measures set out in the action plan are sufficient to terminate or remedy the infringement, and shall set a reasonable period for its implementation. The possible commitment to adhere to relevant codes of conduct shall be taken into account in that decision. The Commission shall subsequently monitor the implementation of the action plan. To that end, the provider of a very large online platform or of a very large online search engine concerned shall communicate the audit report to the Commission without undue delay after it becomes available, and shall keep the Commission up to date on steps taken to implement the action plan. The Commission may, where necessary for such monitoring, require the provider of a very large online platform or of a very large online search engine concerned to provide additional information within a reasonable period set by the Commission.

The Commission shall keep the Board and the Digital Services Coordinators informed about the implementation of the action plan, and about its monitoring thereof.

4. The Commission may take necessary measures in accordance with this Regulation, in particular Article 76(1), point (e), and Article 82(1), where:

(a) the provider of the very large online platform or of the very large online search engine concerned fails to provide any action plan, the audit report, the necessary updates or any additional information required, within the applicable period;
(b) the Commission rejects the proposed action plan because it considers that the measures set out therein are insufficient to terminate or remedy the infringement; or

(c) the Commission considers, on the basis of the audit report, any updates or additional information provided or any other relevant information available to it, that the implementation of the action plan is insufficient to terminate or remedy the infringement.

Article 76
Periodic penalty payments

1. The Commission may adopt a decision, imposing on the provider of the very large online platform or of the very large online search engine concerned or other person referred to in Article 67(1), as applicable, periodic penalty payments not exceeding 5 % of the average daily income or worldwide annual turnover in the preceding financial year per day, calculated from the date appointed by the decision, in order to compel them to:

(a) supply correct and complete information in response to a decision requiring information pursuant to Article 67;
(b) submit to an inspection which it has ordered by decision pursuant to Article 69;
(c) comply with a decision ordering interim measures pursuant to Article 70(1);
(d) comply with commitments made legally binding by a decision pursuant to Article 71(1);
(e) comply with a decision pursuant to Article 73(1), including where applicable the requirements it contains relating to the action plan referred to in Article 75.

2. Where the provider of the very large online platform or of the very large online search engine concerned or other person referred to in Article 67(1) has satisfied the obligation which the periodic penalty payment was intended to enforce, the Commission may fix the definitive amount of the periodic penalty payment at a figure lower than that under the original decision.

Article 77
Limitation period for the imposition of penalties

1. The powers conferred on the Commission by Articles 74 and 76 shall be subject to a limitation period of five years.

2. Time shall begin to run on the day on which the infringement is committed. However, in the case of continuing or repeated infringements, time shall begin to run on the day on which the infringement ceases.

3. Any action taken by the Commission or by the Digital Services Coordinator for the purpose of the investigation or proceedings in respect of an infringement shall interrupt the limitation period for the imposition of fines or periodic penalty payments. Actions which interrupt the limitation period shall include, in particular, the following:

(a) requests for information by the Commission or by a Digital Services Coordinator;
(b) inspection;
(c) the opening of a proceeding by the Commission pursuant to Article 66(1).

4. Each interruption shall start time running afresh. However, the limitation period for the imposition of fines or periodic penalty payments shall expire at the latest on the day on which a period equal to twice the limitation period has elapsed without the Commission having imposed a fine or a periodic penalty payment. That period shall be extended

by the time during which the limitation period has been suspended pursuant to paragraph 5.

5. The limitation period for the imposition of fines or periodic penalty payments shall be suspended for as long as the decision of the Commission is the subject of proceedings pending before the Court of Justice of the European Union.

Article 78
Limitation period for the enforcement of penalties

1. The power of the Commission to enforce decisions taken pursuant to Articles 74 and 76 shall be subject to a limitation period of five years.

2. Time shall begin to run on the day on which the decision becomes final.

3. The limitation period for the enforcement of penalties shall be interrupted:

(a) by notification of a decision varying the original amount of the fine or periodic penalty payment or refusing an application for variation;
(b) by any action of the Commission, or of a Member State acting at the request of the Commission, designed to enforce payment of the fine or periodic penalty payment.

4. Each interruption shall start time running afresh.

5. The limitation period for the enforcement of penalties shall be suspended for so long as:

(a) time to pay is allowed;
(b) enforcement of payment is suspended pursuant to a decision of the Court of Justice of the European Union or to a decision of a national court.

Article 79
Right to be heard and access to the file

1. Before adopting a decision pursuant to Article 73(1), Article 74 or 76, the Commission shall give the provider of the very large online platform or of the very large online search engine concerned or other person referred to in Article 67(1) the opportunity of being heard on:

(a) preliminary findings of the Commission, including any matter to which the Commission has taken objections; and
(b) measures that the Commission may intend to take in view of the preliminary findings referred to point (a).

2. The provider of the very large online platform or of the very large online search engine concerned or other person referred to in Article 67(1) may submit its observations on the Commission's preliminary findings within a reasonable period set by the Commission in its preliminary findings, which may not be less than 14 days.

3. The Commission shall base its decisions only on objections on which the parties concerned have been able to comment.

4. The rights of defence of the parties concerned shall be fully respected in the proceedings. They shall be entitled to have access to the Commission's file under the terms of a negotiated disclosure, subject to the legitimate interest of the provider of the very large online platform or of the very large online search engine or other person con-

cerned in the protection of their business secrets. The Commission shall have the power to adopt decisions setting out such terms of disclosure in case of disagreement between the parties. The right of access to the file of the Commission shall not extend to confidential information and internal documents of the Commission, the Board, Digital Service Coordinators, other competent authorities or other public authorities of the Member States. In particular, the right of access shall not extend to correspondence between the Commission and those authorities. Nothing in this paragraph shall prevent the Commission from disclosing and using information necessary to prove an infringement.

5. The information collected pursuant to Articles 67, 68 and 69 shall be used only for the purpose of this Regulation.

Article 80
Publication of decisions

1. The Commission shall publish the decisions it adopts pursuant to Article 70(1), Article 71(1) and Articles 73 to 76. Such publication shall state the names of the parties and the main content of the decision, including any penalties imposed.

2. The publication shall have regard to the rights and legitimate interests of the provider of the very large online platform or of the very large online search engine concerned, any other person referred to in Article 67(1) and any third parties in the protection of their confidential information.

Article 81
Review by the Court of Justice of the European Union

In accordance with Article 261 TFEU, the Court of Justice of the European Union has unlimited jurisdiction to review decisions by which the Commission has imposed fines or periodic penalty payments. It may cancel, reduce or increase the fine or periodic penalty payment imposed.

Article 82
Requests for access restrictions and cooperation with national courts

1. Where all powers pursuant to this Section to bring about the cessation of an infringement of this Regulation have been exhausted, the infringement persists and causes serious harm which cannot be avoided through the exercise of other powers available under Union or national law, the Commission may request the Digital Services Coordinator of establishment of the provider of the very large online platform or of the very large online search engine concerned to act pursuant to Article 51(3).

Prior to making such request to the Digital Services Coordinator, the Commission shall invite interested parties to submit written observations within a period that shall not be less than 14 working days, describing the measures it intends to request and identifying the intended addressee or addressees thereof.

2. Where the coherent application of this Regulation so requires, the Commission, acting on its own initiative, may submit written observations to the competent judicial authority referred to Article 51(3). With the permission of the judicial authority in question, it may also make oral observations.

For the purpose of the preparation of its observations only, the Commission may request that judicial authority to transmit or ensure the transmission to it of any documents necessary for the assessment of the case.

3. When a national court rules on a matter which is already the subject matter of a decision adopted by the Commission under this Regulation, that national court shall not take any decision which runs counter to that Commission decision. National courts shall also avoid taking decisions which could conflict with a decision contemplated by the Commission in proceedings it has initiated under this Regulation. To that effect, a national court may assess whether it is necessary to stay its proceedings. This is without prejudice to Article 267 TFEU.

Article 83
Implementing acts relating to Commission intervention

In relation to the Commission intervention covered by this Section, the Commission may adopt implementing acts concerning the practical arrangements for:

(a) the proceedings pursuant to Articles 69 and 72;
(b) the hearings provided for in Article 79;
(c) the negotiated disclosure of information provided for in Article 79.

Before the adoption of any measures pursuant to the first paragraph of this Article, the Commission shall publish a draft thereof and invite all interested parties to submit their comments within the period set out therein, which shall not be less than one month. Those implementing acts shall be adopted in accordance with the advisory procedure referred to in Article 88.

SECTION 5
Common provisions on enforcement

Article 84
Professional secrecy

Without prejudice to the exchange and to the use of information referred to in this Chapter, the Commission, the Board, Member States' competent authorities and their respective officials, servants and other persons working under their supervision, and any other natural or legal person involved, including auditors and experts appointed pursuant to Article 72(2), shall not disclose information acquired or exchanged by them pursuant to this Regulation and of the kind covered by the obligation of professional secrecy.

Article 85
Information sharing system

1. The Commission shall establish and maintain a reliable and secure information sharing system supporting communications between Digital Services Coordinators, the Commission and the Board. Other competent authorities may be granted access to this system where necessary for them to carry out the tasks conferred to them in accordance with this Regulation.

2. The Digital Services Coordinators, the Commission and the Board shall use the information sharing system for all communications pursuant to this Regulation.

3. The Commission shall adopt implementing acts laying down the practical and operational arrangements for the functioning of the information sharing system and its interoperability with other relevant systems. Those implementing acts shall be adopted in accordance with the advisory procedure referred to in Article 88.

Article 86
Representation

1. Without prejudice to Directive (EU) 2020/1828 or to any other type of representation under national law, recipients of intermediary services shall at least have the right to mandate a body, organisation or association to exercise the rights conferred by this Regulation on their behalf, provided the body, organisation or association meets all of the following conditions:

(a) it operates on a not-for-profit basis;
(b) it has been properly constituted in accordance with the law of a Member State;
(c) its statutory objectives include a legitimate interest in ensuring that this Regulation is complied with.

2. Providers of online platforms shall take the necessary technical and organisational measures to ensure that complaints submitted by bodies, organisations or associations referred to in paragraph 1 of this Article on behalf of recipients of the service through the mechanisms referred to in Article 20(1) are processed and decided upon with priority and without undue delay.

SECTION 6
Delegated and implementing acts

Article 87
Exercise of the delegation

1. The power to adopt delegated acts is conferred on the Commission subject to the conditions laid down in this Article.

2. The delegation of power referred to in Articles 24, 33, 37, 40 and 43 shall be conferred on the Commission for five years starting from 16 November 2022. The Commission shall draw up a report in respect of the delegation of power not later than nine months before the end of the five-year period. The delegation of power shall be tacitly extended for periods of an identical duration, unless the European Parliament or the Council opposes such extension not later than three months before the end of each period.

3. The delegation of power referred to in Articles 24, 33, 37, 40 and 43 may be revoked at any time by the European Parliament or by the Council. A decision of revocation shall put an end to the delegation of power specified in that decision. It shall take effect the day following that of its publication in the Official Journal of the European Union or at a later date specified therein. It shall not affect the validity of any delegated acts already in force.

4. Before adopting a delegated act, the Commission shall consult experts designated by each Member State in accordance with the principles laid down in the Interinstitutional Agreement of 13 April 2016 on Better Law-Making.

5. As soon as it adopts a delegated act, the Commission shall notify it simultaneously to the European Parliament and to the Council.

6. A delegated act adopted pursuant to Articles 24, 33, 37, 40 and 43 shall enter into force only if no objection has been expressed by either the European Parliament or the Council within a period of three months of notification of that act to the European Parliament and the Council or if, before the expiry of that period, the European Parliament and the Council have both informed the Commission that they will not object. That period shall be extended by three months at the initiative of the European Parliament or of the Council.

Article 88
Committee procedure

1. The Commission shall be assisted by a committee ('the Digital Services Committee'). That Committee shall be a Committee within the meaning of Regulation (EU) No 182/2011.

2. Where reference is made to this paragraph, Article 4 of Regulation (EU) No 182/2011 shall apply.

CHAPTER V
FINAL PROVISIONS

Article 89
Amendments to Directive 2000/31/EC

1. Articles 12 to 15 of Directive 2000/31/EC are deleted.

2. References to Articles 12 to 15 of Directive 2000/31/EC shall be construed as references to Articles 4, 5, 6 and 8 of this Regulation, respectively.

Article 90
Amendment to Directive (EU) 2020/1828

In Annex I to Directive (EU) 2020/1828, the following point is added:

'(68) Regulation (EU) 2022/2065 of the European Parliament and of the Council of 19 October 2022 on a Single Market for Digital Services and amending Directive 2000/31/EC (Digital Services Act) (OJ L 277, 27.10.2022, p. 1).'.

Article 91
Review

1. By 18 February 2027, the Commission shall evaluate and report to the European Parliament, the Council and the European Economic and Social Committee on the po-

tential effect of this Regulation on the development and economic growth of small and medium-sized enterprises.

By 17 November 2025, the Commission shall evaluate and report to the European Parliament, the Council and the European Economic and Social Committee on:

(a) the application of Article 33, including the scope of providers of intermediary services covered by the obligations set out in Section 5 of Chapter III of this Regulation;
(b) the way that this Regulation interacts with other legal acts, in particular the acts referred to in Article 2(3) and (4).

2. By 17 November 2027, and every five years thereafter, the Commission shall evaluate this Regulation, and report to the European Parliament, the Council and the European Economic and Social Committee.

This report shall address in particular:

(a) the application of paragraph 1, second subparagraph, points (a) and (b);
(b) the contribution of this Regulation to the deepening and efficient functioning of the internal market for intermediary services, in particular as regards the cross-border provision of digital services;
(c) the application of Articles 13, 16, 20, 21, 45 and 46;
(d) the scope of the obligations on small and micro enterprises;
(e) the effectiveness of the supervision and enforcement mechanisms;
(f) the impact on the respect for the right to freedom of expression and information.

3. Where appropriate, the report referred to in paragraphs 1 and 2 shall be accompanied by a proposal for amendment of this Regulation.

4. The Commission shall, in the report referred to in paragraph 2 of this Article, also evaluate and report on the annual reports on their activities by the Digital Services Coordinators provided to the Commission and the Board pursuant to Article 55(1).

5. For the purpose of paragraph 2, Member States and the Board shall send information on the request of the Commission.

6. In carrying out the evaluations referred to in paragraph 2, the Commission shall take into account the positions and findings of the European Parliament, the Council, and other relevant bodies or sources, and shall pay specific attention to small and medium-sized enterprises and the position of new competitors.

7. By 18 February 2027, the Commission, after consulting the Board, shall carry out an assessment of the functioning of the Board and of the application of Article 43, and shall report it to the European Parliament, the Council and the European Economic and Social Committee, taking into account the first years of application of the Regulation. On the basis of the findings and taking utmost account of the opinion of the Board, that report shall, where appropriate, be accompanied by a proposal for amendment of this Regulation with regard to the structure of the Board.

Article 92
Anticipated application to providers of very large online platforms and of very large online search engines

This Regulation shall apply to providers of very large online platforms and of very large online search engines designated pursuant to Article 33(4) from four months after the notification to the provider concerned referred to in Article 33(6) where that date is earlier than 17 February 2024.

Article 93
Entry into force and application

1. This Regulation shall enter into force on the twentieth day following that of its publication in the Official Journal of the European Union.

2. This Regulation shall apply from 17 February 2024.

However, Article 24(2), (3) and (6), Article 33(3) to (6), Article 37(7), Article 40(13), Article 43 and Sections 4, 5 and 6 of Chapter IV shall apply from 16 November 2022.

This Regulation shall be binding in its entirety and directly applicable in all Member States.

Done at Strasbourg, 19 October 2022.

For the European Parliament
The President
R. METSOLA

For the Council
The President
M. BEK

Index

Bold numbers refer to chapters, normal ones to margin numbers.